PHILOSOPHY OF MIND

Developments in the philosophy of mind over the last 20 years have dramatically changed the nature of the subject. In this major new introduction, Tim Bayne presents an outstanding overview of many of the key topics, problems, and debates, taking account not only of changes in philosophy of mind itself but also of important developments in the scientific study of the mind.

The following topics are discussed in depth:

- What distinguishes a physicalist conception of the mind?
- Behaviourism, the identity theory, functionalism, and eliminativism as accounts of the mental
- The nature of perception, including the issue of perceptual transparency, the admissible contents of perception, and the question of unconscious perception
- The nature of thought, including the language of thought hypothesis, Searle's Chinese room argument, and the Turing test
- The basis of intentional content
- Externalist accounts of content and the 'extended mind' thesis
- Consciousness-based objections to physicalism, and illusionist and panpsychist conceptions of consciousness
- Theories of consciousness, including methodological issues in the study of consciousness
- Mental causation, including both philosophical and scientific challenges
- The problem(s) of other minds, including knowledge of non-human minds
- Self-knowledge
- Personal identity and the nature of the self

The book features a number of boxes that provide a more in-depth look at particular issues. Also included are chapter summaries, guides to further reading, and a helpful glossary of terms.

Written by a leading figure in the field, *Philosophy of Mind: An Introduction* is an invaluable core text for any student coming to philosophy of mind for the first time.

Tim Bayne is Professor of Philosophy at Monash University, Australia. He is the author of *The Unity of Consciousness* (2010), *Thought: A Very Short Introduction* (2013), and *Philosophy of Religion: A Very Short Introduction* (2018); and an editor of *Delusion and Self-Deception* (2008), *The Oxford Companion to Consciousness* (2009), and *Cognitive Phenomenology* (2011). He is a Senior Fellow in the CIFAR Brain, Mind, and Consciousness program.

'This is a marvelous introduction to the philosophy of mind. It focuses on the foundational issues that have made philosophy of mind such a vital area of inquiry for the last 50 years. And it places those issues in the context of contemporary research in both philosophy and science. The book deftly integrates the scientific work without losing sight of the deep philosophical problems. Bayne also achieves an excellent balance of accessibility and philosophical precision. It is likely to become the standard text on philosophy of mind for years to come.'

– **Shaun Nichols**, *Cornell University, USA*

'This is a superb introduction to the philosophy of mind. Bayne focuses on fundamental aspects of mentality such as perception, thought, intentionality, consciousness, and the self, presenting the central debates in the field in a way that is both empirically informed and up-to-date. Each chapter is lucidly written and provides a skillfully crafted narrative. He has achieved the remarkable feat of writing a highly accessible book without ever sacrificing rigor or simplifying arguments. A jewel that belongs in every classroom!'

– **René Jagnow**, *University of Georgia, USA*

'An ideal introduction to the subject by a leader in the field. It covers the traditional big questions, including the mind-body problem, mental causation, and self-knowledge. But it is also on the cutting edge, featuring detailed discussions of recent hot topics. And it is unique among introductions to the subject in giving a prominent place to both empirical considerations and a priori philosophical arguments. Lucidly written and neatly organized throughout, Bayne's introduction will be a delight for students and teachers alike.'

– **Adam Pautz**, *Brown University, USA*

'Tim Bayne covers a diverse array of both traditional and cutting-edge topics with clarity, depth, and rigor, making this book an excellent introduction to philosophy of mind and a fantastic launching pad for further investigation. Highly readable and accessible, it is a pleasure to read!'

– **Angela Mendelovici**, *Western University, Canada*

'This is a terrific book! Bayne accomplishes the near-impossible task of giving the reader a sense of both the core issues in philosophy of mind, and the current state of the discipline and where it's heading. Written in plain English, it does a very good job of explaining complicated issues in a clear manner.'

– **Raamy Majeed**, *University of Auckland, New Zealand*

'This is a much-needed update to current introductory offerings in the philosophy of mind. Engaging and clear, Bayne presents philosophical problems in ways that will excite and motivate his readers. Most importantly, he demonstrates how empirical work can be used to evaluate philosophical theories, serving as an invaluable role-model for future generations of philosophers of mind.'

– **Jane Suilin Lavelle**, *University of Edinburgh, UK*

PHILOSOPHY OF MIND

An Introduction

Tim Bayne

LONDON AND NEW YORK

First published 2022
by Routledge
2 Park Square, Milton Park, Abingdon, Oxon OX14 4RN

and by Routledge
605 Third Avenue, New York, NY 10158

Routledge is an imprint of the Taylor & Francis Group, an informa business

© 2022 Tim Bayne

The right of Tim Bayne to be identified as author of this work has been asserted by him in accordance with sections 77 and 78 of the Copyright, Designs and Patents Act 1988.

All rights reserved. No part of this book may be reprinted or reproduced or utilised in any form or by any electronic, mechanical, or other means, now known or hereafter invented, including photocopying and recording, or in any information storage or retrieval system, without permission in writing from the publishers.

Trademark notice: Product or corporate names may be trademarks or registered trademarks, and are used only for identification and explanation without intent to infringe.

British Library Cataloguing-in-Publication Data
A catalogue record for this book is available from the British Library

Library of Congress Cataloging-in-Publication Data
A catalog record for this book has been requested

ISBN: 978-0-415-66984-9 (hbk)
ISBN: 978-0-415-66985-6 (pbk)
ISBN: 978-1-003-22534-8 (ebk)

DOI: 10.4324/9781003225348

Typeset in Interstate
by Apex CoVantage, LLC

For Helen

CONTENTS

Acknowledgements — xii
List of figures — xiii
Preface: Just Keep Swimming — xiv

Introduction: a map of the mind — 1

1 Marks of the mental — 6

   1.1   Aspects of mentality 6
   1.2   The privacy of the mental 8
          Box: Brain-reading? 9
          Box: The personal/subpersonal distinction 10
   1.3   Intentionality 11
          Box: The propositional attitudes 13
   1.4   Consciousness 16
          Box: Qualia 17
   1.5   Folk psychology 18
          Box: Folk psychology or folk psychologies? 19
   1.6   Conclusion 20
   Further reading 22
   Study questions 22

2 Physicalism — 24

   2.1   Motivating physicalism 25
   2.2   Hempel's dilemma 26
          Box: Mentality in the foundations? 27
   2.3   Supervenience, emergence, and intelligibility 28
          Box: Two kinds of possibility 29
   2.4   A priori and a posteriori physicalism 31
   2.5   The prospects of physicalism 33
          Box: Ghosts and zombies 34
   2.6   Conclusion 35
   Further reading 35
   Study questions 36

3 How to be a physicalist — 38

- 3.1 Behaviourism 38
- 3.2 The mind-brain identity theory 41
  - Box: Anomalous monism and token identities 41
  - Box: Multiple realization 43
- 3.3 Functionalism 44
  - Box: Constructing an artificial mind 47
- 3.4 Eliminativism 47
  - Box: Eliminativism and incoherence 50
- 3.5 The role of science 51
- 3.6 Conclusion 53
- Further reading 53
- Study questions 54

4 Perception — 56

- 4.1 Three accounts of perception 57
  - Box: Disjunctivism 60
  - Box: Virtual reality 62
- 4.2 Intentionalism and phenomenal character 62
  - Box: Perception and pain 64
- 4.3 Intentionalism: for and against 65
  - Box: Blurry vision 65
- 4.4 The admissible contents of perception 69
- 4.5 Unconscious perception? 71
- 4.6 Conclusion 73
- Further reading 74
- Study questions 75

5 Thought — 77

- 5.1 The varieties of thought 78
  - Box: Alief: between thought and perception? 79
- 5.2 The language of thought hypothesis 81
  - Box: But does it have to be a *language*? 84
- 5.3 Alternatives to the language of thought 84
  - Box: The scaffolding of thought 87
- 5.4 The Chinese room argument 88
- 5.5 The Turing test and the boundaries of thought 90
  - Box: Winning the imitation game? 91
- 5.6 Conclusion 94
- Further reading 95
- Study questions 96

6 Grounding intentionality — 98

- 6.1 Getting situated 99
- 6.2 The tracking approach 101
  - Box: The normativity of content 103
- 6.3 The teleosemantic approach 104
  - Box: Swampman 107
- 6.4 The phenomenal approach 107
  - Box: The puzzle of cognitive phenomenology 110

6.5   The intentional stance   111
 6.6   Conclusion   113
 Further reading   114
 Study questions   115

7 Externalism and the extended mind   117

 7.1   Motivating content externalism   118
 7.2   Responses to the doppelgänger arguments   120
 7.3   Externalism extended   121
       Box: Border problems   122
 7.4   The internalist fights back   123
 7.5   Vehicle externalism and the extended mind   125
       Box: The extended conscious mind?   126
 7.6   Conclusion   129
 Further reading   130
 Study questions   130

8 The metaphysics of consciousness   133

 8.1   Bats, neuroscientists, and zombies   134
       Box: Mind the gaps   136
 8.2   Type-A physicalism and the inscrutability premise   138
       Box: Mysterianism   141
 8.3   Type-B physicalism and the bridging premise   142
       Box: Consciousness and a posteriori necessities   143
 8.4   Illusionism   146
       Box: Chase, Sanborn, and the taste of coffee   147
 8.5   Dualism and Russellian monism   148
       Box: Panprotopsychism?   149
 8.6   Conclusion   150
 Further reading   151
 Study questions   152

9 Theories of consciousness   154

 9.1   First-person methods and third-person methods   155
       Box: Phenomenal overflow?   157
 9.2   Explanatory targets   160
       Box: Global states of consciousness   160
       Box: The neural correlates of consciousness   162
 9.3   Monitoring theories versus first-order theories   163
 9.4   Neural theories versus functional theories   167
       Box: Cortical dominance and cortical deference   168
 9.5   Intentionalism   172
 9.6   Conclusion   174
 Further reading   174
 Study questions   175

10 Mental causation   178

 10.1   Motivating mental causation   179
 10.2   The causal exclusion objection   180
        Box: Token identities (again)   183

    10.3   Causal exclusion and non-reductive physicalism   184
    10.4   Externalism and mental causation   187
    10.5   Libet's challenge   190
            Box: What's it like to raise your hand?   192
    10.6   Conclusion   193
    Further reading   194
    Study questions   194

11 Other minds   196

    11.1   The psychology of mindreading   197
            Box: The theory-theory: little scientists, mental modules   199
    11.2   The conceptual problem of other minds   201
            Box: The beetle in the box   202
    11.3   The sceptical problem of other minds   203
            Box: Solipsism   204
            Box: Detecting consciousness in the 'vegetative state'   206
    11.4   Other kinds of minds I: non-human animals   208
            Box: Plant mentality   209
    11.5   Other kinds of minds II: artificial consciousness   212
            Box: Consciousness in cerebral organoids?   212
    11.6   Conclusion   214
    Further reading   215
    Study questions   216

12 Self-knowledge   218

    12.1   The scope and status of self-knowledge   218
            Box: Avowals and expressivism   221
    12.2   The inner-sense account   221
            Box: Acquaintance   223
    12.3   The inferentialist account   224
    12.4   The deliberative account   226
            Box: Anscombe on agent's knowledge   227
    12.5   Neo-Rylean approaches   228
            Box: Making sense of oneself   230
    12.6   Conclusion   231
    Further reading   232
    Study questions   233

13 The self   234

    13.1   Putting the self to work   235
            Box: Losing oneself   237
    13.2   Dualism   238
    13.3   Animalism   241
            Box: One organism, two selves?   242
    13.4   The psychological approach   243
            Box: Who wants to live forever?   247
    13.5   The self as an illusion   248
            Box: Doing without the self   250
    13.6   Conclusion   250

Further reading 251
Study questions 252

Conclusion: the mind-body problem 255

Glossary 258
Bibliography 263
Index 283

ACKNOWLEDGEMENTS

I have benefited from the support of many people in the course of writing of this book. Thanks are due to Helen Beebee, Yuri Cath, David Chalmers, Andy Clark, Martin Davies, Jordi Fernández, Colin Klein, Uriah Kriegel, Eric Mandelbaum, Daniel Muñoz, Casey O'Callaghan, Marya Schechtman, Nicholas Shea, Susanna Siegel, and Manuel Vargas for their advice and feedback. I am also indebted to my colleagues Monima Chadha, Jakob Hohwy, and Jenny Windt, for their support, encouragement, and wise counsel. Andrew McKilliam, Niccolo Negro, and Iwan Williams read an early draft of this book, and their input improved the manuscript in innumerable respects. I am grateful to each of the five referees for Routledge, whose extensive feedback on the manuscript saved me from numerous errors, and to the very many referees who provided feedback on the original proposal for this volume. Particular thanks are due to Tony Bruce, who not only entrusted me with this project but also kept faith with me during its long and difficult gestation. But my most significant debt of gratitude is owed to Helen Gordon, without whose love and support this book would never have been completed.

FIGURES

8.1	The specific explanatory gap and the generic explanatory gap	137
9.1	Typical stimulus display used in Sperling's partial report task	158
9.2	Cortical deference versus cortical dominance	169
10.1	Apparent causal competition between the mental and the physical	181
10.2	A schematic representation of Yablo's counterexample to EXCLUSION	186
10.3	A schematic representation of Libet's data	190
11.1	*Migrant Mother*, Dorothea Lange (1936)	198

PREFACE

Just Keep Swimming

It is sometimes said that there is no shallow end in the swimming pool of philosophy. As with many aphorisms, this statement is something of a half-truth, for although philosophy does get very deep very quickly, some philosophical texts are certainly more challenging than others. In writing this book, I have tried to make it accessible to readers who have little prior acquaintance with philosophy; that said, this book is not always easy. Certain passages may need to be read slowly, and if you are unfamiliar with philosophical terminology, you may find it helpful to consult the glossary.

The philosopher Ludwig Wittgenstein once remarked that 'light dawns gradually over the whole' (1967, §141). He was talking about understanding in general, but his comment is particularly appropriate with respect to the kind of understanding that is peculiar to philosophy. You may find it helpful to bear Wittgenstein's remark in mind as you proceed. Although the first three chapters are foundational and should, ideally, be read in the order in which they appear, subsequent chapters are relatively free-standing and can be read in any order. Just as the material in earlier chapters will illuminate that found in later chapters, so too the material in later chapters will illuminate that found in earlier chapters. Thus, you might find it helpful to re-read earlier chapters in light of the later ones. The index can also function as a kind of pointer to issues that are discussed across various locations in the book.

But perhaps the best advice that I can offer is to just keep swimming when the discussion gets difficult. Sooner or later you will hit clear water, and when you've got your breath back you can always dive back into the choppy waters that you skimmed over on the first reading.

Introduction
A map of the mind

If you're able to understand this sentence, then it's likely that you already know a good deal about minds. You yourself will have a mind, and you will be familiar with a wide range of mental phenomena: thoughts, perceptions, emotions, moods, and bodily sensations. You will know what it's like to experience pain. You will know that there's a difference between hoping to win the lottery and believing that you've won the lottery. And you'll be able to distinguish things that have a mind (you, your friends, your dog) from those that don't (your shoes, your socks, the chair on which you're sitting). In short, mental phenomena will not be completely mysterious to you in the way in which the chemical structure of zirconium or the nature of dark matter might be.

But it is one thing to have a rough-and-ready grip on mental phenomena and quite another to grasp their fundamental nature. You might know what it feels like to be in pain, but do you know what pains themselves are? Is pain one and the same thing as brain activity, or is pain one thing and brain activity another? (And if pain and brain activity are different things, how exactly are they related?) You might know that there is a difference between hoping that something is the case and believing that it's the case, but what exactly are hopes and beliefs? You might be sure that you have a mind and that your chair doesn't, but there are probably questions about mentality in other creatures about which you are less certain. Are octopuses conscious? Could a computer think? Are crows capable of self-awareness? Thinking, perceiving, and acting come as naturally to us as flying comes to an eagle, but one can think, perceive, and act without ever having reflected on the fundamental nature of thought, perception, or action. After all, eagles know how to fly, but they know nothing about the mechanisms of flight or the principles of aerodynamics.

Philosophical reflection on the mind has a long and venerable history. In Greece, Plato (428/427-348/347 BCE) and Aristotle (384-322 BCE) offered sophisticated accounts of mental activity, as did Śaṅkara (788-820) and Ramanuja (1017-1137) in India and Zhuangzi (4th century BCE) in China. In the medieval period, Al-Fârâbî (ca. 870-950), Avicenna (980-1037), Averroës (1126-98), St. Thomas Aquinas (1225-74), and William of Ockham (1285-1347) all made important contributions to debates about the nature of the mind. The writings of René Descartes (1596-1650), John Locke (1632-1704), and David Hume (1711-76) in the 17th and 18th centuries continue to have a profound influence on how contemporary philosophers view the mind. But although some of these thinkers will make a brief appearance here, this book is not a guide to the history of philosophical reflection on the mind. Instead, our primary

DOI: 10.4324/9781003225348-1

focus will be on contemporary debates in the philosophy of mind. Our aim here is not to eavesdrop on voices from the past, but to participate in an ongoing conversation.[1]

That conversation is informed by the history of the philosophy of mind, but it also is informed by (and in turn informs) debates in a number of other disciplines. On one side of the philosophy of mind lie other areas of philosophical inquiry. Some questions in the philosophy of mind fall under the umbrella of metaphysics, for they are concerned with what exists and the kinds of categories we should include in our conception of reality. Other questions in the philosophy of mind fall under the umbrella of epistemology, for they are concerned with what we can know and how we can know it. We will also encounter questions that fall within the domain of the philosophy of language (How do psychological terms acquire their meaning?), the philosophy of science (What is the relationship between the explanations provided by fundamental physics and those provided by the special sciences, such as biology and psychology?), and ethics and value theory (Can we make sense of moral responsibility if there is no self?).

On the other side of the philosophy of mind lie the sciences of the mind, such as psychology, psychiatry, and neuroscience. The nature of the border between the philosophy of mind and the sciences of the mind is contested. Some philosophers regard the philosophy of mind as largely autonomous of empirical investigation, denying that empirical results could have any bearing on philosophical debates, even in principle. Other philosophers regard the border between the philosophical study of the mind and the scientific study of the mind as vague, ill-defined, and of little fundamental importance. I myself have more sympathy with the second approach, but I do think that there are many questions in the philosophy of mind for which it is very difficult to see precisely how empirical results might be relevant. At any rate, there is a clear difference in emphasis between the questions that are addressed in this book and those that might be addressed in (say) a psychology textbook. Experimental results are front and centre in the scientific study of the mind, whereas philosophical questions arise precisely when an issue cannot be settled (at least not in any direct way) by experiment.

Let us turn now to the structure of this book. The first three chapters are foundational, and should ideally be read in the order in which they appear. (That said, there are sections of Chapters 2 and 3 that could be safely skipped.) Subsequent chapters are relatively independent of each other, and need not be read in the order in which they appear.

Chapter 1 considers the question of what mental phenomena have in common. Why do we group bodily sensations, perceptual experiences, moods, emotions, and thoughts together as mental phenomenon? What features, if any, do these phenomena share? Our discussion of these issues will uncover two central aspects of mentality: intentionality and consciousness. Intentionality concerns the fact that mental states are about or directed towards particular things. For example, my belief that the moon was created by a collision between Earth and another planet is about the moon (and, of course, also about Earth). Consciousness concerns the experiential aspects of the mind. To be conscious is to have a subjective perspective on the world. Much of this book revolves around the twin concerns of intentionality and consciousness. How are these two phenomena related to each other? Can we understand intentionality in terms of consciousness? Can we understand consciousness in terms of intentionality? Or are intentionality and consciousness fundamentally different phenomena that need to be accounted for in their own terms?

In Chapter 2 we turn to an important position called physicalism. The guiding idea behind physicalism is that mental phenomena are no less a part of the physical world than (say) photosynthesis, respiration, or digestion. Although fundamental physics doesn't study digestion as such, digestion is 'nothing over and above' a very complex arrangement of purely physical states and processes. Similarly, the physicalist claims that mental phenomena are 'nothing over and above' very complex arrangements of purely physical states and processes. The debate between physicalism and its opponents is one of the central debates in the philosophy of mind, and it makes an appearance in multiple chapters.

Chapter 3 examines four of the leading frameworks that physicalists have developed for understanding the mind: behaviourism, the identity theory, functionalism, and eliminativism. We consider how these approaches to the mind differ from each other, and we consider some of the main ways in which each approach has been developed. We also reflect on the role played by science in different versions of physicalism.

Although the contrast between consciousness and intentionality is central to the philosophy of mind, it is not the only way of carving up the mind. Another approach to the mind focuses on mental faculties. This is the approach that we adopt in Chapters 4 and 5. In Chapter 4 we examine the nature of perception, exploring questions relating to the experiential character of perception, the kinds of things that can be perceived, and the possibility of unconscious perception. Chapter 5 focuses on thought. We ask how thoughts of various kinds might differ from each other, whether thought involves an internal language of some kind, and what a good test for the presence of thought in an artificial system might look like.

Chapters 6 and 7 focus on intentionality. We begin in Chapter 6 by asking what it is that grounds our capacity to represent various aspects of the world. What makes it the case that a thought about the moon is about the moon rather than (say) Jupiter, Mars, or blue cheese? Philosophers have proposed a number of very different answers to this question. Some theorists appeal to causal and informational relations between an organism and its environment; some theorists argue that evolutionary considerations ought to play a role in accounting for the mind's capacity to be directed towards the world; others focus on consciousness; and still others appeal to the patterns that are manifest in an agent's behaviour. We will subject each of these accounts to scrutiny.

Chapter 7 considers what kind of role, if any, an agent's social and physical environment plays in determining the nature of their thoughts and psychological capacities. Our discussion of this issue is structured in terms of a debate between internalists and externalists. *Internalism* is so named because its advocates hold that an agent's mental states and capacities are fully determined by factors that are internal to them, whereas *externalism* is so named because externalists allow that facts about an agent's history and environment can play a fundamental role in determining their mental states and capacities. In addition to considering the debate between internalists and externalists, Chapter 7 also examines the connections between this debate and other foundational questions in the philosophy of mind.

In Chapter 8 we return to consciousness. Our focus here is on an influential trio of arguments (Thomas Nagel's bat argument, Frank Jackson's knowledge argument, and David Chalmers's zombie argument) that raise doubts about whether consciousness can be reconciled with a commitment to physicalism. The fundamental problem is that there appears to be a gap between physical phenomena (such as brain activity) and consciousness, such that it is difficult to see how, even in principle, physical phenomena could explain the existence of consciousness. As we will see, physicalists have developed a number of very interesting – and very different – responses to the challenge of the explanatory gap. Chapter 8 also considers two alternatives to physicalism: dualism and Russellian monism.

Our focus on consciousness continues in Chapter 9, where we consider a number of questions that straddle the border between the philosophy of mind and the scientific study of consciousness. Should the study of consciousness be based on first-person methods such as introspection, or should it instead employ third-person methods, such as behavioural responses and brain-imaging data? Can we explain why conscious states are conscious, and can we explain the contrast between different kinds of conscious states? Why is there 'something it's like' to feel an itch, and why is 'what it's like' to feel an itch very different from 'what it's like' to smell burnt toast?

In Chapter 10 we turn our attention to mental causation. The assumption that a person's mental states can have an effect on the world is deeply embedded in our explanations of human behaviour, our moral attitudes, and our political and legal institutions. We take it for granted that hunger causes people to eat, jealousy causes them to seek the demise of their rivals, and ophidiophobia (the fear of snakes) causes people to avoid long grass. However, a number of arguments appear to either undermine the possibility of mental causation altogether, or to at least show that a commitment to mental causation is incompatible with various theses about the mind that are highly attractive. In addition to considering these arguments, Chapter 10 also explores an objection to mental causation that arises out of neuroscientific research.

Chapters 11 and 12 focus on issues relating to our knowledge of the mind. We begin in Chapter 11 with the problem (or rather, problems) of other minds. The practice of attributing thoughts and feelings to other people – mindreading, as it is known – is utterly unremarkable, but how exactly do we do it? And does this practice generate knowledge? Can you ever know what I'm thinking or feeling? In addition to considering the challenges posed by the minds of other people, we also consider the challenges associated with identifying mentality in other kinds of creatures. What, if anything, can we know about what it is like to be a bee, an octopus, or a robot?

In Chapter 12 we turn to knowledge of one's own mental states, what philosophers call 'self-knowledge'. The access that you have to your own mental states seems to be very different from the access that you have to my mental states. You might not be sure what I am thinking or feeling, but you are unlikely to harbour doubts about the contents of your own mind. Knowledge of one's own mind seems to be both more extensive and more secure than knowledge of anyone else's mind. The problem of self-knowledge, roughly speaking, is the problem of explaining why knowledge of one's own mind has the distinctive features that it does.

In the final chapter, we turn from the problem of self-knowledge to the problem of the self: what, most fundamentally, are you? Are you an organism? An immaterial substance? A mind? A story? Indeed, are you any kind of *thing* at all? Perhaps, as some philosophers have argued, you are an illusion. You may not be convinced by any of the accounts of the self that we consider, but you will (I hope) come away from our discussion with an appreciation of what the problem of the self involves and why it has proven so challenging to solve.

As you will see, each chapter contains a number of boxes. Some boxes provide background material that might be helpful to readers who are new to philosophy; others discuss theories and perspectives that complement those that are presented in the main text; and still others point to debates in which issues in the philosophy of mind bear on questions that are of more general interest.

My main aim in writing this book is not to convince you to see the mind as I do, but to provide you with a map of the central problems in the philosophy of mind. As with any map, the one provided here is drawn from a particular perspective, and the reader should be aware that much of the ground that we will cover is contested – sometimes deeply so. Theorists don't merely disagree about how best to answer certain questions (although that is certainly true); they also disagree about how various questions are related to each other, about how key terms ought to be used, and even about whether certain questions make any sense. I have noted some of these disagreements where they are particularly important, but for the most part I have simply tried to chart a clear path through the landscape. Each chapter concludes with a Further Reading section for those who want to explore the relevant terrain in more detail.

Enough preamble. Let's get to work.

Note

[1] For the history of the philosophy of mind, see R. Copenhaver and C. Shields, eds. *The History of the Philosophy of Mind* (Routledge, 2019).

1 Marks of the mental

Chapter overview

- Considers three possible 'marks of the mental': privacy, intentionality, and consciousness
- Introduces the relationship between consciousness and intentionality as a key question in the philosophy of mind
- Presents the notion of folk psychology.

1.1 Aspects of mentality

How do minded beings differ from those that lack minds? One feature that distinguishes things with minds from things without minds is that the former have various faculties that the latter lack. Consider, for example, your ability to read the sentences on this page. In order to see these sentences you need to employ the faculty of sight, and in order to comprehend their meaning you must have the capacity to read. Species differ in the kinds of perceptual systems that they possess, but arguably all minded creatures have the capacity to perceive a range of objects and events in their environment.

Other mental capacities are concerned with action. Minded beings are agents, and it seems a pretty safe bet to assume that the evolution of mentality was heavily constrained by the need for smart and efficient action. Your brain is an expensive organ to run – although it weighs only 2% of your total body weight, it demands 20% of your resting metabolic energy – and evolution is unlikely to have fostered the capacity for mentality unless it paid off. Whether it involves reaching for a cup of coffee, looking for a friend in a crowd, or deciding which pant leg to put on first, much of our mental lives is dedicated to the control of behaviour.

The mental capacities of some creatures don't extend much beyond those that are directly implicated in perception and action. Other creatures, however, enjoy a broader suite of mental capacities. We ourselves belong to this second class: not only can we perceive and act, we can also *think*. (Is thinking a kind of acting? Perhaps, but it's certainly a different kind of acting from moving one's body.) We can weigh up competing sources of evidence, we can

DOI: 10.4324/9781003225348-2

consider the consequences of a various plans of action, and we can adopt the perspectives of other creatures. Thought allows us to exploit our perceptual capacities in novel ways. Instead of waiting for the world to present itself for inspection, a thinker can manipulate the world in order to see what would happen under certain conditions. (That, in a nutshell, is what an experiment is.) Thought also enables us to exploit our capacities for action in new ways, and thus massively expand the kind of control we have over our environments.

There are other mental faculties too, of course. There is the faculty of memory, which can perhaps be regarded as a kind of perception of the past. There is emotion, which is bound up in complex ways with perceiving, thinking, and acting. And there is imagination, a faculty that enables us to envisage how things might be in the future or how they might have been had things gone differently. A full understanding of mentality needs to account for each of these faculties and the ways in which they are related to each other.

In addition to considering the contrast between different types of mental faculties, we also need to consider the contrast between different types of mental phenomena. Here, we can distinguish between mental *events*, mental *processes*, and mental *states*.

Mental events are dated, particular, happenings. The paradigmatic examples of mental events are bodily sensations, such as headaches, itches, pains, sensations of thirst and of hunger, and feelings of drowsiness and of lightheadedness. But not all mental events involve the awareness of one's body; indeed, not all mental events are sensory. Some mental events – such as getting a joke or realizing that one has been insulted – are cognitive.

Mental processes unfold over time and often involve transitions between mental events. Consider what is involved in deciding where to go for dinner. You might weigh up the pros and cons of various options and deliberate about what the best course of action is. This is an example of practical reasoning. Other mental processes involve theoretical reasoning. When you encounter authors with divergent views on some topic in the philosophy of mind (as you surely will) then you will need to deliberate as to which of the competing claims is the more plausible. Mental processes can also involve imagery of various kinds. If you've just been presented with plans for renovating your house, you may need to engage in a process of visualization in order to know what the result of the renovations will look like.

The term 'mental state' is employed in different ways within philosophy. Some authors use it to refer solely to what I will call 'standing states': mental phenomena that do not 'unfold over time' in the way in which mental processes do. Beliefs are standing states. Suppose that Bella believes that sloths are herbivores. As long as Bella doesn't forget that sloths are herbivores or change her mind for some reason, she will continue to believe that sloths are herbivores even when she is asleep or is engrossed in doing a jigsaw puzzle and is not thinking about sloths at all. Desires and intentions are also standing states. Just as Bella can believe that sloths are herbivores when dreamlessly asleep, so too she can also desire to learn more about sloths or intend to acquire a pet sloth even when dreamlessly asleep. But although some philosophers reserve the phrase 'mental state' for standing states of the kind that we have just described, others use the phrase in a more inclusive sense that includes not just standing states but also mental events and processes. I generally use the phrase in this broader sense and will refer to standing states as 'standing states'.

Another notion that plays an important role in the philosophy of mind is that of a mental *property*. We each have a great many properties. I have the property of being 5 feet 7 inches tall, of having been to Addis Ababa, and of being a poor swimmer. These are physical properties, but I also have *mental* properties of various kinds. For example, I have the property of *knowing* how tall I am, of *remembering* having been to Addis Ababa, and of *intending* to become a better swimmer.

How do mental properties differ from mental states? Although the nature (i.e., ontology) of properties is a contested matter, for our purposes the crucial point is that different objects can have (or instantiate) the same property. I am not the only person in the world who is 5 feet 7 inches, nor am I the only person to remember having been to Addis Ababa or who intends to become a better swimmer. By contrast, mental states, events, and processes are what philosophers call *particulars*: they are datable and locatable occurrences. Although you and I might both believe that Addis Ababa is in Ethiopia, my belief that Addis Ababa is in Ethiopia is distinct from your belief that Addis Ababa is in Ethiopia.

The relationship between mental states and mental properties is something about which there is much debate. Some theorists take mental states as primitives, and hold that a person has a mental property in virtue of being in a certain mental state. Another approach, and one that I find more attractive, takes mental properties as fundamental, and holds that a mental state can be identified with a particular creature having (or 'instantiating', as we might put it) a mental property at a time. On this view, mental properties are more basic than mental states. Although the distinction between mental states and mental properties is important for certain debates, one can often move back and forth between talk of mental states and talk of mental properties without undue risk of confusion, and I will often do precisely that.

Thus far we have discussed the notion of mental faculties, events, processes, states, and properties, but what of minds themselves? What is the mind? Talk of the mind needs to be handled with care. Placing the definite article before 'mind' suggests that minds are things: objects of a certain kind, on a par perhaps with bricks, bicycles, and bandicoots. But as seductive as that thought might be, it should be regarded with suspicion. Although certain theorists ('substance dualists') conceive of minds as things, this position is very much a minority one within the philosophy of mind, and most philosophers are highly (and, in my view, rightly) suspicious of reifying minds (i.e., treating them as 'things'). In many respects, it is perhaps best to think of the mind as a convenient shorthand for picking out the kinds of mental phenomena that we have surveyed here. That said, we do need to give an account of what distinguishes the mental states of one person from those of another. What makes certain thoughts and feelings yours and other thoughts and feelings mine? This question is bound up with questions about the nature of the self. We consider it in Chapter 13.

1.2 The privacy of the mental

It is all very well to distinguish different kinds of mental phenomena from each other, but what exactly do we mean when we describe something as mental? What distinguishes mental phenomena as a class from non-mental phenomena?

The attempt to find a defining feature of mentality is often referred to as the search for the 'mark of the mental'. The aim of this project is to find a property (or, perhaps, some collection of properties) that is both necessary and sufficient for mentality. In other words, everything that is mental would have it (that's the necessary bit), and anything that has it would be mental (that's the sufficient bit). We might think of the search for the mark (or marks) of the mental as attempting to capture the *essence* of mentality.

One property that has sometimes been touted as a potential mark of the mental is *privacy*. The intuitive idea is that mental phenomena can be distinguished from non-mental phenomena on the basis of the kind of access that one has to them. Suppose that you have a splitting headache. Your access to your own headache isn't mediated by any kind of evidence, but is direct and immediate. But now consider how things stand from my perspective – the third-person perspective. I might be able to tell that you have a headache from what you do and say, but I don't have the kind of direct access to it that you do. So, there seems to be a deep contrast between the kind of access that one has to one's current mental states and the kind of access one has to the mental states of other people (Box: Brain-reading?).

This contrast does not characterize one's access to physical states, for there is no deep asymmetry between the first-person perspective and the third-person perspective when it comes to knowledge of a person's physical states. In principle, you can figure out my height, age, and weight in roughly the same kinds of ways that I can. Indeed, sometimes other people are better informed about one's own height, age, and weight than one is oneself. So, mental phenomena seem to exhibit a kind of privacy that physical phenomena do not.

Box: Brain-reading?

At present, gaining access to another person's mind requires interrogating their behaviour and drawing inferences from what they do and say. However, advances in neuroscience raise the prospect of 'brain-reading' (or 'brain-decoding'), in which information about brain activity is used to identify a person's thoughts. In one study, subjects were told that they would be presented with two numerals (e.g., 3 and 7), and that they were to then either mentally add the presented numbers together or subtract one number from the other. Using functional magnetic resonance imaging (fMRI), the experimenters were able to tell with up to 70% accuracy whether a subject had decided to add the two numbers or subtract one number from the other (Haynes et al. 2007). In a sense, fMRI was being used to engage in a primitive form of mindreading.

At only 70% accuracy, there is arguably no real threat to mental privacy here. The interesting questions revolve around what the future of this kind of technology might be. Could someone armed with a suitably powerful brain decoder know exactly what you're thinking and feeling? Could another person's access to your mental states rival – or even outstrip – your own? Or are there fundamental limits on the kind of access that other people could have to your mental states?

Further reading

Dennett, D. 1978. Brain Writing and Mind Reading. *Brainstorms*. MIT Press.
Haynes, J-D. et al. 2007. Reading Hidden Intentions in the Human Brain. *Current Biology*, 17: 323-28.

Although privacy is certainly an important aspect of mentality, it is doubtful whether it can provide us with a mark of the mental – something that enables us to distinguish mental from non-mental phenomena. There are at least three reasons for this.

First, although neurotypical adult human beings have robust access to many of their own mental states, it is doubtful whether this kind of access extends to all minded creatures. Perhaps young children, people who have suffered from severe brain damage, or certain types of non-human animals lack the capacity to become aware of their own experiences and thoughts. In fact, there are pathologies of adult cognition in which individuals seem to lack full access to their own mental states. For example, individuals who suffer from Anton's syndrome believe that they can see despite the fact that they are largely, and in some cases completely, blind (Forde & Wallesch 2003; Goldenberg et al. 1995). Anton's syndrome is a species of anosognosia, a condition in which patients are unaware of a deficit from which they suffer, such as paralysis, deafness, or aphasia (difficulty producing meaningful speech). Anosognosia is of great philosophical interest, for it puts pressure on the intuitive idea that we always know our own states of mind better than other people do.[1]

Second, the kind of direct access that we have to many kinds of mental phenomena doesn't seem to extend to mental phenomena of all forms. Even if one always has better access to one's own pains, aches, and itches than other people do, one's anger, depression, or grief might be more apparent to others than it is to oneself. Similarly, self-deception can blind a person to their own desires and motivations.

Third, there are mental states to which we lack any kind of first-person access. For example, vision scientists explain why we are susceptible to certain kinds of perceptual illusions by supposing that there are representations in the visual system which 'assume' that objects are illuminated from above. These representations are not states to which you have direct access. Instead, your reasons for ascribing these states to yourself are precisely the same reasons that I have for ascribing them to you; namely, that they explain certain kinds of illusions. Although one could deny that representational states of these kinds are genuine *mental* states (as some theorists do), there are good reasons to adopt a more inclusive conception of what counts as mental, and to hold that mental phenomena don't just include familiar personal-level states such as pains, beliefs, and visual experiences, but also the kinds of subpersonal representational states that are posited by psychologists and neuroscientists to explain our behaviour (see Box: The personal/subpersonal distinction).

Box: The personal/subpersonal distinction

In his book *Content and Consciousness*, Daniel Dennett introduced an important contrast between two types of explanations: personal explanations and subpersonal explanations. The former concern 'people and their sensations and activities', whereas the latter focus on the 'level of brains and events in the nervous system' (Dennett 1969: 93). Dennett claimed that both personal and subpersonal explanations are mental, but he argued that it is important not to confuse subpersonal explanations with personal ones (or vice versa), for they are subject to different kinds of constraints. Corresponding to this distinction between two kinds of explanation is a distinction between two kinds of mental phenomena. Deciding to walk along a boulder-strewn beach involves states and processes at the personal level (it's something that you do), whereas the computations that enable you to successfully navigate your way between the boulders on the beach are subpersonal. Roughly speaking, we might say that subpersonal states are 'in us', whereas personal states are 'for us'.

Although the personal/subpersonal contrast is widely employed, theorists do not always draw the line between the personal and the subpersonal in the same way. Some authors focus on consciousness, arguing that personal level phenomena must be consciously accessible. Others focus on explanatory considerations, arguing that what is distinctive of personal states is their capacity to ground reason-giving explanations. Despite this disagreement about how exactly the contrast between the personal and the subpersonal should be drawn, in practice it is generally clear whether a particular state ought to be classed as personal or subpersonal. Our focus in this book is on personal states, but we will occasionally consider subpersonal states and the relationship between the subpersonal and the personal.

Further reading

Dennett, D. 1969. *Content and Consciousness*. Routledge and Kegan Paul.
Drayson, Z. 2014. The Personal/Subpersonal Distinction. *Philosophy Compass*, 9(5): 338-46.
Hornsby, J. 2000. Personal and Sub-personal: A Defence of Dennett's Early Distinction. *Philosophical Explorations*, 3(1): 6-24.

There is a final point to consider here, and it is perhaps the most important: even if the notion of privacy were to provide us with a *criterion* that distinguished mental phenomena from non-mental phenomena, it wouldn't provide us with a *positive* characterization of mentality. Suppose that you were trying to explain the notion of mentality to someone – a visitor from Mars, for example – who was unacquainted with it. Telling such a person that mental phenomena can be distinguished from non-mental phenomena on the grounds that the former exhibit a kind of privacy that the latter lacks might be of some help to them, but it wouldn't give them much grip on the notion. In looking for a mark of the mental, we don't just want a feature that can help us distinguish mental phenomena from non-mental phenomena; we also want to identify features that might *illuminate* the nature of mentality.

1.3 Intentionality

One proposal that promises to do just that appeals to intentionality, for some theorists claim that all and only mental phenomena are intentional. This thesis is known as *Brentano's thesis* in honour of Franz Brentano (1838-1917), the philosopher who first advocated it. We will consider Brentano's thesis in some detail, but we first need to examine the notion of intentionality, for the term has a technical meaning in the philosophy of mind.

In ordinary life, the word 'intentional' is applied to actions that are purposeful and goal directed. This is *not* the primary meaning of intentionality in the philosophy of mind, although the two notions are related. As the term is used here, a state is intentional in virtue of the fact that it is directed towards a certain object, event, or state of affairs. For example, my belief that Valentina Tereshkova was the first woman in space is about a particular person; namely, Valentina Tereshkova. My belief reaches out and 'points' to her; it latches on to some particular aspect of the world and says something about it. Desires are also intentional, for they too are directed towards particular aspects of the world. My desire to visit Madagascar is about Madagascar and not any other tropical island. Intentionality is not restricted to thoughts, but also characterizes perceptual and emotional episodes. Seeing one's dog bite the mail carrier is directed towards a particular event; namely, the dog's biting of the mail carrier. The mail carrier's fear is also directed towards something; namely, the dog. As Brentano put it, 'in presentation, something is presented, in judgment something is affirmed or denied, in love loved, in hate hated, in desire desired and so on' (1874/1973: 88).

Philosophers have two ways of talking about what is presented in perception, thought, and emotion. Sometimes the term 'object' is used here. In this sense, we can say that my desire to visit Madagascar has as its object Madagascar. Other theorists tend to talk about intentional states in terms of propositional contents (or just 'contents' for short) rather than objects. Here, for example, we might say that what is affirmed in a particular thought is (say) the proposition 'foxes are solitary hunters'. There are deep and difficult questions about precisely how these two ways of describing intentional states are related to each other, but we cannot engage with them here. Instead, we will avail ourselves of both ways of describing intentional states. For example, we can say that the object of my belief that Valentina Tereshkova was the first woman in space is Valentina Tereshkova, and we can also say that the content of this belief is the proposition 'Valentina Tereshkova was the first woman in space'.

What are the objects of intentional states? On the face of things, most intentional states seem to be directed towards ordinary, publicly accessible things. My belief that Valentina Tereshkova was the first woman in space is about a particular Russian; my desire to visit Madagascar is about a particular island just east of Mozambique. An episode of seeing might be directed towards a dog's interaction with a mail carrier, and an episode of hearing might be directed towards the mail carrier's response to that interaction. So far, perhaps, so good, but there are also intentional states whose objects have a more problematic status. Those who go without sleep for long periods often see (or at least seem to see) things that aren't there, and more than one prospector has been hoodwinked into searching for treasure that doesn't exist. Indeed, fiction shows that we can think about non-existent objects while being fully aware of their non-existence. So there is a range of cases in which it does not appear to be possible to identify the object of a mental state with something that is part of the furniture of the world. Otto is afraid of a blue-eyed monster under his bed, but this fact does not entail that there is something (namely, a blue-eyed monster) of which Otto is afraid.

These considerations present us with the following dilemma. On the one hand, there is some inclination to think that intentional states all have the same kinds of objects. Consider, for example, a normal visual experience and a visual hallucination that is indistinguishable from it from the perspective of the subject in question. Intuitively, these two states have the same kind of entities as their objects. On the other hand, hallucinations do not have ordinary physical things as their intentional objects. For example, a visual hallucination of a spider doesn't have a spider as its object. So, if we insist that all intentional states have the same kinds of objects, then we are forced to say that the visual perception of a spider doesn't have a spider as its intentional object either. But that seems implausible, for we want to say that the objects of thought and perception are often ordinary physical objects. When Helen is afraid of spiders, it's real spiders that she's afraid of, not merely the idea or concept of a spider. We won't attempt to solve this dilemma here. The point to appreciate for now is that the nature of intentional objects raises questions that are not easy to answer.

Intentional objects provide part of the structure of intentional states, but they are only part of the story. Another part of the story concerns the ways in which intentional states can be evaluated. Consider the contrast between believing that it will rain tomorrow and desiring that it will rain tomorrow. These two intentional states have the same content (namely, the proposition 'it rains tomorrow'), but they are related to that proposition in very different ways. Believing that it will rain tomorrow is an indicative representation: it says how the world is. As such, it can be evaluated in terms of whether it is true or false. If it does rain tomorrow, then my belief that it will rain tomorrow it true, but if it doesn't rain tomorrow, then my belief is false. By contrast, desiring that it rain tomorrow doesn't purport to say how the world is, but is instead in the business of saying how the world should be. It is an imperative state rather than an indicative one. We don't evaluate desires for whether they are true or false, but instead evaluate them for whether or not they are satisfied. So, one contrast between beliefs and desires is in terms of how they are related to the world: beliefs have truth conditions, whereas desires have satisfaction conditions. Belief and desire are referred to as 'intentional modes' or 'intentional attitudes'. A full account of intentionality would need to say how many intentional attitudes there are, and how they are related to each other (Box: The propositional attitudes).

Box: The propositional attitudes

Because intentional states often have propositions as their contents, intentional attitudes are often referred to as propositional attitudes. (A proposition is simply something that can be true or false.) For example, the belief that Valentina Tereshkova was the first woman in space has the proposition 'Valentina Tereshkova was the first woman in space' as its content, while the desire to visit Madagascar has the proposition 'I visit Madagascar' as its content. In fact, the connection between intentionality and propositional attitudes is so close that it is often assumed that the analysis of intentionality *just is* the analysis of the propositional attitudes.

That assumption is problematic, for many intentional states don't appear to involve attitudes to propositions. For example, loving someone is an intentional state, but Anthony's love for Cleopatra seems to be directed towards Cleopatra herself rather than any proposition that involves Cleopatra. Similarly, Otto's fear of the monster under his bed is directed towards an imagined monster, and doesn't appear to involve any monster-involving proposition. Indeed, perception is intentional, but it is controversial whether it has propositional content. So, although the propositional attitudes play an important role in our understanding of intentionality, there are good reasons to think that the analysis of intentionality is not exhausted by that of the propositional attitudes.

Further reading

Grzankowski, A. 2013. Non-propositional Attitudes. *Philosophy Compass*, 8(12): 1123-37.
Grzankowski, A., and M. Montague. (Eds.) 2018. *Non-propositional Intentionality*. Oxford University Press.
Montague, M. 2007. Against Propositionalism. *Noûs*, 41(3): 503-18.

There is much more to say about intentionality (as we will see in later chapters), but I hope that the foregoing provides enough of a guide to the notion to enable us to return to Brentano's thesis: do all and only mental phenomena exhibit intentionality?

Let us begin with the 'only' part of the equation: is intentionality *restricted* to mental phenomena? Arguably not. Consider any example of language, such as the words that you are currently reading. These words and the sentences that they compose are intentional, for they are directed towards certain things. For example, the word 'language' is about language. Indeed, even sentences that refer to themselves, such as 'This sentence is in English', are intentional. Language - not to mention other representational devices, such as maps, musical scores, and fragments of Morse code - indicates that intentionality is not restricted to mental phenomena.

This objection to Brentano's Thesis is far from decisive, for it can be met by distinguishing two kinds of intentionality: *derived* intentionality and *underived* intentionality. The kind of intentionality that characterizes sentences, maps, musical scores, and so on is derived, for it depends on conventions. The word 'fox' refers to foxes only because English speakers abide by the convention that the word 'fox' refers to foxes. Similarly, an open circle on a subway map might indicate a subway station only because that's the convention adopted by the mapmaker. By contrast, the intentionality that characterizes mental phenomena is *underived*, for it does not depend on conventions. Thoughts don't need to be interpreted in the way in which utterances and inscriptions do. (If they did, a vicious regress would threaten to ensue, for acts of interpretation are themselves intentional, and as such they would in turn require interpretation, and so on.)[2] So, rather than saying that all intentional phenomena are mental, the advocate of Brentano's thesis should instead say that all phenomena that exhibit *underived* intentionality are mental. Although that claim is not universally accepted, in my view it is fairly compelling, and I don't know of any counterexamples to it.

However, the claim that (underived) intentionality suffices for mentality is only one component of Brentano's thesis. The other component of Brentano's thesis is that claim that (underived) intentionality characterizes *all* mental phenomena. Are there (or could there be) mental phenomena that are not about anything at all?

The answer to this question is highly disputed, and much ink has been spilt over it. For reasons that we will explore in later chapters, some theorists think that this is one of the most important questions in the philosophy of mind. We cannot address all of the issues that it raises, but we can consider a couple of the many phenomena that theorists have taken to provide counterexamples to the claim that all mental phenomena are intentional.

If you stare at green dot for 30 seconds or so, and then shift your focus to a blank piece of paper, you will visually experience ('seem to see?') an afterimage – a red dot of roughly the same size as the green dot at which you were staring. Afterimages don't appear to be directed towards objects in the way in which ordinary perceptual experiences are. Nor, on the face things, do they seem to be accessible for accuracy in the way in which ordinary visual experiences are. It is tolerably clear what the world has to be like in order for a visual experience of a green dot to be veridical, but what does the world have to be like in order for a red afterimage experience to be veridical?

Another source of pressure on Brentano's thesis derives from moods. Although many emotions are intentional – one can be sad about the death of a friend, rejoice in the success of a loved one, or be angry at a perceived insult – moods, their close relatives, seem to be objectless. Consider the state of mind sometimes described as generalized anxiety. The term is apt insofar as generalized anxiety doesn't have a specific focus, unlike the forms of anxiety that might be directed towards (say) an upcoming exam, meeting one's boyfriend's parents, or a trip to the proctologist. Those in a state of generalized anxiety are not anxious about any particular object, event, or situation; rather, their mood state seems to be undirected. Euphoria also seems to lack intentional focus. Although euphoria can be directed towards particular events (the exam went swimmingly; you got on with your boyfriend's parents; the appointment with the proctologist was uneventful), it can also be undirected. Sometimes there doesn't seem to be any sensible answer to the question, 'What are you happy about?'

Both of these putative counterexamples to Brentano's thesis are controversial. For example, a number of theorists argue that afterimages *are* intentional, and can be thought of as illusory presentations of phenomena. On some views, what is presented in an afterimage experience is an ordinary physical object (Byrne & Hilbert 2003; Tye 2000a); on other views, what is presented in an afterimage experience is an illusory experience of light (Phillips 2013). Each of these accounts treats afterimage experiences as intentional states, and thus if either of them is right, then afterimages don't constitute a counterexample to Brentano's thesis. To my mind, the objection from moods is significantly more compelling than the objection from afterimages, but even it is not decisive. Some theorists argue that moods are directed towards the world as a whole; others argue that moods are directed towards states of one's own body. We return to moods in Chapter 9.

Although it is controversial whether either afterimages or moods exhibit intentionality, these phenomena do nonetheless indicate that Brentano's Thesis is problematic. This is because the question of whether afterimages or moods are mental clearly doesn't turn on the question of whether they are intentional. (Suppose that someone was able to demonstrate that afterimages aren't intentional. Surely it would be unreasonable to conclude on that basis that they aren't mental!) So, whatever the outcome of the debate surrounding the intentionality of afterimages and moods, the mere fact that their status as intentional is contested (but their status as mental isn't) indicates that there is more to our conception of the mental than intentionality.

1.4 Consciousness

Together with intentionality, the other notion that dominates the philosophy of mind is consciousness. Let us begin by considering the notion of consciousness in its own right before turning to the question of whether consciousness might provide us with a viable mark of the mental.

We ascribe consciousness to two types of things. On the one hand, we describe people – and organisms more generally – as conscious or unconscious. For example, we distinguish between people who in a state of alert wakefulness or are dreaming from those who have been knocked unconscious or who are in a state of dreamless sleep. Exactly which kinds of organisms are capable of consciousness is an open question (see Chapter 11), but it is generally thought that many other mammals (and perhaps also certain non-mammalian species) are conscious. At the same time, we also describe mental states as conscious or unconscious. For example, we can distinguish between the conscious states that one might enjoy when relaxing in a hot bath and listening to music from the unconscious mental states that are implicated in the processing of perceptual input.

Some theorists suggest that the kind of consciousness that characterizes creatures is a very different thing from the kind that characterizes a creature's mental states. In my view, however, there is an intimate connection between what it is for a creature to be conscious and what it is for a mental state to be conscious. As I think of it, creatures are conscious in virtue of having conscious mental states. There are not two different kinds of properties here; instead, there is just a single kind of property that can take more or less specific forms.

There are various ways of distinguishing conscious states from each other. When it comes to sensory forms of consciousness, we often distinguish conscious states from each other by appealing to the objects and/or properties that we are conscious of. For example, one might distinguish between the experience of seeing Nathaniel from the experience of seeing Luka or Asher, and one might distinguish each of these experiences from the experience of tasting coffee or feeling the texture of a dress. We often distinguish conscious thoughts from each other by reference to the fact or state of affairs that the thought is directed towards. For example, one might distinguish being conscious that today is Christmas from being conscious that the dishes haven't been washed.

Consciousness itself is a mysterious phenomenon, and matters are not helped by the fact that a great many terms are used in connection with it. In addition to distinguishing between different kinds of consciousness (such as 'sensory consciousness', 'qualitative consciousness', and 'reflexive consciousness'), there are also a number of terms that are near synonyms of consciousness, such as 'awareness', 'experience', and 'qualia' (Box: Qualia). Some writers hold that there are important distinctions between 'awareness', 'experience', and 'consciousness', whereas others use these labels as terminological variants of each other. We consider the question of how many types of consciousness there might be in later chapters (see in particular Chapter 9). Here, we will focus on the most philosophically important (and controversial) form of consciousness: phenomenal consciousness.

The notion of phenomenal consciousness can't be defined in any non-circular way. We can, however, attempt to point to it by means of the phrase 'what it's like' (Nagel 1974). There is 'something that it is like' for a creature to be in a phenomenally conscious state, and phenomenal states differ from each other in terms of what it's like to be in them. For example, what it's like to taste strawberries differs from what it's like to hear the sound of a didgeridoo, and both of these states differ from what it's like to experience a persistent itch in the middle of one's back. We can also say that these states differ from each other in terms of their phenomenal character. The notion of phenomenal consciousness picks out roughly the same class of phenomena that is picked out by the terms 'sensory consciousness', 'qualitative consciousness', and 'experience', although some theorists argue that there are non-sensory forms of phenomenal consciousness.

Box: Qualia

Of all the contested terms in the philosophy of mind, perhaps none is more contested than *qualia* (singular: *quale*). In its broadest sense, qualia are simply the appearances of things. The qualia associated with the taste of coffee are simply the way in which coffee tastes. Qualia, in this sense of the term, are what give experiences their phenomenal character. Without them, there would nothing that it was like to be in a particular conscious state. Call this the uncontentious notion of qualia.

The existence of uncontentious qualia is pretty much, well, uncontentious, for even the most radical of sceptics allow that our interaction with the world involves various forms of sensory appearance. However, there are also conceptions of qualia that associate qualia with particular features, and the existence of qualia in these more demanding senses is contentious. For example, qualia are often taken to be non-intentional (i.e., not explainable in terms of intentional content); intrinsic (i.e., not definable in terms of their relations to other states); ineffable (i.e., not able to be communicated); and private (i.e., not able to be compared across individuals). The claim that there are sensory appearances that have one or more of these features has been the subject of a long-standing dispute between 'qualiaphiles' (who hold that contentious qualia of some kind exist) and 'qualiaphobes' (who hold that only uncontentious qualia exist).

Subsequent chapters will explore various aspects of the debate between qualiaphiles and qualiaphobes, but I will generally avoid using the term 'qualia'. The issues raised by qualia-talk are certainly important, but they are best tackled using terms (such as 'consciousness' and 'experience') that carry less baggage.

Further reading

Crane, T. 2000. The Origins of Qualia. In Tim Crane and Sarah Patterson (eds.), *The History of the Mind-Body Problem*. Routledge.

Might consciousness provide us with a viable mark of the mental? In other words, are all and only mental phenomena conscious?

The 'only' part of this question is straightforward, for few would deny that if a state is conscious then it is also mental. However, there are good reasons to deny that all mental states are conscious. As we noted earlier in this chapter, someone who is in a dreamless sleep or has been knocked unconscious can (say) believe that sloths are herbivores, want to become a dentist, or intend to grow pumpkins. Of course, a person cannot be *aware* of their belief, desires, and intentions if they are unconscious, but it might still be true to say of them that they have particular beliefs, desires, and intentions. And if that's right, then at least some mental phenomena (namely, standing states) are not necessarily conscious, and consciousness cannot provide us with a mark of the mental.

There is, however, a fall-back position for theorists who are attracted to the view that consciousness is at the heart of mentality. Instead of holding that mental states must be conscious, one could hold that mental states must be *potentially* conscious. This position has been advocated by John Searle (1992). According to Searle's *connection principle*, it is of the essence of mentality that a mental state must be accessible to consciousness. A state that one couldn't be aware of simply wouldn't qualify as a genuine mental state, Searle claims.

Although we could follow Searle in restricting the term 'mental' to states that are accessible to consciousness, it is far from clear what might be gained by that move. Certainly we don't, as a matter of current practice, restrict the domain of the mental to what is consciously accessible. Psychologists and cognitive neuroscientists routinely describe the kinds of complex information processing involved in recognizing a friend, recalling a telephone number, or deciding whether or not Canada is larger than Brazil (it is) as mental, even though these processes involve subpersonal states that are not accessible to consciousness, even in principle. The issue here is not restricted to subpersonal states, for there are also personal-level phenomena that seem to fall foul of Searle's connection principle. Consider character traits, such as being shy or being conscientious. These are simply not the kinds of states that can be conscious or unconscious. (One can, of course, become conscious that one is shy, but that doesn't mean that shyness is itself a conscious state.) Consciousness is one of the most important aspects of mentality, but it does not provide us with a plausible mark of the mental.

1.5 Folk psychology

Although some of the terminology employed in this chapter might be new to you, I hope that the ideas themselves have a familiar feel. The reason for this familiarity is that you, together with the vast majority of your fellow human beings, possess an intuitive conception of the mind. This intuitive conception is sometimes referred to as 'common-sense psychology', 'belief-desire psychology', or 'naïve psychology', but I will use the label that is perhaps most often associated with it: 'folk psychology'.

One way to think of folk psychology is on the model of other everyday (or 'folk') theories of reality, such as folk physics. One needn't have formally studied physics to have an intuitive appreciation of the ways in which certain types of objects behave. Even young children know that when you spill a cup of milk on the floor its contents don't bounce. Similarly, one needn't have studied psychology in order to know that people act on the basis of their beliefs and desires, that they typically experience pain when they are stabbed by something sharp, that they are typically angry when they believe that their trust has been betrayed, and so on. Explaining, understanding, and predicting what someone might do by invoking their perceptions, beliefs, intentions, emotions, and so on is second nature to us. We are not the only creatures on this planet to have minds, but we are one of the few – indeed, perhaps the only – species whose members routinely ascribe mental properties to each other and to themselves.

Folk psychology raises a great number of questions. One question concerns its content. What exactly is the folk-psychological conception of the mind? Is folk psychology committed to the claim that mental states *cause* their actions, or is it committed only to the claim that a person's beliefs explain and rationalize their actions without necessarily causing them? What is the folk-psychological conception of thought? Is folk psychology committed to the idea that thoughts have a language-like structure, or is it non-committal in this respect? Does folk psychology make any claims about how we know the contents of our own minds, or is it agnostic on this issue? At present, these are all open questions. Interestingly, answering them requires treating our own intuitive conception of the mind as a subject of scientific inquiry in its own right (Box: Folk psychology or folk psychologies?).

Box: Folk psychology or folk psychologies?

Philosophers of mind commonly assume that folk psychology is a monolithic entity, and that one person's folk psychology is likely to be essentially the same as another's. However, there is evidence of some degree of folk-psychological variation, both within societies and – perhaps more interestingly – between societies.

One culturally based contrast concerns how people view the relationship between agents and their environment. In the 1970s social psychologists noticed that we generally over-emphasize the degree to which people's behaviour is driven by underlying features of their personality (their character traits) as opposed to features of their environment. Suppose that you are interviewing someone for a job, and they seem to be very anxious. You might assume that their anxiety is due to the fact that they have a nervous disposition (a trait-based explanation) and overlook the fact that job interviews are unusually stressful contexts (a situational explanation). The tendency of people to focus on trait-based explanations of behaviour and ignore situational explanations appeared to be so robust that it was dubbed the 'fundamental attribution error'. However, subsequent research has suggested that the so-called fundamental attribution error is not a universal feature of folk psychology but occurs only in societies that place an emphasis on individual autonomy. Societies that emphasize collective action and conformity to social norms are more inclined to provide situational explanations of behaviour.

In general, however, the conceptual repertoire that we have for thinking about minds seems not to vary a great deal from one society to another, and as far as we know, all human societies explain human behaviour by appeal to desires, thoughts, bodily sensations, intentions, beliefs, and emotions.

Further reading

Henrich, J. et al. 2010. The Weirdest People in the World? *Behavioral and Brain Sciences*, 33(2-3): 61-83.

Lavelle, J. S. 2017. Cross-Cultural Considerations in Social Cognition. In J. Kiverstein (ed.), *The Routledge Handbook of Philosophy of the Social Mind*, Routledge, pp. 172-88.

Lillard, A. 1998. Ethnopsychologies: Cultural Variations in Theories of Mind. *Psychological Bulletin*, 123(1): 3-32.

A second question posed by folk psychology concerns its acquisition. We clearly don't acquire folk psychology on the basis of formal instruction, for even uneducated individuals have an intuitive understanding of mental phenomena. Do we acquire it by a kind of intuitive theorizing, building up a model of human behaviour in the way in which a scientist might? Do we acquire it in the context of learning the meaning of psychological terms – terms such as 'want', 'think', 'know' and 'see'? Or is folk psychology part of our innate endowment? Perhaps all three of these factors play a role in the acquisition of folk psychology.

A third question concerns the application of folk-psychological concepts. One aspect of this question concerns our capacity to apply folk-psychological concepts to other people. What grounds do we typically have for judging that (say) Meg is hungry or Bella is happy, and are these grounds able to generate knowledge of their mental states? Another aspect of this question concerns our capacity to apply folk-psychological concepts to ourselves. How do you know that you are in pain, that you are looking at a sloth, or that you regret not taking the 508 Bus to Moonee Ponds? Here too we can ask whether the methods that we use to apply mental concepts to ourselves – whatever exactly they are – generate knowledge.

A fourth question concerns the accuracy of folk psychology. To what degree is our intuitive conception of the mind correct? No one would claim that folk psychology presents us with a *complete* picture of the mind, for there are clearly many facets of the mind about which folk psychology is silent. We do, however, typically assume that the kinds of mental phenomena posited by folk psychology exist and that what folk psychology says about them is correct, at least in its broad outlines. However, some theorists have argued that we should take seriously the possibility that the very categories of folk psychology fail to refer to genuine features of reality. This view is known as eliminativism. According to eliminativists, some of the key concepts of folk psychology are akin to the aether of ancient physics, a substance that was posited to fill the universe in the region beyond the moon but turned out not to exist.

A final (and related) question concerns the relationship between folk psychology and our understanding of the natural world in general. Folk psychology makes reference to beliefs, desires, decisions, pains, and itches, but what exactly are these things? Are they physical phenomena? If so, then we need to explain why they don't seem to show up in the physical sciences. If, on the other hand, they are non-physical, then we need to explain how they are related to states of the agent's brain, body, and wider environment. More generally, we face questions about how the folk-psychological conception of human nature 'hangs together' with the conception of human nature that is provided by the sciences. Is folk psychology at odds with what we are learning about the human mind from psychology, neuroscience, and evolutionary biology, or is it consistent with (or perhaps even entailed by) findings in these sciences? To use Wilfrid Sellars's (1962) useful terms, we need an account of how the manifest image of the mind that is given to us by folk psychology relates to the scientific image of the mind that is given to us by the cognitive sciences.

1.6 Conclusion

Let's review the progress that we've made in this chapter. Our primary aim was to identify a 'mark of the mental' – a feature that is both necessary and sufficient for something to qualify as a mental phenomenon. We have considered three candidate features: privacy, intentionality, and consciousness – and in each case have found reason to suspect that the proposed feature does not characterize all and only mental phenomena.

One response to this failure would be to argue that we simply haven't looked hard enough, and that there is some feature that we have yet to consider which characterizes all and only mental phenomena. That proposal shouldn't be dismissed, but in my view a more likely possibility is that there is no mark of the mental. This conclusion shouldn't really be that surprising, for there are few interesting phenomena for which necessary and sufficient conditions can be given. Moreover, the fact that we generally agree about whether or not a particular phenomenon is mental doesn't entail that there must be some illuminating account of what makes it mental. Perhaps the concept of mentality is a cluster concept, one whose analysis resists any kind of watertight definition.

Although we haven't managed to discover a mark of the mental, our search has not been in vain, for we have learned a great deal about mentality and the content of folk psychology. In particular, we have identified two central features of the mind: intentionality and consciousness. Perhaps the most important question is not whether intentionality or consciousness might function as plausible marks of the mental, but how these two aspects of mentality are to be understood. What is the place of intentionality and consciousness in the natural world? Can they be accounted for in the same general kinds of ways as (say) digestion, respiration, and photosynthesis, or do they resist ordinary forms of scientific analysis?

A particularly important question here concerns the relationship *between* consciousness and intentionality. From about the middle of the 20th century to roughly the beginning of the 21st century, philosophers tended to view intentionality and consciousness as fundamentally distinct phenomena. Although certain kinds of mental states (such as emotions) were taken to exhibit both intentionality and consciousness, it was widely assumed that mental states could be sorted into two, relatively distinct, classes: those that were intentional (but not phenomenal), and those that were phenomenal (but not intentional). Beliefs, desires and other propositional attitudes were placed in the first category, while perceptual experiences and bodily sensations were placed in the second category. Richard Rorty expressed this 'separatist' conception of mentality vividly:

> The obvious objection to defining the mental as the intentional is that pains are not intentional – they do not represent, they are not *about* anything. The obvious objection to defining the mental as 'the phenomenal' is that beliefs don't feel like anything – they don't have phenomenal properties.
>
> (Rorty 1979: 22)

Over the last three or so decades, however, separatism in the philosophy of mind has come under increasing pressure, and many philosophers now espouse some form of what Terry Horgan and John Tienson (2002) have labelled 'inseparatism'. Inseparatism comes in various flavours, but the basic idea is that intentionality and (phenomenal) consciousness are deeply intertwined and cannot be understood in isolation from each other. Some inseparatists embrace an 'intentionality-first' approach to the mind, arguing that we need to appeal to intentionality in order to understand consciousness. Other inseparatists embrace a 'consciousness-first' approach, arguing that we must appeal to consciousness in order to understand

22 Marks of the mental

intentionality. As we will see, the debate between these two versions of inseparatism – and, indeed, the more fundamental debate between separatism and inseparatism – has implications for many issues in the philosophy of mind, and we will return to it often.

Further reading

The literature on intentionality is immense. A good place to begin is with Michelle Montague's 'Intentionality: From Brentano to Representationalism', in A. Kind (ed.), *Philosophy of Mind in the 20th and 21st Centuries* (Routledge, 2018). Also excellent is Tim Crane's paper 'Intentionality as the Mark of the Mental', in A. O'Hear (ed.), *Current Issues in the Philosophy of Mind* (Cambridge University Press, pp. 229-51, 1998), and his book *The Elements of Mind* (OUP, 2001). The distinction between original and derived intentionality was introduced by John Searle in his paper 'Intentionality and Its Place in Nature', *Synthese*, 61(1): 3-16 (1984), reprinted in his *Consciousness and Language* (Cambridge University Press 2002). For more on afterimages, see Ian Phillips, 'Afterimages and Sensation', *Philosophy and Phenomenological Research*, 87(2): 417-53 (2013) and Robert Schroer, 'Environmental Representationalists and Phosphenes: Putting Our Best Foot Forward', *Southern Journal of Philosophy*, 42: 531-46 (2004). Further readings on moods can be found at the end of Chapter 9.

The literature on consciousness is, if anything, even more voluminous than the literature on intentionality. Two of the most useful collections on the topic are *The Nature of Consciousness: Philosophical Essays*, edited by Ned Block, Owen Flanagan, and Güven Güzeldere (MIT Press, 1997), and *The Oxford Handbook of the Philosophy of Consciousness*, edited by Uriah Kriegel (OUP, 2020). Further readings on consciousness can be found at the end of Chapters 8 and 9.

An excellent overview of folk psychology can be found in 'Folk Psychology', by Stephen Stich and Shaun Nichols, in *The Blackwell Guide to Philosophy of Mind*, edited by S. Stich and Ted A. Warfield (Basil Blackwell, pp. 235-55, 2003). For a discussion of the relationship between folk psychology and scientific psychology, see Heidi Maibom's 'The Mindreader and the Scientist', *Mind and Language*, 18(3): 296-315 (2003) and Barbara von Eckardt's 'Folk Psychology and Scientific Psychology', in Samuel Guttenplan (ed.), *A Companion to the Philosophy of Mind* (Blackwell, pp. 300-307, 1994). Wilfrid S. Sellars's distinction between the manifest and scientific images can be found in his 'Philosophy and the Scientific Image of Man', in Robert Colodny (ed.), *Science, Perception, and Reality* (Humanities Press/Ridgeview, pp. 35-78, 1962).

Study questions

1 What does it mean to say that mental phenomena are private? What are the most serious objections to the claim that all mental phenomena are private?
2 Could brain-scanning devices threaten the privacy of the mental?
3 What is Brentano's thesis? What challenges does it face? Do you think that those challenges are successful, or can a plausible version of Brentano's thesis be defended?
4 Consider the terms 'awareness', 'experience', and 'consciousness'. Do you use these terms as synonyms, or do you distinguish between them in certain ways? If the latter is

the case, in what ways do you distinguish between these terms?
5   What is Searle's connection principle? Do you agree with the objections to it that are presented in this chapter, or do you think that it can be successfully defended from them?
6   This chapter introduces the distinction between personal states and subpersonal states. Explain this distinction in your own words. Do you think that there is a sharp distinction between the personal and subpersonal, or could this contrast be a matter of degree?
7   What is the difference between folk psychology and scientific psychology? How do you think they are, or should be, related to each other?
8   Explain the contrast between separatist and inseparatist approaches to the philosophy of mind. Which of these two approaches seems to you to be more compelling? Why?

Notes

1   For more on anosognosia, see Davies et al. (2005) and de Vignemont (2009).
2   One could hold that mental content is more basic than linguistic content (and doesn't in general depend on conventions) but also think that certain kinds of thoughts (e.g., those that concern imperceptible or fictional objects) are possible only for creatures who have mastered a public language (Carruthers 1996; Clark 1998, 2006). But to allow that certain types of intentionality depend on language is very different from holding that intentionality as such depends on language. For more on the relationship between mental content and linguistic content, see Speaks (2005).

2 Physicalism

Chapter overview

- Introduces the thesis of physicalism and contrasts physicalist conceptions of the mind with other views
- Considers some of the central motivations for physicalism
- Explains an important problem for attempts to characterize physicalism (Hempel's dilemma) and considers some responses to that problem
- Introduces the contrast between a priori and a posteriori conceptions of physicalism.

What is the place of mental phenomena in the natural world? Our focus in this chapter concerns an answer to this question that is variously known as 'physicalism' or 'materialism'.[1] (Although some authors use these labels to refer to different views, I will treat them as synonyms.) The basic idea behind physicalism is that mental phenomena are parts of the natural world in the same basic sense in which temperature and life are. These phenomena might not appear in the physicist's list of what is fundamental, but (the physicalist claims) they are in some sense 'nothing over and above' those fundamental features. As Frank Jackson puts it, 'consciousness and temperature and life, while not appearing in the inventory of physical ingredients, are nothing more than what we get if we put the right ingredients together aright' (Jackson 2006a: 236).

Physicalism is implicated in many of the most important debates in the philosophy of mind. Some of those debates concern the truth of physicalism, while others seek instead to identify the most plausible version of physicalism. We consider debates of both kinds in future chapters. In this chapter, however, our primary focus concerns how to define physicalism. What exactly does it mean to say that mental phenomenal are 'nothing over and above' physical phenomena? But before we turn to that question, we need first to consider questions of motivation. Why should we take physicalism seriously?

2.1 Motivating physicalism

As even committed physicalists recognize, physicalism is unintuitive. After all, mental phenomena seem to be utterly unlike physical phenomena. Physical phenomena are public in the sense that statements about them can (in principle at least) be subject to any number of tests and methods of evaluation. Suppose that someone tells me that there's a fox in the chicken coop. I have various ways of evaluating this claim. For example, I can ask if anyone saw the fox skulking around the chicken coop, I can check for fox prints in the dirt, and I can look for signs of fox fur in the chicken netting. By contrast, it is much more difficult for me to verify the claim that you are *imagining* that the fox has broken into the chicken coop, for on the face of things your act of imagination is a private event to which only you have direct access.

The fact that you appear to have a kind of direct access to the contents of your own mind that no one else has leads naturally to the idea that mental phenomena are radically unlike physical phenomena. This idea is known as dualism, for it holds that reality consists of two fundamentally different types of phenomena: physical phenomena and mental phenomena. Dualism itself comes in two forms: substance dualism and property dualism. Substance dualists hold that there are two kinds of substances, minds (or mental substances) and bodies (physical substances). Substance dualism is also known as Cartesian dualism, in honour of the French philosopher René Descartes (1596-1650), who was one of its most influential advocates. Although substance dualism has its proponents, contemporary dualists are more likely to be property dualists, who typically hold that although all substances are physical, certain kinds of mental properties are non-physical. What exactly it means for a mental property to be non-physical is a question to which we will return.

Although dualism is intuitively attractive, it faces a number of powerful objections. Let's consider three. The first problem is that dualism is difficult to reconcile with the origins of mentality. Just as our physical capacities have been shaped by our evolutionary history, so too have our mental capacities. We know that species with complex minds evolved from species with simpler minds, and that those species in turn evolved from creatures in which mentality was altogether absent. Although it's not inconceivable that this process might have involved the emergence of radically new kinds of states and processes, but it is surely more elegant to suppose that minded systems emerged from non-minded systems in much the way in which living systems emerged from non-living systems, and that you get mindedness 'for free' when you put the right kinds of physical ingredients together aright.

A second motivation for physicalism concerns the relations between mental states and brain states. We know from neuroscience and the treatment of psychiatric conditions that a person's thoughts, moods, perceptual experiences, and bodily sensations depend in intimate ways on the electrical and chemical states of their brain. To account for such dependencies the dualist needs to posit primitive laws of nature, 'psychophysical laws', that relate states of the brain to states of the mind. By contrast, if mental phenomena are nothing over and above physical phenomena, then we can understand why mental states are intimately related to brain states without positing primitive psychophysical laws.

A third motivation for physicalism concerns its capacity to account for causal interaction between the mental and the physical. Mental events are caused by physical events (the pattern of light hitting one's retina enables one to identify the bottles of whisky in the cupboard) and are in turn the cause of physical events (the intention to select a particular bottle typically leads to its retrieval). Physicalism provides - or at least *promises* to provide - a framework that does justice to the causal role of thoughts and experiences. By contrast, it is less clear that dualism can accommodate the possibility of mental causation. The dualist must either deny that mental properties are causally efficacious (a position known as epiphenomenalism), or explain how causal relations between non-physical properties can be accommodated within a conception of the world in which every event appears to have a full causal explanation in physical terms. Neither of these two options is appealing.

There is much more to be said by way of evaluating the case for and against physicalism, but we will leave that task for other chapters. Our focus here is on what exactly it is that the physicalist is committed to. Let's turn now to that topic.

2.2 Hempel's dilemma

Consider again Jackson's claim that physicalism about mentality is the view that mental phenomena are nothing more than what one gets if one puts the right physical ingredients together aright. This claim raises two questions. What does it mean for something to be *physical*, and what does it mean for something to be *nothing over and above* what is physical?

Attempts to say what it is for something to be physical confront a dilemma first noted by Carl Hempel (1905-97). Hempel pointed out that in defining what it is for something to be physical, one seems to have only two choices: either one says that a physical phenomenon is a phenomenon that is recognized by current physics, or one says that it's a phenomenon recognized by 'completed' or 'ideal' physics. Neither of these two options, Hempel (1969, 1980) argued, is attractive.

Appeals to current physics are unsatisfactory, for if the history of physics is any guide, contemporary physical theories are likely to be incorrect in important respects, and many of the properties and particles that they posit may not even exist. And if that is so, then it would follow that any version of physicalism that was defined in terms of current physics would also be incorrect, for mental phenomena obviously couldn't be nothing over and above the fundamental properties and particles posited by current physics if those properties and particles don't exist. Moreover, even if the fundamental properties and particles posited by current physics do exist, neither physicalists nor their detractors would want the truth of physicalism to depend on their existence. After all, the debate over physicalism isn't a debate over whether mental properties are nothing over and above the appropriate arrangement of the phenomena that are posited by current physics.

What about the second option? What would be wrong with defining 'physicalism' in terms of completed or ideal physics? One worry is that there may be no such thing as a completed or ideal physics. Perhaps reality is structured in terms of infinite layers of complexity, with the result that physics can never be complete or ideal, even in principle. A further objection is that even if the notion of a completed or ideal physics is coherent, appealing to it threatens to be vacuous, for – the argument goes – we have no idea what kinds of phenomena a completed or ideal physics might posit. A third problem with this proposal is that it threatens to render physicalism trivially true, for if physics is the science of whatever is fundamental, then it *must* account for mental phenomena in some way (Chomsky 1995). Either mental phenomena will be accounted for in terms of the non-mental phenomenal that appear in the physicist's list of what is fundamental, or – if they cannot be accounted for in those terms – physicists will simply include mental phenomena in their list of what is fundamental. Either way, the objection runs, appealing to a completed or ideal physics in order to define 'physicalism' seems to guarantee that physicalism is true, but that surely can't be right. After all, even physicalists don't think that the truth of physicalism is guaranteed by the meaning of the term! (Box: Mentality in the foundations?).

Box: Mentality in the foundations?

In characterizing physicalism, Jackson assumes that mentality won't be included in the physicist's list of the fundamental ingredients of reality, and that consciousness (like life, temperature, and other macro-level phenomena) comes into existence only when the fundamental forces, fields, and particles of physics are organized in the right kinds of ways. Although Jackson's view is widely endorsed, Russellian monists argue that mentality ought to be included in any inventory of what is fundamental. Named in honour of Bertrand Russell (1872–1970), the philosopher who gave the view its canonical formulation, the Russellian monist holds that consciousness characterizes the intrinsic nature of the fundamental phenomena identified by physics.

Does Russellian monism qualify as a kind of physicalism? Its advocates often argue that it does, and they have a point. After all, if mental properties really do function as the ground of ordinary physical phenomena, then it is not unreasonable to describe them as physical. At the same time, the picture of mentality espoused by the Russellian monist is so very different from that defended by the ordinary physicalist (who takes mental phenomena to be restricted to the macroscopic world in the way in which biological phenomena are), that it invites confusion to describe both conceptions of the mind as versions of physicalism. At any rate, I will reserve the term 'physicalism' for accounts that follow Jackson in holding that mental phenomena are not fundamental. In many respects, Russellian monism has more in common with dualism than it does with physicalism (as I am using the term here). We revisit Russellian monism in Chapter 8.

Further reading

Strawson, G. 2003. Real Materialism. In L. Anthony and N. Hornstein (eds.), *Chomsky and His Critics*. Blackwell, pp. 48–88.

The challenge that Hempel's dilemma poses is significant, but it is not insurmountable. In fact, there are two promising strategies for addressing it.

The first strategy seeks to evade Hempel's dilemma by arguing that even though we might not know the details of future physics, we do know the kinds of phenomena that any future physics will recognize. More importantly, we know the kinds of properties that any future physics *won't* recognize. For one thing, they won't be *normative*, for physics traffics in properties that describe how things are rather than how they ought to be. Nor will they be inherently private or accessible only from the first-person perspective, for physics is concerned with properties that can be captured from any point of view. More positively, we might say that the properties of future physics will be structural and functional, concerned with how objects and their properties interact with each other. This doesn't provide us with anything like a complete characterization of physicalism, but it is enough to provide the debate between physicalists and their detractors with some definition. Those who reject physicalism argue that mental phenomena involve properties (such as normativity, privacy, and subjectivity) that cannot be captured by appeal to purely structural and functional properties, whereas physicalists deny that that is the case.

Another strategy for avoiding Hempel's dilemma looks to characterize physicalism without using the term 'physical' at all. At heart, the physicalist is committed to the idea that mental phenomena are parts of the natural world in the same basic sense in which other natural phenomena are, such as digestion, respiration, and photosynthesis. Developing this thought, we might characterize physicalism as the view that mental phenomena are related to the fundamental elements (objects, properties, processes) of reality in the same general kinds of ways in which (say) digestion, respiration and photosynthesis are. None of these phenomena are truly fundamental–instead, they emerge only when one combines certain (fundamental) elements in the right kinds of ways.

A final point to consider before we move on from Hempel's dilemma concerns two ways in which the term 'physical' is used in the philosophy of mind. In what we might call the narrow sense of the term, a phenomenon is physical if and only if reference to it appears within fundamental physics. In this sense of 'physical', macrophysical objects and their states are not physical, for fundamental physics doesn't talk about (say) the hippocampus or neurotransmitters. There is, however, a broad sense of 'physical' in which the objects, states, and processes described by neuroscience and physiology clearly qualify as physical. In general, I will use the term 'physical' in this broader sense. Where the distinction between these two senses is important it will be explicitly noted.

2.3 Supervenience, emergence, and intelligibility

Having examined the question of what it means for something to be physical, let us turn now to the second question raised by Jackson's characterization of physicalism: what does it mean to say that something is 'nothing over and above' the physical?

One influential answer to this question appeals to the relation of *supervenience* – or rather, to a particular kind of supervenience relation known as *metaphysical supervenience*.[2] Let's begin with supervenience itself before turning to metaphysical supervenience.

Supervenience is a relation between two kinds of properties – the *P*-properties and the *Q*-properties. Suppose that an object's *P*-properties include various physical properties, such as its shape, colour, and size. And suppose that the *Q*-properties include certain aesthetic properties, such as being elegant and being beautiful. Now consider Michelangelo's *David*. Intuitively, anything that has exactly the same *P*-properties as *David* must also have its *Q*-properties. If *David* is elegant, then a perfect physical duplicate of *David* will also be elegant. If two sculptures have different aesthetic properties – if, for example, one of them is elegant and the other gauche – then it must be the case that they also differ in physical properties. Speaking loosely, we might say that if the *Q*-properties supervene on the *P*-properties, then the *P*-properties 'fix' the *Q*-properties. More precisely, we can say that the *Q*-properties supervene on the *P*-properties when there is no difference in *Q*-properties without a difference in *P*-properties.

Appealing to relations of supervenience is particularly useful when one wants to capture the fact that two types of properties are intimately related, but one also wants to remain uncommitted about the precise nature of that relation. This is precisely the situation that occurs in the current context, for theorists might agree that two scenarios cannot differ in their mental features without differing in their physical features but disagree as to *why* exactly mental differences must be accompanied by physical differences (see Chapter 3).

So much for supervenience; what is *metaphysical* supervenience? The supervenience relation comes in two strengths: nomological supervenience and metaphysical supervenience. Nomological supervenience is the weaker of the two relations. To say that the *Q*-properties *nomologically* supervene on the *P*-properties is to say that there can be no difference in *Q*-properties without a difference in *P*-properties within a restricted range of possibilities – roughly, those in which the laws of nature hold. (*Nomos* is Greek for 'law', and hence a relation that depends on laws of nature is known as a nomological relation.) Metaphysical supervenience is stronger than nomological supervenience, for claims about metaphysical supervenience are unrestricted: they hold in every possible world. In other words, if the *Q*-properties metaphysically supervene on the *P*-properties, then it's not possible for two scenarios to differ in their *Q*-properties without differing in their *P*-properties, even in possible worlds in which the laws of nature are very different from those that hold in the actual world (Box: Two kinds of possibility).

Box: Two kinds of possibility

Modal notions such as possibility and necessity are a notorious source of confusion in philosophy. Although many forms of possibility and necessity are invoked in the philosophy of mind, perhaps the most important contrast is between nomological possibility (and necessity) and metaphysical possibility (and necessity).

One way to grasp this distinction is to consider the claim that it's not possible to travel faster than the speed of light. Is this claim true or false? That depends. It's true as long as we are restricting our attention to worlds in which the laws of nature hold. But suppose that that restriction is lifted, and we allow ourselves to consider worlds in

> which the laws of nature are very different from those that obtain in the actual world. In that case, one might say, it *is* possible to travel faster than the speed of light, for there is certainly no incoherence in the idea that the laws of nature might have permitted such a feat. Thus, we might say that although it is nomologically impossible to travel faster than the speed of light (i.e., the laws of nature rule it out), it is metaphysically possible (for the laws of nature might have been different). Similarly, we might want to distinguish the claim that mental properties supervene on physical properties with nomological necessity from the claim that they supervene on physical properties with metaphysical necessity.

With the contrast between nomological supervenience and metaphysical supervenience in hand, let's turn now to the relevance of this distinction for the formulation of physicalism. Nomological supervenience is too weak to capture what is distinctive of physicalism, for dualists can (and typically do) hold that the mental facts nomologically supervene on the physical facts. As we noted earlier in this chapter, dualists can (and typically do) posit psychophysical laws that relate physical properties to mental properties. For example, they might say that there is a law relating a certain kind of activity in the visual cortex to the experience of colour. Physicalism is at odds with the existence of psychophysical laws, for if there are such laws, then it's not the case that mental phenomena are 'nothing more than what we get if we put the right ingredients together aright', as Jackson puts it. Instead, we would need also to posit brute (i.e., primitive) psychophysical laws in order to explain the distribution of mental phenomena. Thus, physicalists are committed to the claim that the mental is metaphysically (and not just nomologically) supervenient on the physical.

Physicalists are committed to the claim that the mental metaphysically supervenes on the physical, but is an appeal to metaphysical supervenience *sufficient* to distinguish physicalism from other conceptions of the mind? In other words, does anyone who takes the mental to metaphysically supervene on the physical qualify as a physicalist?

It is generally thought that the answer to this question is no. The reason for this is best explained by considering a view known as 'British emergentism'. British emergentism was developed by a group of philosophers who were active in Britain in the early decades of the 20th century, most notably Samuel Alexander (1859-1938) and C. D. Broad (1887-1971). Although there is some debate as to what exactly the British emergentists were committed to (McLaughlin 1992), they are generally taken to have held that although the mental is metaphysically supervenient on the physical, no explanation for this relationship can be given. Instead, the supervenience of the mental on the physical must simply be accepted 'with natural piety', as Samuel Alexander (1920) put it.

If endorsing metaphysical supervenience suffices for physicalism, then British emergentism qualifies a kind of physicalism. Although some philosophers would be happy to accept that verdict (Lewis 1983), most argue that British emergentism should not be regarded as any kind of physicalism at all. As Andrew Melnyk puts it:

> If the necessitation of the mental by the physical were just the holding of a brute modal relation between physical phenomena and mental phenomena, then there would be no

sense in which the mental was nothing over and above the physical, no sense in which true descriptions of mental affairs were made true by the antics of physical things, and no sense in which the mental was wholly constituted by the physical.

(Melnyk 2008: 1287-88)

If the metaphysical supervenience of the mental on the physical were primitive and unexplainable, then mental phenomena would be radically unlike other natural phenomena, such as temperature and life. Although temperature and life can be described as emergent phenomena in the sense that they aren't part of the fundamental structure of the physical world, we don't think that their existence has to be accepted 'with natural piety'. Instead, the supervenience of temperature and life on the microphysical facts is something that can be explained and made intelligible. Thus, if the physicalist conception of the mind is, most fundamentally, the claim that mental facts are related to the microphysical facts in the same basic kinds of ways that (say) temperature and life are, then the physicalist ought also to demand that the metaphysical supervenience of the mental on the physical can be made intelligible. (To use Terry Horgan's [1993] attractive neologism, physicalism requires not just supervenience but 'superdupervenience'.) As we will see in the next section, there is some debate as to what exactly the demand for intelligibility requires, but the important point to note for now is that physicalism (as defined here) is committed to it.[3]

2.4 A priori and a posteriori physicalism

We saw in the previous section that physicalism involves an epistemic commitment of some kind. On this conception of the view, being a physicalist requires more than holding that the mental is metaphysically supervient on the physical, it also requires thinking that this relation can be made intelligible in some way. In this section, we consider two very different conceptions of what this notion of 'intelligibility' might involve. On the one side of this debate is a position known as 'a priori physicalism', and on the other side is a position known as 'a posteriori physicalism'.

We can approach this debate by considering 'Laplace's demon', a mythical being with an intellect of unlimited power. Laplace's demon was concocted by the French mathematician Pierre Simon Laplace (1749-1827) to explore the notion of determinism, but we will use it to consider rival conceptions of physicalism.[4] Here is the key question: would a Laplacean demon who was acquainted with all the physical facts be able to 'read off' (i.e., know a priori) all the mental facts? In other words, are the mental facts a priori scrutable from the physical facts? Those who embrace an a priori conception of physicalism answer this question in the affirmative, whereas those who embrace an a posteriori conception of physicalism answer it in the negative.[5]

Note, crucially, that this debate is *not* about whether the truth of physicalism can be established on a priori grounds or whether it can be established only a posteriori. Pretty much everyone holds that the truth of physicalism is an a posteriori matter. The question, rather, is whether the physicalist is committed to the existence of conditionals, knowable a priori, which take one from truths about the fundamental physical features of the world to its mental features. For this reason, neither a priori physicalism nor a posteriori physicalism presupposes the truth of physicalism. As strange as it might sound, one could embrace either a priori physicalism or a posteriori physicalism without actually embracing physicalism, for what it is to be an a priori/a posteriori physicalist is to be committed to a certain view about what physicalists are - or at least should be - committed to. (Somewhat confusingly, physicalists who embrace a priori physicalism are known as 'Type-A physicalists', whereas those who embrace a posteriori physicalism are known as 'Type-B physicalists'.)

Let us return to Laplace's demon. The question, you will recall, is whether the demon - an intellect of unlimited power - would be able to read off all the mental facts from its knowledge of the physical facts. In other words, would such a demon be able to discern the mental features of a world armed with a book that described only its fundamental physical features?

The first issue to consider is what concepts Laplace's demon has. In particular, does it have the concepts of BELIEF, DESIRE, PAIN, and the like? If not, then one might think that any attempt to read off the mental facts from the physical facts must be ill-fated. Without psychological concepts, Laplace's demon wouldn't be able to entertain hypotheses about what the mental facts are, and if it cannot even entertain these hypotheses, then it can hardly tell which of them is true. Let's assume, then, that the demon has all the concepts that it needs. It can (let's suppose) formulate hypotheses about what various entities are thinking, feeling, or trying to do. It can wonder to itself, 'Does this person have a headache?', 'Is this person thinking about Madagascar?', 'Is this person trying to remember a telephone number?' The question is whether Laplace's demon can determine which of these hypotheses is true.

Even by the standards of the philosophy of mind, this question is an abstruse one, and if you find yourself flummoxed by it you are certainly not alone. The following example might help to illuminate what this debate involves. Consider the relationship between the points that constitute figures (e.g., squares, circles, and letters) and the figures that they constitute. As Jackson points out, one can

> ... learn to recognize and name the shapes of closed figures without knowing the formulae that gives the commonality among the points that make up their boundaries. All the same, the locations of those points a priori determine the shapes, and there will be a formula that shows this. This is because finding the formulae satisfied by the points that make up any given shape is an exercise in mathematics, and mathematics is an a priori discipline. In the case of circles it is a very easy exercise; in the case of shape recognition of handwritten words, it is a very hard one tackled by those who write programs to turn handwriting into *Times New Roman*. . . . We are able to recognize the pattern, the commonality, that unites the written a's. That is to say, if α is a name for that shape . . . [then] there is a complex sentence giving [the] location of the boundary points of X that a priori entails 'X is α'. . . . A priori physicalists have to say that the language of psychology is like this but in a much more complex way.
>
> (Jackson 2007: 194-95)

What is contested, as Jackson recognizes, is whether the language of psychology *is* akin to the language of shapes. It is very plausible to suppose that there are analytic truths (i.e., truths that are true merely in virtue of the meanings of the relevant terms) that connect position concepts to shape concepts. Such linkages would explain the appeal of the idea that one can read off shape facts from position facts. But are there analytic connections between the concepts of fundamental physics on the one hand and psychological concepts on the other? Well, it's obvious that there aren't any *direct* analytic truths of this kind, for the simple reason that no one really knows what the fundamental physical truths are. However, some a priori physicalists suggest that there are a priori links between mental concepts and what we might call 'vernacular' physical concepts – that is, concepts drawn from everyday physical discourse – and that such links suffice to establish *indirect* a priori links between the concepts of fundamental physics and those of folk psychology in virtue of analytic connections between the concepts of fundamental physics and those of vernacular physics.

Although the debate between a priori physicalism and a posteriori physicalism concerns the content of physicalism, it does have important implications for the question of whether physicalism is true, for an important family of arguments against physicalism turns on the assumption that physicalists must be a priori physicalists. In essence, these arguments involve an appeal to the idea that a Laplacean demon would not be able to read off a certain class of mental facts from its knowledge of the physical facts. One way to block these arguments would be to argue that a posteriori physicalism is viable, and that the physicalist need not assume that the mental facts are a priori scrutable from the physical facts. Chapter 8 examines these issues in more detail.

2.5 The prospects of physicalism

Let's take a step back from the question of how the thesis of physicalism ought to be formulated, and consider how one might go about putting pressure on it. What kinds of objections might the physicalist face?

Broadly speaking, there are two ways of challenging physicalism. First, one might focus on the modal dimension of physicalism, arguing that there is reason to doubt whether the mental facts are metaphysically supervenient on the physical facts. Indeed, some argue that the mental facts aren't even nomologically supervenient on the physical facts, and that (for example) an individual's decisions can make an impact on the world that is not constrained by physical processes. Neuroscientists often speak as though challenges of this kind represent the most serious threat to physicalism, but such threats tend not to be taken terribly seriously by philosophers of mind. Even philosophers who reject physicalism tend to accept that there is no mental difference in the *actual* world without a physical difference. On the face of things, it seems as though no *empirical* evidence could establish that the laws relating mental phenomena to physical phenomena are merely contingent. But if empirical evidence isn't relevant here, then what kind of evidence could one appeal to?

Many invoke distinctively philosophical methods at this point. More specifically, they argue that thought experiments and appeals to what is (and isn't) conceivable can provide evidence about metaphysical possibility. The idea, in other words, is that the conceivability of certain scenarios can be used to put pressure on the modal dimension of physicalism. The key questions here are whether certain scenarios are indeed conceivable, and whether conceivability is a reliable guide to what is metaphysically possible (Box: Ghosts and zombies).

> **Box: Ghosts and zombies**
>
> Among the many strange creatures that populate the philosophy of mind are ghosts and zombies. Ghosts are 'disembodied minds'—creatures with the mental properties of a normal human being but none of our physical properties. Your ghost twin is a creature that has exactly the same mental properties that you do but none of your physical properties. Zombies are 'anti-ghosts' – bodies without minds, as it were. Zombies have the physical, functional, and behavioural properties of normal human beings, but no mental states. Your zombie twin is indiscernible from you 'from the outside', but there is 'nothing it's like' for your zombie twin to be the creature that it is.
>
> If physicalism is true, then neither ghosts nor zombies exist. Physicalism rules out ghosts on the grounds that minds are nothing over and above physical ingredients. It also rules out zombies, for if mental properties supervene on physical properties, then anything that has the physical properties of a normal human being must also have the mental properties of a normal human being. But does physicalism also rule out the very *possibility* of ghosts and zombies? It certainly rules out the possibility of zombies, for if the mental facts metaphysically supervene on the physical facts, then your zombie twin is metaphysically impossible. It is less clear whether physicalism does (or should) rule out the possibility of ghosts. Some physicalists hold that although ghosts don't exist, they are the kinds of things that could have existed; others deny even the metaphysical possibility of ghosts.
>
> The fact that physicalism rules out the metaphysical possibility of zombies (and perhaps also ghosts) has been used to put pressure on it, for if ghosts and/or zombies are conceivable, and if (as many argue) conceivability is a reliable guide to metaphysical possibility, then the mere conceivability of ghosts and/or zombies would count against the truth of physicalism. We return to these issues in Chapter 8.

The second way of putting pressure on physicalism focuses on its epistemic commitments. Here, the critic might argue that even if the microphysical facts determine the mental facts just as they determine (say) the chemical and biological facts, we cannot explain *why* the mental facts depend on the microphysical facts in the way in which we can explain why the chemical and biological facts depend on the microphysical facts.

Not only do different objections to physicalism focus on distinct aspects of what the physicalist is committed to, they also focus on distinct aspects of mentality. For example, some theorists have argued that the physicalist cannot account for the rationality of the human mind, and that one needs to posit non-physical states and processes in order to explain our capacity for reason. This kind of argument is most famously associated with René Descartes. However, the force of this worry has dissipated – although perhaps not entirely disappeared – with the development of computers and the advent of artificial intelligence.

Other critics focus on intentionality, and the mind's capacity to grasp 'objects', some of which might not even exist. How, one might wonder, could a purely physical system have intentional states? Chapter 6 examines a number of the leading proposals for how intentionality might be accommodated within the framework of physicalism.

In the last couple of decades, debate about the prospects of physicalism has focused not on rationality or intentionality but on consciousness, for it is here that many theorists locate the most serious challenges to physicalism.[6] A number of influential lines of argument purport to show either that the experiential facts aren't necessitated by the physical facts, or that even if they are, we have no means of rendering the relationship between the physical and the mental intelligible. We consider these arguments in Chapter 8.

2.6 Conclusion

Let's retrace our steps. We began this chapter by considering what it is to be a physicalist. Here, we embraced Frank Jackson's conception of physicalism as the view that mental phenomena are nothing over and above what we get if we put the right physical ingredients together aright. The idea, roughly speaking, is that facts about minds are no spookier than other high-level facts, such as those involving respiration, digestion, and photosynthesis. Although respiration, digestion, and photosynthesis don't themselves appear in the physicist's list of the fundamental features of the world, they are (so we tend to believe) 'nothing over and above' the appropriate arrangement of those features.

This gives us an initial grip on what it is to be a physicalist, but it raises two further questions: (1) What does it take for an ingredient to be physical? (2) What does it mean for a phenomenon to be 'nothing over and above' the appropriate arrangement of physical ingredients? Section 2.2 explored the first of these questions through the lens of Hempel's dilemma; while Section 2.3 developed an answer to the second question that appealed to the modal notion of metaphysical supervenience and epistemic notion of intelligibility. In Section 2.4, we examined a debate about what exactly the epistemic commitments of physicalism might entail, and whether the physicalist should hold that the mental facts are a priori scrutable from the physical facts.

In Section 2.5, we distinguished different ways in which one might attempt to put pressure on physicalism, noting that one could focus either on physicalism's modal commitments or its epistemic commitments (or both). We saw too that different aspects of mentality can be identified as posing challenges to physicalism. Our focus in the next chapter, however, is not on the prospects of physicalism as such, but on some of the main ways in which physicalism has been developed. What exactly is the link between mental phenomena and physical phenomena? How *could* the mental facts be 'nothing over and above' the physical facts?

Further reading

For discussion of some of the central motivations for physicalism, see David Papineau's 'The Rise of Physicalism', in G. Gillet and B. Loewer (eds.), *Physicalism and Its Discontents* (CUP, 2001), which also contains a number of other important papers on physicalism. Another important collection of papers on physicalism can be found in a special issue of *Philosophical Studies*, 131(1) (2006); particularly useful here is Terry Horgan's paper 'Materialism: Matters of Definition: Defense and Deconstruction'.

On the question of how to define physicalism, see Alyssa Ney's 'Defining Physicalism', *Philosophy Compass*, 3(5): 1033-48 (2008); Janice Dowell's 'Formulating the Thesis of Physicalism: An Introduction', *Philosophical Studies*, 131(1): 1-23 (2006); and Daniel Stoljar's

Physicalism (Routledge, 2010). For more on Hempel's dilemma in particular, see Barbara Montero's 'The Body Problem', *Noûs*, 33(2): 183-200 (1999).

For objections to supervenience-based conceptions of physicalism, see Barbara Montero's 'Must Physicalism Imply the Supervenience of the Mental on the Physical?', *Journal of Philosophy*, 110(2): 93-110 (2013) and Jessica M. Wilson's 'Supervenience-Based Formulations of Physicalism', *Noûs*, 39(3): 426-59 (2005). For more on the relationship between physicalism and emergentism, see Brian McLaughlin, 'The Rise and Fall of British Emergentism', in A. Beckermann, H. Flohr, and J. Kim (eds.), *Emergence or Reduction? Prospects for Nonreductive Physicalism* (De Gruyter, 1992); James Van Cleve, 'Supervenience and Closure', *Philosophical Studies*, 58: 225-83 (1990); and Jessica M. Wilson, *Metaphysical Emergence* (OUP, 2021).

The literature on a priori and a posteriori physicalism is challenging. One place to start is with Ned Block and Robert Stalnaker's paper 'Conceptual Analysis, Dualism, and the Explanatory Gap', *Philosophical Review*, 108: 1-46 (1999), to which David Chalmers and Frank Jackson's 'Conceptual Analysis and Reductive Explanation', *Philosophical Review*, 110: 315-60 (2001) is a response. See also the chapters by Frank Jackson and Brian McLaughlin in *Contemporary Debates in Philosophy of Mind*, edited by B. McLaughlin and J. Cohen (Blackwell, 2007).

Louise Antony's 'The Mental and the Physical', in Robin Le Poidevin's *The Routledge Companion to Metaphysics* (Routledge, 2009), provides an excellent survey of the basic challenges that intentionality and consciousness pose to physicalism and the various ways in which physicalists have responded to those challenges.

Study questions

1. This chapter presents three motivations for physicalism. What are those motivations, and how convincing are they?
2. What is Hempel's dilemma? Explain exactly why it is a dilemma. What do you think is the best response to it?
3. What is Russellian monism? Explain why some theorists treat it as a species of physicalism whereas others (such as myself) distinguish it from physicalism.
4. What is the difference between nomological and metaphysical supervenience? Why do some theorists think that an appeal to metaphysical supervenience is too weak to capture what is distinctive of physicalism?
5. What, according to the account presented here, is the key difference between physicalism and British emergentism?
6. What is the difference between a priori physicalism and a posteriori physicalism? In answering this question, you might want to consider why each of these positions has the label that it does. You might also want to explain how the notion of a Laplacean demon is relevant here.
7. What, in the philosophical sense, are ghosts and zombies? In what ways are ghosts and zombies relevant to debates concerning physicalism?
8. The final section of this chapter suggested that, broadly speaking, there are two ways of challenging physicalism. What are those two ways? As you read later chapters, make a note of examples of these challenges that you come across.

Notes

1 'Physicalism' is problematic, for it suggests that all truths can be expressed in the language of physics, and that is not a claim that need be associated with this view. 'Materialism' is problematic on the grounds that it suggests that all objects are spatially extended, and that is not a claim that need be associated with this view either. I use 'physicalism' simply because it is entrenched within the current literature.
2 For further discussion of supervenience, see Kim (1984) and Stalnaker (1996).
3 Another approach to defining physicalism involves appeals to a relation that metaphysicians call 'grounding' (often capitalized), which is a relation of ontological explanation. For examples of this approach, see Dasgupta (2014), Ney (2016), and Schaffer (2009). For criticism of grounding-based formulations of physicalism, see Wilson (2018).
4 See Horgan (1983), Byrne (1999), and Chalmers (2012).
5 For defences of a priori physicalism see Chalmers (2012), Chalmers and Jackson (2001), Jackson (2007), Lewis (1994) and Stoljar (2000). For defences of a posteriori physicalism see Block and Stalnaker (1999), Byrne (1999), Levine (2020), and McLaughlin (2007).
6 It wasn't always so. 'Twenty years ago, emotions, qualia, and "raw feels" were held to be the principal stumbling blocks for the materialist [that is, physicalist] program. With these barriers dissolving, the locus of opposition has shifted. Now it is the realm of the intentional, the realm of the propositional attitude, that is most commonly held up as both being irreducible and ineliminable in favour of anything from within a materialist [that is, physicalist] framework' (Churchland 1981: 67–8). The pendulum has well and truly swung the other way since Churchland penned these words, and it is once again consciousness that is regarded as the major impediment to physicalism.

3 How to be a physicalist

> **Chapter overview**
> - Explains the core claims of behaviourism, the mind-brain identity theory, and functionalism
> - Considers eliminativism as an approach to mentality
> - Examines the respective roles of philosophical analysis and scientific inquiry in understanding the mind.

In the previous chapter, we identified physicalism as a key position in the philosophy of mind. According to the physicalist, mental phenomena are 'nothing over and above' physical phenomena. We saw also that one way of explicating that slogan is in terms of metaphysical supervenience, together with the idea that the idea that the metaphysical supervenience of the mental on the physical is not just a brute, unexplainable, fact but can be rendered intelligible.

The aim of this chapter is to consider four of the most influential approaches to the mind: behaviourism, the identity theory, functionalism, and eliminativism. Although not all of these approaches are strictly speaking committed to physicalism, they are all 'physicalism friendly', for each promises both to secure the dependence of the mental on the physical and to provide an explanation for that dependence. We will consider some of the main motivations for each of these theories and some of the central challenges that they face, but our primary focus here isn't on evaluating these positions but on understanding them.

3.1 Behaviourism

We begin with behaviourism, an approach to the mind that had its heyday between the 1930s and 1960s. As the label suggests, behaviourists take behaviour to be the key to mentality. There are, however, different traditions within behaviourism. In psychology, the most influential versions of behaviourism focused on methodological and explanatory issues. For

DOI: 10.4324/9781003225348-4

example, the behaviourists J. B. Watson (1878-1958) and B. F. Skinner (1904-90) held that the study of the mind should focus on the study of an organism's behavioural responses, and the ways in which those responses are altered by its environment and learning history. The psychological behaviourists eschewed reference to inner mental states and processes, arguing that they are not needed for the explanation of human behaviour. Indeed, Watson argued that positing such states wouldn't even be scientifically legitimate.

Although psychological behaviourism has had an influence on the philosophy of mind, the more profound behaviourist influence is due to a view that I will refer to as 'analytical behaviorism'. (It's also known as 'logical behaviourism' and 'philosophical behaviourism'.) Analytical behaviourists held that mental states can be analysed in terms of behavioural dispositions. For example, what it is to believe that it's raining outside just is to be disposed to behave in certain ways – for example, to put one a raincoat before heading outside or nod one's head in response to the question 'Is it raining outside?' The view is so called because its advocates held that an account of the relevant behavioural dispositions is implicit in the meaning of psychological terms, and thus that the behavioural analyses of mental phenomena qualify as analytical truths (claims that are true in virtue of their meaning). Someone who knows what 'pain' means knows that what it is to be in pain is a matter of having (say) the disposition to wince and to move away from a noxious stimulus. Importantly, what counts as behaviour here must be understood in non-psychological terms. Thus, what it is to 'put on one's raincoat' isn't a matter of intentionally putting on something that one believes to be one's raincoat, but is instead to be understood in terms of moving one's limbs so as to make it the case that one is in fact wearing a raincoat.

Behaviourism has a number of motivations, two of which continue to exert a significant influence on the philosophy of mind. The first motivation is epistemic. Our ordinary grounds for ascribing mental states to other people involve close attention to their behaviour – to what they do and say. The fact that Bonnie is smiling provides evidence that she's happy, and the fact that Clyde is yelling is naturally taken to indicate that he's angry. Now, if mental states just are behavioural dispositions (as the analytical behaviourists claimed), then we would have a straightforward account for why we are justified in ascribing happiness to people who smile and anger to people who yell. Whatever the shortcomings of behaviourism, there is clearly much that is attractive in any view of the mental which promises to vindicate our ordinary practice of ascribing mental states to others on the basis of behaviour.

A second, and closely related, motivation for behaviourism is the desire to reject a Cartesian conception of the mental as a private realm that is accessible only from the first-person perspective. In this regard, behaviourism drew significant inspiration from Gilbert Ryle (1900-76) and Ludwig Wittgenstein (1889-1951). Although neither Ryle nor Wittgenstein were full-blooded behaviourists, their accounts of the mind had much in common with behaviourism, and their influence did much to elevate that of behaviourism. Both Ryle and Wittgenstein rejected the dualist conception of the self as an immaterial substance that controls the body – what Ryle's parodied as 'the Ghost in the Machine' in his book *The Concept of Mind* (1949). They also argued that the meaning of our psychological vocabulary cannot be prised apart from its use to describe ordinary activity. As Wittgenstein put it in his *Philosophical Investigations* (1953/2009: §580), 'an "inner processes" stands in need of outward criteria'.

We will shortly consider a number of objections to behaviourism, but let us first reflect on why behaviourism qualifies as a form of physicalism. First, behaviourism satisfies the modal constraint on physicalism, for if mental phenomena are identical to behavioural dispositions then the mental facts are nothing over and above the physical facts. Behaviourism also satisfies the intelligibility constraint, for if mental phenomena are behavioural dispositions then the supervenience of the mental on the physical isn't primitive but can instead be fully explained.

The question, of course, is whether the behaviourist account of mentality is plausible. It certainly has some appeal with respect to certain kinds of mental phenomena. Consider, for example, character traits, such as being shy, curious, or quick-witted. Arguably, all there is to being shy is being disposed to behave in certain kinds of ways in certain contexts. But it is implausible to suppose that mental phenomena in general can be identified with behavioural dispositions in the ways in which analytical behaviourists held. Let us consider three reasons for this.

First, behaviourism struggles to account for the privacy of the mental. As we noted in the first chapter, we seem to enjoy a kind of direct and secure access to certain kinds of mental states. You have a kind of knowledge of your current emotional experiences that I don't (and possibily cannot) share. Similarly, you know what you are currently thinking in ways that I don't. Behaviourism renders the privacy of the mental mysterious, for - in principle at least - a person's behavioural dispositions are accessible from the third-person perspective. Many of those in the behaviourist tradition tend to respond to this challenge by downplaying the privacy of the mental, but few have found that response compelling.

Second, although many mental phenomena are correlated with behavioural responses, this link appears to be neither analytic nor necessary. Consider the relationship between pain and wincing. As it happens, being in pain is correlated with wincing in humans, but it seems perfectly coherent to suppose that there might be creatures for which this correlation fails to hold. Consider super-spartans - a kind of creature that can experience pain, but have none of the behavioural dispositions that we associate with pain (Putnam 1963). Super-spartans not only remain silent when in pain, they aren't even *disposed* to cry or whimper. Behaviourists must rule out the very possibility of super-spartans, but on the face of things super-spartans seem to be perfectly coherent. Equally coherent is the possibility of beings - let's call them 'actors' - who are disposed to produce pain behaviours (i.e., the kind of behaviours that in us are associated with pain) despite the fact that they aren't in pain. But again, if pain is identified with the disposition to produce a range of the behaviours that are associated with pain in us, then it would follow that actors are not a genuine possibility.

A third problem for behaviourism concerns the threat of circularity: to provide a behavioural analysis of one kind of mental state, one must invariably mention other kinds of mental states (Chisholm 1957). I might believe that it's raining outside, but I won't answer the question 'Is it raining outside?' in the affirmative if I desire to hide my weather-related beliefs from you, nor will I take an umbrella with me if I believe that the rain will soon cease and that taking an umbrella is more trouble than it's worth. What one is disposed to do in any particular context depends on one's entire network of beliefs, desires, and intentions, not to mention one's habits and emotional state. Thus, giving a full specification of any one mental state will inevitably involve reference to mental states of other kinds. But if that's right, then the behaviourist hasn't really provided a full account of mentality, or shown how mental phenomena might be 'nothing over and above' physical phenomena.

3.2 The mind-brain identity theory

Although it had relatively few explicit adherents, analytical behaviourism was extremely influential in the philosophy of mind until the late 1950s and early 1960s, at which point it was usurped by the mind-brain identity theory (also known as 'central-state materialism'). Identity theorists argue that mental states – or at least certain classes of mental states – are identical to brain states. For example, the identity theorist might identify pain with a particular kind of activity in the so-called 'pain matrix', a network involving the primary and secondary somatosensory cortices, the insula, and the anterior cingulate cortex, and which is typically active when people experience transient pain (although see page 168). One can find hints of the identity theory in the work of 17th- and 18th-century materialists such as Thomas Hobbes, Julien Offray de La Mettrie, and Baron d'Holbach, but the detailed development of the view did not occur until the middle decades of the 20th century. Some of its most significant advocates include Herbert Feigl (1958), U. T. Place (1956), J.J.C. Smart (1959), David Armstrong (1968), and David Lewis (1966). Although not as dominant as it once was, the identity theory remains influential (Box: Anomalous monism and token identities).

Box: Anomalous monism and token identities

The dominant version of the identity theory is known as the *type* identity theory, for it holds that types of mental states (i.e., mental properties) are identical to types of neural states (i.e., neural properties). However, there is another version of the identity account – the *token* identity theory – which has also been very influential. The token identity theory is associated most closely with a view of the mind known as *anomalous monism*. Developed by Donald Davidson (1917-2003) in the 1970s, the anomalous monist holds that although there are no laws that can be formulated using both physical and mental predicates (that's the 'anomalous' part), every particular mental event is identical to a particular physical event (that's the 'monism' part). According to the anomalous monist, your pain will be identical to a neural event (N^1), and my pain will also identical to a neural event (N^2), but it need not be the case that N^1 and N^2 are instances of a single type of neural state. Together with functionalism (described in the next section), the token identity theory is often described as a kind of non-reductive physicalism, for unlike standard versions of the identity theory it denies that mental properties are identical to neural properties.

What account *does* the anomalous monist give of mental properties? Davidson himself gave no account of them, for he was a nominalist about properties; as he saw it, properties are not part of the fabric of reality. But realism about mental properties is attractive, and anomalous monism's failure to give an account of them represents a sticking point for many.

Further reading

Davidson D. 1970. Mental Events. *Essays on Actions and Events*. Clarendon Press (1980).Macdonald, C. 1989. *Mind-Body Identity Theories*. Routledge.

In its modern guise, the identity theory was a reaction to behaviourism, and there are many respects in which the identity theorist's conception of the mind differs from that of the behaviourist. Analytical behaviourists assumed that the reduction of mental states to behavioural dispositions could be carried out a priori (i.e., independent of empirical investigation) and that the reductions in question were also *analytic* (i.e., followed from the meanings of the relevant terms. Identity theorists such as J. J. C. Smart (1959) rejected both of these commitments, holding that mind-brain identity statements are synthetic and a posteriori rather than analytic and a priori. Just as science has revealed that lightning is identical to electrochemical discharge and that water is identical to H_2O, so too, Smart claimed, the scientific data indicate that particular kinds of mental states are identical to particular kinds of brain states. Other identity theorists, such as Lewis (1966) and Armstrong (1968), did make substantive assumptions about the meanings of folk-psychological terms, but they too held that identifying a mental property with a neural property required scientific investigation and couldn't be established solely on the basis of philosophical analysis.

We will consider objections to the identity theory shortly, but let's first note that the identity theory qualifies as a version of physicalism for the same kind of reasons that behaviourism does. First, it satisfies the modal constraint on physicalism, for if mental states are identical to brain states, then the mental facts will supervene on the microphysical facts given that the facts about brain states presumably supervene on the microphysical facts. The identity theory also satisfies the intelligibility constraint, for if mental states are indeed identical to brain states, then the fact that the mental supervenes on the physical isn't a primitive, unanalysable fact but can instead be fully explained.[1]

The identity theory avoids some of the objections facing behaviourism, but it is vulnerable to others. For one thing, the identity theorist appears to have as much difficulty accommodating the privacy of the mental as the behaviourist does. In the same way that someone else's knowledge of my behavioural dispositions might rival (if not exceed) my own, so too someone else's knowledge of my brain states might rival (if not exceed) my own. But surely, one might think, another person's access to my mental states couldn't outstrip my access, no matter how detailed their knowledge of my brain. Even someone armed with the most accurate neuroimaging device imaginable couldn't know what it's like to be me in the way that I can.

But it is worries about the apparent contingency of the relationship between mental states and brain states that have proven most problematic for the identity theory. Writing in the 1960s and early 1970s, Hilary Putnam (1926–2016) pointed out that if pain is identical to a certain brain state ('the firing of C-fibres', to use his physiologically implausible example), then not only will any creature with firing C-fibres be in pain, but any creature that is in pain will have firing C-fibres (Putnam 1967, 1975a). This conclusion follows from the logic of identity. (If lightning *is* electrochemical discharge, then any instance of lightning must also be an instance of electrochemical discharge and vice versa.) But, Putnam went on to suggest, it is highly improbable that there is a single type of brain state associated with all instances of pain. Instead, he argued, it is surely more plausible to suppose that pain in the octopus (for example) involves neural states and processes that are quite different from those that are implicated in human pain. In essence, Putnam's objection mirrored an objection that was instrumental in the demise of behaviourism; namely, that the behaviour associated with any particular mental state is likely to be only contingently related to it. Putnam's objection has come to be known as the *multiple realization* objection.

It is important to distinguish two versions of the multiple realization objection. One version focuses on the idea that mental properties are *actually* multiply realized. Putnam himself seems to have thought of the objection in these terms. Although it is widely assumed that mental properties are multiply realized, the issue continues to provoke debate (see Box: Multiple realization). Another version of the objection focuses on whether mental properties *could* be multiply realized. Even if pain is in fact associated with a single type of neural state in both humans and non-humans, it seems entirely possible – does it not? – that it could occur in creatures whose brains are very different from ours. Indeed, much science fiction trades on the assumption that a creature could have mental states (of the kinds we have) without having any kind of brain at all. We might call this the multiple realiz*ability* objection.

Box: Multiple realization

Although the multiple realization objection convinced a generation of philosophers to abandon the identity theory, around the turn of the century, a number of theorists began to argue that its merits had been greatly exaggerated. Bechtel and Mundale (1999), for example, pointed out that the issue of multiple realization turns crucially on exactly how states, both mental and physical, are characterized. The case for multiple realization may seem compelling if one contrasts a coarse-grained description of a mental state with a fine-grained description of a neural state. But, they argued, that would surely be illegitimate, and one should instead compare mental states with neural states that are characterized in terms of comparable levels of specificity.

Bechtel and Mundale's point is an important one, although the idea of a 'common grain' for neural and mental taxonomizing is not entirely unproblematic. In my view, however, there is enough evidence of multiple realization to put the identity theory under serious pressure even without settling issues of granularity. In fact, there is good evidence of multiple realization within our own species. The brain is highly plastic, and when an organism is deprived of input in one sensory modality the brain networks that are associated with that modality often take on different jobs. For example, in individuals who have been blind from an early age, areas of the cortex which ordinarily process visual information are recruited for other tasks, such as processing language or the haptic-based identification of objects. These studies indicate that a single brain region or network can be implicated in different types of mental states and processes. We revisit neural plasticity in Chapter 9.

Further reading

Aizawa, K., and C. Gillett. 2009. The (Multiple) Realization of Psychological and Other Properties in the Sciences. *Mind and Language*, 24: 181-208.
Bechtel, W., and J. Mundale. 1999. Multiple Realizability Revisited: Linking Cognitive and Neural States. *Philosophy of Science*, 66(2): 175-207.
Funkhouser, E. 2007. Multiple Realizability. *Philosophy Compass*, 2 (2): 303-15.

If the multiple realizability of pain does not seem altogether convincing to you, consider mental phenomena of other kinds. Mind-brain identity theorists focus on sensations, but if the theory is to provide us with a comprehensive account of the mind, then it must also be applicable to mental phenomena in general. Consider the thought PLATO WAS BORN IN ATHENS. Not only does it seem possible that instances of this type of thought could be associated with brain states of very different kinds, but it also seems possible that a creature made entirely of silicon-based transistors could think PLATO WAS BORN IN ATHENS. But if that is so, then thinking PLATO WAS BORN IN ATHENS cannot be identified with being in a certain kind of neural state.

Building on Putnam's argument, in the mid-1970s Jerry Fodor identified a further challenge to the identity theory. Fodor approached the question of how mental states are related to brain states in terms of a wider debate about the unity of science. How are the special sciences – that is, sciences that apply only to particular domains, such as geology, biology, and psychology – related to each other and to fundamental physics? Fodor argued that it is vanishingly rare for the properties posited by one scientific theory to be identified with the properties posited by another, and that the unity of science doesn't require any such identification. Instead, a unified conception of reality requires only that we can 'explicate the physical mechanisms whereby events conform to the laws of the special sciences' (Fodor 1974: 107). Fodor did not rule out the possibility that certain types of mental properties *could* turn out to be identical to neural properties, but he made a persuasive case for thinking that we shouldn't expect such identifications to be common, and that the physicalist needn't choose between identifying mental phenomena with behavioural dispositions (as behaviourists do) and identifying them with brain states (as identity theorists do).

3.3 Functionalism

The work of Putnam and Fodor didn't just undermine the identity theory, it also provided an alternative to it: functionalism. At its heart, functionalism is the view that mental properties are functional properties, akin to the property of being a camshaft. Something is a camshaft in virtue of its functional profile (i.e., in virtue of what it does or can do). In order to be a camshaft, an object must be able to convert rotational motion to reciprocal motion. What gives a camshaft its identity is not the substance from which it is made – one can fashion a camshaft from many kinds of materials – but the role that it plays within the system in which it is embedded. Similarly, functionalists claim that the identity of a mental state is determined by the role that it plays within the cognitive system (i.e., the mind) in which it is located.[2]

There are various views within functionalism as to how to analyse the notion of a state's functional role. However, the most influential versions of functionalism equate a state's functional role with its causal profile – that is, with the range of states that cause it (its inputs) and the range of states that it in turn causes (its output).[3] Importantly, functionalists hold that both the inputs and the outputs of a mental state invariably include other mental states. For example, pain can be triggered not only by bodily events (such as nerve damage) but also by mental events (such as memories of traumatic events). Similarly, pain has both bodily effects (increased heart rate) and mental effects (forming an intention to buy pain medication). In this respect, then, functionalism embraces a holistic conception of mentality: the identity of a particular kind of mental state is determined by how it is related to other kinds of mental states.[4]

How is functionalism related to physicalism? Functionalism is often described as a kind of non-reductive physicalism, so named because the functionalist doesn't identify mental properties with neural properties (unlike the identity theorist). Instead, functionalists think of the connection between the physical and the mental as mediated by the relation of realization: physical states necessitate mental states because they *realize* them. We can say that a property *F* realizes a property *G* if and only if: (a) *G* is identical to the property of having some property that has a certain functional role; and (b) *F* is a property that plays that functional role (Melnyk 2003). The idea is that a mental property is the second-order property of having some state or other that plays a particular kind of functional role. For example, being in pain will be identified with the second-order property of having some property that plays the pain role (e.g., being triggered by noxious stimuli and in turn triggering pain avoidance behaviour). In principle, this second-order property could be realized by different kind of physical states, for the pain role might be realized by different kinds of physical states in creatures of different kinds. Indeed, functionalists can even allow that the relevant functional roles could – in principle at least – be realized by non-physical properties.

Functionalism in the philosophy of mind is a very broad church, and there are many forms of functionalism. We don't have the space to consider every distinction within the functionalist family, but there are two contrasts that are too important to be left to one side.

The first contrast concerns how the functional roles in question are characterized. Here, the basic distinction is between long-arm functionalists and short-arm functionalists. Long-arm functionalists characterize the relevant functional roles in terms of objects and properties in the world. For example, a long-arm functionalist might distinguish a state that is caused by the perception of elm trees from a state that is caused by the perception of oak trees, even if there is no brain-based difference between these states. In this sense, then, the long-arm functionalist holds that the external world can play a crucial role in fixing the identity of mental states. The short-arm functionalist, by contrast, restricts her attention to causal roles that are internal to the agent. From the perspective of the short-arm functionalist, differences in input and output that are described in terms of features of the environment are irrelevant. Chapter 7 explores in more detail the question of exactly how mental states depend on relations to the environment.

A second important contrast concerns how the functional roles that are essential to the identity of mental states are to be identified. Some theorists hold that these roles can be identified a priori (that is, independent of scientific investigation) because information about them is implicit in our folk theory of the mind. Here is how David Lewis puts this view:

> Think of common-sense psychology [i.e. folk psychology] as a term-introducing scientific theory, though one invented long before there was any such institution as professional science. Collect all the platitudes you can think of regarding the causal relations of mental states, sensory stimuli, and motor responses. . . . Include only platitudes which are common knowledge among us – everyone knows them, everyone knows that everyone else knows them, and so on. For the meanings of our words are common knowledge, and I am going to claim that the names of mental states derive their meaning from these platitudes.
>
> (Lewis 1972: 212)

This version of functionalism is commonly known as 'analytic functionalism', for as Lewis's comments indicate, its advocates often hold that information regarding the functional roles which determine the identities of mental states is derived from the meaning of psychological terms. However, the commitment to analyticity is not essential to this position, and I will refer to it as 'a priori functionalism' in virtue of the fact that its central commitment concerns the a priori availability of the relevant functional roles.

A very different approach to this issue is taken by a view that I will call 'a posteriori functionalism'. The a posteriori functionalist holds that the functional roles which are essential to mental states are not implicit in folk psychology but can be identified only on the basis of scientific investigation. This version of functionalism is often referred to as 'psychofunctionalism', for its advocates typically look to psychology in order to identify the functional roles of mental states. We return to the contrast between a priori functionalism and a posteriori functionalism at the end of this chapter.

Functionalism is widely regarded as a promising account of many kinds of mental states, most notably propositional attitudes such as belief, desire, and intention. Here, it is usually paired with the representational theory of mind, which holds that mental states are relations to internal representations. (We consider various aspects of the representational theory of mind in Chapters 5 and 6.) However, functionalism is significantly more controversial as an account of phenomenal states. One reason for this is that it is these states that pose the most serious privacy-related challenges, and functionalists struggle to account for the privacy of the mind in much the way that behaviourists and identity theorists do. But there is also a second reason why phenomenal states pose a challenge to functionalism – a reason that is unique to functionalism. Functionalism treats mental states as relational: what it is for a mental to be a state of a particular kind is determined by the relations that it bears to perceptual input, behavioural output, and other mental states. Phenomenal states, by contrast, are widely taken to be non-relational (or 'intrinsic', as it is often put). What makes something a pain (for example) seems to be a matter of its particular subjective quality (its 'experiential feel'), and that quality is often taken to be independent of pain's functional profile. We return to this issue in Chapter 9. Our aim in this section has not been to evaluate functionalism, but to explore its central features, and to recognize that it provides physicalists with another conception of how mental phenomena could be nothing over and above physical phenomena (see Box: Constructing an artificial mind).

Box: Constructing an artificial mind

We can highlight the contrast between behaviourism, the identity theory, and functionalism by reflecting on how each account views the task of constructing an artificial mind. From the perspective of behaviourism, building an artificial mind requires constructing an agent with the right set of behavioural dispositions. The physical constitution and causal structure of that agent is relevant to its status as a minded entity only to the extent that it has an impact on the behaviour that the system is disposed to produce. From the perspective of the identity theory, the key to creating an artificial mind is the creation of an 'artificial brain'. What exactly that requires, however, is something of an open question, for brain states can be described at various levels of abstraction, and it is unclear precisely which levels of abstraction the identity theorist will regard as central to mentality. The functionalist will, of course, focus on issues of causal structure, arguing that to construct an artificial mind one need only duplicate the functional roles that characterize our mental states. A key question for the functionalist concerns the degree to which a system's causal structure could differ from that of the human mind and yet still count as supporting mentality. Reflection on the diversity of non-human minds suggests that the functionalist ought to adopt a relatively liberal approach to this issue, although it is unclear just how liberal the functionalist ought to be here.

3.4 Eliminativism

Behaviourism, the identity theory, and functionalism differ from each other in important ways, but they all take for granted the reality of folk-psychological states. A very different tradition within physicalism is known as 'eliminativism', a view that is so named because its advocates reject the very existence of some of the central posits of folk psychology. In the same way that talk of unicorns, fairies, and the phlogiston of 19th-century chemistry simply fails to latch on to anything, so too, eliminativists argue, do certain folk-psychological terms. As the eliminativist sees it, the sciences of the mind don't provide an account of what mental phenomena are; instead, they show that (certain) kinds of mental phenomena *aren't*.

Eliminativism is sometimes equated with reductionism, but there are important differences between these two approaches to the mind. To be an eliminativist about some phenomenon (Xs) is to deny that there are any Xs – or at least, it's to deny that talk of Xs picks out a category that is of genuine scientific interest.[5] To be a reductionist about Xs, in contrast, is to identify Xs with Ys. Science has reduced lightning to electrochemical discharge, whereas it has eliminated the aether from its ontology (i.e., from its catalogue of what exists).[6] Eliminativism is also to be contrasted with revisionism. To be a revisionist about Xs isn't to deny that Xs exist, but to hold that our ordinary beliefs about Xs are mistaken in important respects. Although the contrast between eliminativism and revisionism is clear in principle, it can be difficult to draw in practice. An example of this point is provided by the category of race. Some theorists argue that we should be eliminativists about race, and that the term 'race' fails to refer to any genuine feature of reality. Others argue for revisionism about race, arguing that although our ordinary conceptions of race are deeply mistaken, the term does refer to a genuine feature of reality.

One of the most influential defences of eliminativism is due to Paul Churchland (1981). Churchland's focus is on the propositional attitudes, such as belief, desire, and intention. Although he allows that a physical system could, in principle, have propositional attitudes, Churchland argues that the propositional attitude framework does a very poor job of capturing the dynamics of human psychology – so poor, in fact, that we should conclude that we lack any such states.

Churchland gives a number of arguments for this striking claim, but the one that is of most interest to us here – and the one on which he himself puts most weight – is the *argument from autonomy*: the propositional attitudes should be rejected because they cannot be integrated into the sciences of behaviour, such as evolutionary theory, biology, physiology, and neuroscience. According to Churchland, the propositional attitudes 'stand magnificently alone' from the rest of science, and are 'orthogonal to the background physical science whose long-term claim to explain human behavior seems undeniable' (1981: 76).[7]

At the heart of Churchland's case for eliminativism is the assumption that folk-psychological categories pick out genuine features of reality only if they can be integrated into the sciences of behaviour. That demand might seem eminently reasonable – indeed, one might even think that it is entailed by physicalism – but Churchland's conception of what it is for folk psychological categories to be 'integrated' into science is tendentious. As he sees it, the legitimacy of folk psychology requires that its categories are 'neatly reflected in the framework of neuroscience' (1981: 75). This conception of integration goes well beyond anything that is entailed by a commitment to physicalism. Functionalists, for example, deny that the categories of folk psychology are 'neatly reflected' in those of neuroscience, but they certainly don't take them to stand 'magnificently alone' from them, either.[8]

The thought that psychological categories must be mirrored by those of neuroscience is driven by a certain conception of the unity of science, according to which the categories of 'high-level' (or 'special') sciences are legitimate only if they can be identified with those of 'lower-level' sciences. On this view, biology can be integrated with chemistry only if the categories of biology can be identified with those of chemistry, and chemistry can in turn be integrated with physics only if the categories of chemistry can be identified with those of physics. This conception of the unity of science is treated with suspicion by many. Rather than taking scientific domains to be hierarchically structured and integrated by means of inter-level identities, many philosophers embrace what Nancy Cartwright (1999) calls a 'dappled' view of the world, according to which integration between domains is typically messy and piecemeal. From this perspective, the fact that the categories of folk psychology are orthogonal to those of the background physical sciences is hardly a reason to eliminate them; in fact, orthogonality is to be expected.

A very different version of eliminativism is defended by Daniel Dennett (1978a) in his paper 'Why You Can't Make a Computer That Feels Pain'. Dennett argues that one can't make a computer that feels pain not because pain is some kind of non-physical state, but because pains don't exist. His case begins with the claim that the concept of pain involves two commitments: pains are intrinsically awful ('the awfulness condition'), and they are states to which we have infallible first-person access ('the infallibility condition'). As Dennett points out, there are cases in which these two conditions seem to come into conflict with each other. For example, patients who are given morphine often say that they still experience pain but that it is no longer awful – they no longer mind it. What should we make of such reports? Taking them at face value requires rejecting the awfulness condition, but if we hold fast to the assumption that pains are intrinsically awful then we must accept that those on morphine aren't actually in pain, and that in turn means we have to reject the infallibility condition. Either way, Dennett argues, something has to give: there are no states that are both intrinsically awful and to which we have infallible access.

What should we make of Dennett's position? One question concerns the concept of pain. It's true that we ordinarily assume that pains are intrinsically awful and that we have infallible first-person access to them, but it is arguable that neither feature is *essential* to pain as we ordinarily conceive of it. Perhaps folk psychology allows that we could be wrong on at least one (if not both) of these points and yet still be talking about pain. Perhaps morphine cases involve highly unusual pains (pains that aren't awful), or perhaps they involve failures of self-knowledge (and those on morphine merely *think* that they are in pain). In fact, the idea that pains are not atomic sensations but are rather complex states with sensory, hedonic, and motivational elements is received wisdom in pain science. Although the various aspects of pain usually co-occur, there are conditions – such as those to which Dennett draws our attention – in which only some of these elements are present. In such cases, perhaps there is no fact of the matter as to whether the individual in question is in pain. But to say this is not to deny that pains exist; it's rather to hold that pains are more complex than we thought. To go down this route would be to embrace revisionism rather than eliminativism with respect to pain.

Let's take a step back from the arguments of Churchland and Dennett, and consider how eliminativism might bear on the question of physicalism. It is evident that the truth of eliminativism with respect to a certain folk-psychological term ('x') would alter the dynamic of the debate surrounding physicalism, for if there are no x's then it follows trivially that facts about the x's are nothing over and above the physical facts. Thus, establishing the truth of eliminativism about (say) belief or pain would certainly alter the shape of the problem that confronts the physicalist. However, eliminativism is unlikely to be a 'game changer' in the debate surrounding physicalism unless it can be plausibly applied to the *central* categories of mentality – i.e., intentionality and consciousness. Does anyone take eliminativism with respect to these categories seriously?

Some theorists do. In fact, there are places in which Churchland appears to have as his target not just particular kinds of intentional states (such as belief, desire, and intention) but intentionality as such. And there are places in which Dennett explores – although perhaps stops short of fully endorsing – eliminativism with respect to consciousness itself (e.g., Dennett 1988). These forms of eliminativism are *much* more radical than the restricted forms of eliminativism on which we have focused. We could, perhaps, live with the idea that there are no beliefs, desires, or intentions as long as we had agent-level intentional states of some kind with which to replace them. We might also be able to live with the idea that there are no pains if we had other kinds of conscious states (negative affect, sensations of hurt) to appeal to. But if the notions of intentionality and consciousness were to go, then we really would be lost. Without intentionality, we would lose our grip on the notions of rationality, justification, and truth; without consciousness, we would lose our grip on what it is to be a subject of experience. In my view, eliminativism with respect to intentionality and consciousness are not open questions in the way in which eliminativist accounts of particular mental phenomena might be. We simply find ourselves confronted by consciousness, and the attempt to deny the reality of intentionality threatens to undermine itself (see Box: Eliminativism and incoherence).

Box: Eliminativism and incoherence

A common objection to Churchland's eliminativism is that it is self-referentially incoherent. As it is sometimes put: 'Churchland believes that there are no such things as beliefs, but surely it is pragmatically self-defeating to believe that there are no beliefs'. I have some sympathy with this objection, but as stated it is clearly question-begging, for the eliminativist will obviously deny that their attitude to eliminativism is one of belief. What attitude does the eliminativist take to the truth of eliminativism? That question, the eliminativist will say, can be answered only once we have replaced folk psychology with a better model of the human mind. Until then, we should decline any invitation to say what attitude we ought to take to the proposition 'eliminativism is true'.

Whether this response is justified seems to me to turn on the kind of states the eliminativist sees as replacing the propositional attitudes. There are two options here. The moderate option is that the successor states will be intentional states of some kind; it's just that they won't be the familiar intentional states of folk psychology. Eliminativists who take this path could claim that there is an intentional attitude of some kind – call it 'schmelief' – which we ought to take to the proposition 'eliminativism is true'. A more radical option – and the one that Churchland himself appears to endorse – is that the intentional states of folk psychology will be replaced by *non-intentional* states, such as activation patterns in neuronal assemblies. Eliminativists who take this path have a harder job meeting the incoherence objection, for it is unclear how non-intentional states might relate one to the proposition 'eliminativism is true' (or to any proposition, for that matter).

Further reading

Baker, L. R. 1989. *Saving Belief*. Princeton University Press.
Stich, S. 1983. *From Folk Psychology to Cognitive Science*. MIT Press.

3.5 The role of science

Let's take a step back from the details of the four views of the mind that we have examined and consider a general question that they all face: what is the appropriate role for science in developing an account of the mind? Or, to put the question in a slightly more nuanced form: what are the respective roles of philosophical analysis on the one hand and scientific inquiry on the other?

Analytical behaviourism gives pride of place to philosophical methods in understanding the mind, for they hold that the nature of mental states can be gleaned from an analysis of the meaning of mental terms, and that the meaning of mental terms is accessible from the philosopher's armchair. Thus, analytical behaviourists hold that both the general claim that mental phenomena can be identified with behavioural dispositions, and more specific claims about the behavioural dispositions that are associated with particular mental concepts, can be defended in relative isolation from scientific investigation. (In this respect, analytical behaviourism differs sharply from the scientific behaviourism of Watson and Skinner, which took scientific methods to be absolutely crucial to the study of the mind.) The analytical behaviourist recognizes the importance of science for understanding the categorical basis of our behavioural dispositions, but it is the nature of the dispositions themselves that is what matters as far as the essence of mentality is concerned, and, as they see it, their identification does not require scientific methods.

Identity theorists give different roles to science depending on the version of the identity theory that they espouse. The version of the identity theory defended by Feigl (1958), Place (1956), and Smart (1959) can be described as a 'science-first' approach, for it makes minimal assumptions about what can be gleaned about the nature of the mental by purely armchair methods. As these theorists see it, the justification for thinking that certain psychological terms and certain brain state terms are co-referential (i.e., refer to the same thing) is based on the existence of correlations between the applicability of the relevant psychological terms and the applicability of the relevant brain state terms, together with the claim that the simplest explanation for this correlation is that the psychological terms and the neural terms have a single phenomenon as their subject matter. (The dualist alternative, they point out, would involve positing primitive psychophysical laws.) Although the appeal to simplicity is not a purely scientific consideration (as Smart recognized), the identification of particular mental states with particular brain states is driven by scientific considerations.

In contrast, the version of the identity theory defended by Lewis (1966) and Armstrong (1968) gives a much more prominent role to philosophical analysis, for a crucial component of this view involves a claim about the meaning of psychological terms. On the Lewis-Armstrong view, psychological terms refer to those states (whatever they are) that play a particular functional role. For example, 'pain' refers to the state that plays the pain role. Once the philosophers have completed their functional analysis of the relevant folk-psychological concept, they then hand that analysis to the scientist who is charged with the job of identifying the brain states that realize the role outlined in that analysis. Although the Lewis-Armstrong version of the identity theory takes science to be necessary for identifying the nature of mental phenomena, it is very much a 'philosophy-first' approach to the mind, for armchair considerations are used to get the identity theory up and running, as it were.

In the same way that identity theorists give different roles to science depending on the version of the identity theory that they espouse, so too do functionalists. The key distinction here is between a posteriori functionalism and a priori functionalism. A posteriori functionalists, you will recall, hold that the functional profile unique to each kind of mental state can be discovered only by scientific investigation. We can think of a posteriori functionalism as the functionalist heir to the Feigl-Place-Smart version of the identity theory, for it too makes minimal assumptions about the meaning of mental state terms or the degree to which conceptual analysis can reveal the nature of mental phenomena. By contrast, a priori functionalism can be understood on the model of the Lewis-Armstrong version of the identity theory, for the a priori functionalist relies crucially on conceptual analysis. In fact, the a priori functionalist goes one step further than Lewis and Armstrong did, for Lewis and Armstrong argued that scientific investigation is needed to tell us what mental states *are* (taking mental states to be the entities named by psychological terms), whereas the a priori functionalist holds that philosophical considerations alone are sufficient to reveal the essential nature of mental states. In this sense, then, the a priori functionalist has more in common with the analytical behaviourist than they do with the Lewis-Armstrong identity theorist, for both the analytical behaviourist and the a priori functionalist take the essential nature of mental phenomena to be revealed by philosophical analysis alone.[9]

What attitude does the eliminativist take to these issues? At first sight, one might expect the eliminativist to embrace a profoundly science-first methodology, and to eschew any claims about the meaning of psychological terms or what can be gleaned about psychological concepts from the philosopher's armchair. On closer inspection, however, it becomes evident that philosophical considerations play an important role in arguments for eliminativism. For example, Churchland's argument for eliminativism about the propositional attitudes makes assumptions about what it would take for the terms 'belief' and 'desire' to refer, and the plausibility of these assumptions turns on contested issues in the philosophy of language about the meaning of folk-psychological terms. Dennett's case for eliminativism also relies crucially on an a priori assumption; namely, that the concept of pain is committed to the idea that pain is both intrinsically awful and something to which one has infallible first-person access. Although eliminativists typically downplay the relevance of philosophical methods for understanding the mind, at the back of every argument for eliminativism are assumptions about what it would take for a folk-psychological term to refer, and the plausibility of these assumptions is something to which philosophical methods speak.

3.6 Conclusion

This chapter has focused on four influential accounts of mental phenomena: behaviourism, the identity theory, functionalism, and eliminativism. Each of these accounts provides an answer to this question of how it could be the case that mental phenomena are nothing over and above physical phenomena, although the answers that they provide are quite different from each other.

Behaviourism and the identity theory entail physicalism, for they identify mental phenomena with physical phenomena. Although neither behavioural dispositions nor brain states appear in the physicist's list of what is fundamental, both behavioural dispositions and brain states qualify as physical in a broad sense of the term. The third account of the mind that we considered was functionalism, a view that identifies mental states with functional role states. Although functionalism doesn't entail physicalism, if mental states are in fact realized by physical states, as functionalists hold, then the mental is nothing over and above the physical. At any rate, if functionalism is true, then mental properties are no more mysterious than any other functionally individuated properties, such as the property of being a camshaft. Finally, we considered eliminativism. Eliminativism about a certain class of mental phenomena ('Xs') is the view that X-related talk fails to refer to anything – or at least, that it fails to refer to anything of genuine scientific interest. Eliminativists are physicalists not because they think that the categories of folk psychology can be accounted for in physical terms, but because they believe that the categories of the behavioural sciences will *displace* those of folk psychology.

Although behaviourism, the identity theory, functionalism, and eliminativism are often treated as monolithic positions, that is very far from being the case. In fact, the contrasts between different versions of each account are in many respects as important as the contrasts between the accounts themselves. For example, insofar as they appeal to a priori analysis and claims about the meanings of mental state terms, a priori functionalists have more in common with behaviourists and Lewis-Armstrong identity theorists than they do with a posteriori functionalists, who eschew any such appeal. It is also important to recognize that although these accounts are competitors, it might be possible to mix and match from among them, and to account for different kinds of mental phenomena in different ways. In principle, for example, one might attempt to defend behaviourism as an account of character traits, functionalism as an account of the propositional attitudes, the identity theory as an account of bodily sensations, and eliminativism with respect to the folk-psychological categories of emotion. Whether or not this (or indeed any other) combination of positions is viable is something that I will leave you to consider. The aim of this chapter has not been to defend any particular account of the mind, but to present some of the main physicalist options that are on the table, and to identify some of their main strengths and weaknesses.

Further reading

Although he was by no means a card-carrying philosophical behaviourist, Gilbert Ryle's *The Concept of Mind* (1949) did much to establish the influence of behaviourism in mid-20th-century philosophy of mind. Daniel Dennett's introduction to the 2002 edition (University of Chicago Press) is particularly illuminating on Ryle's influence. Also published in 1949 was Carl Hempel's paper 'The Logical Analysis of Psychology', in H. Feigl and W. Sellars (eds.), *Readings in Philosophical Analysis* (Appleton-Century-Crofts, pp. 373–84), which represents a more orthodox form of analytical behaviourism than Ryle's account does. George Graham's 'Spartans and Behaviorists', *Behaviorism*, 10(2): 137–49 (1982) provides a critical assessment of Putnam's super-spartans objection to behaviourism. For a thought-provoking treatment of behaviourism and the rise of the identity theory, see Sean Crawford's 'The Myth of Logical Behaviourism and the Origins of the Identity Theory', in M. Beaney (ed.) *The Oxford Handbook of the History of Analytic Philosophy* (OUP, 2013).

For reviews of the identity theory, see Brian McLaughlin's 'Type Materialism for Phenomenal Consciousness', in M. Velmans and S. Schneider (eds.), *The Blackwell Companion to Consciousness* (Blackwell, 2007) and Thomas Polger's 'Identity Theories', *Philosophy Compass*, 4(5): 822–34 (2009). For a recent collection of papers on the identity theory, see Simone Gozzano and Christopher Hill (eds.), *New Perspectives on Type Identity* (CUP, 2012).

For more on multiple realization, see Lawrence Shapiro's 'Multiple Realizations', *Journal of Philosophy*, 97: 635–54 (2000). On non-reductive physicalism in general, see Louise Antony's 'Everybody Has Got It: A Defense of Non-Reductive Materialism', in B. McLaughlin and J. Cohen (eds.), *Contemporary Debates in Philosophy of Mind* (Blackwell, 2007); Andrew Melynk's 'Can Physicalism Be Non-Reductive?' *Philosophy Compass*, 3(6): 1281–96 (2008); and Lynne Rudder Baker's 'Non-Reductive Materialism', in A. Beckermann, B. P. McLaughlin, and S. Walter (eds.), *The Oxford Handbook of the Philosophy of Mind* (OUP, 2009).

On functionalism in particular, see Ned Block's 'What Is Functionalism?', in *Readings in Philosophy of Psychology* (vol. 1, 1980); Brian Loar's *Mind and Meaning* (CUP, 1981); and Sydney Shoemaker's 'Some Varieties of Functionalism' (1981), reprinted in his *Identity, Cause and Mind* (CUP, 1984).

For further reading on eliminativism, see Stephen Stich's *From Folk Psychology to Cognitive Science* (MIT Press, 1983). The eliminativism of Stich and Churchland provoked many responses. Two of the most influential were Frank Jackson and Philip Pettit's 'In Defence of Folk Psychology', *Philosophical Studies*, 59: 31–54 (1990) and Terry Horgan and James Woodward's 'Folk Psychology Is Here to Stay', *Philosophical Review*, 94: 197–226 (1985). For another eliminativist treatment of pain, see Valerie Hardcastle's *The Myth of Pain* (MIT Press, 2000). For eliminativist treatments of consciousness more generally, see Elizabeth Irvine and Mark Sprevak's, 'Eliminativism about Consciousness', in U. Kriegel (ed.), *The Oxford Handbook of the Philosophy of Consciousness* (OUP, 348–70, 2020).

Study questions

1. What is the central claim of analytical behaviourism?
2. Explain why the possibility of 'super-spartans' and 'actors' poses a challenge to analytical behaviourism. Might the analytical behaviourist be able to respond to either challenge? If so, how?
3. What is the central difference between the token identity theory and the type identity theory?

4 Explain what Putnam's multiple realization (or 'realizability') objection to the type identity theory is. How does (or might) the identity theorist respond to this objection?
5 What is the relationship between functionalism and physicalism?
6 What is the difference between a priori functionalism and a posteriori functionalism?
7 Why does eliminativist physicalism (materialism) qualify as a version of physicalism?
8 The final section of this chapter considered various accounts of the relationship between philosophical analysis on the one hand and scientific research on the other in identifying the nature of mental states. Which of the positions described in this section do you find most compelling?

Notes

1 One might wonder whether the identity theory isn't actually at odds with the supervenience of the mental on the physical, for one might think that the Q-properties can supervene on the P-properties only if the P-properties are distinct from the Q-properties. However, that worry would be unfounded, for there is nothing in the notion of supervenience which requires that supervenience is a relation between distinct properties.
2 I am focusing here on what is sometimes called 'role functionalism', a view that can be contrasted with 'realizer functionalism'. The term 'realizer functionalism' is sometimes used in connection with the views of Lewis (1966) and Armstrong (1968), for they identify a particular kind of mental phenomenon with the state that realizes a particular functional role. However, I view this position as a version of the identity theory, for although its account of mental state concepts has a functional component, it treats mental states themselves as brain states.
3 Another version of functionalism is known as 'machine functionalism', for it equates mental states with states of a Turing machine. See Kim (2011, chap. 5) for an excellent introduction to machine functionalism.
4 Because functionalism holds that mental states are defined in terms of their relations to other kinds of mental states, it faces the threat of circularity akin to that which troubles behaviourism. However, functionalists have a way of dealing with this problem, known as Ramsification. For discussion, see Lewis (1972).
5 The form of eliminativism on which I'm focusing holds that psychological terms fail to refer to anything. However, there is another version of eliminativism which holds that although folk-psychological terms refer, they don't refer to genuine scientific kinds. Rather than liken psychological terms to 'unicorn' or 'fairy' (as the standard version of eliminativism does), this kind of eliminativist likens them to 'weeds' and 'dirt'. Weeds and dirt exist, but the corresponding categories aren't scientific categories.
6 There is a *kind* of eliminativism involved in reductionism, for if one has reduced the Xs to the Ys, then statements about the Xs can be made using the term 'Y'. However, this kind of elimination is purely linguistic, for what one eliminates isn't the Xs themselves (as in eliminativism) but the term 'X'.
7 'One is reminded', Churchland continues, 'of how alchemy must have looked as elemental chemistry was taking form, how Aristotelean cosmology must have looked as classical mechanics was being articulated, or how the vitalist conception of life must have looked as organic chemistry marched forward' (1981: 76).
8 Churchland is not unaware of the functionalist alternative, but rejects functionalism as 'short-sighted and reactionary' (1981: 78).
9 You may be wondering how these questions are related to the contrast between a priori physicalism and a posteriori physicalism that we discussed in the previous chapter. The issues here are complex, but roughly speaking a posteriori functionalists and identity theorists in the Feigl-Place-Smart tradition tend to be a posteriori physicalists, whereas behaviourists, a priori functionalists, and identity theorists in the Lewis-Armstrong tradition tend to be a priori physicalists.

4 Perception

Chapter overview

- Explains three of the most influential accounts of perception: the content view (representationalism), the sense-data view, and naïve realism
- Introduces the debate over whether the experiential character of perception can be understood in terms of its intentional features (intentionalism)
- Engages with the debate about what kinds of properties can be perceived
- Explores the possibility of unconscious perception.

Perception forms a central part of our mental lives. It is the source of most of what we know and the basis of much of what we value in life. The pleasure of listening to music, of enjoying a freshly baked bagel, and of taking in the rich colours of a sunset is, in large part, directed towards the sensuous nature of perception. It's no wonder, then, that perception has a central place in the philosophy of mind.

We begin in Section 4.1 by considering the nature of perception and perceptual experience more generally. Our focus here is on the content view of perception, which claims that perception is a kind of intentional (or representational) state. The content view is compared and contrasted with two alternative conceptions of perception: the sense-data view and naïve realism. We then turn in Section 4.2 to the relationship between perception as an intentional state and perception as an experiential state, asking how these two aspects of perception are related to each other. Intentionalists hold that the phenomenal character of perception ('what it's like' to perceive) is determined by perception's intentional content. Section 4.3 considers arguments both for and against intentionalism. In Section 4.4, we turn to the question of what kinds of properties can be perceived. The chapter concludes in Section 4.5 by briefly considering whether unconscious perception is possible.

4.1 Three accounts of perception

Consider the following scenario:

> You are looking out a window when you suddenly see a small animal trotting along the road. It seems to be about the size and shape of a medium-sized dog, with a red coat and a large bushy tail. You watch it for a few seconds. Just before it disappears behind a tree you suddenly realize what it is: a fox.

Although foxes might be unusual visitors to your neighbourhood, as perceptual objects they are utterly unremarkable, for visual experience is dominated by what J. L. Austin (1962) called 'moderate-sized dry goods', such as foxes, figs, and flugelhorns. Material things aren't the only objections of vision, for we also see perceptual ephemera of various kinds: rainbows, reflections, shadows, and silhouettes (Crowther & Mac Cumhaill 2018). The diversity of perceptual objects becomes even more apparent if we extend our gaze beyond vision and consider other sensory modalities. It's plausible to suppose that the direct objects of auditory experience aren't ordinary things but the sounds that they produce. Indeed, perhaps we don't really hear physical objects at all, but only the events and processes in which they are implicated. We hear the yelping of the fox, the squelching of the fig, and the playing of the flugelhorn. Consider also the chemical senses of smell (olfaction) and flavour (gustation). Arguably, the objects of smell aren't roses, rhododendrons, or rotten eggs but the odours that they produce, while the objects of taste aren't foods themselves but their flavours. Exclusive attention to vision can blind us to the true variety of perceptual objects.[1]

Perception doesn't just have objects, it also ascribes properties to those objects. For example, the fox might be presented as having a certain shape ('foxy', if one had to try to put it into words) and a certain colour ('dark red'). A sound might be experienced as loud, high-pitched, and rising in tone. Perception also presents its objects as standing in certain relations to oneself. The fox might be presented as being a certain distance from one (say, 30 or so metres), and the sound of the flugelhorn might be heard as coming from behind one.

We can capture these two points – the fact that perception has objects, and that it attributes properties and relations to its objects – by saying that perception has *intentional content*. Perception presents the world as being a certain way, and the content of a particular perceptual episode is the way that it presents the world as being. It is because perception has content that it is a source of information. If it didn't have content (i.e., if it didn't make any claims about how things are), then it couldn't serve as the basis for thought and action.

Because perceptual episodes have content they can be assessed for accuracy (or veridicality). A perceptual episode is accurate (or veridical) when one's environment is the way in which perception represents it as being, and it is inaccurate when (or to the degree to which) one's environment isn't the way in which perception presents it. Roughly speaking, we can say that the content of a perceptual experience determines what it is for that experience to be accurate – its 'accuracy conditions'.

With the notion of perceptual content in hand, we can distinguish between three kinds of cases. The first kind of case is one in which one's environment is indeed populated with the objects that it seems to be and those objects have the properties that they seem to have. We might think of this as 'perception proper'. If the fox scenario is an instance of this kind, then there really is a fox in front of you and it has the kinds of properties that it seems to (e.g., its tail really is as red as it seems to be). In cases of the second kind, you are hallucinating, and your environment doesn't contain the objects that it seems to. For example, perhaps you seem to see a fox only because you have taken hallucinogenic drugs, and there is no such creature in your perceptual environment at all. In this kind of case, you have a perceptual experience, but you are not actually perceiving anything. In cases of the third kind, although the object of your perceptual experience exists, it appears to have properties that it doesn't actually have. For example, you may indeed be looking at a fox, but perhaps its coat is white, and it looks red only because the fox is illuminated by a red streetlight. In this case, you are subject to a perceptual illusion. So we can distinguish three kinds of cases: 'good' cases (in which the contents of perceptual experience are accurate and the objects that one seems to perceive do indeed have the properties that they appear to have) and two kinds of 'bad' cases (one in which the objects of perception don't exist [hallucination] and another in which they exist but are misrepresented in some way [illusion]).

I will refer to the account of perceptual experience that we have just sketched as 'the content view'. (It is also known as the 'representational view'). The claim at the heart of the content view is that perception is akin to belief and other intentional states in that it is first and foremost a relation to intentional contents. When things go well then the contents of perceptual experience match the relevant aspects of one's environment, but when things go awry – as they do in cases of hallucination and illusion – then there is a mismatch between one's environment and the contents of perceptual experience.

The content view is the dominant view in the philosophy of perception, but it is very far from being the only game in town. Let's consider some objections to the content view and in so doing explore two of the most influential alternatives to it: the sense-data view and naïve realism.[2]

Hallucination and the appeal to sense data

Suppose that you seem to see a fox in front of you, but you are in fact hallucinating. Perhaps you are aware that you are hallucinating (as those who hallucinate often are), or perhaps you are unaware that your experience is hallucinatory, and you take yourself to be actually seeing a fox. Either way, it will seem as though there is some object of which you are directly aware. 'There it is', you might think to yourself; 'look how bushy its tail is'. You seem to be referring to something, but what are you referring to? The content view faces a challenge at this point, for there is no object of which you are perceptually aware. You might *think* that your perceptual experience has latched on to an object if you are unaware that you are hallucinating, but you would be wrong. But – the critic continues – surely it's implausible to suppose that your experience has no object at all. Even when one is hallucinating, *something* is always presented in perceptual experience.

Advocates of the sense-data account have a ready response to this objection: the objects of perceptual experience, they hold, are purely *mental* objects, and as such they exist even when one is hallucinating (Ayer 1956; Price 1932; Robinson 1994). These mental objects are the sense data after which the account is named. On this view, there is indeed something that one sees when one hallucinates a fox, but that thing is a private object – a kind of mental image, perhaps – rather than an ordinary observable object. Indeed, sense-data theorists hold that the *only* direct objects of perceptual experience are sense data, for (they claim) we should give a uniform account of the 'good' cases and the 'bad' cases. Even when things go well and there is indeed a fox in your perceptual environment that has the properties that it seems to, according to the sense-data theorist it's not the fox itself that is the direct object of your visual experience. Instead, that honour goes to a sense datum – a kind of mental facsimile of a fox (indeed, the same kind of facsimile of the fox that is the object of your perceptual experience in the hallucination case). On the sense-data account, you only ever see a fox by experiencing a sense datum.

Although the sense-data account was once immensely influential, it has few contemporary advocates. One of the main objections to the view concerns the mysterious nature of sense data themselves. Can they exist unperceived? Can they be misperceived? How many spatial dimensions do they have? It is far from clear that these questions have good answers. Many philosophers also reject the sense-data account on the grounds that it seems to be at odds with the character of perceptual experience. Even in the context of hallucination, the objects of perceptual experience don't appear to be purely mental entities but instead appear to occupy a public space in which they are accessible to the scrutiny of others.

Can we account for hallucination without positing sense data? Content theorists argue that we can. Indeed, from the perspective of the content theorist, the challenge posed by hallucination is really just a special case of the more general challenge posed by our capacity to represent non-existent objects. Sometimes our thoughts latch on to genuine objects, and sometimes they don't. Consider the conquistadors of South America, who spent many years looking for the mythical city of El Dorado. It is true that the conquistadors looked for El Dorado, but (in the relevant sense) false that there was a city for which the conquistadors looked. Similarly, it may be true that the hallucinator sees (better: *seems* to see) a fox in front of them, but it doesn't follow that there is anything (let alone a fox) that they seem to see. Just as the objects of desire – El Dorado, world peace, the perfect cocktail – may not appear in an inventory of what there is, so too the objects of perceptual experience will sometimes be merely intentional (or 'notional', as it is sometimes put). Questions about what it is that one is aware of in the context of hallucination are on a par with questions about what it is that one thinks about in thinking about non-existent objects, and those problems are *everyone's* problems.

Perceptual presence and naïve realism

A second objection to the content view is that it lacks the resources to account for a phenomenon known as *perceptual presence* (Dorsch & Macpherson 2018; Noë 2005). Consider the contrast between perceiving a fox and other ways in which a fox might be 'before one's mind'. Suppose that you hear a commotion outside and infer that a fox has broken into the chicken coop. In this case, you might form the belief that a fox is in the chicken coop. You might even form a visual image of a fox in the chicken coop. Clearly, believing that a fox is in the chicken coop and having a visual image of a fox in the chicken coop are both very different from perceiving a fox in the chicken coop. In perception, some aspect of the world seems to be 'revealed', 'manifest', or 'present' to you, whereas no such claim is true of thought or imagination. That, in a nutshell, is the phenomenon of perceptual presence.

Some theorists argue that the content view cannot account for perceptual presence. Why? Well, the content view treats perception as a representational phenomenon, akin to belief or imagination. But, as we have just noted, the world isn't 'present' to one in either thought or imagination. Thus, the argument runs, how then could the content view explain perceptual presence? How could the world be revealed or made manifest or present to us in perception if perception were just a matter of representing that such-and-such is the case?

Enter naïve realism. According to the naïve realist, aspects of the world itself are constituents of perception. In seeing a fox, one is not related to fox-involving propositional content; instead, one is directly related to a fox itself. When you see a fox jump into a chicken coop, the fox and its activities are essential components of your perceptual experience. Naïve realism is also known as the relational view of perception, for it treats perception as a specific kind of relation – a relation of sensory awareness – between a perceiver and aspects of their environment. According to the naïve realist, the world seems to be present to you in perceptual experience because it *is* present in your perceptual experience. After all, the naïve realist holds that what one perceives is quite literally a constituent of one's experience, and surely one can't get any more 'present' than that![3]

The argument from perceptual presence puts pressure on the content view only if the naïve realist has a better account of perceptual presence than the content theorist. Do they? To answer that question, we need to explore in more detail the approach that each account takes to perceptual presence. Let's begin with naïve realism.

The naïve realist does indeed seem to have a plausible account of perceptual presence to offer when it comes to the good cases. But what about the bad cases? Consider again a case in which the fox's coat looks red only because it is illuminated by a red street light. How could the redness of the fox's coat account for the fact that it seems to be 'present' if the coat itself *isn't* red? Worse still is the hallucination case, in which there is no object at all that might account for the fox's presence. Thus, naïve realism struggles to account for perceptual presence in cases of illusion and hallucination. The fact that naïve realism focuses on the good cases (and has rather little to say about the bad cases) is arguably a weakness with the view in and of itself (Box: Disjunctivism), but it's particularly problematic here given that perceptual presence characterizes both the good and bad cases.[4]

Box: Disjunctivism

Naïve realists deny that cases of genuine perception and cases of hallucination are instances of the same basic kind of mental state. This is a direct consequence of their view, for in cases of genuine perception one's experience is partly constituted by the perceptual object, whereas in hallucination there is no such object to play a constituting role. In denying that genuine perception and hallucination are instances of a common kind, naïve realists endorse a view known as *disjunctivism*. From the first-person perspective, one might know that one is either in perceptual contact with the world or merely hallucinating (this is the 'either/or' after which the view is named), but it doesn't follow that there is a single type of state in common to both perception and hallucination – or so disjunctivists argue.

Both sense-data theorists and content theorists reject disjunctivism, for they hold that cases of genuine perception and hallucination are both instances of the same fundamental kind of mental state. The sense-data view holds that that fundamental kind should be characterized in terms of relations to sense data, while the content view holds that that fundamental kind should be characterized in terms of intentional content. Naïve realists give various accounts of hallucination, but in general they characterize it in epistemic terms. As they see it, hallucinations have no positive nature of their own, and all we can say about them is that they are the kinds of states that are not easily distinguished from certain kinds of perceptual experiences.

Further reading

Byrne, A., and H. Logue. 2009. *Disjunctivism*. MIT Press.
Haddock, A., and F. Macpherson. 2008. *Disjunctivism: Perception, Action, Knowledge*. Oxford University Press.
Soteriou, M. 2016. *Disjunctivism*. Routledge.

How might the content theorist account for perceptual presence? Broadly speaking, there are two options open to them. The first involves the notion of an intentional attitude (or mode). Consider the difference between *desiring* that there is cake for dinner and *believing* that there is cake for dinner. These two states have the same content (*that there is cake for dinner*), but they involve different attitudes to that content. Thus, one might argue that perceptual experience involves a sense of presence because perception involves taking a distinctive attitude – 'sensory awareness', one might call it – to a certain content. The attitude of sensory awareness would be akin to judgment in that both attitudes involve taking things to be thus-and-so, but they would differ insofar as sensory awareness purports to put one into direct contact with the world in the way that judgment doesn't.[5]

The second factor that the content theorist might appeal to in order to account for perceptual presence concerns the distinctive features of perceptual *content*. There are various aspects of perceptual content which might be invoked here, but perhaps the most compelling account involves an appeal to the representation of perceptual constancies. Suppose that you are looking at a coin, which is tilted towards you at a certain angle. The angle that the coin displays to you will change depending on how you are related to it. If either you or the coin were to move relative to each other, then the appearance of the coin would change in distinctive and predictable ways. Our perceptual experience is acutely sensitive to these contingencies and represents both the way that the coin looks from a particular point of view and the underlying properties that explain why the coin looks the way that it does from various perspectives. Arguably, neither imagination nor thought is characterized by the representation of perceptual constancies in this way (Box: Virtual reality).

Box: Virtual reality

One of the most powerful methods for studying the sense of perceptual presence involves the use of virtual reality (VR) technology. A truly rewarding VR experience would be immersive and would share the revelatory character of ordinary perceptual experience. By modifying the parameters of VR systems, we can learn a lot about what generates the sense of presence. Does the sense of presence require the visual scene to be presented in great detail, or can it be generated with only minimal amounts of perceptual detail? Does the sense of presence require the kinds of perceptual constancies that are familiar from our ordinary perceptual interaction with the world, or can it be generated with novel perceptual constancies that apply only within the confines of the virtual world? And how important is the role of multimodal integration (i.e., integration between different sensory modalities) in the generation of perceptual presence? In addition to the fact that VR allows us to study perceptual presence in new and exciting ways, it also provides a further challenge to naïve realism, for whatever exactly the objects of VR experience are, they don't appear to be the kinds of ordinary physical objects that naïve realists appeal to as explaining perceptual presence.

Further reading

Sanchez-Vives, M., and M. Slater. 2005. From Presence to Consciousness through Virtual Reality. *Nature Reviews Neuroscience*, 6: 332-39.

There is much more to be said regarding the debate between the content view, the sense-data view, and naïve realism, but we must leave that task for another occasion. I will proceed on the assumption that the content view is correct - or at least undefeated by the two objections that we have considered here. Our next task is to consider the relationship between the content of perception and its phenomenal character.

4.2 Intentionalism and phenomenal character

The previous section focused on the idea that perception has intentional content: it represents the world as being a certain way. Putting it another way, we can say that perceptual experiences can be evaluated for accuracy. But perception doesn't just have an intentional dimension - it also has an experiential dimension. There is something distinctive about what it's like to see a fox, and what it's like to see a fox is different from what it's like to taste a fig or to hear a flugelhorn. How is the experiential dimension of perception – its 'phenomenal character', as it is often known – related to its intentional features? Are these two aspects of perception independent of each other, or are they deeply intertwined – perhaps two sides of a single coin?

Intentionalists (also known as 'representationalists') hold that the intentional properties of perception and its phenomenal character are very closely related. Some intentionalists identify the phenomenal character of perception with its intentional properties; others hold only that the phenomenal character of perception supervenes on (i.e., is fixed by) its intentional properties. Here we will focus on supervenience intentionalism, the weaker of the two views. If this form of intentionalism is correct, then no two perceptual experiences can differ in phenomenal character without differing in intentional properties. Fix a perceptual experience's intentional properties and one fixes its phenomenal character.

Intentionalism can be contrasted with a view that I will refer to as 'sensationalism'. The sensationalist holds that there are aspects of the phenomenal character of perception that outrun its intentional features. These aspects are often referred to as *qualia* (singular: *quale*), and for this reason sensationalists are sometimes known as 'qualiaphiles'. As we noted in Chapter 1 (p. 17), the term 'qualia' is best avoided because it is used in so many different ways. Thus, I will refer to these non-representational properties as 'sensational properties' or simply 'sensations'.

It is useful to distinguish between two types of sensations. (In making this distinction, we need not assume that either kind of sensation actually exists; the distinction is merely a conceptual one.) One kind of sensation is used by the machinery of perception to represent certain features in the world. The Scottish philosopher Thomas Reid (1710-96) held that sensations of heat and cold function in this way. Although these sensations are not inherently intentional, in us they function to indicate objective properties of objects. In principle, however, these sensations could have been used to represent different properties. For example, sensations of cold could have been used to represent the property that is actually represented by sensations of heat and vice versa. Following Ned Block (1996, 2003a), let's call sensations that function in this way 'mental paint'.[6] Sensations of this kind can be contrasted with sensations that don't serve any representational function at all. Block calls these sensations 'mental latex' in honour of the fact that latex is the element in paint that is representationally inert (unlike the pigment).

So, intentionalists deny that perception involves sensational properties, whereas sensationalists ('qualiaphiles') hold that perception involves sensational properties of some kind – either mental paint or mental latex (or both).

The debate between intentionalists and sensationalists is a central debate in the philosophy of perception. In part, this is because it is a focal point in a broader debate about the relationship between intentionality and phenomenal consciousness (or 'phenomenality', as it is sometimes put). According to some theorists, *all* forms of phenomenal character are determined by intentional properties. In order to evaluate this kind of unrestricted intentionalism, we would need to consider not just perceptual experience but the experiences associated with bodily sensations, moods, and emotions. Addressing that issue goes beyond the scope of this chapter, but it is something to which we return in Chapter 9. Here, our focus is on what we might call 'perceptual intentionalism', according to which the phenomenal character of *perceptual* experience supervenes on its intentional properties (Box: Perception and pain).

Box: Perception and pain

The paradigmatic forms of perceptual experience are those associated with the five traditional senses: vision, audition, touch, smell, and taste. However, many other mental states are perception-like in important respects. For example, bodily experiences of various kinds – itches, tickles, aches, and feelings of thirst, hunger, and tiredness – can be regarded as broadly perceptual in nature. In contrast to the traditional senses (which provide one with information about external objects), the bodily senses are forms of interoception, for their job is to provide one with information about the state of one's own body.

The bodily sensation that has received more philosophical attention than any other is pain. Pains have often been regarded as non-intentional experiences or 'raw feels'. Indeed, we saw in Chapter 1 that the allegedly non-intentional nature of pains has sometimes been used to argue that intentionality isn't the mark of the mental. Many theorists, however, argue that pains are intentional states. The standard intentionalist account of pain holds that pains are representations of damage to a particular region or part of one's body (e.g., Cutter & Tye 2011). On this view, experiences of pain can be assessed for accuracy in the manner of visual experiences. A pain will be veridical if the part of the body that is represented as damaged is indeed damaged, whereas it will be non-veridical if the relevant part of the body is either undamaged or doesn't exist. A putative example of a non-veridical pain experience is provided by the phenomenon of phantom pain, in which a person experiences pain 'in' a limb that was absent from birth or has been amputated.

Recently, this 'indicative' version of intentionalism has been challenged by another kind of intentionalist account of pain known as the 'imperative view'. The imperative view agrees that pains are intentional states, but it takes pains to be states that tell the agent what to do – or, as the case may be, what *not* to do – rather than states that tell the agent how things are. On this view, the pain associated with a broken ankle might be thought of as a negative imperative that commands against moving it in a way that would put weight on it (Klein 2015). Thus, the debate surrounding about pain isn't just about whether pains are intentional, but about what kinds of intentional states they might be: are they indicatives that tell us how things are or imperatives that tell us what (not) to do?

Further reading

Aydede, M. 2009. Is Feeling Pain the Perception of Something? *Journal of Philosophy*, 106(10): 531–67.
Grahek, N. 2007. *Feeling Pain and Being in Pain*. MIT Press.
Klein, C. 2015. *What the Body Commands: The Imperative Theory of Pain*. MIT Press.

4.3 Intentionalism: for and against

Having identified what (perceptual) intentionalism says, let us now consider whether we should accept it. One of the most influential arguments for intentionalism begins with the following passage by Gilbert Harman:

> When you see a tree, you do not experience any features as intrinsic features of your experience. Look at a tree and try to turn your attention to intrinsic features of your visual experience. I predict you will find that the only features there to turn your attention to will be features of the presented tree.
>
> (Harman 1990: 667)

The intrinsic features that Harman refers to are what we are calling sensational properties. These are properties *of* an experience rather than properties that are represented *by* (or *in*) an experience. The idea here is that when one attends to an experience, the only features that one can identify are features that are attributed to the objects of that experience. The motion, shape, and colour of which you are directly aware aren't experienced as properties of you yourself (or of your experience), but are instead experienced as properties of the objects around you. This phenomenon is known as the transparency (or diaphanousness) of perceptual experience.[7]

Harman, together with a number of other theorists, claims that perceptual transparency provides an argument for intentionalism.[8] We can put this 'transparency argument' as follows:

1. Transparency characterizes all perceptual experiences: we are never introspectively aware of any perceptual features as sensational properties (intrinsic features of our experience).
2. If there are sensational features of perception, then introspection ought to reveal them *as* intrinsic properties of experience (rather than apparent properties of external objects).
3. So, we have no reason to believe that there are sensational properties.

Let's begin with the first premise, the *transparency thesis*. Transparency certainly seems to characterize *most* perceptual experiences, but does it characterize *all* perceptual experiences? Some argue that although we typically see through our experiences and focus on the world as it is presented in perception, we *can* become aware of (and attend to) intrinsic features of our experience. Indeed, even G. E. Moore (1873-1958), the philosopher who first brought the phenomenon of perceptual transparency to philosophical prominence, claimed that there is a non-intentional element to experience that can be identified 'if we look attentively enough, and if we know that there is something to look for' (Moore 1903). However, I am willing to grant the first premise of the transparency argument, for none of the scenarios that are advanced as counterexamples to the transparency thesis seems to me to be convincing (Box: Blurry vision).

Box: Blurry vision

One of the many visual phenomena that have been raised as counterexamples to the transparency thesis is blurry vision. As one critic has put it, 'visual experiences can become blurry, as when one removes one's glasses, without their objects appearing to have become fuzzy. Their objects look different, of course, but do not look to have changed' (Bach 1997: 467). Can the intentionalist account for blurry vision? If so, how?

Earlier in the chapter, we noted that vision represents both intrinsic properties (having a certain shape) and relational properties (being a certain distance from a person). Blurriness is clearly not an intrinsic property of an object, nor does vision represent it as such. But perhaps blurriness is a relational feature – akin, perhaps, to being 30 metres from a person. To see an object blurrily, then, is to visually represent it with a lower degree of precision than one would ordinarily represent it. Thus, the contrast between seeing the world with one's glasses on and seeing it without them is (roughly) the difference between having a high-resolution representation of the world and having a low-resolution representation of the world. In this sense, then, blurry vision is no counterexample to transparency.

Further reading

Pace, M. 2007. Blurred Vision and the Transparency of Experience. *Pacific Philosophical Quarterly*, 88(3): 328-54.
Smith. A. D. 2008. Translucent Experiences. *Philosophical Studies*, 140(2): 197-212.
Tye, M. 2000. *Consciousness, Color, and Content*. MIT Press.

What about the second premise of the transparency argument? Are sensationalists committed to the claim that sensational features ought to be introspectively detectable as such?

Arguably not. To see why, consider again the contrast between 'mental paint' and 'mental latex'. The transparency argument assumes that sensational properties (intrinsic properties of experience) would need to be representationally idle in the way in which mental latex is, but the sensationalist need not make that assumption. Instead, they could hold that all sensational properties carry representational content, although precisely what content they carry might vary from case to case. Thus – this line of thought continues – it is no surprise that introspection fails to reveal sensational properties *as* sensational properties, for we 'see' right through their sensational nature and focus instead on those features of the world that sensations represent. In short, the sensationalist could accept the transparency thesis, but argue that the features of which we are directly aware in introspection are in fact intrinsic properties of experience even though they are not presented to us as such.[9] (Of course, if sensational properties aren't presented to us as intrinsic, then we would lose one of the main motivations for thinking that they are intrinsic.)

There is much more to be said about the transparency argument, but let us turn our attention now to arguments against intentionalism. What reasons might there be to think that the phenomenal character of perception fails to supervene on its intentional properties?

One objection to intentionalism concerns what Aristotle called the common-sensibles: properties, such as shape, that can be perceived by more than one modality (Block 1996; Lopes 2000; O'Dea 2006). Suppose that you can both see and feel a coin. Your visual experience presents the coin as circular, as does your haptic experience. Intuitively, there is a clear contrast between what it's like to see a coin as circular and what it's like to feel it as circular. But – the objection runs – the intentionalist cannot capture this contrast, for if the phenomenal character of perception is determined by its intentional content, then the experience of seeing a coin as circular ought to be indistinguishable from the experience of feeling it as circular. Call this the *common-sensibles objection*.

One response to this objection would be to restrict the scope of the view and to hold that phenomenal character is determined by intentional content only *within* a sensory modality. This position is known as intramodal intentionalism (Crane 2003; Lycan 1987, 1996; Harman 1996; Neander 1998). Intramodal intentionalists hold that any phenomenal difference between experiences belonging to the same perceptual modality will always be accompanied by an intentional difference, but they allow that the features that distinguish (say) visual experiences from auditory ones might be sensational (i.e., non-intentional).

Intramodal intentionalism can certainly avoid the objection from common-sensibles, but by allowing that certain aspects of phenomenal character depend on sensational features it threatens to rob intentionalism of much that is most interesting – and, indeed, important – about it. Can the intentionalist block the common-sensibles objection without embracing intramodal intentionalism?

I think so. First, note that neither vision nor touch represents shape alone; instead, each modality represents shape only in the context of representing other properties, some of which are unique to it. For example, the visual experience of shape is integrated with the experience of colour (but not of pressure), while the haptic experience of shape is integrated with the experiences of pressure (but not of colour). (In Aristotelian terms, colour and pressure are *proper sensibles*, for each feature is accessible only via a single modality.) Second, touch and vision represent a coin's shape with different degrees of precision; typically, vision represents size with more precision than touch does. Third, vision and touch each contain self-representational content that distinguishes them from each other. Vision doesn't just represent a coin as being thus-and-so, it also contains information to the effect that the representation of the coin is mediated by the movements of one's eyes and head; similarly, haptic experiences represent the fact that they involve the movement of a certain body part (such as one's fingers). So, there are at least three ways in which the intentionalist can account for the evident contrast between vision and touch.[10]

Another objection to intentionalism appeals to the idea that perceptual properties (such as colours) might appear differently to different people. Scenarios of this kind are known as 'inverted spectrum scenarios' (Shoemaker 1982) and have been discussed since at least the 17th Century. For example, John Locke (1632–1704) entertained the possibility that the experiences that a violet produces in one person should be the same as the experiences that a marigold produces in another person and vice-versa (Locke 1690: II xxxii.15).

Consider a variant on Locke's proposal, in which red objects produce in Bonnie the kinds of colour experiences that green objects produce in Clyde. This spectrum inversion is systematic, and doesn't show up in their behaviour. They both refer to red things as 'red' and green things as 'green', and when asked to sort objects on the basis of colour each of them groups fire engines with rubies and tomatoes and limes with bok choi and frogs.

Suppose that Bonnie and Clyde are looking at a fire engine in ordinary conditions. Surely, one might think, their colour experiences have the same content. They both agree that the fire engine appears to be the same colour as other paradigmatically red objects. And if one of them misrepresents the fire engine's colour, then who would that be? Is Bonnie's experience accurate and Clyde's experience inaccurate, or is Clyde's experience accurate and Bonnie's experience inaccurate? Neither answer is attractive. But if Bonnie and Clyde both represent the fire engine as having the same colour, then intentionalism is in trouble, for (by hypothesis) Bonnie and Clyde are colour inverts: they experience the fire engine's colour *differently*.

Intentionalists have developed a number of responses to the challenge of inverted spectra. One of the most promising allows that spectrum inversion is possible (i.e., objects which look red to Bonnie could look green to Clyde and vice versa) but denies that their colour experiences would have the same content. Why might that be? Well, consider a dispositional conception of colour, according to which an object is red just in case it reliably produces certain kinds of experiences ('red experiences') in perceivers of a certain kind in normal conditions. This account allows that a fire engine could be both fully red and fully green, for it might reliably produce one kind of experience ('phenomenal red') when individuals like Bonnie view it and another kind of experience ('phenomenal green') when individuals like Clyde view it. Treating colours as dispositional properties thus appears to allow for the possibility of spectrum inversion without undermining intentionalism.

This is an elegant proposal, but it faces at least one problem: how are we to understand the notions of 'phenomenal red' and 'phenomenal blue'? It looks as though these terms will have to refer to sensational properties – i.e., non-intentional properties of visual experience itself rather than properties of external objects. But if the intentionalist needs to posit sensational properties in order to account for spectrum inversion, then they are in trouble, for intentionalism just is the claim that there are no sensational properties.

The fundamental challenge posed by the inverted spectrum objection goes well beyond the experience of colour. Since Galileo, many theorists have distinguished two kinds of perceptual qualities: qualities that objects have in their own right (primary qualities) and qualities that can be understood only in terms of their dispositions to produce certain kinds of experiences in us (secondary qualities). Colour is often treated as a secondary quality, but so too are scents, flavours, and certain aspects of auditory experience such as pitch and beat. According to many, what we are aware of when we experience secondary qualities resides 'only in the mind' (i.e., as intrinsic features of experience). Secondary qualities pose a problem for intentionalism. If the intentionalist treats apparently secondary qualities as actually primary qualities, then they need to provide an account of what it is for something to have the property in question. If, on the other hand, they allow that apparently secondary qualifies are properties of experience (and not properties of the *objects* of experience), then they need to explain why they haven't in effect rejected the core tenet of intentionalism, which is that the phenomenal character of perception supervenes on its intentional properties. The lesson, perhaps, is not that the inverted spectrum objection succeeds, but that it shows just how difficult it is for intentionalists to account for all forms of perceptual phenomenology.[11]

4.4 The admissible contents of perception

Let's return to the fox. What exactly do you see when you look at the fox? What properties of the fox are directly given to you in your visual experience? You see the fox as having a certain colour, as being a certain shape and size, and as moving in a certain direction. But is that all you see? Do you see the fox *as a fox*? Do you see it as *being about to jump over a fence*? Do you see it as *the same fox as the one that ate the chickens last week*?

Some theorists answer all of these questions in the negative. As they see it, visual experience acquaints us with only a very limited range of properties, such as shape, texture, colour, and motion. I will call such views 'conservative' accounts of visual experience. Other theorists – whom I will label 'liberals' – hold that perception can acquaint us with a much wider range of properties. In other words, liberals have a much richer conception of the kinds of properties that can be presented in perception than conservatives do. (For this reason, the liberal view is sometimes referred to as a 'rich' view, while the conservative view is sometimes referred to as the 'thin' or 'austere' view.) For example, some liberals argue that causal properties can be visually represented, and that one can see a toddler's movements as (say) breaking a glass. Some liberals argue that mental properties can be visually presented, and that one can see joy on a person's face. Some liberals argue that possibilities for action can be visually presented, and that one can see the edibility of an apple. And some liberals argue that moral properties can be visually presented, and that one can see the injustice in a situation.[12]

The debate between conservatives and liberals concerns the kinds of contents (i.e., properties) that can enter into the contents of direct perception. (For this reason, it is often called the 'admissible contents debate'.) We can contrast direct perception with what is sometimes called *indirect* perception, in which one makes inferences about the environment by integrating the content of perception with background belief (Dretske 2010). Suppose that you are looking at an analogue speedometer, which is pointing to '100 kph'. Although you directly perceive only that the speedometer is pointing to a certain mark on the dial, if you know how a speedometer works then you can infer on the basis of your visual experience that you are travelling at 100 kph. For experienced drivers this inference might be tacit (automatic, effortless, and immediate), but it will be an inference nonetheless. If you suspect that your speedometer is malfunctioning, then although you will still see that the dial points to '100 kph', you will no longer use that information to infer that you are travelling at 100 kph.

How might we identify the kinds of properties that can (and cannot) be directly presented in visual experience? One approach would be to consider our use of such words as 'looks', 'seems', and 'appears'. Consider the fact that one might say that something 'looks like a fig', 'seems to be edible', or 'appears to be wrong'. One might argue that our tendency to use locutions like these shows that the liberal view is implicit in our everyday view of perception, even if it doesn't actually provide evidence for the truth of the account.

However, it would be a mistake to try to read off an account of perceptual content from our use of 'looks', 'seems', or 'appears'. That is because these terms are used not merely to refer to those properties that are directly presented in perception (the 'phenomenal use'), but also to compare the objects of perception with other objects (the 'comparative use'). To say that something looks like a fig might mean only that it looks similar to other figs, and that could be true even if the property *being a fig* isn't presented in visual experience.[13]

A more promising argument for liberalism appeals to Susanna Siegel's *phenomenal contrast* method (Siegel 2006, 2007). Phenomenal contrast arguments proceed in two steps. The first step involves specifying two scenarios, A and B, which are assumed to differ phenomenally (the 'phenomenal contrast'). In the second step, one argues that the best explanation for the phenomenal contrast identified in step 1 requires positing 'high-level' perceptual content of some kind (i.e., the kind of content that conservatives claim is not present in perceptual experience).

Siegel (2006) puts her phenomenal contrast method to work as follows. Consider someone (let's call her 'Kylie') who becomes an arborist. As part of her training, Kylie learns to recognize pines by sight. Now, contrast Kylie's visual experience when looking at pines as a novice (state A) with a visual experience that she has when looking at pines once she has learnt to recognize them by sight (state B). It is plausible to suppose that there's a phenomenal contrast between state A and state B: that the process of perceptual learning has changed how pines look (in the phenomenal sense of the term) to Kylie. Siegel argues that the best explanation for this change requires accepting that *being a pine tree* is now directly presented in Kylie's visual experience.

In responding to Siegel's argument, conservatives have two options open to them: a *high road* and a *low road*. Those who adopt the high road argue that phenomenal contrasts are best explained in terms of the kinds of judgments that one is disposed to make. As a novice, Kylie wasn't in a position to classify trees as pines merely on the basis of seeing them, but as an experienced arborist, she is. Conservatives who adopt the low-road response argue that phenomenal contrasts can be accounted for in terms that appeal only to differences in how low-level features (such as colour, shape, orientation, and texture) are represented. According to this proposal, learning to recognize pine trees by sight doesn't involve perceptually representing the property *being a pine tree*, but instead involves only an increased sensitivity to those low-level features that are diagnostic of pines (such as the shape of a tree's leaves or the texture of its bark). This account allows that one can use the contents of visual experience to infer that something is a pine tree (indirect perception), but it denies that *being a pine tree* is directly given in the contents of visual experience.

What should we make of these two lines of response? One problem with the high-road response is that it doesn't explain why perceptual learning leads to changes in the judgments that one is disposed to make. The natural thing to say is that as an expert arborist, Kylie is able to make judgments about trees that she was unable to make as a novice precisely because pines now look differently to her. But that explanation is not available to the high-road conservative, for the high-road theorist holds that the way pines look to Kylie hasn't changed at all. The low-road response is perhaps more plausible, for phenomenal contrasts typically (perhaps invariably) involve changes to the way in which one attends to particular details of an object or scene. At the time same, it is far from clear that such changes can fully account for the phenomenal contrast between how pines looked to Kylie prior to her training and how they appear to her now.

The question of whether the property of being a pine tree can be directly given in perceptual experience isn't, perhaps, terribly momentous, but it does provide an elegant entry point into the admissible contents debate, and that debate certainly does bear on a number of important issues, such as the relationship between perception and thought, the epistemic power of perceptual experience, and the role of concepts in perception. Indeed, the admissible contents debate even raises questions about the very notion of perceptual content, and how exactly the contrast between 'direct perception' and 'indirect perception' should be drawn.

4.5 Unconscious perception?

Thus far we have focused on aspects of the experiential nature of perception – that is, on the nature of perception as a mode of consciousness. But is all perception conscious, or is it possible to perceive an object without being conscious of it?

Although philosophers have traditionally assumed that perception is essentially conscious, psychologists and neuroscientists tend to think that perception can be, and often is, unconscious. Debate about the possibility of unconscious perception centres around the interpretation of various experimental findings, the most famous of which involves blindsight. Blindsight is a rare condition in which damage to area V1 of the primary visual cortex causes impairments relating to an area of the visual field (the 'blindfield'). Individuals with blindsight claim to be unaware of stimuli that are presented in the blindfield, but are often able to discriminate those stimuli from other stimuli under forced choice conditions with remarkable accuracy. For example, a blindsight subject may be well above chance in distinguishing vertical lines from horizontal ones, all the time insisting that he 'doesn't see' the lines and is merely guessing (Weiskrantz 1998).

Other alleged examples of unconscious perception involve studies that use a technique known as continuous flash suppression (CFS), in which a high-contrast rapidly changing Mondrian is presented to one eye and a target image is presented to the other eye. The Mondrian 'captures' visual experience and prevents information about a target stimulus from breaking through to visual awareness for a period of time (often 10 seconds or longer). But despite the fact that information about the target stimulus doesn't reach awareness, studies have shown that it is represented by the subject's visual system and can have an impact on the subject's behaviour. One CFS study used images of male and female nudes as targets, and found that although subjects weren't conscious of the images, the images did influence their visual attention (Jiang et al. 2006). Importantly, the nature of that influence depended on the gender and sexual orientation of the subject: the attention of heterosexual males was captured by the images of female nudes and repelled by images of male nudes, whereas the attention of heterosexual females and gay males was captured by the images of male nudes and repelled by the images of female nudes.

Does either blindsight or the results of this CFS study establish the existence of unconscious perception? As Ian Phillips (2018) has pointed out, to answer this question in the affirmative, one would need to show that subjects were genuinely unaware of the relevant stimuli (the *unconscious condition*) and that they really did perceive it (the *perception condition*). Let's consider whether either blindsight or Jiang et al.'s CFS study meets both of these conditions.

The traditional view of blindsight as involving the complete absence of visual experience is supported by the fact that when subjects are asked whether they saw the stimulus or not, they usually say that they didn't see anything. However, it has been argued that blindsight subjects retain some kind of degraded visual experience in their blindfield (Cowey 2010; Overgaard 2012; Phillips 2021). According to this proposal, subjects deny seeing stimuli that have been presented in their blindfield not because they are completely unaware of them, but because their awareness of them is weak and indistinct, falling below their criterion for what it is to 'see' something. Interestingly, when subjects are encouraged to report their visual experiences with a 4-point scale that includes not only 'not seen' at one end of the scale and 'clear image' at the other end but also two intermediate categories ('weak glimpse' and 'almost clear'), then the contrast between their reports and their capacity to distinguish stimuli essentially disappears (Overgaard et al. 2008).[14]

Worries about whether subjects might actually have been conscious of the target stimuli have less force in the case of the Jiang et al. CFS study, for not only did the subjects insist that they saw nothing other than the Mondrian, they were at chance when asked to guess which of two nudes had been presented as the target. The question here is whether this study meets the *perception condition*.

As Phillips (2018) points out, perception is a personal-level phenomenon. Seeing requires processing in the visual system, but it is not the visual system (or its parts) that sees: it is organisms that see. Thus, we need to consider what it would take for representations in the visual system to qualify as, or give rise to, personal-level states.

One approach holds that a state is personal only if it provides the agent with conscious access to its environment. States whose contents don't enter consciousness might modulate the agent's behaviour in some way, but they aren't genuinely personal level – they aren't 'for' the agent. This conception of what it takes to be personal-level certainly rules out the possibility of unconscious perception, but appealing to it in this context is arguably question-begging. After all, anyone who takes the possibility of unconscious perception seriously is unlikely to think that the boundary between the personal and the subpersonal is marked by what is consciously accessible.

A more promising proposal is that a state is personal-level only if it is able to provide reasons for thought and action. ('Why did you jump up from your chair?' 'Because I saw a fox'.) This account wouldn't automatically rule out the possibility of unconscious perception, but it would cast doubt on the claim that the Jiang et al. study provides evidence of unconscious perception, for although the subjects in that study had visual representations of the nudes which influenced their behaviour, those representations did not provide them with reasons to act in the ways that they did.

The debate regarding the possibility of unconscious perception is of interest in its own right, but it is also raises important questions about the category of perception, and indeed the nature of psychological categories more generally. On the one hand, perception and the related notions of seeing, hearing, and so on are part of our everyday framework for understanding the mind: they are folk concepts. At the same time, perception and its modalities are the objects of scientific study. The debate about unconscious perception forces us to ask whether the nature of perception is fixed by the role that the category of perception plays in folk psychology, or whether it is answerable to the sciences of the mind, and thus potentially open to revision in the light of findings in neuroscience and psychology.

4.6 Conclusion

Let's revisit some of the major themes of this chapter. We began by considering three of the main accounts of perception: the content view, the sense-data view, and naïve realism. The sense-data view captures the intuitive thought that even in hallucination there is some kind of perceptual object, whereas hallucination is commonly taken to be a problem for the content view. However, we saw that sense data are inherently mysterious, and that hallucination doesn't pose any kind of distinctive problem for the content theorist. (Explaining our capacity to represent non-existent objects is everyone's problem.) The main motivation for naïve realism involves an appeal to the phenomenon of perceptual presence. However, I argued both that the content theorists can explain why perception is characterized by a sense of presence, and that there are instances of perceptual presence that the naïve realist cannot accommodate. Although the content view has many critics, in my view it is the most compelling account that we have of perception.

We then turned to the question of how the contents of perception relate to its phenomenal character. Intentionalists hold that the phenomenal character of perception is either identical to, or at least supervenient on, its intentional content. If intentionalism is right, then perceptual experiences with the same intentional content must have the same phenomenal character. In Section 4.3, we first explored the transparency argument in favour of intentionalism and then considered two arguments against intentionalism: the common-sensibles argument and the inverted-spectrum argument. I suggested that the second of these two objections is more powerful than the first, although even it is far from decisive.

In the second half of this chapter we turned to two debates that straddle the border between philosophy and the scientific study of the mind. The first of these debates concerns the admissible contents of perception, and the question of what kinds of properties can be directly perceived. We examined phenomenal contrast arguments for the claim that perception can include high-level properties (such as being a pine tree), and considered two ways in which conservatives might respond to such arguments. We then turned to the debate regarding the possibility of unconscious perception, focusing on blindsight and studies that employ continuous flash suppression (CFS). We saw that it is an open question whether blindsight subjects really are unaware of stimuli in their blindfield, and that it is also an open question whether the subjects in Jiang et al.'s CFS study genuinely perceived the nudes of which they were unaware. Indeed, we saw that unconscious perception might turn out to be impossible for reasons that ultimately derive from the fact that it is a personal, rather than a subpersonal, phenomenon.

Further reading

Perception has been a lively area in recent philosophy of mind, and there are a number of excellent collections on the topic. Among the three best volumes are Tamar Gendler and John Hawthorne (eds.), *Perceptual Experience* (OUP, 2006); Bence Nanay (ed.), *Perceiving the World* (OUP, 2010); and Berit Brogaard, *Does Perception Have Content?* (OUP, 2014). *The Oxford Handbook of the Philosophy of Perception* (OUP, 2015), edited by Mohan Matthen, contains authoritative discussion of the issues covered in this chapter and a great many more.

For general introductions to the philosophy of perception see William Fish's *Philosophy of Perception: A Contemporary Introduction* (Routledge, 2010) and Adam Pautz's *The Puzzle of Perception* (Routledge, 2021). Among the many excellent monographs on perception are Mohan Matthen's *Seeing, Doing, and Knowing* (OUP, 2005) and J. Christopher Maloney's *What It Is Like to Perceive: Direct Realism and the Phenomenal Character of Perception* (OUP, 2018). *The Senses* (OUP, 2011), edited by Fiona Macpherson, contains a number of excellent essays on non-visual perception.

For more on hallucination see Fiona Macpherson and Dimitris Platchias (eds.), *Hallucination* (MIT Press, 2013). For more on naïve realism see James Genone's 'Recent Work on Naïve Realism', *American Philosophical Quarterly*, 53(1): 1-25 (2016) and Heather Logue's 'Why Naïve Realism?', *Proceedings of the Aristotelian Society*, 112(2): 211-37 (2012). For more on perceptual presence see Alva Noë's 'Real Presence', *Philosophical Topics*, 33: 235-64 (2005); Dan Cavedon-Taylor's 'Perceptual Content and Sensorimotor Expectations', *Philosophical Quarterly*, 61: 383-91 (2011); and Sam Wilkinson's 'Distinguishing Volumetric Content from Perceptual Presence within a Predictive Processing Framework', *Phenomenology and the Cognitive Sciences*, 19: 791-800 (2020).

For more on intentionalism see Michael Tye's *Consciousness, Color, and Content* (MIT Press, 2000); Alex Byrne's 'Intentionalism Defended', *Philosophical Review*, 110 (2): 199-240 (2001); and Jeff Speaks's *The Phenomenal and the Representational* (OUP, 2015).

For an excellent entry point into the admissible contents question, see the debate between Susanna Siegel and Alex Byrne in their paper 'Rich or Thin?', in B. Nanay (ed.), *Current Controversies in the Philosophy of Perception* (Routledge, 2016). For more on Siegel's phenomenal contrast method see her *The Contents of Visual Experience* (2010, OUP) and her paper 'How Can We Discover the Contents of Experience?' *Southern Journal of Philosophy*, 45 (Supplement): 127-42 (2007). An excellent collection of papers on the topic of perceptual content is *The Admissible Contents of Experience* (Wiley-Blackwell, 2011), edited by Katherine Hawley and Fiona Macpherson. For more on perceptual learning see Kevin Connolly's *Perceptual Learning* (OUP, 2019) and Adrienne Prettyman's 'Perceptual Learning', *WIREs Cognitive Science*, 20(1), e1489 (2019).

For more on unconscious perception see Berit Brogaard's 'Are There Unconscious Perceptual Processes?, *Consciousness and Cognition*, 20(2): 449-63 (2011); Henry Taylor's 'Fuzziness in the Mind: Can Perception Be Unconscious?' *Philosophy and Phenomenological Research*, 101(2): 383-98 (2020); and Joshua Shepherd and Myrto Mylopoulos's 'Unconscious Perception and Central Coordinating Agency', *Philosophical Studies* (forthcoming). Also excellent is the debate between Ian Phillips and Ned Block in *Current Controversies in Philosophy of Perception*, edited by Bence Nanay (Routledge, 2016).

Study questions

1. This chapter distinguishes three accounts of perception: the content (or representational) view, the sense-data view, and naïve realism. What is distinctive about each view? What are their respective strengths and weaknesses?
2. What is disjunctivism? How is it relevant to the debate between the content view, the sense-data view, and naïve realism?
3. What is perceptual presence? Explain how naïve realism and the content view attempt to account for it. Evaluate their proposals.
4. What are intentionalist (representationalist) accounts of perceptual experience committed to? How does intentionalism relate to the debate between separatism and inseparatism that was discussed in Chapter 1?
5. What is the perceptual transparency argument for intentionalism? Does it succeed?
6. Section 4.4 provides an overview of the debate between those who have a conservative (austere, thin) view of perceptual content and those who have a liberal (rich, thick) view of it. Which position do you find most compelling, and why?
7. Explain and evaluate Siegel's pine tree argument for a liberal (rich, thick) account of perceptual content.
8. Why is the border between the personal and the subpersonal relevant to the debate regarding unconscious perception? How do you think that the personal/subpersonal border should be drawn?

Notes

1. On auditory experience, see Casati and Dokic (2005), O'Callaghan (2007), Matthen (2010), and Nudds and O'Callaghan (2009). On olfactory experience, see Barwich (2020), Batty (2010, 2011) and Cavedon-Taylor (2018). On flavour, see Auvray and Spence (2008), Smith (2015a), and Richardson (2013).
2. For defences of the content view, see Brogaard (2014), Nanay (2015), Pautz (2010, 2020), Siegel (2010a, 2010b), Searle (1983), and Schellenberg (2011).
3. For defences of naïve realism (although not always under that name), see Brewer (2011), Campbell (2002), Fish (2009), Johnston (2014), Martin (2002, 2004), and Travis (2004).
4. Note that perceptual presence might not characterize all instances of hallucination, but the argument presented here doesn't require that it does. All that's required is that some instances of hallucination involve perceptual presence.
5. Some content theorists deny that there *is* a difference between perception and judgment, holding that perception just is a kind of belief (Byrne 2009; Glüer 2009, 2014). Advocates of this version of the content view clearly cannot account for perceptual presence by appealing to a distinctive kind of perceptual attitude.
6. I believe that the first use of 'mental paint' in connection with perceptual phenomenology occurs in Harman (1990), although Harman uses it in a slightly broader way than Block does.
7. Although contemporary discussion of this idea derives from Harman (1990), a notion of perceptual transparency – although perhaps not quite the one that Harman had in mind – dates back to a 1903 paper by G. E. Moore, 'The Refutation of Idealism'.
8. See also Byrne (2001), Dretske (1995), Speaks (2009), and Tye (2002).
9. For more on the transparency argument, see Kind (2003), Martin (2002), Siewert (2004), Speaks (2009), Stoljar (2004), and van Cleve (2015).
10. For another line of response that the intentionalist might take to this problem, see the Fregean version of intentionalism developed by Thompson (2008, 2009) and Chalmers (2004b).

76 *Perception*

11 For other alleged counterexamples, see Macpherson (2006), Nickel (2007), and Peacocke (1983). Tye (2003) provides a response to many of the alleged counterexamples to intentionalism. For more on spectrum inversion, see Cohen (2001), Horgan (1984a), and Speaks (2011).
12 On causation, see Beebee (2003), Butterfill (2009), Nudds (2001), and Rips (2011). On mental states, see Carruthers (2015), Cassam (2007), Smith (2015b), and Green (2010). On affordances and dispositional properties, see Siegel (2014) and Nanay (2011). On moral properties, see Audi (2013) and Cullison (2010). See also Church (2010) for the claim that reasons can be perceived.
13 For more on looks talk, see Brogaard (2015) and Martin (2010).
14 It is also worth noting that some blindsight patients do report some form of awareness even when using a dichotomous scale, referring to 'visual pin pricks' (Richards 1973), 'dark shadows' (Barbur et al. 1980), and 'white halos' (Perenin and Jeannerod 1978).

5 Thought

Chapter overview

- Introduces the language of thought (LOT) hypothesis and evaluates the central arguments for it
- Explains and evaluates John Searle's Chinese room argument against the LOT hypothesis
- Introduces the Turing test and considers some of its strengths and weaknesses.

'Man is only a reed, the most feeble thing in nature, but he is a thinking reed'. So wrote the 17th-century philosopher and mathematician Blaise Pascal in his volume *Pensees* (§347). Thought is indeed one of our most notable attributes. But although we spend much of our time thinking, we rarely turn our cognitive faculties on themselves and consider their own nature. That is our task here.

Our discussion will revolve around two closely related questions. The first concerns the analysis of human thought. What does it take for creatures like us to have the kinds of thoughts that we do? This question is in many ways a question for psychologists and neuroscientists, but philosophers have had a great deal to say about it (as we shall see). A second – and more recognizably philosophical – question concerns the nature of thought as such. What are the essential features of thought? What would it take for an animal or an artificial neural network to think? DeepMind's AlphaZero can outplay humans in chess, and IBM's Watson has beaten the world's best players of the quiz show *Jeopardy!*, but are AlphaZero or Watson genuine thinkers?

We begin in Section 5.1 by distinguishing between thoughts of different kinds, and by asking what might distinguish thoughts from mental phenomena of other kinds. In Section 5.2 we explore the language of thought hypothesis (LOT). According to LOT, thoughts involve symbols in an internal representational system ('Mentalese'), and thinking involves nothing more than the manipulation of these symbols. LOT is influential, but it is also highly controversial. One challenge to LOT is that the manipulation of language-like symbols isn't necessary for thought; another challenge is that the manipulation of language-like symbols

DOI: 10.4324/9781003225348-6

doesn't suffice for thought. Section 5.3 considers challenges of the first kind, while Section 5.4 considers a challenge of the second kind. The chapter concludes with the question of how we might test for the presence of thought in an artificial system.

5.1 The varieties of thought

The term 'thought' is used in a variety of senses. In its widest sense, any mental state – memory, perception, intention, judgment, and so on – qualifies as a thought. However, philosophers tend to use 'thought' in a narrower sense that excludes bodily sensations, moods, and perceptual states. Deciding what to have for dinner, wishing that the rain would stop, and realizing that an argument is invalid are all paradigmatic instances of thought in this sense of the term.

Is it possible to provide necessary and sufficient conditions for thought (or for being a thinker)? Probably not, but this should come as no surprise, for it is rarely possible to provide necessary and sufficient conditions for any philosophically interesting phenomenon. Instead of searching for a definition of 'thought', let's focus on identifying some of its core features, features that distinguish thought from other mental phenomena.

First, thought is *stimulus independent*. Consider the contrast between seeing a fox and merely thinking about a fox. In order to see a fox, there must be a direct causal connection between the fox and you. By contrast, no such causal connection is needed in order to think about a fox. Further, in order to see a fox, certain environmental conditions must obtain. For example, the fox cannot be occluded, and it must fall within one's visual field. No such factors interfere with one's capacity to think about a fox. Because thought allows a creature to represent its environment in a stimulus-independent manner, a creature with the capacity for thought can control its environment in ways that creatures which rely only on perception cannot.

Second, thought is *abstract*. It is amodal (i.e., not tied to any particular sensory system) and allows one to grasp aspects of the world that cannot be perceived. One can see the colour of a fox's coat and hear its yelping, but only a creature with the power of thought can understand the evolutionary history of the fox or figure out how to fox-proof the chicken coop. We can think about things that are too distant from us in space or time to be perceived, and we can think about things (such as numbers and fictional entities) that are imperceptible in principle. As long as one has a means of locking on to an object – a name ('Genghis Khan'), a demonstrative ('that thing next to the teapot'), or a description ('the square root of 2') – one can think about it.

Third, thought is *open-ended*. The faculty of thought allows one to draw on information derived from multiple sensory modalities and to integrate it with background beliefs, desires, and other propositional attitudes to generate new thoughts and novel plans of action. Thought allows one to grasp the relevance of an unexpected discovery and to draw connections between topics that are normally unrelated. Section 5.2 considers the open-ended nature of thought in more detail.

One question raised by the foregoing concerns the nature of the border between perception and thought. Traditionally, philosophers have tended to treat this border as sharp and clear-cut. Extended mental processes, such as deciding what to order from a menu, might involve complex interactions between perception (looking at various items on the menu) and thought (wondering what a dish might contain or what it might taste like), but according to this view, no individual mental phenomenon can fall between perception proper and thought proper. Contemporary theorists, however, often view the border between perception and thought as nebulous and somewhat ill-defined, allowing that there might be phenomena that fall somewhere between paradigmatic perception on the one hand and paradigmatic thought on the other (Box: Alief: between thought and perception?).

Box: Alief: between thought and perception?

The Grand Canyon Skywalk is an enclosed viewing platform with a glass floor that extends 70 feet out into the Grand Canyon and allows one to look directly onto the canyon floor. Those who venture out onto it often experience vertigo. In some cases the vertigo is so overwhelming that people find themselves unable to walk to the middle of the viewing platform despite having paid for that privilege. How are we to understand this phenomenon? As Tamar Gendler (2008a, 2008b) has observed, appealing to what a person believes doesn't get us very far, for those who experience vertigo surely believe that the platform is perfectly safe. After all, why would they pay to step onto it if they had even the slightest doubt about its safety?

Gendler argues that in order to explain a person's reluctance to venture out onto Skywalk we need to posit a novel type of mental state that she calls 'alief'. Aliefs represent features of one's environment as having certain properties (e.g., as dangerous), they generate characteristic affective responses (e.g., feelings of anxiety and fear), and they activate various motor routines (e.g., muscle contractions associated with hesitation and retreat). Aliefs are akin to beliefs in that they guide the agent's behaviour, but unlike beliefs they are not subject to rational control. Reflecting on the evident safety of Skywalk might reinforce the belief that it is safe, but it won't suppress the queasy feeling in one's stomach or reduce the shaking of one's knees. Beliefs can be freely integrated with each other to form new beliefs (they are 'inferentially promiscuous'), whereas aliefs only enter into associative relations. Aliefs are akin to thoughts in certain ways, but in other respects they are more like perceptual states.

Gendler's arguments for the existence of aliefs has generated much discussion, and not everyone is convinced that the notion of alief must be added to our psychological arsenal. But whether or not the case for aliefs is ultimately successful, Gendler's work raises important questions about the nature of the border between thought and perception.

Further reading

Currie, G., and A. Ichino. 2012. Aliefs Don't Exist, though Some of Their Relatives Do. *Analysis Reviews*, 72(4): 788-98.
Mandelbaum, E. 2013. Against Alief. *Philosophical Studies*, 165(1): 197-211.
Nagel, J. 2012. Gendler on Alief. *Analysis Reviews*, 72(4): 774-88.

The three features of thought that we have just identified are not peculiar to (mature) human thought but (to some degree at least) characterize thought in general. Thus, we can use them to guide our reflection on the kinds of organisms that qualify as thinkers. As an example of this approach, consider the capacity that baboons have to represent social relations in their troop. The social world of female baboons involves a two-tiered hierarchy of status, in which families are ranked in relation to each other and the females within each family are ranked in relation to each other (Cheney & Seyfarth 2007). It is important for baboons to be able to keep track of these rankings, for an individual's rank plays a pivotal role in determining how that individual will interact with other individuals (and how they will interact with it). Behavioural evidence suggests that baboons are able to do this.

As Elisabeth Camp (2009) has argued, the baboon's representations of its social world seem to qualify as thoughts. These representations are independent of the baboon's immediate perceptual environment, and thus satisfy the constraint of stimulus independence. They are abstract, for the properties that they track (such as being of subordinate status) are not perceptually manifest. And they are (somewhat) open-ended, for baboons can represent a great number of relations between the members of their troop - not only those that are predictable but also those that are unexpected and incongruous.

In suggesting that baboons can think we are not committed to the claim that the baboon's capacities for thought rival our own. Our self-bestowed title *Homo sapiens* is not unjustified, for no other species matches us when it comes to thought. We are the only species to have created the social institutions associated with law, government, and religion; the only species to have developed complex tools and technologies; and the only species to have produced a sophisticated material culture. But although other species - not to mention the immature members of our own species - lack the capacity to entertain the range of thoughts that are distinctive of mature human cognition, there is no reason to think that the capacity for thought is uniquely human.

Thus far we have focused on thoughts as mental states (or events) in their own right, but we should also recognize that thoughts are commonly embedded in *trains of thought*: sequences in which thoughts are related to each other in various way. Some trains of thoughts involve only *associative* relations. As David Hume (1711-76) observed in a chapter of his book *An Enquiry Concerning Human Understanding* titled 'Of the Association of Ideas': 'thoughts introduce each other with a certain degree of method and regularity'. To use Hume's own example, the thought of a picture might lead one to think of the object depicted in the picture. Associative thinking is familiar from daydreams and other forms of mind-wandering. Other trains of thought are characterized by logical and evidential relations. Consider the sequence of thoughts: 'Hypatia is a human'; 'All humans are mortal'; therefore 'Hypatia is mortal'. The elements in this sequence are inferentially connected, for if the first two thoughts are true then the third thought must also be true. This train of thought is very different from an associative train of thought, in which (say) a thought about a graveyard might elicit thoughts about Hypatia's morality. Associative trains of thought are useful for problem-solving and creativity, but the power of thought derives from its capacity to track the logical and evidential relations between propositions. Indeed, the term 'thinking' is sometimes reserved for the activity of keeping track of such relations (i.e., reasoning).

Some reasoning is automatic, intuitive, and fast. Reasoning of this kind has much in common with perception and occurs mostly unconsciously (although its results are typically available to consciousness). But reasoning can also be controlled, reflective, and slow. Psychologists often refer to the contrast between reasoning that is automatic, intuitive, and fast and reasoning that is controlled, reflected, and slow as the distinction between 'system 1' reasoning and 'system 2' reasoning. However, it is controversial whether these two modes of reasoning involve distinct systems or whether they involve using a single suite of systems in distinct ways.[1] Arguably the distinction between these two modes of reasoning is not hard and fast but instead marks out two ends of a continuum, with many instances of thought falling somewhere between the purely automatic and the purely controlled.

The contrast between automatic and controlled thought is most clearly revealed by cognitive illusions. These are cases in which our intuitions about a problem are at odds with our reflectively endorsed judgments. Consider the well-known *bat-and-ball problem* (Kahneman & Frederick 2002):

> *Bat and Ball Problem*: A bat and a ball cost $1.10 in total. The bat costs $1.00 more than the ball. How much does the ball cost?

Most people's intuitive response is that the ball costs 10 cents. However, on reflection, it's evident that the ball must cost 5 cents and the bat $1.05. (If the ball cost 10 cents and the bat costs $1.00 more than the ball, then the bat would cost $1.10 and together they would cost $1.20.) What's striking, however, is that we remain primed to provide the wrong answer even when we know that it's wrong. In the same way that one's experience of a visual illusion is not penetrated by one's knowledge that it's an illusion, so too one's intuitive response to the bat-and-ball problem is not penetrated by one's reflective understanding. We share the capacity for automatic thought with the members of many other species, but the capacity for controlled thought may be a distinctively human trait. (We return to this theme in Section 5.4.)

5.2 The language of thought hypothesis

How is the capacity for thought to be explained? The most influential answer to this question is that thought involves the manipulation of sentences in a kind of inner language, what is sometimes called 'Mentalese'. Mentalese is not a public language in the way that English, Mandarin, or Portuguese is – instead, it's a purely private language. The idea that thought involves an inner language dates back to the Middle Ages but was given its canonical defence by Jerry Fodor (1935-2017) in his 1975 book *The Language of Thought*. The view (or at least close relatives of it) trades under a number of names (e.g., 'the representational theory of the mind', 'the computer model of the mind', 'the computational theory of the mind', 'the symbol-system hypothesis', 'sententialism'), but I will refer to it as the 'language of thought hypothesis', or LOT for short.

Central to LOT is the idea of a symbol (or representation). Symbols have both syntactic and semantic properties. A syntactic (or formal) property is a property that a purely physical system could be sensitive to and which is correlated with a semantic property. Some of the most familiar syntactic properties are shapes. Consider, for example, the following three tokens (or instances) of a familiar English word:

    fox   FOX   *fox*

These three tokens of the word 'fox' differ in various ways, yet each is a recognizable instance of that English symbol in virtue of its shape. Not all differences in shape are syntactically relevant - there are subtle differences between the shape of 'fox' and that of 'FOX' and *'fox'* - but all three symbols belong to the same syntactic category (unlike, say, 'fox' and 'socks'). Natural languages don't limit themselves to shapes but also employ phonological properties (for speech) and movement properties (in signing) as syntactic properties. In principle, a symbol system could employ physical properties of any kind (e.g., temperature, weight, or electric charge) as syntactic properties.

    A semantic (or content) property of a symbol concerns its meaning. To a first approximation, we can say that the meaning of a symbol is a matter of what it refers to. Thus, 'fox' means fox. The story is more complicated than this, for some symbols don't refer to anything (e.g., 'Santa Claus'), and there are symbols that refer to the same object but which intuitively differ in meaning (e.g., 'Dr. Dre', 'Andre Young'), but we will leave these complications to one side here.

    Let's turn now to the LOT hypothesis itself. We can think of LOT as comprising two claims: a claim about the nature of *thoughts* and a claim about the nature of *thinking*. In a nutshell, LOT holds that thoughts are sentences in a language of thought, and that thinking involves syntactically governed transitions between sentences in a language of thought. Let's unpack these claims.

    What does it mean to say that thoughts are sentences in a language of thought? Consider the thought THE FOX ATE THE CHICKENS. Just as the sentence 'The fox ate the chickens' is built up out of symbols ('fox', 'ate', and 'chickens') that have distinct contents, so too (the advocate of LOT claims) the thought THE FOX ATE THE CHICKENS is built up out of symbols with distinct contents. Thinking that the fox ate the chickens involves activating mental symbols that refer to foxes, chickens, and the relation of eating. The key idea here is that thoughts themselves are compositional, and that corresponding to each of a thought's semantic components is a symbol whose content makes a discrete contribution to its overall meaning. In the same way that the word 'fox' makes the same contribution to the various sentences in which it occurs ('Foxes are ingenious predators', 'Foxes are mammals', etc.), so too a single kind of mental symbol (/fox/) makes a uniform contribution to the various thoughts about foxes that a person might have. That, at any rate, is what LOT claims.[2]

    What about *thinking*? What does it mean to say that thinking involves syntactically governed transitions between sentences in a language of thought? Suppose that I think FOXES ARE MORTAL and MARTHA IS A FOX, and that these two thoughts lead me to form the thought MARTHA IS MORTAL. LOT explains this transition in thought by appealing to the syntactic properties of the relevant symbols. A mechanism that is sensitive to these properties can generate the third thought when provided with the first two thoughts. According to LOT, our brain is such a mechanism. Viewed abstractly, its principles of operation mirror those of the post office's automated address reader. Although the reader doesn't know anything about Mrs. Kahn or Mr. Jones, it is able to sort their mail correctly because it is sensitive to the syntactical differences between the names 'Mrs. Kahn' and 'Mr. Jones'. As John Haugeland (1985: 106) memorably put it, 'If you take care of the syntax, the semantics will take care of itself'.

That, in essence, is how LOT accounts for thought. The basic idea is that thoughts are symbol structures, and thinking involves the manipulation of these structures on the basis of their syntactic properties. Does thinking *feel* like it involves symbol manipulation? Probably not, although it's not exactly clear what symbol manipulation would feel like. But in any case, the issue is irrelevant, for LOT doesn't make any claims about what it feels like to think. Instead, LOT is an account of the machinery of thought.

Advocates of the LOT hypothesis have different conceptions of the scope of the account. One approach – we might call it the 'essentialist view' – treats LOT as an account of the nature of thought as such (see, e.g., Davies 1992, 1998). According to the essentialist, no creature could be a thinker unless it had some version of a language of thought. By contrast, the non-essentialist version of LOT (as defended by Fodor) treats it as an empirical claim about the nature of human thought and allows that thought could occur in the absence of Mentalese. The contrast between these two views has important consequences. Most obviously, it bears on the analysis of non-human thought. If the essentialist version of LOT were right, then the question of whether a certain kind of AI system qualifies as a thinker would need to be addressed by asking whether it has a language of thought. By contrast, if the LOT hypothesis were regarded as only one possible way in which thought can be realized, then we couldn't draw any conclusions about whether an AI system was a thinker from its failure to employ language-like representations. We will focus on the non-essentialist version of LOT, for it is this form of the view that has had the most influence.

Having seen what the LOT hypothesis says, let us consider what might be said in favour of it. The most influential arguments for LOT are Fodor's arguments from productivity and systematicity. The productivity and systematicity of thought are both aspects of what we earlier referred to as its open-ended nature. Thought is productive in that there don't seem to be any principled limits on the range of thoughts that we can entertain. Fodor puts the point as follows:

> The thoughts that one actually entertains in the course of a mental life comprise a relatively unsystematic subset drawn from a vastly larger variety of thoughts that one could have entertained had an occasion for them arisen. For example, it has probably never occurred to you before that no grass grows on kangaroos. But, once your attention is drawn to the point, it's an idea that you are quite capable of entertaining, one which, in fact, you are probably inclined to endorse.
>
> (Fodor 1985: 89)

The systematicity of thought has two faces. The first is that the capacity to think certain thoughts comes along with the capacity to think other thoughts. As Fodor points out, we don't find people who can think MARY LOVES JOHN but cannot think JOHN LOVES MARY. The second face of systematicity is that inferential capacities are systematically related to each other. For example, we don't find people who can infer *P* from *P&Q* but cannot infer *Q* from *P&Q*.[3]

Fodor argues that the productivity and systematicity of thought are best explained by supposing that thought is compositional. The model here is provided by our linguistic capacities. Linguistic capacities are systematic, for if you know what 'Mary loves John' means, then you also know what 'John loves Mary' means. They are also productive (in principle at least), for you are able to understand sentences you have not previously encountered. ('Would Ben Jonson have knifed a man on account of some literary disagreement if he had not been bearded to the eyebrows?' - P. G. Wodehouse.) The systematicity and productivity of language derives from its compositionality. Knowing a natural language involves knowing the meaning of a set of representations (the words) and the rules for combining those representations into larger units of meaning (i.e., sentences). Thus, Fodor argues, our cognitive capacities are systematic and productive because cognition involves a set of atomic symbols (the 'words' of Mentalese) and the capacity to combine those atoms into larger representational units, namely, thoughts (Box: But does it have to be a *language*?).[4]

Box: But does it have to be a *language*?

One might be convinced that thought is compositional but wonder whether its format must really be *linguistic*. After all, sentences aren't the only kind of representations with compositional structure. Perhaps the format of thought has more in common with that of maps or graphs than languages. Maps and graphs are representational systems that support certain forms of systematicity and productivity, but their format is not linguistic.

This question brings to the surface two uses of the term 'the language of thought': a broad use and a narrow use. The narrow use requires that a representational system must have a linguistic format if it is to qualify as a genuine language of thought. This seems to have been Fodor's use of the phrase. Other theorists use 'the language of thought' in a more inclusive manner, according to which any system of mental representations that supports compositional structure counts as a kind of language of thought. The important issue isn't how 'the language of thought' should be used - after all, it's just a label - but to note that there are broader and narrower conceptions of what exactly the language of thought hypothesis is. The key issue is whether the arguments for LOT support the narrow version of the thesis or the broader version of it - assuming, of course, that they succeed at all.

Further reading

Camp, E. 2007. Thinking with Maps. *Philosophical Perspectives*, 21(1): 145-82.
Frankland, S. M., and J. Greene. 2020. Concepts and Compositionality: In Search of the Brain's Language of Thought. *Annual Review of Psychology*, 71: 273-303.
Rescorla, M. 2009. Cognitive Maps and the Language of Thought. *British Journal for the Philosophy of Science*, 60(2): 377-407.

5.3 Alternatives to the language of thought

Although neither systematicity nor productivity is an entirely straightforward phenomenon, it is evident that thought - at least mature human thought - exhibits a significant degree of systematicity and productivity. But does LOT provide the only (or even the best) explanation of this fact?

One challenge to LOT derives from connectionist models of cognitive architecture. These models were first developed in the 1980s and over time have given rise to the deep-learning networks that drive voice- and face-recognition systems (Buckner 2019; Lake et al. 2017; LeCun et al. 2015). Instead of a central processor and symbolic representations that are stored in memory, a connectionist network involves layers of nodes that bear weighted connections to one another. Learning changes the weights on these nodes, and computation in a connectionist network involves activating the network nodes, with a node's activation level being dependent upon the weighted activations of the nodes to which it is connected. Crucially, in a network processing is both distributed and parallel – hence connectionist architectures are known as parallel distributed processing architectures (Rumelhart et al. 1987). By contrast, in a LOT-based architecture computation is typically localized and serial. With the rise of connectionism, the LOT approach to cognition has become known as the classical approach to cognition.

Connectionism suggests an alternative account of thought to that provided by LOT. Because representation in a network is distributed across the network, a network can represent THE CAT SAT ON THE MAT and THE CAT CHASED THE DOG without these representations having any common element. The overall state of the network might encode the content THE CAT SAT ON THE MAT, but there may be no component of the network that represents the cat (or the mat, for that matter). Although the *contents* of thought will have constituents – the thought THE CAT SAT ON THE MAT 'contains' the concepts CAT, SAT, and MAT – the structure of thoughts themselves may not reflect the structure of their contents. In a LOT-based architecture, by contrast, systems that represent THE CAT SAT ON THE MAT and THE CAT CHASED THE DOG will have a common element; namely, the symbol CAT.

The mere fact that connectionism is an alternative to the classical LOT-based approach doesn't itself undermine the LOT hypothesis, for it might be argued that the LOT hypothesis does a better job of explaining the crucial features of thought than connectionist accounts do. Indeed, that is precisely the claim made by Fodor and a number of his colleagues (Fodor & Pylyshyn 1988; Fodor & McLaughlin 1990). In order to account for the systematicity of thought, they argued, there must be a higher level of description of any connectionist network according to which it can be thought of as implementing a language of thought. In a nutshell, Fodor and his colleagues responded to the connectionist challenge with a dilemma: either connectionist networks are mere implementations of a LOT-based architecture (in which case they aren't genuine rivals to LOT), or they are genuine rivals to LOT but fail to account for the systematicity of thought. Let's call this the *systematicity argument*.[5]

Evaluating the systematicity argument requires turning the spotlight on systematicity itself. Let us grant that mature human thought is systematic. In other words, let's grant Fodor's claim that you just don't find people who can think MARY LOVES JOHN but not JOHN LOVES MARY. Let's also grant that connectionism as such lacks the resources to explain this fact. (Although connectionist networks *can* exhibit systematicity, there is nothing in their structure which would lead one to predict that a connectionist network will exhibit systematicity.) The crucial question is this: should an account of the architecture of thought *guarantee* systematicity?

Arguably not. An account of the architecture of thought must obviously be *consistent* with whatever features it displays (including, of course, systematicity), but these features need not be *entailed* by thought's fundamental nature. Indeed, Fodor himself must allow for the possibility of LOT-based architectures that fail to exhibit systematicity, for he holds that although both animals and infants have a LOT, neither animal thought nor infant thought is systematic in the relevant sense. And surely Fodor is right to grant that systematicity is not an essential feature of thought. As Dennett (1991a: 27) has noted, 'There are organisms of whom one would say with little hesitation that they think a lion wants to eat them, but where there is no reason at all to think they could "frame the thought" that they want to eat the lion!'[6] But if the advocate of LOT must invoke other factors to explain why mature human thought is systematic, then they are hardly in a position to complain when connectionists do likewise!

How might we explain the systematicity (and productivity) of mature human thought? It's tempting to look to *natural* language. Non-linguistic creatures may be capable of thought about certain domains (social relations between the members of its group, the location of different types of food, the uses for different types of tools, and so on), but – so this proposal runs – only creatures who have mastered a natural language have cognitive capacities that are truly productive and systematic.[7] Natural language accounts of thought are often contrasted with the classical and connectionist accounts, but it is possible to see them as complementing rather than competing with those accounts. Thoughts themselves might be sentences in a language of thought or states of a connectionist network, but perhaps the distinctive features of mature human thought – its systematicity and productivity – are explained by the compositional structure of natural language.

Does this mean that we think *in* (natural) language? Not necessarily, although perhaps a significant portion of human thought does take the form of inner speech (Langland-Hassan & Vicente 2018; Lupyan 2012). Instead of supposing that thought is literally encoded in natural language, we might think of natural language as shaping and sculpting our cognitive capacities. Perhaps we don't find people who can think JOHN LOVES MARY but not MARY LOVES JOHN because the capacity to understand the sentence 'John loves Mary' is acquired in tandem with the capacity to understand the sentence 'Mary loves John'. And the fact that language makes possible representations that relate very different domains may explain our capacity to grasp such connections in thought. The mastery of terms for logical properties ('all', 'some', 'no') and evidential properties ('therefore', 'if. . . then', 'because') both expands the range of thoughts that are available to us and enables us to link thoughts together into arguments. More recent additions to the arsenal of natural language – such as the formal machinery associated with logic, probability theory, and the canons of good scientific reasoning – are likely to have further contributed to the productivity and systematicity of human thought (Box: The scaffolding of thought).

Box: The scaffolding of thought

If language makes a cognitive contribution to thought, then the question arises as to *how* it makes this contribution.

One possibility is that the use of symbols enables a creature to transform problems that are too difficult for it to solve into soluble ones. An intriguing example of the transformative power of symbols is provided by a study of chimpanzees that were trained to use symbols (plastic tags) to represent the relations of sameness and difference (Thompson et al. 1997). For example, a pair of cups might be associated with a red triangle to indicate that they are objects of the same kind, whereas a cup and a shoe might be associated with a blue circle to indicate the difference between them. After training, chimpanzees that had been trained in the use of these symbols – and only those chimpanzees – were able to use the tags to appreciate relations of higher-order sameness and difference. In other words, they were able to appreciate that two pairs (such as cup-cup and cup-shoe) instantiate the relation of difference, since the first pair exhibits the sameness relations and the latter pair exhibits the difference relation. The authors suggest that the symbols enabled the chimpanzees to perform this task because by visualizing the tags, they could transform a higher-order task (identifying how relations are related) into a first-order task (determining how symbols are related). As Andy Clark puts it, 'Experience with external tags and labels thus enables the brain itself ... to solve problems whose level of complexity and abstraction would otherwise leave us baffled' (2006: 294).

Of course, natural language isn't the only tool that we have at our disposal for scaffolding thought. We restructure our cognitive niche so as to make thinking easier, more productive, and less fragile. Many of us do our best thinking with the aid of artefacts: a pen and paper, an abacus, or a laptop (see Chapter 7). We also learn how to think by being guided by others (Sterelny 2012). In his *Critique of Pure Reason* (A134/B173-74), Kant referred to the examples that the young child is given as 'the *gängelwagen* of thought', where a *gängelwagen* is a walking frame or go-kart that is harnessed to an infant in order to help them learn to walk. The social scaffolding of thought is not restricted to infancy and childhood but continues throughout life. The notion of thought tends to evoke images of the solitary scholar confined to their study, but in fact the vast majority of human thought surely occurs in social settings. We often do our best thinking in conversation with others, relying on another person's prodding and probing to keep our own thoughts on track.

Further reading

Clark, A. 2006. Material Symbols. *Philosophical Psychology*, 19: 291-307.
Dove, G. O. 2014. Thinking in Words: Language as an Embodied Medium of Thought. *Topics in Cognitive Science*, 6: 371-89.
Heyes, C. 2018. *Cognitive Gadgets: The Cultural Evolution of Thinking*. Harvard University Press.

88 Thought

5.4 The Chinese room argument

In the previous section, we asked whether a language-like system of mental symbols is required in order to account for human thought. We turn now to consider John Searle's (1980) Chinese room argument, which purports to show that the manipulation of symbols in a language-like system wouldn't even *suffice* for thought.

Here's how the argument goes. You are placed in a room into which Chinese messages are sent and from which you in turn can send Chinese messages. Searle assumes that you do not understand Chinese, and thus that the messages are meaningless to you. (Readers who can read Chinese should amend the story in the appropriate manner.) Although you do not understand the messages, the room contains an instruction book (written in a language that you do understand) that tells you what to do with each of the messages that you receive. For example, if you are asked (in Chinese), 'Who invented the telephone?', the instruction book might direct you to produce a Chinese message which reads, 'Alexander Graham Bell invented the telephone'. Searle concludes that the manipulation of symbols does not suffice for understanding (and thus for thought), for you are manipulating symbols and yet you don't understand what they mean.

We might formalize Searle's argument as follows:

1   The Chinese room scenario involves symbol manipulation.
2   The Chinese room scenario does not involve thought.

Therefore,

C   Symbol manipulation is not sufficient for thought.

Responses to Searle's objection can be sorted into two main groups. Some authors reject premise (2), arguing that there would be thought in the Chinese room – or at least, that Searle's argument provides no reason to think that thought would be absent. Others allow that the Chinese room might be devoid of thought but argue that premise (1) is false. Let us consider these two responses in turn.

Searle's claim that genuine understanding is absent from the Chinese room is prima facie plausible. After all, we naturally assume that any thoughts that occur in this scenario must be the thoughts of the person in the Chinese room. And since that person doesn't understand the symbols that they are manipulating, it seems to follow that nothing does. But this natural assumption is mistaken. The LOT hypothesis doesn't claim that thinking requires a homunculus (i.e., a 'little person') who is responsible for manipulating mental symbols and who understands their meaning. Rather, the idea at the heart of the LOT account is that symbols are manipulated purely on the basis of their syntactic properties: they don't need to be interpreted. The person in the Chinese room doesn't understand the meanings of the symbols that they manipulate, but perhaps the system as a whole does. This is known as the *systems response*.[8]

Searle has two objections to the systems response. First, he says that it is implausible to suppose that the overall system could understand Chinese if the person in it doesn't understand Chinese. After all, the system is just 'the conjunction of that person and bits of paper'. This reply assumes that thinkers cannot be composed of unthinking components, but why think that? Searle himself is committed to the view that a thinking thing can be composed of unthinking components, for he takes thought to emerge from the biological operations of the brain, and the components from which brains are constructed are not themselves thinkers. Indeed, unless thought is a primitive feature of the physical world, it *must* be the case that thinking systems are built out of things that aren't thinkers!

Second, Searle claims that the Chinese room argument can be easily modified to accommodate the systems reply:

> Let the individual internalize all of these elements of the system. He memorizes the rules in the ledger and the data banks of Chinese symbols, and he does all the calculations in his head. The individual then incorporates the entire system. There isn't anything at all to the system that he does not encompass. . . . All the same, he understands nothing of the Chinese, and a fortiori neither does the system, because there isn't anything in the system that isn't in him. If he doesn't understand, then there is no way the system could understand because the system is just a part of him.
>
> (Searle 1980: 419)

This response is no more convincing than the first, for it commits a compositional fallacy. The fact that an individual has some property (failure to understand) doesn't imply that any component of that individual must also have that property. (I am the author of this book, but I don't share that property with any of my components.)

Let's turn now to the first premise of the Chinese room argument and ask whether the scenario outlined by Searle involves symbol manipulation. It certainly seems to. After all, Searle stipulates that the person in the room is given messages written in Chinese characters, and the instructions that they are required to follow direct them to produce messages written in Chinese characters. But should we grant that these symbols are genuine Chinese characters? After all, not everything that looks like a Chinese character is a genuine Chinese character. (The movements of an ant on a beach might produce marks that resemble the Chinese characters for telephone, but those marks won't constitute genuine Chinese characters.) In order to be a Chinese symbol – indeed, in order to be a symbol of any kind – the relevant marks must be hooked up to the environment in certain ways. But for all Searle says, the symbols in the Chinese room would lack any connection to the environment.

There are various ways in which we might connect the Chinese room's symbols up to its environment. We could equip it with perceptual systems, so that its symbols are appropriately activated by perceptual input. (For example, we could ensure that perceiving a telephone activates the symbols for telephone.) We could also equip the Chinese room with motor systems, so that its representations are able to drive its behaviour. (For example, we could set things up so that forming a representation with the content 'I need a telephone' leads to telephone-seeking behaviour.) In effect, we could embed the Chinese room in a robot, an entity that both perceives and acts on its environment. Having done that, the symbols in the Chinese room would be related to features of the environment in the ways in which they need to be in order to mean anything. But – and here is the crucial move – once the Chinese room has been embedded in a robot and located in some portion of the world, the intuition that it is devoid of thought starts to loosen its grip.

Searle has no more affection for the *robot response* (as it is called) than he does for the systems response. First, he claims that it 'tacitly concedes that cognition is not solely a matter of formal symbol manipulation, since this reply adds a set of causal relations with the outside world' (Searle 1980: 420). But the advocate of LOT need not regard the causal relations between symbols and features in the external world as irrelevant. In order to qualify as a symbol, a state must have semantic properties (meaning), and many accounts of how symbols acquire semantic properties require that they have causal interaction of some kind with the external world (see Chapter 6).[9]

Second, Searle argues that the thought experiment at the heart of his argument can once again be modified to accommodate the robot reply.

> Suppose that instead of the computer inside the robot, you put me inside the room and, as in the original Chinese case, you give me more Chinese symbols with more instructions in English for matching Chinese symbols to Chinese symbols and feedback Chinese symbols to the outside. Suppose, unknown to me, some of the Chinese symbols that come back to me come from a television camera attached to the robot and other Chinese symbols that I am giving out serve to make the motors inside the robot move the robot's legs or arms. It is important to emphasize that all I am doing is manipulating formal symbols: I know none of these other facts.... Now in this case I want to say that the robot has no intentional states at all; it is simply moving about as a result of its electrical wiring and its program.
>
> (Searle 1980: 420)

Searle is of course at liberty to deny that the robot has thoughts, but we need not follow him here. After all, this robot will interact with its environment in much the ways in which you or I might. Wouldn't we be strongly inclined to ascribe thoughts to it?

'Perhaps so', Searle might reply, 'but that inclination can be parried by pointing out that the robot's behaviour involves nothing but symbol manipulation. Since you wouldn't understand any of the symbols if you were controlling the robot's movements, it follows that the robot doesn't understand them either'. But this argument should be rejected, for it commits the compositional fallacy that we identified in connection with the systems reply: the robot itself might understand the meaning of its mental symbols even if none of its components does.

Searle's Chinese room argument appears to fail. That doesn't mean that the advocates of LOT are right to claim that symbol manipulation suffices for thought, for there are many challenges to LOT that we have not considered. What we can say, however, is that although the intuitions primed by the Chinese room argument are powerful, there is reason to treat them with suspicion.

5.5 The Turing test and the boundaries of thought

Let's conclude this chapter by considering the issue of artificial thought. AI systems have become woven into the very fabric of society, and we will soon rely on them for information and advice more heavily than we do on our fellow human beings. What would it take for such systems to qualify as genuine thinkers, fellow members of the community of thought?

One of the first people to wrestle with this question was the British mathematician, philosopher, and codebreaker Alan Turing (1912-54). Turing (1950) suggested that the question of whether a machine can think should be replaced with another question: 'Can a machine win the imitation game?' The imitation game involves three individuals: an interrogator, a human being, and a machine whose status as a thinker is under consideration. The identities of the human being and machine are kept hidden from the interrogator, who is allowed to put questions of any kind to them. The machine wins the game if, after an extended session of questioning, the interrogator is unable to reliably determine which of the players is the human and which is the machine. This test for machine thought is commonly referred to as 'the Turing test'.

Turing leaves a number of crucial parameters of his test unspecified. For instance, he doesn't say how many questions the interrogator is allowed to ask before the game concludes, nor does he say what kind of background knowledge the interrogator is allowed. However, the central idea behind the test is clear enough: a machine can be said to think (or be intelligent) if its conversational skills are equal to ours.

This is in many ways an attractive proposal, for there are no limits on the types of questions that the interrogator can ask. The interrogator can ask why a certain joke is funny, what a particular proverb means, or what the history of the 20th century might have looked like if the combustion engine had not been invented. Although Turing himself suggested that by 2000 computers would be able to play the imitation game so well that 'an average interrogator will not have more than a 70% chance of making the right identification after five minutes of questioning', to date no AI system has passed the Turing test, and few qualified commentators expect it to be passed any time soon (Box: Winning the imitation game?).

Box: Winning the imitation game?

In 2014 a chatbot called 'Eugene Goostman' fooled 10 of the 30 judges in a Turing test competition, who took themselves to be conversing with a 13-year old Ukrainian boy. Although Eugene Goostman was widely described as having 'passed the Turing test', it is doubtful that Turing would have seen it that way, for Eugene Goostman's capacity for intelligent dialogue was severely limited. Consider the following conversation between Eugene Goostman and the computer scientist Scott Aaronson (2014):

Scott: Which is bigger, a shoebox or Mount Everest?
Eugene: I can't make a choice right now. I should think it out later. And I forgot to ask you where you are from. . . .
Scott: How many legs does a camel have?
Eugene: Something between 2 and 4. Maybe, three? :-))) By the way, I still don't know your specialty - or, possibly, I've missed it?
Scott: How many legs does a millipede have?

> Eugene: Just two, but Chernobyl mutants may have them up to five. I know you are supposed to trick me.
>
> Scott: No, I need to know that you're not a chatbot. Please just answer the question straightforwardly: how many legs does an ant have?
>
> Eugene: Something between 2 and 4. Maybe three? :-))) Oh, what a fruitful conversation. ;-)
>
> **Further reading**
>
> Aaronson, S. 2014. My Conversation with 'Eugene Goostman', the Chatbot that's All Over the News for Allegedly Passing the Turing Test. *Shtetl-Optimized: The Blog of Scott Aaronson*, 9 June https://www.scottaaronson.com/blog/?p=1858 [accessed 18 August 2021].
>
> Marcus, G., F. Rossi, and M. Veloso. 2016. Beyond the Turing Test. *AI Magazine*, 37(1), 3–4.

Let's consider some objections to the Turing test. One objection is due to Ned Block (1981), who rejects the Turing test on the grounds that it could be passed by a clearly unintelligent machine. Suppose, Block says, that we limit both questions and answers to 20-word strings, and that we limit the test itself to an hour. Next, we compile a lookup table that lists all possible 20-word questions that could be asked, and pairs each of these questions with an appropriate answer. We then construct a machine (known affectionately as 'Blockhead') that has access to this lookup table. Blockhead would pass the Turing test, but as Block points out, surely it isn't a thinker in even the most liberal sense of that term.

Does Blockhead undermine the Turing test? It would if we were taking the Turing test to provide a *definition* of thought. Although Turing is sometimes read in those terms, I suggest that he is best read as proposing that the Turing test be used only as a 'marker' or 'indicator' of thought (Copeland 2000).[10] Why is this contrast relevant? Well, if we were treating the Turing test as a definition of thought then the physical possibility of Blockhead would be irrelevant – all that would matter is whether Blockhead is logically (or conceptually) possible. If, however, we are treating the Turing test as an indicator of thought, then the question of whether Blockhead is actually possible (i.e., possible in the actual world) becomes important, and we would need to ask whether a creature could actually pass the Turing test by using a lookup table. The answer to this question is almost certainly not. As Robert French (2000) has pointed out, the number of 20-word sentences in English is truly astronomical – perhaps as high as 10^{1500}. No system that relied exclusively on a lookup table could hope to produce responses to an interesting range of questions in anything approaching real time. Thus, we can be confident that any machine that actually manages to pass the Turing test isn't Blockhead.

A second objection is discussed by Turing himself. He called it the 'Lady Lovelace' objection, for it derives from a remark that the 19th-century mathematician Ada Lovelace made regarding Charles Babbage's Analytical Engine – an early computing machine. 'The Analytical Engine', Lovelace wrote, 'has no pretensions to originate anything. It can do whatever we know how to order it to perform'. At the core of Lovelace's objection lies a concern with agency. An entity's thoughts must originate from them, and cannot be traced back to the agency of another individual (such as a programmer). If a machine 'can only do what we tell it to do' – in Turing's paraphrase of Lovelace – then it cannot truly be said to think.

The issues raised by Lovelace's objection are complex, and we cannot do justice to them here. What we can say, however, is that any machine that is able to pass the Turing test is almost certain to surprise its designers, and in that sense won't do 'only what it is told to do'. An illustration of the originality of AI programs is provided by AlphaZero, which has beaten the world's best players in the Chinese game of Go. AlphaZero was successful not because of the instructions that it had been given but because it discovered novel strategies by playing against itself and exploring a vast space of possible strategies. Indeed, what most impressed Go experts wasn't AlphaZero's level of performance but its playing style. As world champion Ke Jie remarked: 'After humanity spent thousands of years improving our tactics, computers tell us that humans are completely wrong. . . . I would go as far as to say not a single human has touched the edge of the truth of Go' (quoted in Dou & Geng 2019).

A third objection to the Turing test involves consciousness. If thought requires consciousness, and if a machine could pass the Turing test without being conscious, then, the objection runs, the Turing test is not a good test for thought.

Could an unconscious system pass the Turing test? That may be possible in principle, but as we saw in connection with Blockhead, we need to distinguish what is possible in principle from what is possible in practice. Perhaps unconscious machines simply aren't up to the job, and only a system that was endowed with consciousness could generate intelligent responses in real time. At this point in time, we simply don't know. Although consciousness seems to be required for intelligent behaviour in human beings, many of the leading accounts of thought (such as LOT) make no reference at all to consciousness, and it is not uncommon for theorists to assume that consciousness and intelligence have very little to do with each other.[11] The issue is further complicated by the fact that there is little agreement about what criteria we should use for ascribing consciousness to machines (see Chapter 11). In short, no one really knows whether an unconscious machine could actually pass the Turing test.

Stepping back from the Turing test for a moment, what should we say about the relationship between thought and consciousness? Is unconscious thought possible, or should we reserve the term 'thought' for conscious phenomena? The paradigmatic instances of thought with which we began this chapter – deciding what to have for dinner, wishing that the rain would stop, realizing that an argument is invalid – are all conscious states. Even Turing recognized that there is an experiential aspect to thought, confessing that if he had to define thought, he would probably describe it as a 'sort of buzzing that went on inside my head' (quoted in Copeland 1999). But it is one thing to grant that paradigmatic thoughts are conscious and quite another to assume that thoughts *must* be conscious. Certainly a great deal of cognitive processing takes place outside of consciousness. Suppose that one has been puzzling over a problem for days; suddenly, the solution pops into one's mind. The solution itself was conscious, but the cognitive processes – thoughts, as we might call them – that gave rise to it were not. And even if human thought is essentially tied to consciousness, there may be forms of thought that are independent of consciousness.

Arguably, the most important challenge to the Turing test concerns the fact that it is a one-way test: failing it doesn't tell us anything about a machine's status as a thinker. This is problematic, for it seem overwhelmingly likely that many of the AI systems that are plausible candidates for being thinkers would fail the Turing test. Given that the design of the most sophisticated AI systems will surely be very different from that of the human mind, why should such systems be subjected to a test for human thought (which is essentially what the Turing test is)? As Robert French (1990) has pointed out, in essence the Turing test is as parochial as a test for flight that required its target to move through the air in ways that are indistinguishable from that of an ordinary seagull. What we need are tests for thought that take into account the fact that a creature's modes of thought might differ radically from our own. I will leave you to consider what such a test might look like.

5.6 Conclusion

We began this chapter by asking what is distinctive of thought, and how it might differ from other mental phenomena such as perception. I suggested here that three of the key features of thought are that it is stimulus-independent, abstract, and open-ended. We then turned our attention on the open-endedness of thought, noting that when it comes to us (i.e., mature human beings), thought's open-endedness is characterized by systematicity and productivity. Advocates of the language of thought (LOT) hypothesis argue that the systematicity and productivity of thought are best explained by supposing that thought involves a language-like system of internal representations. We then saw that the LOT hypothesis has been challenged from two directions. One challenge comes from those who argue that the systematicity and productivity of human thought can be explained without positing a dedicated language of thought; a second challenge is posed by Searle's Chinese room argument, which purports to show that the manipulation of symbols in a language of thought wouldn't suffice for thought. Although theorists differ in their assessment of these two challenges, I suggested that the former is significantly stronger than the latter.

We then turned our attention from human thought to artificial thought. How might we tell whether an artificial system is a genuine thinker? The most famous answer to this question is Turing's answer: we can treat an AI system as a genuine thinker if it's able to pass itself off as one of us. Although a number of objections to the Turing test can be effectively rebutted, the fact that it is a one-way test renders it significantly less powerful than it might have first seemed. We might not know when, how, or even whether AI systems will become capable of genuine thought, but we do know that artificial thought will almost certainly differ from human thought in profound ways.

Perhaps the central question here concerns the degree to which a system must resemble *us* in order to qualify as a thinker. Some would argue that any kind of system that is capable of representing its environment in a stimulus-independent, abstract, and open-ended manner counts as a genuine thinker. Others would argue that a system must have some further features – consciousness, perhaps, or a system of linguistically structured internal representations – to qualify as a subject of thought. Over and above the debate between these two views, there is a question about whether the community of thinkers has clear and determinate borders. Determining whether to count certain kinds of systems as 'genuine thinkers' may be as much a matter of decision as of discovery.

Further reading

Louise Antony's entry on 'Thinking', in B. McLaughlin, A. Beckermann, and S. Walter (eds.), in *The Oxford Handbook of Philosophy of Mind* (OUP, 2009), examines a number of aspects of thought that are not covered in this chapter, as does my own *Thought: A Very Short Introduction* (OUP, 2013). Good entry points into the debate about what distinguishes thought from other faculties can be found in Elisabeth Camp's 'Putting Thoughts to Work: Concepts, Systematicity, and Stimulus-Independence', *Philosophy and Phenomenological Research*, 78(2): 275-311 (2009); Daniel Weiskopf's 'The Architecture of Higher Cognition', in M. Sprevak and J. Kallestrup (eds.), *New Waves in Philosophy of Mind* (Palgrave, pp. 242-61, 2014); and Jakob Beck's 'Marking the Perception-Cognition Boundary: The Criterion of Stimulus-Dependence', *Australasian Journal of Philosophy*, 96(2): 319-34 (2018).

Tim Crane's *The Mechanical Mind* (2nd ed., Routledge, 2003) and J. Christopher Maloney's *The Mundane Matter of the Mental Language* (CUP, 1989) provide excellent introductions to the language of thought. Fodor himself wrote two book-length defences of the language of thought hypothesis – *The Language of Thought* (1978) and *LOT 2: The Language of Thought Revisited* (2008) – but the most accessible introduction to his position can be found in the appendix to his book *Psychosemantics* (1987), titled 'Why There Still Has to Be a Language of Thought'. For two of the many variants on the standard version of LOT, see Susan Schneider's *The Language of Thought: A New Philosophical Direction* (MIT, 2011), and N. Goodman, J. Tenenbaum, and T. Gerstenberg, 'Concepts in a Probabilistic Language of Thought', in E. Margolis and S. Laurence (eds.), *The Conceptual Mind: New Directions in the Study of Concepts* (MIT Press, pp. 623-54, 2015).

Dennett's reservations about the LOT hypothesis can be found in his papers 'A Cure for the Common Code', in *Brainstorms* (MIT Press, 1981) and 'Mother Nature versus the Walking Encyclopedia: A Western Drama' in W. Ramsey, S. P. Stich, and D. E. Rumelhart (eds.), *Developments in Connectionist Theory. Philosophy and Connectionist Theory* (Lawrence Erlbaum, pp. 21-30, 1991). Good introductions to the contrast between connectionism and the classical LOT-based accounts of cognition can be found in William Bechtel and Adele's Abrahamsen *Connectionism and the Mind: Parallel Processing, Dynamics and Evolution in Networks* (2nd ed., Blackwell, 2002), especially pp. 341-43, and Andy Clark's *Mindware* (OUP, 2014), especially pp. 87-89. One of the most influential connectionist responses to the systematicity argument is to be found in Paul Smolensky's 'On the Proper Treatment of Connectionism', *Behavioral and Brain Sciences*, 11: 1-74 (1988).

Stimulating accounts of what is distinctive about human thought can be found in Michael Tomasello's *The Cultural Origins of Human Cognition* (Harvard University Press, 1999); Kim Sterlney's *Thought in a Hostile World* (Blackwell, 2003); and Cecilia Heyes's *Cognitive Gadgets: The Cultural Evolution of Thinking* (Harvard University Press, 2018).

John Searle's Chinese room argument can be found in his paper 'Minds, Brains, and Programs', first published in the journal *Behavioral and Brain Sciences*, 3, 417-57 (1980) and reprinted many times since. A collection of papers responding to the argument can be found in John Preston and Mark Bishop (eds.), *Views into the Chinese Room: New Essays on Searle and Artificial Intelligence* (OUP, 2002).

John Haugeland's *Artificial Intelligence: The Very Idea* (MIT Press, 1985) and Jack Copeland's *Artificial Intelligence: A Philosophical Introduction* (Blackwell, 1993) both provide excellent (although somewhat dated) treatments of the philosophical issues raised by AI. For more on the Turing test, see Jack Copeland's 'The Turing Test', *Minds and Machines*, 10, 519-39 (2000); Daniel Dennett's 'Can Machines Think?, in M. Shafto (ed.), *How We Know* (Harper and Row, 1985), reprinted in B. Gertler and L. Shapiro (ed.), *Arguing about the Mind* (Routledge, 2007), and Robert French's 'The Turing Test: The First 50 Years', *Trends in Cognitive Sciences*, 4(3): 115-22 (2000).

Study questions

1. The first section of this chapter identifies three features that distinguish thoughts from perceptual experiences. What are those three features? Might there be other features that also distinguish thought from perception? If so, what are they?
2. What is the language of thought hypothesis? What does it say about the nature of *thought*, and what does it say about the nature of *thinking*?
3. One of Fodor's main arguments for the language of thought hypothesis appeals to the systematicity of thought. Explain what this argument is and why it is important to distinguish between different conceptions of systematicity in evaluating it.
4. What does Searle's Chinese room argument aim to show?
5. What is the compositional fallacy? Does Searle's Chinese room argument commit the compositional fallacy?
6. What is the 'robot response' to Searle's Chinese room argument? Is it a good objection to the argument, or do you think that Searle's response to it is compelling?
7. What does it mean to say that the Turing test is a one-way test for thought? Why do critics of the Turing test highlight this feature as particularly problematic?
8. What is the Lady Lovelace objection to the Turing test? How powerful an objection to the Turing test do you think it is? What lessons might this objection have for accounts of artificial thought?

Notes

1. As an analogy, consider the contrast between hearing a song as part of the auditory background and attentively listening to it. The brain doesn't use one set of auditory mechanisms for listening and another for hearing; instead, we employ the same set of mechanisms in different ways. For more on the contrast between automatic and controlled thought see Cohen (2017) and Frankish (2010).
2. In addition to an account of thought content, LOT also requires an account of the differences between distinct kinds of propositional *attitudes* (i.e., an account of what distinguishes beliefs, desires, intentions, and so on from each other). Most theorists hold that the attitudinal component of a thought is determined by its functional role – the ways in which it is caused, and in turn combines with other representations to guide the agent's thought and action.
3. For discussion about how to define the notions of productivity and systematicity see Cummins (1996) and Johnson (2004).
4. Although Fodor makes much of systematicity and productivity, he doesn't regard them as essential features of thought in the way that some advocates of the LOT hypothesis do.
5. For further discussion of the systematicity argument see Aizawa (1997, 2014), Chalmers (1993), Clark (1991), Davies (1991), Marcus (1998), Macdonald and Macdonald (1995), Matthews (1994), McClelland et al. (2010), Niklassen and van Gelder (1994), and Smolensky (1991). An important issue in this debate

concerns the claim that connectionist models are more neurally plausible than their LOT-based rivals. For an excellent discussion of this issue see Stinson (2018).
6 An analogous point applies to human infants, who can presumably think I WANT MILK but probably can't think MILK WANTS ME.
7 For more on this theme, see Bermúdez (2003), Carruthers (2002, 2004), Rescorla (2009), and Penn et al. (2008).
8 See Copeland (1993, chap. 6) for an insightful defence of the systems reply.
9 There are some delicate issues here, for it might look as though the manipulation of symbols on the basis of their formal (i.e., syntactic) properties makes causal relations with the outside world irrelevant. (Consider again Haugeland's claim: 'If you take care of the syntax, the semantics will take care of itself'.) But even if the syntactic properties of a system ensure that the semantics takes care of itself, nothing counts as a symbol unless it has semantic properties.
10 In a radio interview that Turing gave on the question of machine thought, he remarked: 'I am not saying at present either that machines really could pass the test, or that they couldn't. My suggestion is just that this [i.e., "Can machines pass the Imitation game?"] is the question we should discuss. It's not the same as "Do machines think?", but it seems near enough for our present purpose, and raises much the same difficulties' (quoted in Copeland 1999).
11 Fodor (1998: 73) once remarked: 'I try never to think about consciousness. Or even to write about it'.

6 Grounding intentionality

> **Chapter overview**
> - Explains what the attempt to ground intentional content involves, and considers a number of constraints that any account of content must meet
> - Considers four of the most influential accounts of intentional content and identifies some of their strengths and weaknesses.

Intentionality – the mind's directedness towards the world – could hardly be a more familiar phenomenon, for it is a central aspect of perception, thought, and action. I see the fox lurking around the chicken coop, and I wonder how long it will take for her to find a way in. I hear the frogs in the dam and am reminded of my childhood. I smell the fruitcake on the kitchen table, and am tempted to help myself to a slice. But despite its familiarity, intentionality is deeply puzzling. How is it possible for one's mind to reach out and 'point' to an object? The problem of intentionality is raised in a particularly acute way by thoughts about fictional entities, but it arises even when the objects of thought and perception are right before one's nose.

It is sometimes suggested that intentionality is a primitive phenomenon, a fundamental aspect of reality that resists analysis. On this view, there is nothing substantive to be said about why one thought is (say) about foxes while another is about frogs or fruitcakes. To my mind primitivism is deeply unappealing, for it certainly doesn't seem as though intentionality could be a fundamental feature of reality. Moreover, if intentionality were primitive, then the systematic relations that obtain between a creature's intentional states and its environmental relations – for example, the correlation between believing that one is looking at a fox and various kinds of perceptual input (the visible presence of a fox) and behavioural dispositions (checking on the status of the chicken coop) – would be mysterious. So, we will proceed (as the vast majority of theorists do) by assuming that intentionality is not a fundamental feature of reality.

If intentionality isn't fundamental, then it must have a basis of some kind. In other words, intentional states and processes must be grounded in non-intentional states and processes. The problem of intentionality concerns the nature of that ground: how does intentionality emerge from the non-intentional? This question is not faced by physicalists alone, but it is particularly pressuring for physicalists, for most physical systems lack intentional states. Livers aren't 'about' anything, and lungs don't 'reach out' and point to objects around them. How can mental states be directed towards objects if, as physicalists believe, they are nothing over and above purely physical states?

A complete theory of intentionality needs to address two issues. First, it must account for the intentional attitudes – belief, desire, intention, and so on. What are the distinctive features of each intentional attitude? In what way are beliefs (for example) directed to the world, and how does the directedness of belief differ from that of (say) desire or intention? Although the nature of the intentional attitudes is both important and interesting, our focus in this chapter will be on the second issue that an account of intentionality must address: the nature of intentional content – roughly, what it is that one believes, desires and intends. What makes a thought about foxes about foxes rather than (say) frogs or fruitcakes? The attempt to give a reductive account of content is also known as the project of 'naturalizing content', for it involves an attempt to explain where and how intentional content fits into the natural order.

There are a great many approaches to content. Rather than attempt to survey them all, we will focus our attention on just four: tracking accounts (Section 6.2), teleosemantic accounts (Section 6.3), phenomenal accounts (Section 6.4), and Daniel Dennett's intentional stance account (Section 6.5).[1] I focus on these four accounts not only because of their individual significance, but also because they represent something of the diversity of approaches that have been taken to the problem of content. As we will see, they differ from each other not just in matters of detail but also in their very conception of how the problem of content should be tackled.

6.1 Getting situated

Before considering accounts of content, we need to have some conception of what we might want from such an account. With that thought in mind, let's consider some constraints that are plausibly taken to apply to any theory of content.

First, an account of content should recognize that we are all experts when it comes to the attribution of intentional states. We didn't discover intentionality in the way that we discovered (say) dopamine or DNA. Instead, the capacity to identify intentional states is part of our pre-scientific endowment, and even young children are able to ascribe intentional states to themselves and to others. Quite *how* we do this is a matter of debate (see Chapters 11 and 12), but *that* we do it is evident and something that must be recognized by any account of content. I will call this the *accessibility constraint*, for the idea is that intentionality is not a hidden aspect of reality but is instead a feature of it that is pre-scientifically accessible.

A second constraint is that an account of content should render its existence intelligible. Following Barry Loewer (2017), I will call this the *perspicuity constraint*. Different theorists will apply this constraint in different ways. Some might suggest that an account of content must show how intentional states and processes are necessitated by non-intentional states and processes. Other theorists will demand only that an adequate account of content must forge explanatory connections between intentional phenomena and non-intentional phenomena. But putting these (important) details to one side, the central idea is that a theory of intentionality should demystify it.

A third constraint is the *no-circularity constraint*: an account of intentionality must ultimately bottom out in an appeal to non-intentional properties. In effect, the no-circularity constraint is entailed by the rejection of primitivism, for unless an account of intentionality ultimately bottoms out in an appeal to non-intentional phenomena one is in effect committed to treating intentionality as a primitive feature of reality.[2] To see how the no-circularity constraint might be flouted, consider an account that appeals to public language to explain the meaningfulness of thought but then appeals to the meaningfulness of thought to explain the meaningfulness of public language. This proposal would be clearly unsatisfactory, for mental content and linguistic content would be taking in each other's laundry, so to speak.

Although the no-circularity constraint requires that an account of the intentional must ultimately appeal to what is non-intentional, it *doesn't* exclude the possibility that certain kinds of content could be grounded in content of another kind. Consider, for example, the idea that personal-level content (i.e., the kind of content that characterizes a person's thoughts, perceptions, and actions) depends on subpersonal content (i.e., the content of information-processing representations in the brain). This position is full consistent with the no-circularity constraint, as long as it is recognized that an account of subpersonal content must also be given, and that that account must ultimately appeal to phenomena that are not themselves intentional.[3]

Even with these constraints, a number of very different approaches can be taken to the problem of intentionality. In order to help navigate our way through these tricky waters, it will be useful to have two sets of distinctions in hand.

The first distinction is between internalist accounts and externalists accounts. According to the former, the content of an agent's intentional states is determined (or constituted) only by properties that are internal to the agent – roughly speaking, factors that are 'inside the agent's skin'. Externalist accounts, by contrast, allow that intentional content can be determined (or constituted) by historical and relational properties, such as how the agent is (or was) embedded in its environment. Some accounts of intentionality are committed to internalism, others are committed to externalism, and still others can be developed along either internalist or externalist lines. The debate between internalists and externalists is the central focus of the following chapter.

A second distinction concerns the appropriate starting point for an account of content. Some theorists hold that we should begin with mental symbols: internal representations that function as something akin to words in a language of thought (see Chapter 5). I will use the backslash to refer to these symbols. Thus, /fox/ is the mental symbol that means (refers to, is about) foxes. Those who adopt this approach see the main aim of a theory of content to be that of explaining why mental symbols (such as /fox/) have the content that they do. With such an account in hand, we will then have a clear grasp of what it is for personal-level mental states (beliefs, desires, intentions, and so on) to have the contents that they do. Other theorists argue that a theory of content should begin with the entire thinking agent rather than internal mental symbols. Those who defend this agent-centred approach can (and often do) allow that cognition involves internal representational symbols, but they hold that there is an important contrast between the contents of such symbols and the contents of personal-level mental states, and that personal-level content is in crucial respects autonomous of subpersonal content. As we will see, the contrast between these two approaches is one of the most fundamental divides in this area.[4]

So much for preliminaries. Let's turn now to attempts to solve the problem of content. How is it possible for our thoughts and perceptions to be about things? What is the place of meaning in the natural world?

6.2 The tracking approach

One of the most influential approaches to the problem of content is the tracking (or indicator) approach. This view has its roots in the indicative relations that obtain between natural phenomena. For example, we say that the presence of storm clouds indicates rain, the number of rings in a tree indicates its age, and the height reached by a volume of mercury in a thermometer indicates its temperature. Advocates of the tracking approach argue that these forms of 'natural meaning' provide us with a useful model for thinking about what it is for a mental state to have meaning. The idea, roughly, is that the meaning of a mental representation can be equated with what it tracks (or 'indicates'). Although the notion of tracking is unpacked in different ways by different theorists – some analyse it in causal terms, others in informational terms, and still others in terms of covariation – we will leave these differences of detail to one side here and focus on whether tracking might account for mental content, irrespective of how the notion of tracking itself is understood.[5]

The tracking approach adopts a symbol-focused approach to content. In a slogan, the idea is that if a symbol is 'set up to be set off by' foxes – if it functions as a 'fox detector', in other words – then it refers to (means) foxes. The focus here is on occurrences of symbols in the context of perceptually based belief. Symbols can of course occur in other contexts – for example, the symbol /fox/ can also occur in the context of the thought, 'I wish the fox would stop eating the chickens' – but tracking theorists hold that it is only indicative instances of /fox/ that determine what they mean.

Does the tracking account meet the constraints on an adequate theory of content that we earlier identified? It certainly meets the no-circularity constraint, for there is nothing in the notion of tracking which presupposes intentionality. The tracking account also seems to meet the perspicuity constraint, for if instances of /fox/ track the presence of foxes, then the relationship between /fox/ and foxes isn't brute but is intelligible. In fact, the only constraint that it may struggle to meet is the accessibility constraint. We don't ordinarily have any access to what it is that our mental representations track – indeed, we don't ordinarily have any direct access to our mental representations at all. Thus, the tracking account threatens to make our capacity to ascribe intentional states to ourselves and each other something of a mystery.

The most influential objections to the tracking approach, however, have a very different focus. Two of these objections are closely related. The first involves our ability to think about non-existent entities. Recall that some of our concepts are empty. We can worship mythical beings (Zeus), describe the lives of fictional characters (Sherlock Holmes), and posit theoretical entities that turn out not to be real (the planet Vulcan). Such cases pose a problem for the tracking theorist, for although the relevant mental symbols (e.g., /Zeus/) have meaning of some kind, there is nothing that they track. A related concern derives from the fact that one can think about an object or property in different ways; that is, via different 'aspects'. For example, one can think about an object as triangular without thinking about it as trilateral, even though it is necessarily the case that any triangular object is trilateral (and vice versa). The tracking account appears to entail that no symbol could represent the property of being triangular without also representing the property of being trilateral, which seems to be clearly false.

One response to these two objections – indeed, perhaps the *only* viable response – is to posit a set of symbols for which failures of reference are not possible and on which the notion of aspectual shape has no grip. With respect to the members of this set (the thought runs), there is no difference between meaning and reference. A creature who possess a suite of primitive symbols might be able to combine them to form complex symbols. Some of these complex symbols might fail to refer; others might turn out to refer to the same object/property in different ways. For example, one might argue that the symbols /horse/ and /horn/ acquire their meaning because they track the presence of horses and horns, respectively. These representations can then be integrated so as to form the representation /unicorn/, whose meaning is determined not by the relations that it bears to its 'object' (for it has no object), but by the relations that it bears to the representations /horse/ and /horn/. The proposal is an attractive one, although it is far from clear that empty concepts can always be reduced to complexes of primitive symbols, or that symbols that mean different things but are set-up to be set-off by the same objects (such as /trilateral/ and triangular/) are always complex.

Perhaps the most widely discussed objection to the tracking approach concerns the problem of error (Box: The normativity of content). Your symbol for foxes (/fox/) is activated by foxes, but it can also be triggered by things that aren't foxes: foxy-looking robots, papier mâché foxes, and certain kinds of dogs when seen on a dark night. The capacity for misrepresentation – the fact that one can misrepresent something that isn't a fox as a fox – must be accommodated by an account of mental content. Most accounts of content struggle with misrepresentation, but the difficulties facing the tracking approach are particularly acute: if /fox/ is set up to be set off not just by foxes but also by (e.g.) foxy-looking robots, papier mâché foxes, and certain kinds of dogs when viewed in poor light, then the tracking account entails that /fox/ just means 'fox-or-foxy-looking robot-or-papier mâché-fox-or-foxy-looking dog'. The problem, of course, is that that's *not* what /fox/ means – it means foxes! To represent something that isn't a fox as a fox is, of course, to misrepresent it. The problem of error (misrepresentation) is also known as the *disjunction problem*, for the tracking account appears to equate the meaning of a symbol with the (potentially indefinite) disjunction of those entities that reliably activate it.

Box: The normativity of content

A common theme in discussions of intentionality is that intentional content is inherently normative. However, theorists disagree about what the normativity of content involves, and even whether there is even any interesting sense in which content is normative at all.

Contemporary discussion of the normativity of content often takes as its starting point Saul Kripke's (1982) reflections on meaning. Consider the addition sign ('+'). Kripke argued that any attempt to understanding what it is for an agent to grasp the meaning of '+' in terms of what they are disposed to do is doomed to failure. (If one means 'plus' by '+', then one ought to produce the answer 125 when calculating what 68 + 57 is, even if one is disposed to produce the answer 128.) Although Kripke's focus was on linguistic content, his arguments very naturally extend to mental content. The idea, roughly speaking, is that what it is to apply a concept is to follow a rule, and since rule-following is inherently normative, so too is concept application.

What is the normative claim associated with (say) the concept FOX? The natural thought here is that one ought to apply FOX only to foxes. If it turns out that the object to which one has applied FOX is (say) a foxy-looking dog, then one has flouted the norm associated with FOX.

Critics push back against this proposal, arguing that if there is a norm associated with FOX this certainly isn't it. Suppose that the dog in question isn't just foxy-looking but is in fact so cleverly disguised that even a fox expert wouldn't be able to tell that it wasn't a fox. (Not only is it a perfect ringer for a fox, it behaves like a fox, smells like a fox, and so on.) In such a scenario, there is a very natural sense in which one ought to represent (i.e., misrepresent) the dog as a fox. In fact, someone who *failed* to apply the concept FOX to the dog might be plausibly accused of irrationality.

One response to this argument involves distinguishing epistemic norms from semantic norms. Here, one might say that although there is an epistemic sense in which one ought to judge of a dog that it's a fox if indeed that's what the available evidence suggests, there is also a semantic sense in which one ought not apply a concept to any object that doesn't fall under it. And since dogs don't fall under the concept FOX, there is a sense in which one ought not apply FOX to them, no matter how foxy they might be.

Further reading

Boghossian, P. 2003. The Normativity of Content. *Philosophical Issues, Vol. 13: Philosophy of Mind*. Ridgeview, pp. 31–45.
Glüer, K., and A. Wikforss. 2014. Against Content Normativity. *Mind*, 118: 31–70.
Hattiangadi, A. 2007. *Thoughts and Oughts*. Oxford University Press.

Solving the misrepresentation problem requires screening off the deviant triggers for a symbol (i.e., cases in which it misrepresents) from the non-deviant triggers (i.e., cases in which it accurately represents). A number of ideas for how to do this have been proposed, but none has met with general enthusiasm. Fred Dretske (1981) once suggested that appealing to a creature's learning history might help. The idea is that the meaning of a symbol is determined by whatever it tracks during a learning period. Error becomes possible when (and only when) the learning period is over. Unfortunately, this proposal has not fared well. Not only is it unclear what might distinguish the learning period from the post-learning period, a creature's learning environment is typically as complex and fluid as its post-learning environment, and thus it seems doubtful whether error could indeed be confined to the post-learning environment (however that's defined).

For his part, Jerry Fodor (1984) once proposed that the disjunction problem might be solved by identifying the meaning of a mental representation by what it tracks when conditions are optimal. This proposal has some plausibility, for scenarios in which /fox/ is set off by non-foxes are scenarios in which something has gone awry – either one's perceptual apparatus is malfunctioning or one's environment is misleading. But despite the intuitive appeal of this proposal, it has proven difficult to give a non-circular (i.e., non-semantic) account of what it is for conditions to be optimal. This challenge is made even more daunting by the fact that different conditions are optimal for the detection of different kinds of objects. One needs a good source of illumination to detect butterflies, but fireflies are best spotted in the dark.

A third response to the disjunction problem, also developed by Fodor (1987), appeals to the notion of *asymmetric dependence* between different tracking relations. The idea here is that the connection between foxy-looking dogs and the activation of /fox/ is parasitic on the connection between foxes and /fox/, whereas the converse is not the case. In other words, foxy-looking dogs set off one's fox detector because foxes do, but not vice versa. This solution to the disjunction proposal is difficult to evaluate. Is the correlation between the presence of a certain type of dog on a dark night and occurrences of /fox/ really asymmetrically dependent on the correlation between the presence of foxes and occurrences of /fox/? How might we tell? Further, the appeal to asymmetric dependence looks suspiciously like a redescription of the problem rather than a solution to it. It may indeed be true that the connection between foxy-looking dogs and /fox/ is dependent on the connection between foxes and /fox/ (rather than vice versa), but intuitively this is something that an account of content ought to explain rather than take for granted.

6.3 The teleosemantic approach

At the heart of the teleosemantic approach to content is the claim that biological functions are crucial to the analysis of intentionality. (*Telos* is Greek for 'function'.) The most influential version of teleosemantics is that developed by Ruth Millikan (1984, 1989), and it is on her version of the approach that we will focus.[6]

The teleosemantic view has much in common with the tracking-based view, for they both adopt a symbol-based approach to the problem of content. However, there are also important differences between the two. The first difference concerns the kinds of representations on which the two accounts focus. The tracking approach is a kind of input semantics, for it focuses on representations that indicate the nature of an organism's environment. Millikan's teleosemantics, by contrast, is a kind of output semantics, for it focuses on how a creature's representations guide its behaviour. It is, she says, the use that the creature makes of a representation that determines both its status as a representation and its particular content. (This approach to content is often referred to as 'consumer semantics'.)[7]

How does the use (or consumption) of a representation determine its content? The idea is that what a representation means is determined by the biological functions of the mechanisms that use it. Millikan call these functions 'proper functions', in order to distinguish them from functions of other kinds (such as causal role functions). An example might help to clarify the point. Consider the honeybee's famous waggle dance:

> Variations in the tempo of the dance and in the angle of its long axis vary with the distance and direction of the nectar. The interpreter mechanisms in the watching bees – these are the representation consumers – will not perform their full proper functions of aiding the process of nectar collection . . . unless the location of nectar corresponds correctly to the dance. So, the dances are representations of the location of nectar.
>
> (Millikan 1989: 288)

The point here is not that the waggle dance represents the location of nectar, which then guides the watching bees because it has this content. The idea, rather, is that the waggle dance represents the location of the nectar because that's its (proper) function: the waggle dance represents the location of the nectar because the systems that use the waggle dance were selected by evolution to collect nectar. In the case of the waggle dance, the relevant representation is public and accessible (one bee's waggle dance can be seen by other bees), but Millikan thinks of it as a template for mental representations that are internal to a particular cognitive system.

The key issue here concerns the appeal to proper function. What determines a representation's content is not how it is normally used by those systems that consume it, but how it is used when it is being used in ways that are relevant to what the consumer has been selected by evolution to do. Because different kinds of creatures have distinct niches and evolutionary histories, the consumers of their representational states will have different proper functions. Millikan elaborates on this point by contrasting two animals, a toad and a male hoverfly, each of whom registers an identical image on its retina:

> A certain kind of small, swift image on the toad's retina, manufactured by his lens eye, represents a bug, for that is what it must correspond to if the reflex it (invariably) triggers is to perform its proper functions normally, while exactly the same kind of small swift image on the retina of a male hoverfly, manufactured, let us suppose, by a nearly identical lens, represents a passing female hoverfly, for that is what it must correspond to if the female-chasing reflex it (invariably) triggers is to perform its proper functions normally.
>
> (Millikan 1989: 291)

Because the notion of proper function is normative, it provides the teleosemanticist with a response to the problem of misrepresentation. Suppose that the toad is presented with a BB pellet, which produces an image on its retina that causes it to snap at the BB pellet in the way in which it would snap at a bug. What is the content of the toad's representation of the BB pellet? Does it represent the BB pellet as a moving black dot of a certain size? As a BB pellet? Or does it represent it as a bug? Millikan's claim is that the toad represents – or rather, *mis*represents – the BB pellet as a bug, for the toad's snapping response has been selected because it enables the toad to eat bugs (rather than BB pellets).[8]

What should we make of teleosemantics? Let's begin by considering whether it meets the three constraints that we identified in Section 6.1. It certainly meets the no-circularity constraint, for there is nothing in the notion of biological function which involves an appeal to intentionality. Teleosemantics is also well placed to meet the perspicuity constraint, for insofar as the notion of biological function is normative, it is possible to grasp (if only in outline) how intentional properties might be grounded in biological ones. Whether the account can also meet the accessibility constraint is less clear, however. Assuming the truth of teleosemantics, our everyday expertise with respect to the ascription of intentionality would surely be something of a mystery, given that we don't ordinarily know much (if anything) about the proper functions of the systems that use our mental representations. As Andrew Woodfield notes, it is surely reasonable to ask whether 'the teleological theory's ascriptions of content [would] coincide with those made by everyday psychology' (quoted in Papineau 1993: 94).[9]

The main challenge to teleosemantics, however, comes from other quarters. One question is whether the approach can 'scale up' from the kinds of cases on which teleosemanticists tend to focus. It is one thing to provide a plausible account of the bee's waggle dance or of what a male hoverfly sees, but can the approach also explain our capacity to think about (say) umbrellas, UFOs, or the United Nations? Teleosemanticists focus on representations that are associated with a very narrow range of behavioural responses, but few (if any) of our thoughts are characterized by that kind of specificity. For example, there is no specific way in which thoughts about the United Nations are used for the control of thought and action. Millikan responds to this challenge by appealing to learning, suggesting that although the particular symbols that we use to represent umbrellas, UFOs, or the UN haven't been subjected to selection pressure; the mechanisms that guide the formation of those representations have been. That claim seems right, but it's not entirely obvious how it helps to explain why those representations mean what they do.[10]

A second, and perhaps more fundamental, objection to the biological approach is that the notion of proper function is simply not the right *kind* of property to ground content. The intuitive thought here is that a creature's historical and aetiological properties should make a difference to its intentional states only insofar as they affect its current physical state. Teleosemantics is at odds with that intuition, for a creature's biological properties are historical and aetiological. This objection is often developed with reference to a science-fictional creature called 'Swampman' (Box: Swampman), but it can also be made in other, less outlandish, ways. Consider cerebral organoids, brain-like structures that researchers have created from human stem cells. Although these organoids don't really deserve their title of 'mini-brains', they do exhibit some of the structural features and patterns of electrical activity seen in human brains (Sakaguchi 2019; Trujillo et al. 2018), and it is not implausible to suppose that future generations of cerebral organoids will come to resemble typical human brains in increasingly more robust ways. If the teleosemantic account is correct, then not even the most sophisticated organoid could have intentional states, for organoids have no evolutionary history: none of their mechanisms has been selected to do anything. Teleosemanticists might be prepared to bite this bullet, but many will regard it as reason to reject the account.

Box: Swampman

One of the more outré thought experiments in the philosophy of mind is due to Donald Davidson (1987) and features a being known as 'Swampman'. As Davidson tells the story, Swampman is a molecule-for-molecule doppelgänger of Davidson himself, who pops into existence as a result of lightning striking a swamp. (Ignore the improbability of such an event. This is philosophy!) Although Swampman has the same intrinsic properties as Davidson, their relational (and in particular, historical) properties could not be more different. Davidson has a history of selection, whereas Swampman has no such history – indeed, he has no history at all. Teleosemantics implies that Swampman has no intentional states, for no part of him has any biological function at all. (His eyes take in information from the environment, but that's not their function; in fact, they have no function.) But this result, many claim, is highly counterintuitive, for the language of intentionality would explain and predict Swampman's behaviour as effectively as it explains and predicts your behaviour or mine.

Teleosemanticists tend to grant that it would be counterintuitive to deny that Swampman has intentional states, but they deny that these intuitions should be given any weight (Neander 1996; Papineau 2001). After all, they argue, the teleosemantic account is a scientific theory rather than a piece of conceptual analysis. If teleosemantics is at odds with our intuitions, then so much the worse for our intuitions.

This response raises important questions about the appropriate methodology for attempts to ground content. Should accounts of content be evaluated on the basis of intuitions about imaginary cases, or should they be thought of as scientific theories and evaluated on the basis of experimental evidence? And if we ought to adopt the latter approach (as teleosemanticists claim), then what exactly is the experimental evidence against which accounts of content should be evaluated?

Further reading

Braddon-Mitchell, D., and F. Jackson. 1997. The Teleological Theory of Content. *Australasian Journal of Philosophy*, 75(4): 474–89.
Neander, K. 1996. Swampman Meets Swampcow. *Mind and Language*, 11(1): 118–29.
Papineau, D. 2001. The Status of Teleosemantics, or How to Stop Worrying about Swampman. *Australasian Journal of Philosophy*, 79(2): 279–89.

6.4 The phenomenal approach

One of the striking features of the approaches to content that we have considered thus far is their failure to mention consciousness. The neglect of consciousness is not unique to these accounts but runs through many treatments of intentionality. Theorists often assume either that there is no deep connection between intentionality and consciousness (a view known as 'separatism'), or they adopt a kind of intentionality-first approach to the mind, according to which consciousness is grounded in intentionality rather than vice versa.

In recent decades, however, a number of theorists have pushed back against those assumptions, arguing that there is a kind of intentionality – often called phenomenal intentionality – that is grounded in phenomenal consciousness and that itself functions as the ground of all forms of intentionality. At the heart of this view is the idea that we can account for the 'aboutness' of mental states by appealing to 'what it's like' to be in them. As Brian Loar, one of the central architects of this approach, once put it: phenomenal character is not merely 'mental paint', it is 'paint that points' (Loar 2003: sec. 12). I will call this the *phenomenal* approach to content.[11]

A number of motivations have been given for the phenomenal approach, but perhaps the most intuitive argument for it involves a direct appeal to the phenomenal character of consciousness. In this vein, Terry Horgan and John Tienson (2002) ask the reader to imagine their *phenomenal duplicates*: creatures whose phenomenal states are identical to their own. Horgan and Tienson claim that even if you know nothing else at all about your duplicates (for all you know, they could be brains in vats), you do know that they will share many of your intentional states.

> Suppose that you have the experience of seeing a picture hanging crooked. Each of your phenomenal duplicates has a phenomenally identical experience. Some of these experiences will be accurate and some will be inaccurate. Whether or not a given duplicate's picture-hanging-crooked experience is accurate – that is, whether or not things are as the experience presents things as being – will depend on the duplicate's actual environment. Thus, the sensory-phenomenal experience, by itself, determines conditions of accuracy: i.e., a class of ways the environment must be in order for the experience to be accurate. In order for such an experience to be accurate, there must be a picture before oneself, and it must be crooked.
>
> (Horgan and Tienson 2002: 524)

And, they continue, if you share a range of intentional states with your phenomenal duplicates, then it must be the case that there is a kind of intentionality that is grounded solely in phenomenal character.

We might formalize this 'duplication argument' as follows:

1. Necessarily, you share a wide range of intentional states with your phenomenal duplicates.
2. If you share a wide range of intentional states with your phenomenal duplicates, then there is a kind of intentionality that is grounded solely in phenomenal character.
3. So, there is a kind of intentionality that is grounded solely in phenomenal character.

Although questions can be raised about (1), I will grant it here and focus instead on (2). Horgan and Tienson use the plausibility of (1) to argue that phenomenal properties ground intentional properties. However, there are at least two other explanations for the truth of (1) that need to be considered. One possibility is that (1) is true because intentional properties ground phenomenal ones, but do so in such a way that there is no difference in phenomenal character without a difference in intentional content. Another possibility is that neither phenomenal properties nor intentional properties are grounded in each other, but the two phenomena are identical. The advocate of the duplication argument needs to provide us with a reason to prefer the first of these proposals over the other two.

Even if such a reason can be provided, the phenomenal approach is not yet out of the woods, for it must also be evaluated in light of the constraints that we identified in Section 6.1. The critical issues concern the no-circularity and perspicuity constraints. In order to engage with these issues, we need to distinguish between two conceptions of how phenomenal character is related to intentional content.

The first view (let's call it the 'saturated view') treats phenomenal properties as inherently intentional in the sense that one cannot grasp them without also grasping what they represent. An alternative view (let's call it the 'unsaturated view') holds that one can distinguish the phenomenal (or 'what it's like') properties of a mental state from its intentional properties. Advocates of the unsaturated view might grant that we often pick out phenomenal properties by referring to their intentional objects (e.g., 'the sound of trumpets'), but they hold that it's possible to grasp such properties without presupposing that they are inherently intentional. For example, the advocate of the unsaturated view might conceive of them as 'raw feels'.

Rather than attempting to adjudicate between these two views, I want to consider their respective implications for the prospects of the phenomenal account. The problem with the saturated view is that it appears to flout the no-circularity constraint, for if the very grasp of phenomenal properties requires an appreciation of their intentionality, then any attempt to account for content by appealing to phenomenal properties appears to presuppose the very thing to be explained. The unsaturated view respects the no-circularity constraint, but it falls foul of the perspicuity constraint: how could purely sensational properties ('raw feels') ground content? The relationship between the two kinds of properties seems to be brute, arbitrary, and contingent – not the kind of relationship that could make intentionality intelligible. Even if phenomenal properties are a kind of 'paint that points' (to use Loar's expression), in virtue of what does one shade of phenomenal paint point to (say) foxes and another to dogs rather than vice versa? Particularly challenging here is the normativity of content, for there is not even a whiff of normativity about phenomenal properties.[12]

A further challenge facing the phenomenal approach concerns its capacity to account for the intentionality of *thought*. The problem here is that many theorists are deflationists about the phenomenology of thought, arguing that thought content isn't associated with any kind of distinctive phenomenology in the way that perceptual content is. Some deflationists deny that thought is phenomenally conscious at all; others hold that the phenomenology of thought is exclusively sensory, and derives from the mental imagery and bodily sensations that happen to be associated with thought (e.g., Robinson 2011; Tye & Wright 2011; Prinz 2011). But, the objection runs, if thought lacks any kind of phenomenal character of its own, then its content cannot be grounded in phenomenal consciousness.

Phenomenal theorists respond to this objection in one of two ways. Some push back against deflationist accounts of the phenomenology of thought, arguing that thoughts do have a distinctive kind of phenomenal character, a kind of 'cognitive phenomenology' (Box: The puzzle of cognitive phenomenology). According to Horgan and Tienson (2002), for example, the phenomenal character of thought reflects not only the attitude of the thought (e.g., the fact that it's a belief) but also its intentional content (e.g., that fact that it's a belief *that the fox is about to break into the chicken coop*). Others, such as Angela Mendelovici (2018), attempt to sidestep the cognitive phenomenology debate by grounding the intentionality of thought in the intentionality of perception, and then grounding the intentionality of perception in its phenomenal character. This strategy avoids making controversial assumptions about the phenomenal character of thought, but it faces problems of its own, for it is from clear that the intentionality of thought can be reduced to that of perception.

Box: The puzzle of cognitive phenomenology

At the heart of the cognitive phenomenology debate is the question of what kind(s) of phenomenal character attaches to thought. Following Kriegel (2015), we can distinguish three positions: eliminativism, reductionism, and primitivism. The eliminativist denies that thoughts have any phenomenal character at all. On this view, there is 'nothing that it's like' to (say) wonder what might have happened had President Kennedy not been assassinated (at least, not in the experiential sense of 'what it's like'). Reductionists hold that thoughts do have a phenomenology, but they take the phenomenology of thought to be purely sensory. On this view, what it's like to wonder what might have happened had Kennedy not been assassinated might involve (say) feelings of regret for missed opportunities, or visual imagery of President Johnson's inauguration. Finally, primitivists hold that there is a distinctive, non-sensory phenomenology (often known as 'cognitive phenomenology') associated with thought. This view allows that wondering what might have happened had Kennedy not been assassinated could involve sensory experiences of various kinds, but it denies that such states exhaust the phenomenology of thought.

The debate surrounding cognitive phenomenology is puzzling, for the existence of phenomenal properties is widely assumed to be introspectively evident. Primitivists claim that attentive introspection reveals the existence of irreducible forms of cognitive phenomenology, but eliminativists and reductionists claim to find no trace of such properties in their own experience. Perhaps cognitive phenomenology exists but is elusive in the way that sensory phenomenology isn't. Or perhaps the phenomenology of thought involves only collections of sensory experiences, and primitivists mistake those collections for a distinctive kind of non-sensory phenomenology. Or perhaps the debate is in part verbal, and theorists have different conceptions of what cognitive phenomenology would be. To fully resolve the debate regarding cognitive phenomenology, we need to understand why it generates such profound disagreement.

Further reading

Bayne, T. 2022. The Puzzle of Cognitive Phenomenology. In *Oxford Studies in Philosophy of Mind*, vol. 2. Oxford University Press, 3-35.
Kriegel, U. 2015. Cognitive Phenomenology. In *The Varieties of Consciousness*. Oxford University Press.
Smithies, D. 2013. The Nature of Cognitive Phenomenology. *Philosophy Compass*, 8(8): 744-54.

6.5 The intentional stance

We turn now to an account of content that contrasts sharply with both the symbol-focused approach taken by tracking semantics and teleosemantics and the consciousness-first orientation of the phenomenal account: Daniel Dennett's intentional systems theory (IST). The intentional systems theory is a version of interpretivism, an approach to content which holds that the possession of intentional states is to be understood in terms of the appropriateness of a certain kind of interpretation.[13]

IST has two components. The first is concerned with 'mindreading'; that is, with how we attribute intentionality. According to Dennett, we ascribe intentional states to an agent by adopting a certain perspective on their behaviour – what Dennett calls 'the intentional stance'.

> Here is how it works: first you decide to treat the object whose behavior is to be predicted as a rational agent; then you figure out what beliefs that agent ought to have, given its place in the world and its purpose. Then you figure out what desires it ought to have, on the same considerations, and finally you predict that this rational agent will act to further its goals in the light of its beliefs. A little practical reasoning from the chosen set of beliefs and desires will in most instances yield a decision about what the agent ought to do; that is what you predict the agent will do.
>
> (Dennett 1987: 17)

By ascribing intentional states to an agent, one acquires the capacity to make sense of its behaviour. To take a simple example, if I take you to both believe that there is beer in the fridge and to desire a beer, then I won't be puzzled as to why you've gone to the fridge. Indeed, that's precisely what I would expect you to do.[14]

The second component of IST is an account of intentionality itself, according to which there is nothing more to being an intentional system than what falls out of the intentional stance. Systems on which the intentional stance has no purchase don't have intentional states, whereas systems that can be usefully modelled by the intentional stance do. Moreover, the particular intentional states that a system has are precisely those that are best ascribed to it from the perspective of the intentional stance. If my behaviour is best explained by taking me to believe that there is beer in the fridge, then it follows that I do in fact believe that there is beer in the fridge.

A key component of Dennett's account is that it is holistic. Whether or not the ascription of a particular intentional state to an agent is warranted depends on the agent's overall behavioural profile, and on what other intentional states it might be appropriate to ascribe to them. What a person says will typically provide important constraints on the interpretation of their behaviour, but non-verbal behaviour can be equally important. Suppose that someone finds every possible excuse for not learning to drive, even when they have ample reason to do so. It might be reasonable to think that they are afraid of driving, even in the face of their claims to the contrary.

Unlike the phenomenal account, IST has no particular interest in an agent's conscious states. Indeed, as far as IST is concerned, an intentional agent need not even *be* conscious. Nor does IST have any particular interest in an agent's internal representations. Dennett allows that we may need to posit internal mental representations in order to explain an agent's cognitive capacities, but he argues that the legitimacy of the intentional stance doesn't require such representations, and he denies that they are the primary bearers of intentional content (see esp. Dennett 1978b).

What are we to make of IST? Perhaps the most common criticism is that it is really a form of eliminativism, and that it in effect denies the reality of intentionality. John Heil (1998), for example, claims that on Dennett's account, intentional states are akin to the lines of latitude and longitude that cartographers put on maps. Such lines aren't part of the fabric of reality in the way that mountains and rivers are; they are projections onto reality. The objection is that IST provides only an instrumentalist treatment of intentionality: rather than treating intentional states as genuine features of reality (as the realist does), it treats them as merely useful predictive devices – states that exist only in the eye (or the mind) of the interpreter.

Although this reading of IST is certainly encouraged by Dennett's talk of 'the intentional stance', Dennett (1991c) himself explicitly rejects it. On Dennett's view, the reality of the propositional attitudes consists in the patterns of behaviour that the intentional stance latches on to. These patterns are not merely useful predictive devices, nor do they exist only in the mind of an ascriber. Instead, they are objective features of reality. Dennett (1987) illustrates this point with a fable of super-smart Martians. Although the Martians have no inkling of the intentional stance, they are able to predict our behaviour on the basis of their exhaustive knowledge of our physical properties. (Your capacity to predict that I will go to the fridge is based on your knowledge of what I believe and desire, whereas the Martian's capacity to predict that I will go to the fridge is based on its knowledge of my brain states and how those states will conspire with perceptual input to produce behaviour.) Would the existence of super-smart Martians rob us of intentionality? Surely not, says Dennett. The behavioural patterns that underwrite the utility of the intentional stance are objective features of us, despite the Martians' ignorance of them.

A more serious challenge to Dennett's account is that it is too liberal and ascribes intentionality to systems that are clearly not intentional. Consider the lowly thermostat. Adopting the intentional stance affords some grip on its behaviour, for one can explain why and when a thermostat switches itself on by thinking of it as having beliefs (the room is not yet 20°C) and desires (that the room be at least 20°C). But although it might be useful to treat a thermostat as though it has intentional states, surely (the objection runs) it doesn't *really* have intentional states. The thermostat doesn't believe that the room is less than 20°C, nor does it want the room to be above 20°C. The force of this worry goes well beyond thermostats, for it is often useful to take the intentional stance towards systems that are not intuitively regarded as having mental states. For example, we describe a government as having *decided to close its borders*, a company as *trying to avoid paying tax*, and a computer as *wanting to reboot*, but we don't tend to think of governments, companies, or computers as having genuine intentional states. In short, the objection is that IST ignores the fundamental difference between metaphorical ascriptions of intentionality ('as if' intentionality, as it is sometimes put) and the genuine article.

In response, Dennett grants that there are qualitative differences between us and the lowly thermostat, but he denies that any 'bright line' separates genuine intentionality from merely 'as if' intentionality. Instead, taking the intentional stance towards an entity becomes increasingly useful as its behavioural repertoire becomes increasingly complex. Thermostats aren't usefully modelled by the intentional stance, but more complex artefacts such as chess-playing programs might be. The problem with this response is that it seems to involve a commitment to the kind of instrumentalist treatment of intentionality from which Dennett wants to distance himself.[15]

Another challenge to IST concerns its capacity to account for the explanatory role of intentional states. Suppose that someone has asked why Max jumped into the swimming pool. In response, you might tell them that Max thought that her pants were on fire, and (understandably) wanted to put the flames out. In ascribing certain beliefs and desires to Max we seem to be providing a causal explanation of her behaviour. But if intentional states are just patterns of behaviour (as Dennett's account holds), then it is unclear how they might also provide causal explanations. After all, a pattern isn't ordinarily thought of as a cause of its instances.

The force of this objection depends on the kinds of explanations that we require of intentional states. It seems unlikely that the interpretational approach can accommodate the explanatory role of intentionality if we think of intentional states as providing *causal* explanations of behaviour. But the interpretationalist may argue that attributions of intentionality provide explanations of a different kind. Perhaps appealing to Max's beliefs and desires explains her actions by locating them within a certain kind of model (Godfrey-Smith 2005). Even if this model doesn't identify the causes of behaviour, it might provide explanations of the kind that support counterfactual reasoning, telling us what Max would have done if there had been some other way of extinguishing the flames.

6.6 Conclusion

We have considered a number of very different approaches to the problem of intentional content. The tracking and teleosemantic accounts adopt a symbol-based approach to the issue, arguing that the central job for a theory of content is to assign content to particular mental representations. As we saw, tracking semantics assigns content to a representation on the basis of what it is set up to track (or indicate), whereas Millikan's version of teleosemantics assigns content to a representation on the basis of how it is used – or rather, how it is used when the mechanisms that are consuming it are doing what they have been selected to do. We saw that tracking accounts have difficulty in accounting for the possibility of misrepresentation, while teleosemantic accounts face questions about whether they can scale up, and explain not just the kinds of contents that might govern the behaviour of the hoverfly but also those that characterize mature human thought.

In the second half of this chapter we turned to the phenomenal and interpretational approaches to content. Both of these approaches reject the symbol-based starting point of the tracking and teleosemantic accounts, but they have little else in common. The phenomenal approach attempts to ground intentional content in the phenomenal character of an agent's mental states, while the interpretational approach holds that content is determined by the interpretation that makes best sense of the target's behaviour. We saw that a central challenge facing the phenomenal approach concerns the relationship between phenomenal properties and intentional properties: if phenomenal properties are inherently intentional, then the approach appears to be circular, but if phenomenal properties are not inherently intentional, then it's unclear how they could provide perspicuous explanations of intentional content. For its part, Dennett's IST faces questions about whether its treatment of intentionality is sufficiently realist, and whether it can account for the explanatory role of intentional states.

Let us bring this chapter to a close by returning to a question that we have encountered at various points along the way: how should a theory of content be evaluated? Should we rely on intuitions about the kinds of contents a system can (or cannot) have, or should accounts of content be treated like scientific theories, and evaluated on the basis of their predictive power and explanatory fertility? Most theorists tend to assume that distinctively philosophical considerations have a legitimate role to play in evaluating accounts of content, whereas others argue that theories of content ought to be viewed as scientific proposals, and that philosophical considerations should be afforded little to no weight here. Once again we confront difficult questions about the nature of the border between philosophical reflection on the mind and its scientific study.

Further reading

Good overviews of the problem of content can be found in Barry Loewer's 'A Guide to Naturalizing Semantics', in Bob Hale, Crispin Wright, and Alexander Miller (eds.), *A Companion to the Philosophy of Language* (2nd ed., CUP, 108-26, 2017) and Dan Ryder's, 'Problems of Representation II: Naturalizing Content', in Francisco Garzon and John Symons (eds.), *The Routledge Companion to the Philosophy of Psychology* (2nd ed., Routledge, pp. 251-79, 2019). Peter Godfrey-Smith's 'On Folk Psychology and Mental Representation', in H. Clapin, P. Staines, and P. Slezak (eds.), *Representation in Mind* (Elsevier, pp. 147-62, 2004), contains a thought-provoking discussion of the relationship between symbol-based approaches to mental representation and folk psychology.

For more on tracking approaches to content, see Paul Boghossian's 'Naturalizing Content', in Barry Loewer and Georges Rey (eds.), *Meaning in Mind: Fodor and His Critics* (Basil Blackwell, pp. 65-86, 1990); Angela Mendelovici's 'Reliable Misrepresentation and Tracking Theories of Mental Representation', *Philosophical Studies*, 165: 142-43 (2013); and Robert Rupert's 'Causal Theories of Mental Content', *Philosophy Compass*, 3(2): 353-80 (2008).

An excellent overview of teleosemantics can be found in Karen Neander's 'Teleological Theories of Mental Content: Can Darwin Solve the Problem of Intentionality?', in M. Ruse (ed.), *The Oxford Handbook of Philosophy of Biology* (OUP, 2008). Ruth Millikan's 'Compare and Contrast Dretske, Fodor, and Millikan on Teleosemantics', *Philosophical Topics*, 18(2): 151-61 (1990) is also very helpful. *Teleosemantics*, edited by Graham Macdonald and David Papineau (OUP, 2006), contains a fine collection of papers on precisely that topic, and the editors' introduction provides a useful map of the relevant debates. Recent work in the teleosemantic tradition includes Manolo Martínez's 'Teleosemantics and Indeterminacy', *Dialectica*, 67(4): 427-53 (2013); Karen Neander's *A Mark of the Mental: In Defense of Informational Teleosemantics* (MIT Press, 2017); and Nicholas Shea's *Representation in Cognitive Science* (OUP, 2018).

An important collection of papers on the phenomenal approach to content is contained in *Phenomenal Intentionality* (OUP, 2013), edited by Uriah Kriegel. Kriegel's introduction to the volume is particularly illuminating. See also his own monograph, *The Sources of Intentionality*

(OUP, 2011), for an important defence of the view. For critical discussion of the phenomenal approach see Adam Pautz's 'Does Phenomenology Ground Mental Content?', in U. Kriegel (ed.), *Phenomenal Intentionality* (OUP, 2013) and Robert Wilson's 'Intentionality and Phenomenology', *Pacific Philosophical Quarterly*, 84(4): 413–31 (2003).

For further reflection on Dennett's intentional stance, see *Philosophical Topics, Vol. 22, No. 1/2, The Philosophy of Daniel Dennett* (1994), particularly Brian McLaughlin and John O'Leary-Hawthorne's, 'Dennett's Logical Behaviorism'. More recent discussions of intentionality that bear on the tenability of the intentional stance include Holly Anderson, 'Patterns, Information, and Causation', *Journal of Philosophy*, 114(11): 592–622 (2017) and Abel Suñé and Manolo Martínez, 'Real Patterns and Indispensability', *Synthese*, 198: 4315–30 (2019).

Study questions

1   The opening section of this chapter presents a number of assumptions that, it is argued, ought to constrain attempts to ground intentionality. What are those assumptions? Do you agree that these assumptions should govern attempts to ground intentionality?
2   What is the distinction between symbol-centred and agent-centred approaches to the problem of content?
3   What is the misrepresentation (or disjunction) problem for tracking accounts of content? What are some of the ways in which theorists have attempted to solve it?
4   What is distinctive about the teleosemantic approach to content?
5   What is the Swampman objection to teleosemantics? Do you think that teleosemanticists have an adequate response to that challenge? If so, what is it?
6   What is Horgan and Tienson's duplication argument for the phenomenal approach to intentionality? Is the argument successful?
7   Explain why Dennett's intentional systems theory is often accused of being too liberal. Do you think that this charge is justified?
8   What is the normativity of content? Do any of the accounts of content considered in this chapter can provide an adequate treatment of it? If not, how might the normativity of content be accounted for?

Notes

1   There are a number of important accounts of content that we cannot consider here, such as inferential role (also known as conceptual role) accounts and structural resemblance accounts. For discussion, see Cummins (1989), Loewer (2017), Ryder (2019), and Shea (2013).
2   Arguably this constraint is entailed by the perspicuity constraint, for if our account of intentionality presupposes intentionality, we haven't really rendered it intelligible. Nonetheless, it is useful to separate out the no-circularity constraint as an independent constraint.
3   'There can be no intentionality grinning up at us from the bottom of the beer mug', to modify a well-known expression of J. L. Austin's.
4   There are also important distinctions between symbol-based approaches to content, for some focus on the assignment of content to particular, atomic symbols (the 'words' of the language of thought), whereas others argue that the primary target of analysis should be full propositional attitude states, such as the belief that foxes are mammals.

5   Classic discussion of tracking semantics can be found in Dretske (1981, 1988), Fodor (1987), and Stampe (1977). More recent work in this tradition can be found in Godfrey-Smith (2020), Rupert (1999), Usher (2001), and Weissglass (2020)
6   For other accounts of content that appeal to biological function, see Dretske (1995), Papineau (1984), Ryder (2004), and Neander (2017).
7   Note that there are also input-based versions of teleosemantics. For examples, see Dretske (1995), Neander (1995, 2017).
8   Note, however, that not all teleosemanticists agree with this verdict. See Neander (2006) for discussion.
9   See Papineau (1993: 97–8) for a reply, and see Jackson (2006b) for a response to Papineau's reply.
10 For more on the problem of scaling up, see Martínez (2013).
11 The roots of this approach are to be found in Horgan and Tienson (2002), Loar (2003), Siewert (1998), and Strawson (1994). More recent contributions include Farkas (2008a), Goff (2012), Kriegel (2011), Mendelovici (2018), Pitt (2004), and Strawson (2011).
12 Some theorists might be tempted to draw on the tools discussed in Sections 6.2 and 6.3, suggesting that perhaps phenomenal states point to particular objects rather than others because of (say) their informational or biological properties. (For example, one might suggest that a certain experience means 'fox' because it covaries with the presence of foxes.) But views of this kind are not versions of the phenomenal approach as it is usually developed, for phenomenal theorists typically hold that a phenomenal state is associated with a certain intentional property irrespective of the agent's relations to its environment.
13 For other interpretational accounts, see David Lewis (1974) and Donald Davidson (1973, 1974).
14 Dennett focuses almost exclusively on the attribution of intentional states to other creatures and says very little about self-attribution. It is interesting to consider what account IST can give of knowledge of one's own intentional states. It is also worth noting that the intentional stance is not the only game in town when it comes to explaining our ability to ascribe mental states to other people. We consider a number of alternatives in Chapter 11.
15 This objection raises the very interesting question of whether intentionality admits of indeterminacy and vagueness. Dennett assumes that it does, as (presumably) do most advocates of the tracking and teleosemantic accounts. By contrast, advocates of the phenomenal approach tend to claim that a sharp line divides non-intentional states and systems from intentional states and systems, and that the sharpness of this line derives from the sharpness of the line dividing the phenomenal from the non-phenomenal.

7 Externalism and the extended mind

Chapter overview

- Introduces the debate between content internalists and content externalists
- Explains influential arguments for externalism due to Hilary Putnam and Tyler Burge (the doppelgänger arguments)
- Provides an overview of some of the main objections to content externalism
- Introduces the extended mind hypothesis (vehicle externalism) and evaluates an influential argument for it due to Andy Clark and David Chalmers.

The conception of the mind embraced by dualism is individualistic. According to the dualist, mental states are states of an immaterial self, and the mind's operations are only causally related to the body and the external environment. Although the physicalists of the early to mid-20th century rejected Descartes's dualism, they tended to take his individualism for granted. They recognized that an individual's environment plays a role in explaining why they have the mental states and capacities that they do, but they generally assumed that an account of the fundamental nature of the mental need not appeal to anything beyond the borders of the individual's skull (or at least, their skin). A brain in a vat could, so the thought went, have the same mental states that you and I enjoy.

This position is known as 'internalism'. Although internalism in the philosophy of mind is alive and kicking, many philosophers have been persuaded that extra-cranial facts can (and often do) play a fundamental role in determining the nature of our mental states. According to externalists, an agent's mental states are not determined solely by what happens within their skin, but depend – not merely causally but constitutively – on the nature of their environment. This chapter examines the debate between internalists and externalists.

Our discussion unfolds in two stages. In the first half of the chapter, we focus on a form of externalism known as 'content externalism'.[1] (It is also referred to as 'semantic externalism'.) As the label indicates, content externalists focus on the question of what determines the content (or meaning) of a person's mental states. Traditional (internalist) conceptions of content assume that the contents of one's mental states are determined solely by what goes on within one's head (or at least one's skin), but in the 1970s and '80s an influential pair of arguments due to Hilary Putnam and Tyler Burge convinced many that content can be determined by extra-cranial factors. In the second half of this chapter, we turn our attention to a version of externalism that focus on the location of mental phenomena themselves. 'Vehicle externalists', as the advocates of this view are known, argue that the physical states and processes that underpin cognition are not skin-bound but can extend beyond the agent and incorporate features of their immediate environment.[2]

7.1 Motivating content externalism

The debate between internalists and externalists rests on a distinction between two kinds of properties: intrinsic properties and relational properties. The property of being 6 feet tall is an intrinsic property, for being 6 feet tall doesn't depend on one's history or how one is embedded in one's environment. By contrast, the property of being a mother is a relational (or non-intrinsic) property, for one is a mother only if one is suitably related to another person (one's offspring). Internalists claim that an agent's mental properties supervene on their intrinsic properties. If you fix a person's intrinsic properties, you thereby fix their mental properties. Externalists, by contrast, hold that mental properties are relational properties and don't supervene on a person's intrinsic properties. As externalists see it, mental properties are more like *being a mother* than they are like *being 6 feet tall*.[3]

There are certain kinds of mental phenomena for which externalism is relatively uncontroversial. For example, externalism is clearly true of knowledge, for knowing that Mars has two moons depends on how many moons Mars actually has, and that's clearly an extra-cranial state of affairs. Externalism also seems to be true of perceptual states, such as seeing. In order to see a fox, one must be causally related to a fox in an appropriate manner. If you have merely hallucinated a fox or have mistaken a cleverly disguised dog for a fox, then you haven't seen a fox (although you might *think* that you've seen a fox). The controversial question isn't whether externalism is true of certain kinds of attitudes (states such as knowing and perceiving) but whether it is true of certain kinds of mental *contents*.

There are two very different ways of motivating content externalism. The first involves appealing to an account of how content is grounded. As we saw in the previous chapter, although some theories of content are committed to internalism, others are either explicitly committed to externalism or are at least 'externalism friendly'. Consider, for example, a simple kind of tracking semantics, according to which the meaning of a representation is determined by what it tracks (Section 6.2). On this view, the capacity to think about foxes involves having representations that track the presence of foxes. That might not require the existence of foxes – arguably something can be 'set up to be set off by' foxes, even if there are no foxes for it to set off – but it does seem to imply that the content of a thought isn't determined by what's in the head. A commitment to externalism is even more explicit in the teleosemantic tradition (Section 6.3), according to which the meaning of a representation is determined by the biological functions of the system in which it is embedded. Indeed, even Dennett's interpretational account of content is committed to externalism (Section 6.5), for the interpretation of an agent's behaviour is constrained by their physical and social environment (see Dennett 1982). In fact, the only account of content that we discussed in the previous chapter that isn't 'externalism friendly' is the phenomenal approach (Section 6.4). Although no account of content is unproblematic, the fact that many of the leading views are most naturally developed in terms of externalism is certainly a consideration in its favour. More generally, the idea that our capacity to think about the world is dependent on our interaction with it is a compelling one.

But although they are important, theory-based considerations have not been the driving force behind the widespread enthusiasm for externalism. Instead, that honour goes to a series of arguments developed by Hilary Putnam and Tyler Burge in the 1970s and '80s. I will call them the *doppelgänger arguments*, for they appeal to intuitions about the mental states of doppelgängers, i.e., individuals who are perfect twins with respect to their intrinsic properties. Doppelgängers are a useful device here, for internalists hold that they must have the same mental states, whereas externalists allow that doppelgängers can differ in mental properties in virtue of the fact that an agent's mental states aren't fixed by their intrinsic properties.

Putnam's (1975b) argument features Oscar and Twin-Oscar, two individuals who have the same intrinsic properties but reside in different environments.[4] Oscar inhabits Earth, whereas Twin-Oscar resides on Twin Earth, a planet just like Earth apart from the fact that on Twin Earth the clear, tasteless, odourless substance that falls from the sky and fills the rivers and lakes and oceans isn't H_2O but another substance that Putnam calls 'XYZ'. It is 1750, and neither on Earth nor on Twin Earth has chemistry been developed to the point at which H_2O can be distinguished from XYZ. (The two substances are superficially identical, and it takes specialized chemical analysis to distinguish them.) Does 'water' have the same meaning on Earth as it does on Twin Earth? Putnam says no. On Earth, water refers to the substance that is predominantly H_2O, whereas on Twin Earth, water refers to XYZ and not H_2O. If, for example, there were a single puddle of XYZ on Earth, then it would not be water as Oscar and his fellow Earthlings use the term. Similarly, if there were a single puddle of H_2O on Twin Earth, then it would not be water as Twin-Oscar and his fellow Twin-Earthlings use that term, for 'water' in their mouths refers exclusively to H_2O. If a Twin-Earthling were to point at some H_2O and say 'That's water' (as we might put it), then she would be wrong.

Although Putnam's paper is one of the key texts in the rise of externalism, he didn't actually defend externalism about *mental* content. Instead, his focus was on linguistic content, the meaning of public language terms.[5] But if the meaning of our sentences reflects the meaning of our thoughts, then it is but a short step from externalism about linguistic content to externalism about mental content, and many have found that step attractive. Putnam's tale of Oscar and his twin, it is widely thought, doesn't just show that what goes in our heads can fail to fix the contents of our words; it also shows that it can fail to fix the contents of our thoughts (McGinn 1988). This is the version of Putnam's argument on which we will focus.

We will explore responses to Putnam's argument shortly, but let's first consider Burge's doppelgänger argument for externalism (which he calls 'anti-individualism') (Burge 1979, 1986).[6] Imagine a person (let's call him 'Bert') who thinks that he has arthritis in his thigh (as we would put it). Bert's belief is false. As Bert's doctor tells him, arthritis is an inflammation of the joints, and one cannot have arthritis in one's thigh. Now consider another individual (let's call him 'Ernie'), who is in the same internal states as Bert and shares his history (narrowly construed), but lives in a community in which the term 'arthritis' is used for a different disease ('tharthritis'). Unlike arthritis, tharthritis *can* afflict the thigh. Burge argues that Bert's and Ernie's thoughts have different contents despite the fact that they are doppelgängers: Bert's thoughts are about arthritis, whereas Ernie's thoughts are about tharthritis. The upshot, Burge concludes, is that the contents of an agent's thoughts can change even when their intrinsic properties (their 'qualitative experiences, physiological states and behaviorally described stimuli and responses') are unchanged. Burge labels his version of content externalism 'anti-individualism' to capture the constitutive role that an individual's social context plays in fixing the contents of thought.

The kind of externalism that Burge defends is significantly more ambitious and wide-ranging in scope than that which is motivated by Putnam's argument. The force of Putnam's argument is restricted to natural-kind concepts, such as WATER, ELM, and MOLYBDENUM. Burge's argument, by contrast, 'can get under way in any case where it is intuitively possible to attribute a mental state or event whose content involves a notion that the subject incompletely understands' (1979: 79). The notion of incomplete understanding is crucial to the case for externalism, for it provides the space in which an agent's context can play a role in determining the contents of their thoughts.[7]

7.2 Responses to the doppelgänger arguments

Broadly speaking, responses to the doppelgänger arguments can be grouped into three camps. Those in the first camp accept the arguments and embrace externalism, holding that the contents of thought don't depend solely on what goes on in a person's head. Some of those in this camp are more radical than others. Less radical externalists take externalism to apply only to the contents of thought and are internalists when it comes to mental phenomena of other kinds. More radical externalists take externalism to apply not only to the contents of thought but also to perceptual content; indeed, some theorists even argue that *phenomenal* properties aren't fixed by what's in the head (see Section 7.3).

Those in the second camp reject the doppelgänger arguments and embrace internalism. They typically argue either that we have no reason to trust the intuitions on which these arguments rest, or that although these intuitions are not untrustworthy as such, they can be accommodated without embracing externalism.[8] Those who adopt the latter response often lean heavily on the contrast between mental content and the linguistic expression of that content. They grant that we need to use public language terms in order to describe the contents of our thoughts, and that because these terms are embedded in social contexts those who use them may have only a partial grasp of their meaning. But, they argue, the contents of thoughts themselves do not constitutively depend on external factors, and the idea that an agent might have an incomplete understanding of their own concepts should be resisted. On this view, what agents fail to grasp is not the meaning of their own thoughts but how the meaning of those thoughts relates to the meaning of the sentences in which they are expressed.

A third response to the doppelgänger arguments involves a kind of pluralism about content. Those in this camp hold that there is a kind of content about which externalists are right (wide or broad content), and there is also a kind of content about which internalists are right (narrow content). Let's consider this position in a little more detail.[9]

A useful place to begin is with terms (and their associated concepts) that clearly have two dimensions of meaning. Consider, for example, 'I'. In one sense, 'I' means the same thing no matter who thinks it, but there is another sense in which 'I' means one thing when you use it and another thing when I use it. (After all, the thought 'I am tall' might be true when you think it but false when I think it.) In the same way that 'I' has two dimensions of meaning, so too one might argue that natural-kind terms such as 'water' and the concepts with which they are associated also have two dimensions of meaning (e.g., Chalmers 2002). The narrow content of the concept WATER might be something like 'the watery stuff (clear, drinkable, etc.) found in the lakes, ponds, and oceans around here'. Oscar and his twin will have mental states with the same narrow content. However, the watery stuff that surrounds Oscar is H_2O, whereas the watery stuff that surrounds his twin is XYZ. Thus, the wide content of their water concepts will differ: the wide content of Oscar's concept refers to H_2O, whereas the wide content of his twin's concept refers to XYZ.

The idea that there are two kinds of contents isn't just motivated by our intuitions about doppelgänger cases, but it can also be motivated by reflecting on the kind of work that we want the notion of mental content to do. On the one hand, we appeal to content in order to explain an agent's behaviour and to capture their perspective on the world. The notion of content that is needed for this is arguably narrow. Intuitively, Oscar and his twin have the same perspective on the world, and any content-based explanation of behaviour that applies to one of them will also apply to the other. On the other hand, we also appeal to content in order to capture how an agent is related to their environment, and the notion of content that is needed here is arguably broad. And if attributions of content are in the business of making explicit the relations between an agent and their environment, then we should expect that there will be a type of content that can differ between doppelgängers who are located in different contexts.

7.3 Externalism extended

The doppelgänger arguments developed by Putnam and Burge focus on the contents of thought, but it is natural to ask whether and how they might be extended to other mental phenomena. If the contents of thought don't depend on what's in the head, then perhaps the contents of perception don't either.

The most attractive form of externalism about perceptual content involves an appeal to features of an agent's natural (as opposed to social) environment. Consider a Twin Earth argument developed by Burge (1986), in which Twin Earth differs from Earth in that the kinds of visual experiences that represent cracks on Earth instead represent shadows. In this scenario, Bert (who is on Earth) and Ernie (on Twin Earth) could have qualitatively identical visual experiences, but Bert's visual experiences will represent cracks as cracks whereas Ernie's will represent shadows as shadows (Davies 1997; McGinn 1988). The intuitive thought here is that if Bert were to move to Twin Earth and Ernie to Earth, then Bert's visual experiences would represent shadows as cracks while Ernie's visual experiences would represent cracks as shadows – at least for a period of time.

Externalism about perceptual content is more radical than externalism about thought content, but there is a version of externalism that is more radical still: phenomenal externalism (Dretske 1996; Lycan 2001b). Phenomenal externalists hold that it's not just the content of thought (and perception) that's broad, phenomenal character – the 'what it's like' of conscious experience – is too. As one defence of the view puts it, it's not just meanings that ain't in the head – qualia ain't either! (Byrne & Tye 2006).

Phenomenal externalism is a profoundly counterintuitive view. After all, it is one thing to think that the content of one's 'water' or 'arthritis' thoughts depends on extracranial factors, but it is quite another to think that what it's like to see water or experience arthritic pain also depends on such factors. Phenomenal externalists typically grant that the view is indeed counterintuitive, but they argue that it follows from two highly plausible theses. The first thesis is intentionalism about phenomenal properties – the claim that the phenomenal character of an experience is determined by its intentional content. On this view, what it's like to (say) look at the waves rolling in on a beach is a matter of what one's visual experience represents. The second thesis is that all content is broad. Put these two theses together, phenomenal externalists point out, and it follows that even the 'what it's like-ness' of consciousness can depend on what's outside the head.

Needless to say, this argument is controversial. Some theorists accept intentionalism about phenomenal properties, but deny that the intentional properties on which phenomenal properties supervene are themselves wide. For example, Pautz (2006) invokes evidence from cognitive science to argue that the environment plays only a causal role in determining the subjective nature of perception. Other theorists reject intentionalism, arguing that phenomenal properties can't be fixed by intentional properties precisely because phenomenal properties are narrow but intentional properties are wide (see, e.g., Papineau 2014). But both intentionalism and externalism about perceptual content are attractive positions, and the fact that their conjunction leads directly to phenomenal externalism provides a strong argument for taking it seriously, despite its counterintuitiveness (Box: Border problems).[10]

Box: Border problems

One of the many fascinating issues raised by phenomenal externalism concerns the question of where and how to locate the border between the internal and the external. Most discussions of content externalism focus on the skin (or the skull), defining doppelgängers as individuals who have exactly the same intrinsic physical properties from the skin on in. But it was always clear that this proposal was just a convenient fiction: Oscar and his twin couldn't have exactly the same intrinsic properties because Oscar's body will contain H_2O whereas his twin's body will contain XYZ, yet this fact doesn't appear to undermine their status as doppelgängers (as Putnam recognized).

In effect, the conception of a doppelgänger required by the arguments of Putnam and Burge requires only the notion of subjective indiscriminability. What matters isn't whether Oscar and his twin have the same intrinsic physical properties, but whether they have the same subjective, first-person perspective (Farkas 2003). Put in these terms, internalism can be understood as the claim that any two individuals with the same type of subjective perspective have the same thought contents, whereas externalism allows that individuals with the same type of subjective perspective – 'phenomenal twins', we might call them – can have thoughts with different contents.

This way of setting things up does a good job of capturing the debate between internalism and externalism as it applies to both thought and perceptual content, but it clearly fails when applied to the question of *phenomenal* externalism. One cannot appeal to what phenomenal twins have in common if the very question at issue concerns what it takes to qualify as a phenomenal twin. Absent a better proposal, the border between the internal and the external may need to be drawn at the skin when it comes to the debate regarding phenomenal states.

Further reading

Farkas, K. 2003. What Is Externalism? *Philosophical Studies*, 112(3): 187–208.
Gertler, B. 2012. Understanding the Internalism-Externalism Debate: What Is the Boundary of the Thinker? *Philosophical Perspectives*, 26(1): 51–75.
Gomes, A., and M. Parrott. 2021. On Being Internally the Same. *Oxford Studies in Philosophy of Mind*, vol. 1. Oxford University Press, 315–40.

7.4 The internalist fights back

Thus far we have focused on arguments for externalism and have ignored the case for internalism. It is time to remedy that neglect.

One argument for internalism concerns mental causation. The kinds of environmental features that externalists take to determine the identity of one's mental states are – so the thought goes – surely irrelevant to their causal powers. Thus, the objection runs, externalists must either reject the reality of mental causation altogether, or at the very least deny that mental states are causally efficacious in virtue of their content. Either way, critics argue, the externalist is committed to a counterintuitive conception of mental causation. This is an important objection, but we will defer discussion of it to Chapter 10, for it is best dealt with in the context of an examination of mental causation.

Let's consider instead an argument for internalism that focuses on an apparent tension between externalism and the kind of knowledge that we have of the contents of our own thoughts, what philosophers call 'self-knowledge'. Suppose that you are currently thinking WATER IS WET. Intuitively, you seem to have direct, unmediated access to the contents of your thought. Your access to the fact that you're thinking WATER IS WET is a priori rather than a posteriori. It is a kind of armchair knowledge, for it is available to you without your needing to rise from your armchair. Your access to your own thoughts also has a distinctive kind of authority. You are, we tend to assume, in a much better position to say what it is that you are thinking than anyone else is.

Both the directness and the authority of self-knowledge appear to be threatened by externalism (McKinsey 1991). The directness of self-knowledge is threatened, for if your thoughts depend on the nature of your environment, then, it seems, knowing what one is thinking would require knowledge of one's environment. The authority of self-knowledge is threatened for similar reasons. Those who know more about your environment than you do might be better placed to identify the contents of your thoughts than you yourself are.

The tension between self-knowledge and externalism can be highlighted by reflecting on scenarios in which an agent (Oscar) is moved, without his knowledge, from Earth to Twin Earth (Burge 1988; Boghossian 1989). Externalists hold that immediately after the move from Earth to Twin Earth, Oscar's terms refer to what they referred to on Earth (e.g., 'water' refers to H_2O), but that after a period of time they come to refer to the watery stuff on Twin Earth (namely, XYZ). (For this reason, these scenarios are often called 'slow-switching scenarios'.) Now, if the meaning of Oscar's words reflects the meaning of his thoughts, then at some point his thoughts will switch from being about H_2O to being about XYZ. But, crucially, Oscar is unaware that he has been transported from Earth to Twin Earth, and thus has no reason to think that the contents of his water-related thoughts have changed. Intuitively, Oscar has no a priori access to whether his water-related thoughts are H_2O thoughts or XYZ thoughts. To figure that out, he must leave his armchair and investigate the nature of the watery stuff around him. Moreover, someone who is aware that Oscar has been moved to Twin Earth would know the content of Oscar's thoughts better than Oscar himself does. And that, one might argue, undermines the intuitive view that we have a distinctive kind of authority with respect to the contents of our own thoughts.[11]

Responses to this tension cluster into three main categories. Some argue that the apparent tension between self-knowledge (as traditionally understood) and externalism is a genuine one, and conclude that the traditional view of self-knowledge ought to be rejected on the grounds that the case for externalism is stronger than that for self-knowledge. Others argue that externalism is at odds with self-knowledge, but argue that it is externalism rather than the traditional view of self-knowledge that ought to be jettisoned. (Those who adopt this position can allow that there is a kind of wide content for which authoritative self-knowledge doesn't hold, but they insist that the argument from self-knowledge shows that there is a kind of content that is narrow.) A third group of theorists argue that the tension between externalism and self-knowledge is more apparent than real. Let us explore this compatibilist position in more detail.

The idea that externalism and authoritative self-knowledge are compatible has been defended in various ways. One defence appeals to the idea that self-knowledge involves redeploying the contents of thought in a reflective manner (Burge 1988, 1996; see also Brueckner 2007). On this proposal, one can know that one is thinking WATER IS WET by simply redeploying the content of that very thought reflexively, and thus embedding the content of the first-order thought in a second-order thought. In this way, 'I am thinking water is wet' would be akin to Descartes' famous cogito ('I think, therefore I am'), a thought whose very existence guarantees its truth. Crucially, if self-knowledge involves the redeployment of content, then it is both a priori (for it doesn't require any knowledge of the world over and above that which is provided by the first-order state), and authoritative (for the very having of the second-order thought provides access to the first-order thought).

Although this defence of compatibilism has been influential, many argue that it fails to address the fundamental tension between externalism and the demands of self-knowledge. Self-knowledge, they hold, requires a certain kind of discriminatory ability, in which one can tell (from the armchair, and with authority) which of two closely related thoughts one is thinking. Oscar lacks this capacity, for he cannot tell whether he is currently thinking H_2O is wet or XYZ is wet. As Jessica Brown (2004) has argued, even if an agent is able to reflexively redeploy the contents of their thoughts, externalism entails that differences between thoughts

Externalism and the extended mind 125

won't always be transparent (i.e., available from the armchair) to an agent. And if intentional differences aren't always transparent, then (the argument runs) there is a fundamental sense in which the demands of self-knowledge aren't satisfied.

This objection raises many issues that we cannot pursue here, but we can note two points. First, even if Oscar cannot discriminate his XYZ thoughts from his H_2O thoughts, there are many other thoughts that he can distinguish these thoughts from. For his example, he can distinguish the thought 'H_2O is wet' from the thought 'H_2O is not wet', and he can distinguish both of these thoughts from the thought 'Penguins are birds'. Thus, even if externalism entails that the content of thought is not *fully* transparent, it certainly doesn't entail that the content of thought is opaque from the first-person perspective. The second point to note is that Oscar's situation is unusual, and the fact that he lacks a certain kind of self-knowledge doesn't imply that we too (who, presumably, haven't travelled from Earth to Twin Earth) lack self-knowledge. Perhaps externalism does indeed threaten self-knowledge, but only with respect to agents who find themselves in deceptive environments. Authoritative self-knowledge might be easier to come by for those of us for whom the watery stuff has only ever been H_2O. This line of thought won't satisfy those who assume that we have authoritative self-knowledge irrespective of our environment, but perhaps the lesson of externalism is that that assumption should be rejected.[12]

7.5 Vehicle externalism and the extended mind

The kind of externalism on which we have focused thus far (content externalism) holds that the environment plays a constitutive role in determining the intentional content (and, perhaps, phenomenal character) of our mental states, but it is silent on the location of mental states themselves. We turn now to a form of externalism - often known as 'vehicle externalism' - that focuses on where mentation itself occurs. According to vehicle externalists, the very machinery of mentation is not restricted to the brain but extends out into the body and the immediate environment. As one of its advocates puts it, 'the mind reaches - or at least *can* reach, *sometimes* - beyond the limits of the body out into the world' (Noë 2004: 221).

In the same way that arguments based on thought experiments have played an important role in motivating content externalism, so too they have loomed large in discussions of vehicle externalism. Perhaps the most influential of such arguments is due to Andy Clark and David Chalmers (1998). It features Otto and Inga, two individuals who are trying to get to the Museum of Modern Art (MoMA) in New York City. Inga finds her way to MoMA by consulting her memory. Otto, however, has Alzheimer's disease, and gets to MoMA by relying on information about MoMA's location that he has written down in a notebook. Clark and Chalmers argue that because the information in Otto's notebook plays the same action-guiding role as the information that is encoded in Inga's brain, it ought to count as part of Otto's long-term memory, and thus as part of his mind. The boundaries of Otto's mind, they argue, extend beyond his skin. For this reason, the hypothesis of vehicle externalism is also known as the 'extended mind hypothesis'.

We will consider the MoMA argument (as I will call it) shortly, but let's first reflect on three features of the extended mind hypothesis.[13]

First, it is fundamentally different from the content externalism associated with the work of Putnam and Burge. Content externalists take the environment to bear on the identity conditions of certain types of mental states, whereas advocates of the extended mind hypothesis are interested in the material basis of mentality. As a parallel, consider two kinds of questions that one can ask about a coin. One question concerns what makes a particular coin the kind of coin that it is. That is the kind of question on which content externalists focus. Another question is where exactly a particular coin is located; what parcel of space-time does it occupy? That is the kind of question on which vehicle externalists focus.[14]

Second, the extended mind thesis goes beyond the claim that an agent's environment can have a profound impact on their cognitive capacities (Haugeland 1998; Sterelny 2010; Stotz 2010). A well-structured environment enables an agent to carry out tasks that they would otherwise be unable to perform – at least, not with their usual degree of speed and accuracy. (Consider what it's like to cook in an unfamiliar kitchen.) We create our own cognitive niches, refashioning our world so as to facilitate the efficient retrieval and manipulation of information. That claim – which is known as the *embedded* mind thesis – is relatively uncontroversial and is accepted by even the harshest critics of the extended mind thesis. The extended mind thesis is not about whether tools and environmental cues *augment* cognition, but whether they are incorporated into cognition as part of its *constitutive* basis.

Third, the extended mind thesis can be developed in more or less comprehensive ways. Clark and Chalmers defend a relatively modest form of vehicle externalism, arguing only that the vehicles of dispositional belief and unconscious cognitive processing extend beyond the skin. Other theorists, however, argue that even the vehicles of *consciousness* extend beyond the head to incorporate the body and perhaps even the perceptual environment. This version of vehicle externalism – dubbed by Andy Clark (2009) the *extended conscious mind* hypothesis – is significantly more controversial than the version of vehicle externalism defended by Clark and Chalmers, and cannot easily be motivated by the kinds of parity arguments that they deploy (Box: The extended conscious mind?).

Box: The extended conscious mind?

According to the extended conscious mind (ECM) hypothesis, the physical substrate of consciousness (in particular, perceptual consciousness) cuts across the brain-body-world divisions. In Susan Hurley's memorable phrase, the advocate of ECM denies that the skin is a kind of 'magical membrane', arguing that 'in principle what explains phenomenal qualities can be distributed within the brain, among brain and body, or among brain, body, and embedding environment, depending on the explanatory dynamics' (Hurley 2010: 116).

One might be tempted to dismiss ECM on the grounds that dream experience is clearly produced by brain-bound processes. However, this objection would be far too quick, for only the most radical versions of ECM deny that consciousness *can* arise from brain-based activity alone. Instead, most versions of ECM hold only that consciousness need not be confined to the brain but can 'loop out' into the body and environment. Moreover, given that the kinds of experiences that occur in sleep differ in fairly fundamental ways from those that characterize waking awareness, it wouldn't be unreasonable to suggest that the former might not be brain-bound even if the latter are. For parallel reasons, the fact that neuroscientist can trigger certain types of experiences by directly stimulating the brain isn't evidence that experience in general is brain-bound.

What about the case for ECM? One of the most influential arguments for ECM is due to Kevin O'Regan and Alva Noë (2001), who argue that there is a tension between the sparseness with which the visual system represents the environment and the apparent richness of visual phenomenology. This tension, they argue, can be resolved by denying that visual experience is fully determined by activity in the visual system, and embracing instead an 'enactivist' conception of consciousness, according to which visual experience involves a temporally extended process of skilful exploration of the environment. Critics push back against this argument in two ways. Some take issue with O'Regan and Noë's claims about the poverty of representations in the visual system, arguing that there is enough complexity in the contents of brain-bound representations to account for the richness of visual phenomenology. Others argue that the apparent richness of visual phenomenology is an illusion and that the bandwidth of visual experience is actually highly impoverished.

Further reading

Noë, A. 2009. *Out of Our Heads. Why You Are Not Your Brain and Other Lessons from the Biology of Consciousness*. Hill and Wang.
Vold, K. In Press. Can Consciousness Extend? *Philosophical Topics*, 48/1.
Vold, K. 2020. Can Consciousness Extend? *Philosophical Topics*, 48/1: 243-264.
Thompson, E. 2014. *Waking, Dreaming, Being*. Columbia University Press.

Let's return to Otto and Inga. At the heart of the MoMA argument is the claim that 'insofar as beliefs and desires are characterized by their explanatory roles, Otto's and Inga's cases seem to be on a par: the essential causal dynamics of the two cases mirror each other precisely' (Clark & Chalmers 1998: 13). To reject the essential parity between Otto and Inga, Clark and Chalmers claim, would be to engage in a form of 'neurochauvinism'.[15]

Do the causal dynamics of the Otto and Inga cases mirror each other precisely? There are certainly important respects in which the causal role of the information in Otto's notebook is akin to the causal role of the information in Inga's biological memory. As Clark and Chalmers point out, Otto's reliance on his notebook might be 'automatic and unreflective' in much the way in which Inga's reliance on her biologically based recall is. In the same way that Inga's memory is (generally) available to her as and when she needs it, so too Otto's notebook is (generally) ready to hand. And just as Otto's notebook can be damaged, so too Inga's biological memory can also be compromised.

So far, perhaps so good. But there are also respects in which Otto's situation differs from Inga's. Consider, for example, the kinds of content that Otto and Inga use to arrive at MoMA. Otto needs to interpret the representations in his notebook, for they have their content only in virtue of the conventions that govern English. In contrast, no such interpretation is needed in Inga's case, for the representations that guide her have 'underived' content. This difference, some have argued, undermines the MoMA argument, for genuine cognition requires underived content (Adams & Aizawa 2001; Fodor 2009).

Extended mind theorists respond to this objection in various ways. Some theorists express doubt about the very idea of underived (or 'original') intentionality, suggesting that all content depends on convention and interpretation (e.g., Clark 2005). Another response – and one that I myself find more compelling – allows that mental content is typically underived, but resists the assumption that cognition is restricted to states with underived content. As Menary (2010) points out, there is strong evidence that certain brain-based cognitive processes (such as those involved in mental arithmetic) use natural language representations. Thus, any attempt to argue that Otto's notebook-based processing isn't genuinely mental because it involves underived content would threaten to exclude many processes that seem to clearly qualify as cognitive.

Another respect in which Otto's situation differs from Inga's concerns the profile of their behavioural capacities. As an example of this difference, consider what psychologists call the recency and primacy effects, in which the recall of words that have just been presented in a list of to-be-recalled words is typically better for words at the start (the primacy effect) and the end (the recency effect) of the list than it is for words in the middle of the list. As Frederick Adams and Kenneth Aizawa (2008) point out, if we were to present 20 words to Inga in succession, then would expect her to be more likely to recall words that occur at the start and the end of the list than those that occur in the middle. However, we wouldn't expect to see these effects in Otto's performance, for he would be able to write each word down as it was presented to him.

What should we make of this objection? It is certainly true that Inga's 'biological memory' operates very differently from Otto's 'artefactual memory'. The critical question is whether these differences disqualify Otto's use of his notebook as counting as a kind of memory. As far as I can see, they don't. At most, the kinds of differences that Adams and Aizawa point to show that the study of (ordinary) human memory won't apply to Otto. But that is something that the advocate of the extended mind hypothesis will concede, for it is no part of their view that extended mental processes have precisely the same functional profile as their internal analogues. Indeed, as John Sutton (2010) has noted, extended cognitive processes are often valuable precisely *because* their functional profile differs from that of purely internal ones. The point on which the advocate of the extended mind hypothesis should insist is only that any differences between the brain-bound processes of the kind on which Inga relies and the world-involving processes of the kind on which Otto relies are not essential to their identities as mental states of a certain kind.

To my mind, the most powerful argument objection to the MoMA argument is due to Daniel Weiskopf (2008), who argues that the information stored in Otto's notebook is too passive to qualify as the material basis of belief. As Weiskopf points out, we expect beliefs to be dynamically integrated with each other, in the sense that changes in any one region of a person's web of belief will typically trigger changes in other regions of that web. For example, if one learns that two people are married, then one will typically believe that they share the same address. If one subsequently discovers that the individuals in question are no longer married, then one will (again, typically) believe that they are unlikely to share the same address. Although this kind of updating doesn't always occur, it is part of the nature of belief that it ought to occur; when it does occur, it usually does so automatically, without conscious involvement. But, Weiskopf argues, the information that is stored in Otto's notebook will not be dynamically integrated with the rest of his mental life in this way. Inserting information into Otto's notebook won't automatically trigger adjustments to other parts of his mental economy, nor will changes in other parts of his mental economy have an automatic impact on the information encoded in his notebook. Thus, to the extent that the information in Otto's notebook isn't actively integrated into Otto's cognitive economy, it doesn't qualify a genuine belief.

Weiskopf's argument puts pressure on the idea that Otto's notebook counts as part of his mind, but it doesn't undermine the claim that the boundaries of the mind *could* extend beyond the skull. Perhaps the technology of the future will allow for dynamic integration of the kind required for genuine 'active externalism'. Indeed, the devices with which we each interact on a daily basis may already be active enough to qualify as parts of our mind, for they don't merely store information but also reach out and capture our attention, alerting us to upcoming appointments, incoming email, and changes to our heart-rate and blood-sugar level.

7.6 Conclusion

This chapter has explored one of the most discussed questions in the philosophy of mind over the last half century: are an agent's mental states 'brain-bound'? Externalists answer this question in the negative, arguing that there is a fundamental sense in which an individual's thoughts and/or perceptions depend on the environment in which they are embedded. Content externalists focus on the role that the environment plays in determining the contents of thought (and, perhaps, perception), whereas vehicle externalists focus on the role that the environment plays in grounding the very machinery of thought (and, perhaps, perception).

Externalism has received extensive attention not merely because of its inherent interest, but because its fortunes are intertwined with many of the most fundamental issues in the philosophy of mind. Content externalism raises questions about the relationship between linguistic content and mental content, and the degree to which the meaning of one's thoughts can come apart from the meaning of one's words. It raises questions about the relationship between intentionality and consciousness, and whether the phenomenal character of perception is fixed by its intentional content. And it raises questions about the scope and status of self-knowledge, and what it means for an agent to be authoritative with respect to their own thoughts.

Vehicle externalism too provokes questions that go far beyond its immediate concern with the boundaries of the mind. It raises questions about the relationship between derived and underived intentionality, and the role of natural language representations in mental processing. It raises questions about the nature of mental categories, and whether individual propositional attitudes must be automatically integrated into one's overall cognitive economy. And, finally, it raises questions about the material basis of consciousness, and whether there are properties of brains which render them uniquely capable of supporting experience. It's no wonder, then, that externalism has received as much attention as it has.

Further reading

For an excellent overview of the debate regarding content internalism and externalism, see Sarah Sawyer's 'Internalism and Externalism in Mind', in J. Garvey (ed.), *The Continuum Companion to the Philosophy of Mind* (Continuum International Publishing Group, pp. 133-50, 2011). For more on the question of whether there is a viable notion of narrow (internalist) content, see the papers by Sawyer and Gabriel Segal in B. McLaughlin and J. Cohen (eds.), *Contemporary Debates in Philosophy of Mind* (Blackwell, 2007). Also helpful are the chapters by Segal ('Narrow content') and Frances Egan ('Wide content') in B. McLaughlin, A. Beckermann, and S. Walter (eds.), *The Oxford Handbook of Philosophy of Mind* (OUP, 2009). For book-length studies of the internalism/externalism debate, see Joseph Mendola's *Anti-externalism* (OUP, 2008) and Juhani Yli-Vakkuri and John Hawthorne's *Narrow Content* (OUP, 2018).

For more on the alleged conflict between content externalism and privileged first-person access to the contents of one's thoughts, see Cynthia Macdonald's 'Externalism and First-Person Authority', *Synthese*, 104(1): 99-122 (1995); Jessica Brown's 'Semantic Externalism and Self-Knowledge', in B. McLaughlin, A. Beckermann, and S. Walter (eds.), *Oxford Handbook of Philosophy of Mind* (OUP, 2009) and the chapters by Anthony Brueckner and Michael McKinsey in B. McLaughlin and J. Cohen (eds.), *Contemporary Debates in Philosophy of Mind* (Blackwell, 2007). Two excellent collections of papers on externalism and self-knowledge are S. Nuccetelli's (ed.), *New Essays on Externalism and Self-Knowledge* (MIT Press, 2003) and Sanford C. Goldberg's (ed.), *Externalism, Self-Knowledge and Skepticism: New Essays* (CUP, 2015).

Introductions to the extended mind can be found in Richard Menary's *Cognitive Integration: Mind and Cognition Unbounded* (Palgrave Macmillan, 2007) and Anthony Chemero's *Radical Embodied Cognitive Science* (MIT Press, 2009). More critical treatments of the approach can be found in Rob Rupert's *Cognitive Systems and the Extended Mind* (OUP, 2009) and Fred Adams and Ken Aizawa's *The Bounds of Cognition* (Blackwell, 2008). Also critical (and rather fun) is Fodor's 'Where Is My Mind?' *London Review of Books*, 31(3) (2009). Brie Gertler provides an illuminating analysis of Clark and Chalmers's MoMA argument in her paper 'Overextending the Mind?', in B. Gertler and L. Shapiro (eds.), *Arguing about the Mind* (Routledge, 2007). For more on externalist approaches to consciousness, see Jesse Prinz's 'Is consciousness embodied?', in P. Robbins and M. Aydede (Eds) *The Cambridge Handbook of Situated Cognition* (CUP, 2009); David Ward's 'Enjoying the Spread: Conscious Externalism Reconsidered', *Mind*, 121(483): 731-51 (2012); and Diego Cosmelli and Evan Thompson's 'Embodiment or Envatment?: Reflections on the Bodily Basis of Consciousness', in J. Stewart, O. Gapenne, and E. A. Di Paolo (eds.), *Enaction: Toward a New Paradigm for Cognitive Science* (MIT Press, 2010).

Study questions

1. How does the kind of externalism that is motivated by the doppelgänger arguments (content externalism) differ from the kind of externalism that is motivated by the MoMA argument (vehicle externalism)?
2. In what ways does Putnam's argument for content externalism differ from Burge's? Which of the two arguments do you find more plausible?
3. It is sometimes suggested that the doppelgänger arguments conflate mental content with linguistic content (i.e., the content of public language representations). Evaluate this claim.

4   Discussions of externalism typically draw the border between the internal and the external at the agent's skin. Why is this conception of the relevant border problematic? Where and how should the border between the 'inner' and the 'outer' be located?
5   What do phenomenal externalists mean when they say that 'qualia aren't in the head'? Explain and evaluate the primary argument for phenomenal externalism.
6   Is there is a conflict between content externalism and self-knowledge?
7   Some theorists object to Clark and Chalmers's MoMA argument on the grounds that the representations in Otto's notebook have only underived (or original) intentionality. Is this a good objection?
8   What would it take to provide experimental evidence for or against the extended conscious mind (ECM) hypothesis?

Notes

1 Content externalism is also known as what-externalism (Hurley 2010), passive externalism (Clark & Chalmers 1998), and taxonomic externalism (Wilson 2004).
2 Vehicle externalism is also known as how-externalism (Hurley 2010), active externalism (Clark & Chalmers 1998), and locational externalism (Wilson 2004).
3 For an exception, see Hurley (2010), who argues that the debate is first and foremost a debate about the *explanation* of mental phenomena, and that it is not best understood in terms of supervenience.
4 This isn't *quite* right. For reasons that will soon become clear, Oscar and his twin cannot be perfect doppelgängers.
5 Putnam actually assumed that the thoughts of Oscar and his twin have the same contents, and that only the meanings of their words differ. As he put it: 'The extension of the term "water" (and, in fact, its meaning, in the preanalytical usage of the term) is not a function of the psychological state of the speaker by itself' (Putnam 1975b: 585).
6 Burge's argument doesn't actually invoke doppelgängers but instead contrasts a single individual in two contexts (one in which 'arthritis' is used to refer to arthritis and another in which it is used to refer to tharthritis). However, this point seems to me to be merely superficial, and I present Burge's argument in terms of doppelgängers in order to bring out the deep commonalities between it and Putnam's argument.
7 The notion of incomplete understanding is also an important theme in Millikan's work on concepts. See in particular Millikan (2000) and Millikan (2010). For more on incomplete understanding see Wikforss (2004).
8 See, e.g., Bach (1987), Crane (1991), Farkas (2008b), Mendola (2008), Patterson (1990), and Segal (2000).
9 Versions of this approach can be found in Block (1986), Chalmers (2002), Fodor (1987), Loar (1988), and White (1982). For discussion, see Mendola (2008) and Stalnaker (1989, 1990).
10 Naïve realism (Section 4.1) provides another route to phenomenal externalism (or at least something very much like it).
11 A parallel challenge is that the truth of content externalism would render access to the world too easy. If one has a priori access to the fact that one is (say) thinking about water, and if one also has a priori access to the fact that one can think about water only if the world contains water, then (one might argue) one would also have a priori access to the fact that water exists,. But (the objection continues), surely knowledge that there is water is not a priori but requires empirical investigation. For discussion see (e.g.) McKinsey (1991), Brown (1995), Boghossian (1997) and Sawyer (1998).
12 For more on self-knowledge and discriminability, see Brown (2008), Hohwy (2002), and Goldberg (2006).
13 Clark and Chalmers were not the first to develop ideas of this kind, and a number of other defences of the extended mind hypothesis appeared at roughly the same time, including Dennett (1996), Haugeland (1998; originally published 1995), Hurley (1998), Hutchins (1995), McClamrock (1995), and Wilson (1994).

14 See Rupert (2004) for an insightful discussion of the contrast between content externalism and vehicle externalism.
15 More generally, Clark and Chalmers argue that our approach to the mind ought to be governed by what they call the *parity principle*: 'If, as we confront some task, a part of the world functions as a process which, *were it done in the head*, we would have no hesitation in recognizing as part of the cognitive process, then that part of the world *is* (so we claim) part of the cognitive process' (1998: 8).

8 The metaphysics of consciousness

Chapter overview

- Introduces three influential consciousness-based challenges to physicalism: Nagel's bat argument, Jackson's knowledge argument, and Chalmers's zombie argument
- Considers the two central strategies that physicalists have developed for responding to those challenges: Type-A strategies and Type-B strategies
- Examines illusionist accounts of consciousness
- Provides an overview of two non-physicalist accounts of the metaphysics of consciousness: dualism and Russellian monism.

Physicalism has been challenged on various grounds. Some argue that the nature of human freedom is at odds with the claims of physicalism. Others argue that physicalism cannot account for intentionality and our capacity to think about things that don't exist. But for many, the most serious challenges to physicalism derive from consciousness. The physicalist might be able to account for our capacity to act freely or to think about non-existent objects, but, so the argument runs, she cannot account for what it's like to see the sun going down, soak in a warm bath, or listen to the opening lines of Billie Holiday's *Strange Fruit*.

This chapter focuses on three consciousness-based objections to physicalism: Thomas Nagel's bat argument, Frank Jackson's knowledge argument, and David Chalmers's zombie argument. I will call these arguments *the anti-physicalist arguments*. A common thread runs through them, for they all attempt to make vivid the idea that there is a deep – and potentially unbridgeable – gap between knowledge of the physical world and knowledge of consciousness. The existence of such a gap appears to pose a problem for physicalism, for the physicalist holds that the mental realm is nothing over and above material form and structure. If the physicalist denies that a complete description of the mental can be derived from a complete description of the world's physical properties, then it looks as though something over and above the physical facts must determine the mental facts.

DOI: 10.4324/9781003225348-9

We begin (Section 8.1) by introducing the three anti-physicalist arguments. Sections 8.2 and 8.3 examine the two dominant strategies for responding to them: the Type-A strategy and the Type-B strategy. In Section 8.4, we consider another physicalist response to the challenge of consciousness: illusionism. The chapter concludes (Section 8.5) by discussing two non-physicalist conceptions of consciousness: dualism and Russellian monism.

8.1 Bats, neuroscientists, and zombies

The bat

In his paper 'What Is It Like to Be a Bat?', Thomas Nagel argues that the inscrutability of the bat's conscious perspective creates a problem for physicalism. Although we can reasonably assume (says Nagel) that bats are conscious, no amount of information about a bat's neurophysiology or its behavioural capacities will tell us what kind of experiences a bat has. Nagel allows that we can imagine what it would be like for *us* to echolocate, but he argues that that would fall short of providing us with any insight into what it's like *for a bat* to echolocate. As Nagel sees it, the fundamental problem here concerns our inability to form concepts that can capture the bat's perspective. Because our capacity to form concepts of experience is restricted to the kinds of experiences that we have, alien forms of experience of the kind that the bat might have will be beyond our capacity to grasp. Nagel concludes that facts about what it is like for a certain type of organism to be the organism that it is are accessible only from a certain point of view.[1]

But if that it is so, Nagel argues, then physicalism is faced with a profound challenge. As he puts it:

> If physicalism is to be defended, the phenomenological features must themselves be given a physical account. But when we examine their subjective character it seems that such a result is impossible. The reason is that every subjective phenomenon is essentially connected with a single point of view, and it seems inevitable that an objective, physical theory will abandon that point of view.
>
> (1974: 437)

Nagel himself doesn't argue that physicalism is false – 'It would', he says, 'be truer to say that physicalism is a position we cannot understand because we do not at present have any conception of how it might be true' (1974: 446) – but his discussion does provide the materials for an objection to physicalism. We might call it the 'bat argument':

1. The phenomenological features of an organism's experiences are accessible only from one point of view (namely, the point of view had by organisms of that very type).
2. If physicalism were true, then the phenomenological features of an organism's experiences would not be accessible only from a single point of view.

Therefore,

C Physicalism is false.

The neuroscientist

Mary, a brilliant neuroscientist in the distant future, is an expert in the perception of colour (Jackson 1982). Neuroscience is basically complete at this point, and Mary's knowledge of the physical processes involved in colour perception is exhaustive: she knows everything there is to know about how we perceive colour. But Mary has been confined to a black-and-white room for her entire life. She has never seen colours, nor has she experienced colour imagery. One day she is released from her room and experiences a world of coloured objects. What happens when Mary first sees red?

According to Jackson, Mary learns *what it's like to see red*. Learning what it's like to see red involves learning a fact that was not accessible to Mary whilst she was confined to her black-and-white room. But if that is right (the argument continues), then what it's like to see red cannot be a physical fact, for Mary knew all the relevant physical facts. This argument is known as the knowledge argument, and can be formulated thus:

1   Mary learns something when she first sees red.
2   If physicalism were true, then Mary would not learn anything new when she first sees red.

Therefore,

C   Physicalism is false.

The zombie

As we noted in Chapter 2, philosophical zombies differ from the zombies of popular culture and science fiction. The zombies of B-grade films are slow and sluggish, and can be identified by their thousand-yard stare and bloody eyes. Philosophical zombies, by contrast, are utterly unremarkable, for they are indiscernible from ordinary humans (Kirk 1974, 2005; Chalmers 1996). In fact, your zombie twin has exactly the same physical, functional, and behavioural properties that you do. The only thing that distinguishes you from your zombie twin is the fact that you are conscious but your zombie twin isn't.

Zombies pose a challenge to physicalism, for physicalists are committed to the metaphysical impossibility of zombies. Why is that? Well, the physicalist holds that the physical facts strongly (i.e., metaphysically) necessitate the phenomenal facts, and if that is so, then any creature that is your physical (functional, behavioural) twin must also be your phenomenal twin.[2] In other words, they must be conscious. But if a creature is conscious, then by definition, it isn't a zombie. Thus, physicalism rules out the possibility of you having a zombie twin. But – the zombie argument continues – there is good reason to think that zombies are metaphysically possible, for they are conceivable. Given the laws of nature, it might not be possible for your zombie twin to exist in the actual world, but it is – so the zombie argument holds – the kind of thing that *could* have existed. There is, as philosophers like to say, 'a possible world' in which you have a zombie twin (Chalmers 1996).

We can formulate the zombie argument as follows:

1   Zombies are conceivable.
2   If zombies are conceivable, then they are metaphysically possible.

3 Zombies are metaphysically possible. (From 1 and 2)
4 If physicalism were true, then zombies would not be metaphysically possible.

Therefore,

C Physicalism is false. (From 3 and 4)

Let us take stock. Although there are important differences between these three anti-physicalist arguments, it is what they have in common that is most striking. All three arguments attempt to make vivid what Joseph Levine (1983; 2009) has called the 'explanatory gap' intuition, according to which there is no deep explanatory connection between phenomenal states and physical/functional states. The experiences associated with soaking in a warm bath might be correlated with a certain kind of physical/functional state, but there seems to be no way of removing the sense of contingency that surrounds the relationship between physical/functional states on the one hand and consciousness on the other.

The explanatory gap – or rather, gaps (Box: Mind the gaps) – is at the root of what David Chalmers (1995) has famously dubbed 'the hard problem': how can the experiential dimensions of consciousness be accounted for in physical terms? Chalmers contrasts 'the hard problem' of consciousness with 'the easy problems' associated with consciousness, such as how to explain our ability to identify objects, integrate information, and report on our internal states. Chalmers labels these problems 'easy' not because he wishes to trivialize them, but because we have a conception of how they might be solved and have well-established methods for tackling them. Neither of these claims, he argues, is true of the hard problem.

Box: Mind the gaps

Although he coined the phrase, Joseph Levine wasn't the first to notice the explanatory gap, and earlier discussions of it can be found in Tyndall (1871), Broad (1925), and Ewing (1962). Indeed, it is even possible to see the explanatory gap at work in Leibniz's (1714/1989) argument that thinking, feeling, and perceiving cannot be explained in mechanical terms.

Two kinds of explanatory gaps can be distinguished: a *specific* explanatory gap and a *generic* explanatory gap (see Figure 8.1). The specific explanatory gap involves explaining why a certain type of physical/functional state is associated with a certain type of conscious state rather than another. For example, one might ask why one kind of physical/functional state (N1) is associated with the experience of tasting chocolate while a second kind of physical/functional state (N2) is associated with the experience of hearing an oboe. The generic explanatory gap involves explaining why certain types of physical/functional states (N1 and N2) are associated with conscious states (of any kind) while others (N3) aren't.

Corresponding to these two explanatory gaps are two versions of the 'hard problem' (Chalmers 1996). There is the specific hard problem of explaining why what it's like to (say) taste chocolate is different from what it's like to (say) hear an oboe, and there is the generic hard problem of explaining why it's like anything at all for an agent when she tastes chocolate or hears an oboe.

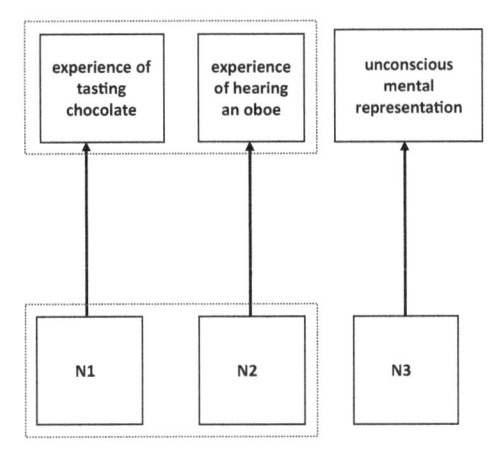

Figure 8.1 The specific explanatory gap and the generic explanatory gap

Further reading

Chalmers, D. 2008. The Hard Problem of Consciousness. In M. Velmans and S. Schneider (eds.), *The Blackwell Companion to Consciousness*. Wiley-Blackwell.

Levine, J. 2009. The Explanatory Gap. In B. McLaughlin, A. Beckermann, and S. Walter (eds.), *The Oxford Handbook of Philosophy of Mind*. Oxford University Press.

We can capture the common thread that unites the anti-physicalist arguments by appealing to the notion of a priori scrutability (Chalmers 2012). Roughly speaking, one proposition (P) is a priori scrutable from another (Q) just in case the truth of P is deducible from the truth of Q. This idea is sometimes put in terms of what a Laplacean demon (Horgan 1983; Byrne 1999) – that is, a being with unlimited time and computational power, and who has the necessary concepts – would be able to deduce by reasoning alone (from its armchair, as it were). If the Laplacean demon would be able to deduce Q from P, then Q is a priori scrutable from P; if not, then Q is inscrutable from P. (The proposition 'There are squares' is a priori scrutable from the proposition 'There are closed, 4-sided, figures with internal angles of 90 degrees'. By contrast, the proposition 'There are koalas' is not a priori scrutable from the proposition 'There are closed, 4-sided, figures with internal angles of 90 degrees'.) The fact that the phenomenal truths don't appear to be a priori scrutable from the physical truths poses a prima facie challenge to physicalism, for if the phenomenal truths are 'nothing over and above' the physical truths then, one might think, they ought to be a priori scrutable from them.

We can encapsulate this line of thought in terms of *the inscrutability argument*:

1   If physicalism were true, then the phenomenal truths would be a priori scrutable from the physical truths. (The bridging premise)
2   The phenomenal truths are not a priori scrutable from the physical truths. (The inscrutability premise)

Therefore,

C   Physicalism is false.

Responses to the inscrutability argument (and, by extension, each of the three anti-physicalist arguments) can be divided into two broad classes. Type-B physicalists reject the bridging premise (premise 1), arguing that the physicalist need not assume that the phenomenal truths can be read off from the physical truths. Type-A physicalists reject the inscrutability premise (premise 2), arguing instead that the phenomenal truths are (or at least might be) a priori scrutable from the physical truths. We begin with Type-A physicalism and the prospects of the inscrutability presmise.

8.2 Type-A physicalism and the inscrutability premise

Each of the anti-physicalist arguments assumes that there are questions about consciousness that even complete knowledge of the physical facts would leave unanswered. Type-A physicalists push back against that assumption. For all we know, they argue, a complete description of a bat's physical profile *would* enable one to work out what it's like to be a bat; Mary would be able to work out what it's like to see red before leaving her black-and-white room; and a comprehensive understanding of the brain would render the zombie hypothesis inconceivable.

Type-A physicalists have developed three somewhat independent strategies for undermining the inscrutability premise. In discussing these strategies, I will generally focus on the knowledge argument, and will leave it as an exercise for the reader to consider how they might be applied to the other anti-physicalist arguments.

The ability hypothesis

Despite her exhaustive knowledge of the psychology and neuroscience of colour perception, we assume that Mary would learn something (namely, what it's like to see red) when she first sees strawberries. Advocates of the knowledge argument hold that if this is right, then physicalism is in trouble, for how could Mary learn anything if what it's like to see red is a physical fact, and, by hypothesis, Mary already knows all of the relevant physical facts?

According to advocates of the *ability hypothesis* (Nemirow 1990, 2007; Lewis 1997), the answer involves recognizing that what Mary acquires when she first sees red isn't knowledge of new facts or propositions but of something else altogether. What Mary learns can't be propositional, they argue, for she would learn something new when leaving her black-and-white room no matter what information she had:

> Let parapsychology be the science of all the non-physical things, properties, causal processes, laws of nature and so forth that may be required to explain the things we do.... Black-and-white Mary may study all the parapsychology as well as all the psychophysics of colour vision, but she still won't know what it's like.
>
> (Lewis 1997: 289)

In short, book learning won't help Mary, whatever it is that we put in the books. But if that is so, then what Mary learns can't just be a matter of information. What, then, *does* Mary learn?

According to the ability hypothesis, Mary acquires know-how. Learning what it's like to see red isn't a matter of acquiring new information ('know-that'), but of acquiring a new set of skills. It's akin to learning how to use chopsticks, learning how to recognize a C-38 locomotive, and learning how to wriggle your ears. It's a matter of acquiring new abilities. What abilities? Roughly, abilities to remember, imagine, and recognize certain types of experiences. In this way the ability hypothesis promises to capture the intuition that Mary learns something when she leaves her black-and-white room, without giving up on the idea that the phenomenal truths can be deduced from the physical truths. But is it plausible to suppose that phenomenal knowledge (i.e., the kind of knowledge that Mary acquires when she leaves her black-and-white room) is merely a kind of know-how?

One reason to think that phenomenal knowledge isn't just a kind of know-how is that it can be used to support conditionals (Loar 1997; Lycan 1995). For example, one can think to oneself, 'If strawberries hadn't tasted like *this*, then I wouldn't have liked them as much as I do'. However, if phenomenal knowledge is knowledge of how to do something, then it's unclear how it could support conditionals of this kind. Another reason to think that phenomenal knowledge is propositional is that it enables one to form new hypotheses, as when one wonders whether strawberries taste like *this* to someone else. But perhaps the strongest objections to the ability hypothesis is due to Martine Nida-Rümelin (1996a, 1998).

Nida-Rümelin invites us to imagine another expert neuroscientist, Marianna, who is restricted to a black-and-white room from which she too is eventually liberated. However, instead of being released into an environment of ordinary objects such as tomatoes and fire engines, Marianna's first experience of colour is restricted to abstract paintings. We can imagine that she sees swatches of red, yellow, and blue. Intuitively, Marianna learns what it's like to see red, yellow, and blue. She is now in a position to pose new questions to herself, such as 'Do strawberries look like *this* [red] or *that* [yellow]?' However, only when she interacts with a world of coloured objects will she be in a position to answer these questions. ('Ah - so *that's* what strawberries look like!'). The key point here is that even when one knows what it's like to see red (as Marianna does once she's seen the paintings), there can still be open questions (such as 'What do strawberries look like?') that one may be unable to answer. But if that is so, then what Mary learns when she leaves her black-and-white room isn't restricted to know-how, but must also include know-that.

There is much more to say about the ability hypothesis, but let's turn now to a pair of Type-A responses which assume, as most physicalists do, that phenomenal knowledge is a species of propositional knowledge.[3]

Failures of imagination and the optimistic induction

'Imagine a neuroscientist of the future', Jackson says, 'who has complete knowledge of the neurophysiology of colour perception'. We nod our heads and take ourselves to have done precisely that. Although we don't (of course!) know what Mary knows, we assume that we know the *kinds* of things that she knows, such as information about the structure and function of neural processes. We also assume that no amount of knowledge of that kind would enable Mary to work out 'what it's like' to see red. In short, we assume that Mary would be *surprised* when she first sees strawberries.

But, we might ask, why assume that our intuitions about Mary's responses are trustworthy? Given our ignorance of neurophysiology, wouldn't it be more reasonable to say that we really have no idea what Mary might be able to figure out from inside her black-and-white room? And how could we possibly know what a Laplacean demon would (or, as the case may be, wouldn't) be able to derive from the set of all the fundamental physical truths? After all, we don't know what the fundamental physical truths are, nor are we Laplacean demons! Perhaps our inability to imagine how the explanatory gap could be bridged is nothing more than a cognitive failing on our part rather than a deep insight into the nature of reality (Churchland 1996; Dennett 2006).

This kind of pessimism about the reliability of our intuitions is often accompanied by a rosy optimism about the progress of science. Here, for example, is Searle:

> The 'mystery' of consciousness today is in roughly the same shape that the mystery of life was in before the development of molecular biology or the mystery of electromagnetism was before Clerk-Maxwell's equations. It seems mysterious because we do not know how the system of neurophysiology/consciousness works, and an adequate knowledge of how it works would remove the mystery ... given a full understanding of the brain, it seems to me likely that we would think it obvious that if the brain was in a certain sort of state, it had to be conscious.
>
> (Searle 1992: 102)

The appeal to life is a familiar theme in responses of this kind. The vitalists of the 19th century thought that life posed an unbridgeable explanatory gap, for they couldn't imagine how living organisms could be built up out of inanimate parts. However, we now know that they were wrong. The lesson here (the argument continues) is twofold: not only should we treat the intuition that consciousness poses an unbridgeable explanatory gap with suspicion, we also have good reason to think that science will demystify consciousness just as it has demystified life. Call this latter claim the 'optimistic induction'.[4]

There is much to be said for the optimistic induction, for science does indeed have an excellent track record of solving problems that baffled previous generations. At the same time, there are reasons to think that the problem of consciousness is unique in important respects, and that lessons gleaned from the study of other phenomena (such as life) might not apply to consciousness. Arguably, the concept of life is a purely structural and functional concept. Roughly speaking, to judge that something is alive is to judge that has homeostatic mechanisms which function to maintain the integrity of its borders. The vitalists concluded that life couldn't be reductively understood, for they couldn't imagine how these structural and functional features could be explained. We now know that they were suffering from a failure of imagination. The concept of consciousness, by contrast, doesn't appear to be purely structural and functional. Indeed, that is arguably one of lessons of the anti-physicalist arguments. (If the concept of consciousness were purely structural and functional, then zombies ought to be inconceivable.) As interesting as the history of the study of life is, it may have little bearing on the metaphysics of consciousness (Box: Mysterianism).

Box: Mysterianism

Those who push back against the optimistic induction often draw attention to the fact that we are cognitively limited creatures, and that the solution to the problem of consciousness may be beyond our ken. In the same way that foxes might know a lot about chickens but lack the cognitive machinery to master number theory or quantum mechanics, so too, it is reasonable to assume that there are problems that we ourselves lack the cognitive machinery to solve. According to some theorists, such as Colin McGinn, the problem of consciousness is precisely one such problem. This view is known as 'Mysterianism'. The idea here is not that consciousness is inherently mysterious – indeed, McGinn explicitly compares it to life, arguing that consciousness too 'must be a natural phenomenon, naturally arising from certain organizations of matter' (McGinn 1989: 353) – but that it is intractably mysterious to us. We have the mental machinery to formulate the problem of consciousness (in some sense, at least), but we lack the intellectual powers to solve it.

Further reading

McGinn, C. 1989. Can We Solve the Mind-Body Problem? *Mind*, 98: 349–66.
Stoljar, D. 2006. *Ignorance and Imagination*. Oxford University Press.

Intentionalism

The advocate of the optimistic induction holds that the materials for bridging the explanatory will come from developments in our understanding of the brain. A rather different Type-A strategy holds that focusing on the brain as such won't close the explanatory gap, but that we should instead focus on the relationship between the phenomenal aspects of the mind and its intentional (or, as it is more commonly put, representational) properties.

According to intentionalists, the phenomenal character of an experience is determined by its intentional properties. We first encountered intentionalism in Chapter 4. Our focus there was on intentionalism as an account of the phenomenal character of perception, but here we are interested in a version of intentionalism that has unrestricted scope and applies to phenomenal properties of all kinds.

To see how intentionalism might bear on the anti-physicalist arguments, let's consider a response to Nagel developed by Kathleen Akins (1993a, 1993b). Akins argues that the key to answering Nagel's question is to identify the bat's representational capacities. What features of the world is the bat sensitive to? What properties of its environment does it react to? What can it do with the information that it receives from its senses? Answering questions of this kind, Akins argues, will enable us to get a grip on what, if anything, it's like (for a bat) to be a bat. The thought here is that the gap between the physical and the phenomenal isn't going to be closed by focusing on the bat's neural activity as such, but by attending to how that activity enables the bat to represent its environment.[5]

Intentionalism is controversial. Many argue that there are aspects of perceptual phenomenology that aren't determined by intentional properties (as we noted in Chapter 4), and even those who hold that all *perceptual* phenomenology is intentional often express doubt about the intentionalist's treatment of other forms of experience, such as those involving bodily sensations and moods (see Chapter 9). Indeed, the anti-physicalist arguments are themselves a source of resistance to intentionalism, for they are often taken to show that the phenomenal character of an agent's experiences can't be captured by appealing to their intentional features.

Even if intentionalism can help to close the specific explanatory gap, it is unclear that it has the resources to close the generic explanatory gap. In other words, even if the intentionalist can explain why a certain kind of state feels like *this* rather than *that*, it is a further question whether she can also explain why certain kinds of representational states 'feel like' anything at all. And until intentionalists can answer *that* question, they won't have fully addressed the problem of consciousness.

8.3 Type-B physicalism and the bridging premise

Let us leave Type-A physicalism to one side and turn to Type-B physicalism. Type-B physicalists reject the bridging premise, arguing that physicalists need not assume that the phenomenal truths are a priori scrutable from the physical truths. The existence of a conceptual or epistemic gap between the physical and the phenomenal, the Type-B physicalist argues, is perfectly consistent with the absence of any kind of ontological gap between the physical and the phenomenal.

Broadly speaking, two Type-B strategies can be distinguished. Advocates of the first strategy argue that explanatory gaps aren't unique to consciousness, and that the truths of the special sciences (such as biology, chemistry, and psychology) are not generally derivable from the truths of fundamental physics. Advocates of the second strategy allow that there is a kind of explanatory gap that is (more or less) unique to consciousness, but that consciousness has features which allow the physicalist to explain away the appearance of this gap. Let's consider these two strategies in turn.

Physicalism and the appeal to a priori scrutability

At the heart of the problem of consciousness is the idea that consciousness poses a kind of challenge to physicalism that other high-level phenomena (digestion, respiration, photosynthesis, etc.) do not. After all, if garden-variety physical truths such as 'Fido is digesting his dinner' aren't derivable from the fundamental physical truths, then the claim that the phenomenal truths aren't derivable from the fundamental physical truths wouldn't really be newsworthy. Instead, the rational response would surely be to deny that physicalism about a domain requires that the truths of that domain must be a priori scrutable from the fundamental physical truths.

Are garden-variety physical truths derivable from the fundamental physical truths? A number of philosophers say no.[6] Scientific reductions, they argue, are typically 'gappy', for high-level properties can rarely be derived from more fundamental levels of description. Even a Laplacean demon, they claim, wouldn't be able to establish the truth of 'Water is H_2O' from its armchair. Other theorists – known as 'a priori physicalists' – deny that fully reductive explanations of high-level phenomena are 'gappy'.[7] As they see it, 'Water is H_2O' is a posteriori only because *we* lack access to the totality of the physical facts. From the perspective of a Laplacean demon the truth of that proposition would be a priori scrutable from the fundamental physical truths, for (this line of thought continues) water can be identified with (roughly) the colourless, odourless stuff that falls from the sky around here and fills the oceans, lakes, and rivers, and it will be evident to anyone who has the concept WATER and knows all the fundamental physical truths that H_2O meets that description and hence is water. The debate between these two positions echoes the debate between a priori physicalists and a posteriori physicalists that we encountered in Chapter 2 (Section 2.4), and is part of a larger debate about the status of posteriori claims in the philosophy of mind (Box: Consciousness and a posteriori necessities).

Box: Consciousness and a posteriori necessities

Prior to Saul Kripke's (1980) *Naming and Necessity*, it was generally assumed that if a statement was a posteriori than it was contingent and vice versa. This posed a challenge to identity theorists, for the identities that they posited were clearly a posteriori rather than a priori, and thus they felt compelled to conclude that mind-brain identities must be contingent.

However, Kripke showed (or at least seemed to show) that statements such as 'Water is H_2O' and 'Heat is molecular motion' can be both necessarily true and a posteriori. Building on Kripke's work, many physicalists argued that the identification of conscious states with brain states could also be treated as a posteriori necessities. In the same way that it is conceivable that water might not have been H_2O despite the fact that it is necessarily H_2O, so too – the argument goes – it is conceivable that consciousness might not have been a physical process, despite the fact that the identity between consciousness and certain physical processes is necessary.

However, the suggestion that mind-brain identity claims could be both a posteriori and necessary has proven controversial. Kripke (1980) himself rejected it on the grounds that there is a crucial difference between a posteriori necessities such as 'Water is H_2O' and putative mind-brain identities such as 'Pain is the firing of C-fibres'. In the former case, the appearance of contingency can be explained away, for what we conceive of when we conceive of a scenario in which water isn't H_2O is the existence of something ('watery stuff') that seems to be water but isn't. However, no parallel explanation can be provided in the case of mind-brain identities. Pain, Kripke argues, 'is not picked out by one of its accidental properties; rather, it is picked out by the property of being pain itself, but its immediate phenomenological quality' (Kripke 1980: 152) Thus, Kripke concludes, there is no way to explain away the appearance of contingency that accompanies putative mind-brain identity statements. Questions regarding the nature of a posteriori necessities and the role that they might play in the defence of physicalism remain highly contested.

Further reading

Chalmers, D. J. 2009. The Two-Dimensional Argument against Materialism. In B. McLaughlin (ed.), *Oxford Handbook of the Philosophy of Mind*. Oxford University Press, 313-39.

Goff, P., and D. Papineau. 2014. What's Wrong with Strong Necessities? *Philosophical Studies*, 167(3): 749-62.

Levine, J. 1998. Conceivability and the Metaphysics of Mind. *Noûs*, 32(4): 449-80.

This debate surrounding the a priori scrutability of high-level truths is a complex one, and we cannot attempt to settle it here. There is, however, one point to note by way of an interim verdict: even if 'explanatory gaps' are ubiquitous and high-level truths are not in general derivable from those of fundamental physics, there does seem to be something unique about the *kind* of gap posed by consciousness. Fully reductive explanations in other domains may not deliver a priori scrutability, but they do seem to demystify their targets in ways in which no reductive account of consciousness could. Or at least, so it is natural to think.

The phenomenal concept strategy

A second Type-B strategy assumes that the gap between the physical/functional and the phenomenal is unique (or at least almost so), and can be accounted for only by appealing to resources that are peculiar to consciousness. Lucky, advocates of this approach argue, such resources exist, for there are distinctive features of consciousness which explain why there seems to be a fundamental gap between the physical facts and the phenomenal facts.

Let's return to Mary in her black-and-white room. As you will recall, the knowledge argument rests on the claim that if physicalism were true, then Mary wouldn't learn anything when she first experiences red, for if what it's like to experience red is a physical fact, then Mary must have already known what it's like to experience red before leaving her room. This argument presupposes something like the following principle:

The Substitution Principle: If S knows fact P, and fact P is fact Q, then S knows fact Q.

The substitution principle is false, for one can know a single fact in different ways (via different 'modes of presentation', as it is sometimes said). For example, one can know that Michael Caine starred in *The Italian Job* without knowing that Maurice Micklewhite Jr. starred in *The Italian Job*, for one might be unaware that Michael Caine is Maurice Micklewhite Jr.

According to the phenomenal concept strategy (PCS), in the same way that facts about Michael Caine/Maurice Micklewhite Jr. can be known in two ways, so too can facts about experiences. The ordinary way of knowing about experiences involves the use of phenomenal concepts.[8] Phenomenal concepts refer to experiences in terms of what it's like have them (rather than in terms of their causal roles or their physical nature, for example). But because phenomenal concepts can be acquired only by having an experience of the relevant kind (or at least one that is very similar to it), Mary isn't able to represent experiences of red via a phenomenal concept until she leaves her room. However, pre-release Mary can represent experiences of red via the kinds of concepts used in science, i.e., in terms of a physical or functional concept. Thus, advocates of the PCS hold, when Mary leaves her black-and-white room for the first time she doesn't learn any new facts about experiences of red, for prior to her release she was able to represent all the relevant facts using her physical/functional concepts. What she acquires, instead, is the capacity to represent those facts in new ways, via phenomenal concepts. For this reason, the PCS is sometimes referred to as the 'new knowledge/old fact' response. The key idea here is that the explanatory gap doesn't reflect a gap between different types of phenomena (as the dualist thinks), but instead derives from a kind of incommensurability between different ways of representing or conceptualizing a single phenomenon.[9]

Critics have raised two types of objections to the PCS. One objection concerns the very notion of a 'phenomenal concept', and the idea that one can form concepts on the basis of introspective attention to the character of one's own experiences. Arguably, it must be possible for any concept to be misapplied (i.e., to be applied to an object that doesn't fall under it). But – the worry goes – if the content of a phenomenal concept is exhausted by the character of the experience to which one is attending, then it is not clear that phenomenal concepts *could* be misapplied – at least when it comes to the first-person case. As Wittgenstein put it, 'Whatever is going to seem right to me is right, and that only means that here we can't talk about right' (1953/2009: §258). To invoke one of Wittgenstein's metaphors, first-person uses of phenomenal concepts can be likened to the claim of someone who says that they know how tall they are by laying their hand on top of their head (1953/2009: §279). Although the position of one's hand must indeed correspond to one's height, 'measuring' one's height in this way involves no independent content, and thus fails to qualify as a cognitive achievement in the way that the application of a concept must.[10]

Leaving worries about the notion of a phenomenal concept to one side, it is a further question whether phenomenal concepts could do the work that the PCS demands of them. The problem here is that failing to realize that two concepts are co-referential (i.e., refer to the same thing) typically involves ignorance of some additional fact. One can believe that Michael Caine starred in *The Italian Job* without believing that Maurice Micklewhite Jr. starred in *The Italian Job*, but only if there are certain facts of which one is unaware (such as that the names 'Michael Caine' and 'Maurice Micklewhite Jr.' refer to the same person). But if that is right, then it seems as though the proponent of the PCS must grant that Mary does learn a new fact when she first sees red, if only the fact that her phenomenal concept of red and her physical/functional concept of red are co-referential. That fact isn't quite the same fact that Jackson claimed that Mary learns when she first leaves her black-and-white room (namely, what it's like to see red), but as long as Mary learns *a new* fact when she first sees red, then the PCS is in trouble, for the point of the PCS is to explain how Mary can gain propositional knowledge without allowing that she learns any new facts at all.[11]

8.4 Illusionism

There is another physicalist response to the challenge of consciousness that doesn't fit neatly under either the 'Type-A' or 'Type-B' headings: illusionism. Illusionists argue that the aim of a science of consciousness shouldn't be to close the explanatory gap or to solve the hard problem, but to explain away the intuitions that lie behind these puzzles. The illusionist grants that we appear to have phenomenal states, but they argue that this appearance is mistaken: there are no phenomenal states. An analogy with stage magic may be instructive (Dennett 2016). Consider a magician who appears to produce a rabbit from an empty hat. It would be a mistake (of course) to take this appearance at face value, and to assume that what needs to be explained is how a live rabbit could emerge from an empty hat. Instead, what needs to be explained is how a rabbit could *seem* to emerge from an empty hat. Similarly, the illusionist claims, we shouldn't attempt to explain why phenomenal states exist. Instead, what needs to be explained is how the brain generates the illusion of phenomenality. The illusionist's slogan is, 'Don't fall for the trick!'

Although illusionists certainly adopt eliminativist language at times, for the most part they don't deny that consciousness exists, or that it has a subjective character, or that there is something it is like to (say) see colours, hear sounds, or smell odours (Dennett 1991b; Frankish 2016a). What the illusionist denies is that consciousness involves properties which are private, intrinsic, ineffable and with which we are directly acquainted. Although the distinction between consciousness and experience on the one hand and phenomenal properties on the other is potentially confusing – after all, Block (1995) introduced the term 'phenomenal consciousness' by saying that it's a synonym for 'experience' – the illusionist proposal is (tolerably) clear: instead of trying to explain why experiences have phenomenal properties, we should instead try to explain why they seem to have phenomenal properties (even though they don't) (Box: Chase, Sanborn, and the taste of coffee).[12]

Illusionism strikes many people as absurd and outrageous – perhaps even outright incoherent. In my view, however, it ought to be taken as seriously as any other approach to the problem of consciousness. Arguably, it avoids the problems facing both Type-A and Type-B physicalists. As we have seen, Type-A physicalists are vulnerable to the charge that they fail to take the explanatory gap seriously, while Type-B physicalists are vulnerable to the charge that they lack the tools to close the explanatory gap. The illusionist can argue that she takes the explanatory gap as seriously as the dualist does (for the illusionist can allow that the existence of phenomenal states would indeed be at odds with physicalism), but she avoids having to actually close the gap since she regards phenomenality as fictitious. Illusionism may be the view for you if you have physicalist sympathies but find neither Type-A nor Type-B physicalism compelling.[13]

> **Box: Chase, Sanborn, and the taste of coffee**
>
> One of the many intuition pumps that Dennett employs to motivate the case for illusionism is the story of Chase and Sanborn, two coffee tasters who have spent many years together working for Maxwell House coffee. Chase and Sanborn agree that something about their experience of coffee has changed, but they disagree – or at least appear to disagree – about what this change involves. Dennett (1988) imagines the following conversation between them:
>
> Chase: 'The coffee tastes the same as it did 6 years ago, but I no longer like it. My tastes have changed'.
>
> Sanborn: 'My tastes haven't changed, but my tasters have. Maxwell House coffee doesn't taste to me the way it used to taste; if it did, I'd still love it'.
>
> If phenomenal states are directly apprehensible, then both Chase and Sanborn should be right in their judgments about 'the taste' of the coffee. But, Dennett points out, there is little reason to think that one of them has phenomenal states that the other lacks, for their reactions to coffee are now identical. They can distinguish the taste of coffee from the taste of other substances, and they have the same suite of affective responses to coffee. But if 'the taste of coffee' is simply a convenient way of referring to how one is disposed to respond to coffee, then one has in effect given up on the idea that experiences of coffee involve properties that are both private (i.e., can be detected only by the subject who has them) and intrinsic (i.e., do not depend on anything other than the experience itself). The 'qualiaphile' can insist that the taste of coffee is directly apprehensible, but then they must deny that it is intrinsic. Alternatively, they can insist that the taste of coffee is intrinsic, but then they must deny that it is directly apprehensible. What they cannot do, Dennett argues, is insist that 'the taste of coffee' is both intrinsic and directly apprehensible. Dennett is here echoing a claim made by Brian Farrell many years earlier: although we can contrast 'experience' with 'behaviour' if behaviour is understood in terms of what one does and says, it is less clear that the contrast between experience and behaviour can be sustained when the latter notion is broadened to include 'the covert verbal and other responses of the person, his response readinesses, all of his relevant bodily states, and all of the possible discriminations he can make' (Farrell 1950: 177).
>
> **Further reading**
>
> Dennett, D. 1988. Quining Qualia. In A. J. Marcel and E. Bisiach (eds.), *Consciousness in Contemporary Science*. Oxford University Press.
> Farrell, B. A. 1950. Experience. *Mind*, 59: 170-98.

But for all its attractiveness, illusionism also faces a number of powerful objections. For one thing, there seems to be a crucial difference between stage magic and consciousness. In the former, we have good grip on what an illusion is, and of what it would be for how things are to differ from how they seem. The magician does indeed seem to produce a rabbit from an empty box, but we know that this seeming fails to reflect reality, even if we can't quite figure out how the trick was done. When it comes to consciousness, however, it is less clear that we have a grip on what the difference between appearance and reality might involve. Consciousness, one is tempted to say, *just is* a matter of how things seem.[14]

The key issue here, it seems to me, is whether the illusionist can explain (away) the appearance of phenomenal properties. Illusionists claim that such an explanation can be provided, but thus far they have only hinted at what it might look like (see Frankish 2016a, 2016b; Dennett 2016). If those hints can be turned into a fully worked-out account, then the force of their position may well be irresistible, for if the best explanations of the intuitions that drive the anti-physicalist arguments do not themselves require the existence of phenomenal consciousness then those arguments will have been undermined. However, it is important to recognize that illusionists really do need to account for these intuitions and not simply dismiss them. Just as accounting for the magician's trick requires recognizing that the rabbit really does seem to have been produced from an empty hat, so too accounting for consciousness requires recognizing that there really does seem to be a profound gap between brain activity and the magic of consciousness.

8.5 Dualism and Russellian monism

Let us turn now from the case against physicalist accounts of consciousness to the question of whether non-physicalist treatments of consciousness might fare any better.

Traditionally, the most influential alternative to physicalism has been dualism. Some dualists posit two kinds of non-physical phenomena: mental substances and mental properties. Most contemporary dualists, however, eschew any commitment to non-physical substances, and restrict the scope of their dualism to mental properties. (Indeed, some dualists accept that certain kinds of mental properties can be accounted for in physical terms, and argue only that phenomenal properties are non-physical.) According to the dualist, the connections between physical properties and phenomenal properties are merely contingent and involve the operation of primitive correlations between physical/functional properties and mental ones.

The chief stumbling block for dualism is often said to be mental causation. The problem, in a nutshell, is that if every event has a fully sufficient physical cause (as it appears to), then there seems to be no work for mental properties to do (unless, of course, mental properties are physical properties, as the physicalist holds). My own view is that this challenge is far from fatal. As we will see in Chapter 10, many versions of physicalism *also* face problems in providing a plausible account of mental causation, and it is far from clear that the challenges that dualists face in attempting to make sense of mental causation are more serious than those faced by many physicalists.

To my mind, the most serious objection to dualism is the fact that it treats conscious states as 'nomological danglers', to use Herbert Feigl's (1958) memorable phrase. Instead of being integrated into our broader conception of reality in the way in which other high-level properties such as digestion, respiration, and photosynthesis are, the dualist takes them to 'dangle' from primitive psychophysical laws. Consciousness, on this view, is a kind of ontological oddball, a metaphysical freak. Although some are untroubled by this kind of 'experiential exceptionalism', others – myself included – hanker for a tidier metaphysics.

Russellian monism promises to provide just that. So named because its classical formulation can be found in Bertrand Russell's *The Analysis of Mind* (1921), the Russellian monist holds that consciousness is a fundamental feature of the universe, for it constitutes the categorical or intrinsic nature of the physical world. If there is just one kind of categorical property (consciousness), then – the Russellian monist argues – the nature of microscopic things (such as quarks and electrons) is continuous with the nature of macroscopic things (such as organisms), and reality would be deeply unified. The view is sometimes known as 'dual-aspect monism', for it conceives of matter as having two aspects: a phenomenal aspect, which is directly accessible only from the first-person perspective, and a physical aspect, which is accessible from the third-person perspective.[15]

Russellian monism has some attractive features. Because the Russellian monist denies that consciousness emerges from the organization of physical phenomena in the way that (say) life, digestion, and respiration do, the view doesn't face the kinds of explanatory gap(s) that confront the physicalist. Further, because Russellian monists view physical reality as inherently conscious, they needn't posit primitive psychophysical laws in the way that dualists must. Yet another apparent benefit of Russellian monism is that it promises to fill a gap in our knowledge of the physical world that cannot be plugged by physics (or any other branch of science). According to the Russellian monist, science reveals only the dispositional properties of the physical world and can tell us nothing about the intrinsic or categorical basis of those properties. Instead, our knowledge of matter's categorical basis is provided by our knowledge of consciousness itself. On this view, physics can tell what the fundamental features of the world *do*, but the only knowledge we have of what those features are in and of themselves is that which is available from the first person-perspective.

But Russellian monism also has some deeply unattractive features too. Most obviously, it leads fairly directly to panpsychism, the view that consciousness is distributed across the universe and is present in all material objects. If, as the Russellian monist holds, consciousness is embedded in the very fabric of fundamental reality, then there must be a sliver of experience in every electron, a quantum of qualia in every quark. It goes without saying that panpsychism is highly counterintuitive. (If you think it's tough imagining what it's like to be a bat, try imagining what it's like to be a quark!) Taking panpsychism seriously would require stripping consciousness of its connections to biological processes, to perception, and to the control of behaviour. We might conceivably have reason to do that if panpsychists could explain the various features of consciousness that need to be accounted for, but to date no such explanation has been provided, nor have panpsychists provided a roadmap as to how it might be identified (see Box: Panprotopsychism?).[16]

Box: Panprotopsychism?

Some Russellian monists argue that worries about the counterintuitive nature of panpsychism can be met (or at least assuaged) by holding that the categorical basis of physical world involves only what they call 'protophenomenal' properties. This version of Russellian monism is sometimes referred to as 'neutral monism', for it takes the fundamental nature of the world to be neither physical nor phenomenal.

Neutral monism avoids the implication that quarks are conscious, but it has problems of its own. For one thing, the notion of a protophenomenal property is defined only negatively (it's neither phenomenal nor physical), and positive characterizations of it are elusive. A second problem is that neutral monism doesn't close the explanatory gap but merely relocates it, for protophenomenal concepts are conceptually independent of phenomenal concepts in much the way in which physical-functional concepts are.

Further reading

Stubenberg, L. 2016. Neutral Monism and Panpsychism. In G. Bruntrup and L. Jaskolla (eds.), *Panpsychism: Contemporary Perspectives*. Oxford University Press.

Leaving panpsychism to one side, Russellian monists face a further challenge in the form of the *combination problem*. At its core, the combination problem involves explaining how the experiences of fundamental physical entities necessitate the experiences of organisms such as us.[17] There are different aspects to this problem. One aspect concerns the emergence of conscious organisms. How do macro-subjects (such as you and I) emerge from micro-subjects (such as quarks)? Another aspect concerns the emergence of the kinds of experiences that ordinary organisms have. Assuming that there is something that it's like to be a quark, surely what it's like to be a quark is very different from what it's like to be you or me (or, presumably, any other organism). How, then, do the experiences of micro-subjects 'combine' to form the experiences of macro-subjects? To date, Russellian monists have not provided plausible answers to these questions. Worse, it is far from clear that the macro-conscious facts will be a priori scrutable from the micro-conscious facts. And if they aren't, then Russellian monism won't deliver on its promise to provide a unified view of reality.

The combination problem seems to me to be every bit as serious as the problems posed by the explanatory gap. (Indeed, it is in its own way a kind of explanatory gap problem.) It doesn't seem to be the kind of problem that could be solved by purely armchair methods, nor does it seem amenable to scientific investigation. After all, the Russellian monist conceives of phenomenal properties as purely categorical, and by the Russellian monist's own lights, categorical properties are insulated from empirical inquiry. Rather than opening up a new frontier in the study of consciousness, I suspect that Russellian monism will turn out to be little more than a metaphysical cul-de-sac.

8.6 Conclusion

This chapter has focused on three influential objections to physicalism: the bat argument, the knowledge argument, and the zombie argument. I have suggested that each argument is, in essence, a variation on the inscrutability argument: if physicalism were true, then the phenomenal truths would be a priori scrutable from the physical truths, but they're not.

As we have seen, physicalists have developed three kinds of responses to the anti-physicalist arguments. Type-A physicalists argue that the explanatory gap between the physical truths and the phenomenal truths will be bridged – or at least, that we have no reason to rule out that possibility. Type-B physicalists allow that there is an unbridgeable gap between the physical and the phenomenal, but they argue that this gap is purely epistemic, and that there is no corresponding ontological gap. Illusionists side with dualists in thinking that phenomenal states would indeed pose a deep and potentially unbridgeable explanatory gap were they to exist, but – they argue – phenomenal states don't exist.

Finally, we briefly considered two alternatives to physicalism: dualism and Russellian monism. We saw that dualism requires brute psychophysical laws and that such laws would have no parallels in other domains. Russellian monism avoids brute psychophysical laws, but it has difficulties of its own, most obviously in explaining how the kinds of conscious states that supposedly obtain at the level of fundamental physics would be able to generate the kinds of conscious states that you and I enjoy. The 'hard problem' of consciousness is certainly well-named, for there are no easy answers as to how to accommodate consciousness within our overall conception of reality.

Further reading

For an excellent overview of the anti-physicalist arguments see Brie Gertler's 'Dualism: How Epistemic Issues Drive Debates about the Ontology of Consciousness', in U. Kriegel (ed.), *The Oxford Handbook of the Philosophy of Consciousness* (OUP, 2020). Another engaging entry point into the literature on consciousness is provided by *A Dialogue on Consciousness* (OUP, 2009) by Torin Alter and Robert Howell.

For a response to Nagel's bat argument, see Kathleen Akins's 'A Bat without Qualities?' in Martin Davies and Glyn Humphreys (eds.), *Consciousness: Psychological and Philosophical Essays* (Blackwell, pp. 258-73, 1993). Also illuminating is Peter Godfrey-Smith's 'On Being an Octopus' (http://bostonreview.net/books-ideas/peter-godfrey-smith-being-octopus), which uses the octopus as a lens through which to explore Nagel's challenge.

For the knowledge argument see *There's Something about Mary: Essays on Phenomenal Consciousness and Frank Jackson's Knowledge Argument*, edited by Peter Ludlow, Yujin Nagasawa, and Daniel Stoljar (MIT Press; 2004). The introduction to this volume is particularly helpful for navigating one's way through the literature on the knowledge argument, as is Robert van Gulick's chapter 'So Many Ways of Saying No to Mary'. For more on phenomenal concepts and the phenomenal concept strategy see Katalin Balog's 'Phenomenal Concepts', in A. Beckermann, B. McLaughlin, and S. Walter (eds.), *The Oxford Handbook of Philosophy of Mind* (OUP, 2009); John Perry's *Knowledge, Possibility and Consciousness* (MIT Press, 2001); and Pär Sundström's 'Phenomenal Concepts', *Philosophy Compass*, 6(4): 267-81 (2011).

For the zombie argument and the explanatory gap more generally, see *Explaining Consciousness: The Hard Problem* (MIT Press, 1997), edited by Jonathan Shear, which includes David Chalmers's influential paper 'Facing Up to the Problem of Consciousness', together with 26 responses from a variety of perspectives.

The best entry point into illusionism is Keith Frankish's 'Illusionism as a Theory of Consciousness', *Journal of Consciousness Studies*, 23(11-12): 11-39 (2016), which is published alongside 17 commentaries together with Frankish's reply to those commentaries.

For a deep dive into Russellian monism, see Philip Goff's *Consciousness and Fundamental Reality* (OUP, 2017) and *Consciousness in the Physical World: Perspectives on Russellian Monism* (OUP, 2015), edited by Torin Alter and Yujin Nagasawa. For the contemporary discussion of panpsychism see William Seager's (ed.), *The Routledge Handbook of Panpsychism* (Routledge, 2019) and *Panpsychism: Contemporary Perspectives* (OUP, 2016), edited by Godehard Bruntrup and Ludwig Jaskolla. For discussion of the combination problem in particular see Luke Roelofs's *Combining Minds: How to Think about Composite Subjectivity* (OUP, 2019).

Study questions

1. The box 'Mind the Gaps' distinguishes the specific explanatory gap from the generic explanatory gap. What does this difference involve?
2. What is the zombie argument against physicalism? What is the difference between Type-A physicalist responses to the zombie argument and Type-B physicalist responses?
3. What is a Laplacean demon? What role does the appeal to a Laplacean demon play in the inscrutability argument?
4. What is the ability hypothesis response to Jackson's knowledge argument? What challenges does it face?
5. What is the optimistic induction? What role does it play in the defence of Type-A physicalism?
6. What is a phenomenal concept, and why do some Type-B physicalists think that phenomenal concepts provide the solution to the knowledge argument?
7. What is illusionism? Evaluate its plausibility as a response to the problem of consciousness.
8. What is Russellian monism? Does it provide a better account of the metaphysics of consciousness than either traditional forms of physicalism or traditional forms of dualism?

Notes

1. Although Nagel assumes that echolocation is alien to human experience, that assumption is almost certainly false, for blind individuals have been found to use echolocation to navigate (Thaler & Goodale 2016). In fact, Schwitzgebel and Gordon (2011) point out that there is evidence that we all have the capacity to echolocate, albeit in a rather rudimentary form.
2. Strictly speaking, this isn't quite right, for it assumes that an individual's phenomenal properties must supervene on their intrinsic physical properties. A physicalist could reject that assumption, and hold that although worlds that are physical duplicates must also be phenomenal duplicates, individuals could be physical twins without being phenomenal twins on the grounds that phenomenal properties depend in part on features of an agent's environmental (see Chapter 7, especially Section 7.3). I ignore this complication here.
3. For more on the ability hypothesis, see Alter (2001), Cath (2009), Papineau (2002), Tye (2000b), and van Gulick (2004).
4. This phrase is meant to echo what Larry Laudan (1981) called 'the pessimistic induction', according to which the fact that most previous scientific theories have turned out to be false gives us reason to think that current scientific theories are also false.
5. Jackson (2003) develops a representationalist response to his own knowledge argument. For critical discussion, see Alter (2007) and Davies (2012).
6. See, e.g., Block and Stalnaker (1999), Byrne (1999), Crane (2010), Hill and McLaughlin (1999), Levine (2020), McLaughlin (2007), Polger (2008), and Schaffer (2017).

7 See, e.g., Chalmers and Jackson (2001), Gertler (2002), and Jackson (2003).
8 See, e.g., Balog (2012), Horgan (1984b), Loar (1997), Papineau (2002), Perry (2001), and Tye (1999).
9 Another way to approach the phenomenal concept strategy is in terms of a distinction between two types of learning: learning a fact and learning a proposition. If physicalism is the view that all the facts are physical facts (i.e., all the facts can be described via physical concepts), then physicalism is consistent with the claim that Mary learns something new when she leaves the room, as long as we read this as the claim that she learns a new proposition. In this context, facts are objective: they involve no reference to our conceptual structures, whereas propositions are constructed out of our concepts.
10 For discussion, see Papineau (2011). For other worries about the notion of a phenomenal concept, see Ball (2009), Crane (2005), and Macdonald (2004).
11 Are there any scenarios in which one learns that two terms are co-referential but doesn't also learn a new fact? Perhaps. The most likely cases here are those that involve indexicals, such as 'I', 'here', and 'now'. Arguably, even complete knowledge of the physical world wouldn't enable me to work out that 'I' and 'Tim Bayne' refer to the same person; that 'here' and 'Times Square' refer to the same place, or that 'now' and '1 January 2022' refer to the same time. Thus if phenomenal concepts are a type of indexical, then perhaps we could explain why even a Laplacean demon would be unable to read off the phenomenal truths from the physical truths, even if the phenomenal facts are nothing over and above the physical facts. For discussion of the relationship between phenomenal concepts and indexicals, see Chalmers (2004a), Ismael (1999), Lycan (1990), McGinn (1983), McMullen (1985), Perry (2001), and Stalnaker (2008).
12 Although illusionists think of phenomenal properties as the (putative) properties of experiences, I myself think of them as properties of selves (or subjects of experience). As far as I can tell, nothing of substance turns on this issue here, and I will adopt the illusionists' conception of things here.
13 Put in terms of the inscrutability argument, the illusionist can allow that phenomenal truths wouldn't be a priori scrutable from the physical truths (unlike the Type-A physicalist), *and* they can agree that the truth of physicalism would require the phenomenal truths to be a priori scrutable from the physical truths (unlike the Type-B physicalist). As the illusionist sees it, where the inscrutability argument (and, indeed, both Type-A and Type-B physicalists) goes wrong is in assuming that there *are* phenomenal truths.
14 Some theorists develop this idea is in terms of the idea that we aren't aware of our experiences by representing them, but are instead directly acquainted with them, where acquaintance is an unmediated mode of access to an object that reveals its nature (see Chapter 12, Box: Acquaintance). The problem with this response, however, is that the notion of acquaintance is mysterious, and it is entirely unclear how it might be understood in scientific terms.
15 For more on Russellian monism see Goff (2017a), Goff and Coleman (2020), Mørch (2017), Pereboom (2014), Strawson (2006), and Stoljar (2014). For more on panpsychism specifically see Chalmers (2016), Coleman (2016), Goff (2017b), Nagel (1979), and Seager (1995).
16 Goff and Coleman (2020: 306): 'What is it like to be a quark? Panpsychism is a broad theoretical framework, and it will take time to fill in the details. Compare: It took decades of hard work to bridge the gap between the basic principles of Darwinian evolution by natural selection and modern genetics'. It did indeed take decades to fill in the Darwinian story, but even in Darwin's day it was pretty clear what kinds of details were missing and how they might, in principle, at least, be filled in. Nothing comparable obtains in the case of panpsychism. What possible experiment could tell us what it's like to be a quark?
17 Chalmers (2016), Roelofs (2019), and Seager (1995).

9 Theories of consciousness

Chapter overview

- Introduces some of the methodological challenges posed by the study of consciousness
- Distinguishes a number of explanatory targets for the science of consciousness
- Explores some of the arguments for and against three of the most influential approaches to consciousness: monitoring theories, neural theories, and functionalist theories
- Introduces intentionalism (representationalism) as an account of the character of consciousness.

In the previous chapter we explored various issues in the metaphysics of consciousness, focusing on the challenge posed by reconciling consciousness with physicalism. Although that challenge remains in the background here, this chapter focuses on a cluster of issues that are more directly concerned with the explanation of consciousness. As we will see, these issues straddle the boundary between philosophy and the science of consciousness.

We begin (Section 9.1) by asking what kinds of data the science of consciousness should collect. Should it restrict itself to first-person (or 'subjective' methods) involving introspection, or should it instead focus on third-person (or 'objective') methods? Each approach is problematic, albeit for different reasons. Section 9.2 considers how many aspects of consciousness there are and distinguishes a number of distinct explanatory targets for a science of consciousness. Section 9.3 examines two of the most influential approaches to consciousness: monitoring approaches and first-order approaches. Monitoring accounts hold that mental states are conscious in virtue of being represented in a certain kind of way, whereas first-order accounts reject that claim. In Section 9.4, we consider two kinds of first-order theories of consciousness: neural theories and functional theories. The chapter concludes by considering intentionalism (also known as 'representationalism'), an account of consciousness that focuses specifically on the phenomenal character of consciousness.

DOI: 10.4324/9781003225348-10

9.1 First-person methods and third-person methods

To develop an account of consciousness we need to be able to identify instances of it. We needn't (of course) be able to settle all questions about the kinds of conscious states (if any) a creature is in before we can evaluate theories of consciousness, but uncertainty about how to detect consciousness will certainly 'problematize' our capacity to study it. Thus, one of the key aims of the science of consciousness is to find adequate ways of identifying consciousness.

Approaches to this question can be (roughly) grouped into two camps. Some argue that introspection is really the only appropriate tool for studying consciousness, and that the science of consciousness should rely first-and-foremost on first-person (or 'subjective') methods. Others argue that introspection is fundamentally problematic and should be avoided as much as possible (if not altogether). As they see it, the science of consciousness should focus on third-person (or 'objective') methods, such as an agent's behavioural capacities, cognitive processes, and neurophysiological responses. Let's begin by considering the status of first-person methods.

First-person methods

The assumption that the study of consciousness must ultimately rely on first-person reports is both compelling and widely endorsed.[1] As the neuroscientist Chris Frith and his colleagues once put it, 'to discover what someone is conscious of we need them to give us some form of report about their subjective experience' (Frith et al. 1999: 107). But despite its influence, there are many powerful objections to the scientific use of introspection.

Some argue that introspection is inherently unscientific because its operations are not subject to public scrutiny in the way that genuinely scientific methods must be. This worry goes back to the earliest days of psychology, and in recent decades it has been forcefully articulated by Daniel Dennett (1991b). We might put it as follows:

1 Only public methods of measurement are scientifically legitimate.
2 Introspection is not a public method of measurement.
3 Therefore, introspection is not scientifically legitimate.

Let's call this *the argument from public availability*.

The argument is not unattractive, for there seems to be a sharp contrast between introspection on the one hand and the kinds of third-person methods employed by science on the other. Suppose that I claim that Hyperion, the tallest known tree in the world, is over 115 metres in height. In principle, any suitably positioned person could evaluate this claim, for facts about the height of a tree are publicly accessible. In contrast, it is much more difficult to see how anyone else might evaluate my claim to have a headache. My behaviour and physiological states might have some bearing on the plausibility of my claim to have a headache, but they won't be authoritative in the way in which measuring the height of Hyperion is. Because the objects of introspection are private, the accuracy of introspective reports can't be independently verified. But no science can take its data purely on trust – can it?

Let's begin with (2), and the claim that introspective reports cannot be verified. As headaches illustrate, it is certainly very difficult to verify certain types of introspective reports. But the accuracy of other types of introspective reports *can* be checked, at least in a certain manner of speaking. Indeed, Dennett (1991b) himself provides a simple but compelling illustration of how this might occur. Fixate on a point directly ahead of you, and slowly move a playing card from the periphery of your visual field to its centre. Chances are, you won't be able to accurately report the colour of the card until it is almost at the centre of your visual field. But before carrying out this exercise, most people have the (introspectively based) belief that they experience colour right to the edges of the visual field. This exercise illustrates one way in which the accuracy of certain introspectively-based beliefs (e.g., 'I can see colour to the edge of my visual field') can be verified, namely, by checking their coherence against other introspectively-based beliefs ('I cannot tell what colour this playing card is').

Of course, using some introspective beliefs to check the accuracy of other introspective beliefs doesn't provide a truly independent test of the reliability of introspection. Arguably, no such test can be provided, for any method of verifying introspection must ultimately take introspection itself for granted. But does that mean that the use of introspection is inherently unscientific? Maybe not. Perhaps it is perfectly legitimate to treat introspection as a legitimate source of data even if its operations aren't public (in the relevant sense). After all, there are certain scientific methods for which it is very difficult to provide truly independent justification. Consider, for example, the use of reason. It's not possible to convince a sceptic who argues that reasoning is unscientific, for any attempt to justify the use of reason must itself employ reasoning, and will thus presuppose the validity of the very method that is in question. But surely it would be unreasonable to decry the scientific use of reason. Similarly, one might argue that introspection too is a legitimate tool of scientific inquiry even if it is in some sense 'private'.[2]

Some theorists are willing to accept that introspection is not *inherently* unscientific, but they argue that there are good reasons to think that it is in fact too unreliable to provide a secure foundation for the science of consciousness. Eric Schwitzgebel has developed a sophisticated case for precisely this view, arguing that 'the introspection of current conscious experience is faulty, untrustworthy, and misleading – not just *possibly* mistaken, but massively and pervasively' (2008: 259; emphasis in original).

Schwitzgebel provides a number of arguments for this thesis, the most powerful of which is the *argument from introspective disagreement*. Consider the debate about conscious thought. Some people claim that there is a kind of phenomenal character distinctive to thought (cognitive phenomenology), whereas others claim that the only kind of phenomenal character associated with thought is that which belongs to the images and bodily feelings that accompany thought (see Chapter 6). We encountered another introspective disagreement in Chapter 4, where we saw that some theorists take perception to be purely transparent (or diaphanous), presenting only the apparent properties of objects, whereas others claim that in perception one seems to be aware of intrinsic features of perceptual experience itself. Yet another introspective dispute concerns our experience of the self, and whether we are (or even seem to be) directly acquainted with a self in experience (see Chapter 13). These disputes, Schwitzgebel argues, undermine the assumption that we have reliable first-person access to our own conscious states.

There are two ways of resisting Schwitzgebel's conclusion. On the one hand, one might take issue with his analysis of these (and other) introspective disputes. For example, it might be argued that some of these disputes are merely verbal rather than substantive (theorists have the same kinds of experiences but merely describe them in different ways), or that they derive from differences in phenomenology itself (disputants are right about their own experiences but wrong to assume that their experience is representative of human experience in general). On the other hand, one might grant Schwitzgebel's analysis of the introspective disputes on which he focuses, but argue that introspection's unreliability in some domains should not undermine our faith in introspection more generally. Schwitzgebel focuses on the *tough* cases (cases in which introspection seems to lead to intractable disagreement), but there are also *easy* cases (cases in which doubt about the deliverances of introspection would seem to be irrational). Pinch one of your fingers and focus on how your finger feels. Is it really plausible that you might be making a 'gross and enduring mistake' about the character of this experience?[3] Perhaps the science of consciousness can get along with a qualified trust in introspection.

In my view, the most serious problem with first-person methods is not that they are inherently unscientific or even that they are generally unreliable, but that they are often unavailable. Ordinary adult humans in the state of waking awareness can usually report their experiences (but see Box: Phenomenal overflow?), but such capacities are severely compromised in the context of sleep, serious brain damage, and many drug-induced states. Moreover, there are many apparently conscious creatures (such as human infants and non-human animals) that lack even the capacity to produce introspective reports. A science of consciousness that relied only on introspective report would be severely impoverished indeed, for it would be able to draw its data from only a very small (and perhaps unrepresentative) sample of conscious creatures.

Box: Phenomenal overflow?

Over the last couple of decades, Ned Block (2007, 2014) has argued that the contents of phenomenal consciousness 'overflow' that which is directly available to introspection. Block's defence of the overflow thesis owes much to an experiment conducted by George Sperling in 1960 (Sperling 1960). The experiment had two stages. First, subjects saw a grid containing 12 items (letters or numerals) arranged in three rows of four items (see Figure 9.1). The grid was presented only briefly (say, 250 milliseconds), and participants were required to identify as many of the 12 items as they could. Although participants often said that they saw 'all' (or at least 'most') of the items, they were usually able to identify only four or so. Stage two involved a 'partial-report' condition, in which participants heard a tone immediately *after* the visual display disappeared. A high tone indicated that the top row was to be reported, a middle tone indicated that the middle row was to be reported, and a low tone indicated that the bottom row was to be reported. Participants were typically able to identify about three of the four items in the cued row.

U	I	V	F
X	L	G	Q
B	S	W	K

Figure 9.1 Typical stimulus display used in Sperling's partial report task

Source: Sperling (1960)

Block argues that these (and related) findings show that participants are aware of more than they can report. His first argument appeals to the fact that participants in these experiments often say that they were aware of all (or most) of the presented items (despite being unable to report more than four). His second (and weightier) argument appeals to the fact that on cued trials participants could typically report three of the four items in the cued row. Because the cue is presented *after* the display was removed, Block argues that it couldn't have affected a subject's awareness of the display, and thus that participants were conscious of the identities of roughly nine of the presented items despite having had introspective access to only four or so.

Both of these arguments have been challenged. In response to the first, Stazicker (2011) suggests that when participants report having been aware of 'all (or at least most) of the items', perhaps they meant only that they were aware of them in a generic fashion – that is, as letter- or number-like rather than as particular letters or numbers (a '9', for example). Responding to the second argument, Phillips (2011) argues that although the tone occured after the display was removed, hearing the tone might nonetheless have altered how the participants saw the display, and thus that a crucial assumption of Block's argument – namely, that a participant's experience of the grid is independent of the cue – might be false. The debate regarding the possibility of phenomenal overflow is ongoing.

Further reading

Gross, S., and J. Flombaum. 2017. Does Perceptual Consciousness Overflow Cognitive Access? The Challenge from Probabilistic, Hierarchical Processes. *Mind and Language*, 32(3): 358-91.

Phillips, I. 2011. Perception and Iconic Memory: What Sperling Doesn't Show. *Mind and Language*, 26(4): 381-411.

Stazicker, J. 2011. Attention, Visual Consciousness, and Indeterminacy. *Mind and Language*, 26(2): 156-84.

Third-person methods

We have seen that the scientific use of introspection faces three challenges: it is inherently unscientific, it is unreliable, and it can be employed only in a restricted range of cases. The force of each challenge is open to debate, but taken as a group they provide ample motivation for the development of third-person methods for identifying consciousness.[4] Such methods would enable us to both sidestep concerns about the trustworthiness of introspection and to study consciousness in creatures that are unable to produce introspective reports. The problem, however, is that it is unclear what form third-person methods should take. What kinds of third-person data should be treated as markers (or indicators) of consciousness?

A very liberal approach to this issue would treat the capacity to make perceptually based discrimination as a marker of consciousness. On this view, any creature that can reliably discriminate (say) vertical lines from horizontal lines should be regarded as being conscious of the lines and their orientations. However, many argue that this approach is too liberal, often appealing to data derived from the study of blindsight. As we noted in Chapter 4, blindsight is a condition in which damage to area VI of the primary visual cortex causes a deficit in the capacity of patients to perceive stimuli that are presented in a certain region of the patient's visual field (the blindfield). Although individuals with blindsight say that they are unaware of stimuli in their blindfield, they are often highly accurate in discriminating them from each other when forced to do so. Although the interpretation of blindsight is controversial, the crucial issue here isn't what to make of the subject's reports, but what to make of their discriminatory capacities. Should we regard the subject's ability to reliably distinguish vertical lines from horizontal ones as evidence that they were conscious of the orientation of the lines? It is far from obvious that we should.

Another proposed marker of consciousness is the capacity for metacognition – what Larry Weiskrantz (1998: 84) once called 'off-line commentary'. The idea here is that consciousness might involve the capacity to adopt a certain kind of attitude to one's world-directed mental states and to represent them in distinctive ways. A creature with metacognitive capacities is able to track the quality of its perceptual information and to opt out of a certain kind of task when it lacks confidence in its capacity to perform it well. Studies have shown that human infants have metacognitive capacities (Goupil et al. 2016; Goupil & Kouider 2016), as do the members of a number of non-human species (Smith 2009; Smith et al. 2003; but see Carruthers 2008).

Yet another proposed third-person marker of consciousness is the capacity to use representations in the context of intentional control. Unconscious information may be able to control and tweak behaviours that have already been selected, but perhaps consciousness is required for the initiation of goal-directed agency (Bayne 2013; Dretske 2006). In this regard, it is noteworthy that instruction-following is routinely used as a marker for consciousness in medical contexts. Clinicians looking for evidence of consciousness in a sedated or brain-damaged patient might give the patient a simple instruction, such as 'Raise your right hand'. Patients who are able to follow commands are regarded as conscious, presumably on the grounds that compliance requires conscious awareness of the command and its meaning.

Although metacognition and intentional control are often employed as markers of consciousness, there are open questions about their legitimacy and scope. Both capacities seem to be closely associated with consciousness in human beings, but it is less clear how closely tied they are to consciousness in other species. Perhaps there are species that are capable of metacognition and/or intentional agency but have no conscious states of any kind; and perhaps there are creatures that have conscious states but are capable of neither metacognition nor intentional agency. And even if consciousness turns out to be necessarily connected to metacognition and intentional agency in the biological realm, it seems entirely conceivable that an AI system could possess the capacity for metacognition and/or intentional control without being conscious, and vice versa.

The fundamental problem here is that third-person markers of consciousness need to be validated, and, on the face of things, validating a third-person marker of consciousness requires correlating it with introspective reports. But if that is right, then it seems as though third-person methods for studying consciousness must inherit whatever epistemic authority they have from their relations to first-person methods. And if that is right, then the science of consciousness must remain fundamentally dependent on introspection, whatever its frailties.

9.2 Explanatory targets

Let us turn now from the challenge of detecting consciousness to the question of what it is that we should expect a theory of consciousness to explain. Consciousness is a multifaceted phenomenon. Although some theories of consciousness aim to explain every facet of it, others are more selective and focus only on particular aspects of consciousness. What follows is my map of the terrain, but the reader should be aware that we are entering contested territory, and theorists carve it up in very different ways.

One facet of consciousness is the generic property of being conscious. An account of generic consciousness would tell us the conditions in which consciousness occurs, and why consciousness is lost as the result of certain types of brain damage but not others. It would tell us how consciousness is distributed (Are mice conscious? What about octopuses?) and what it would take to construct a conscious agent.

What do we mean by 'consciousness' in this sense? I will equate being conscious with having an experiential point of view – with there being 'something that it's like' for the creature in question to be the creature that it is. There are other notions of consciousness; for example, in some contexts, consciousness is used to refer to the state of wakefulness. This is a perfectly legitimate sense of 'consciousness', but it is not the one on which the science of consciousness focuses. Importantly, wakefulness can dissociate from having a subjective point of view, for not only is it possible to have a subjective point of view without being awake, it is also possible to be awake without having a subjective point of view. Subjective experience without wakefulness occurs during dreaming, one of various global states of consciousness (see Box: Global states of consciousness), and wakefulness without subjective experience occurs in the vegetative state (also known as the 'unresponsive wakefulness syndrome').

Box: Global states of consciousness

In addition to fine-grained conscious states (often referred to as 'conscious contents'), such as hearing a trumpet, tasting coffee, and feeling pain, consciousness is also characterized by global states of consciousness. Global states concern an individual's overall subjective perspective. Ordinary waking awareness is the global state that is most familiar to us, but other global states occur in association with sleep, meditation, drowsiness, brain damage, and the use of psychedelic drugs.

One influential view equates differences in global states with differences in levels of consciousness (Laureys 2005). On this account, departures from the state of ordinary waking awareness involve a change in the degree to which the subject is conscious. Most of these departures (such as REM dreaming) are taken to involve decreased levels of consciousness, but some global states (in particular the psychedelic state) are sometimes taken to involve an increase in the subject's ordinary level of consciousness. Although it is influential, the levels-based view of global states is controversial. Even if consciousness can come in degrees (and that is not obvious), it is far from clear that distinctions between global states can be equated with are always accompanied by differences in degrees of consciousness.

Further reading

Bayne, T., J. Hohwy, and A. Owen. 2016. Are There Levels of Consciousness? *Trends in Cognitive Sciences*, 20(6): 405-13.

Laureys, S. 2005. The Neural Correlate of (Un)awareness: Lessons from the Vegetative State. *Trends in Cognitive Sciences*, 9: 556-59.

Although some theories of consciousness focus on generic consciousness, most focus on the question of what it is for a particular mental state to be conscious (state consciousness). At any given time, vast amounts of mental processing might be taking place in an organism, but only some of the states involved in that processing are conscious. Why are some mental states conscious whereas others are not? Accounts of state consciousness (as I shall call them) aim to answer this question.[5]

Theorists disagree as to whether we should expect a single account of state consciousness. Some theorists hold that the term 'consciousness' has basically just one sense when applied to mental states, and that bodily sensations, thoughts, perceptions, and emotional states are all conscious in the same manner. Others claim that there are fundamentally different senses in which mental states are conscious, and that it would simply be a mistake to expect that a single account of consciousness might apply to both thoughts and bodily sensations.[6] But although there is debate about how many kinds of state consciousness we should distinguish, almost everyone accepts that the most interesting and important form of state consciousness is *phenomenal consciousness*, the kind of consciousness that there is 'something it is like' to undergo.[7] Phenomenal consciousness is paradigmatically associated with sensory states such as perceptual experiences, bodily sensations, and experiences of moods and emotions, and it lies at the heart of debates about the metaphysics of consciousness (see Chapter 8).

An account of state consciousness will tell us what it is that distinguishes conscious states from unconscious ones, but it won't tell us what distinguishes one kind of conscious state from another. Thus, we need to distinguish a third target for the science of consciousness: *phenomenal character*. An account of phenomenal character will explain why the phenomenal (experiential, subjective) character associated with seeing a sunflower is very different from that which is associated with hearing a trombone or having a hangover. Accounts of phenomenal character are sometimes referred to as accounts of 'qualia' (see Chapter 1, Box: Qualia). Some theories aim to explain why a mental state is conscious but say nothing about why it has the phenomenal character that it does; others aim to account for a state's phenomenal character but say nothing about why it is conscious in the first place.

Another contrast between theories concerns the range of creatures with which they are concerned. Some theories focus on consciousness as it occurs in human beings, and have little (or even nothing) to say about consciousness in non-human animals or artificial systems. Others are more ambitious, and aim to account for all possible forms of consciousness. In between these two positions lie views of intermediate scope. For example, a theory might aim to address all forms of organically based consciousness but say nothing about what it would take for an artificial system to be conscious. Theories that are primarily motivated by a priori arguments tend to be advanced as accounts of consciousness in general, whereas those that are motivated by empirical research tend to have a more restricted scope.

A final distinction returns us to the metaphysical issues that we examined in the previous chapter. The theories that we will discuss are often advanced as versions of physicalism, and it is possible to view the debate between them as a debate between competing forms of physicalism. However, most (if not all) of these theories also admit of dualist interpretations. Consider, for example, a neural theory of consciousness, according to which consciousness involves integrating activity in sensory areas at the back of the brain with activity in executive processes at the front of the brain. Physicalist versions of this view will *identify* consciousness with the relevant kind of neural integration, whereas the dualist will hold that although consciousness is something over and above neural integration, neural integration of the relevant kind functions as the physical basis of consciousness. More generally, physicalists will view the accounts discussed in this chapter as accounts of the nature of consciousness itself, whereas dualists will view them as accounts of the correlates of consciousness (Box: The neural correlates of consciousness).

Box: The neural correlates of consciousness

The search for the physical basis of consciousness is often described as the search for the *neural correlates of consciousness* (NCCs). The NCC label is potentially misleading, for in looking for the neural correlates of consciousness scientists aren't interested in just any old brain activity which happens to be correlated with consciousness. Instead, the focus is on the brain activity that is directly implicated in consciousness, rather than that which might be correlated with consciousness but is causally upstream or downstream of consciousness. According to one influential characterization, a neural state (N) is the NCC of conscious state C if and only if N is sufficient for C and no proper part (or component) of N suffices for C (Chalmers 2000).

Despite its misleading connotations, the NCC label has stuck because it allows scientists and philosophers to communicate without begging disputed questions about precisely how neural activity is related to consciousness. For example, Melanie and Martine might agree that an area of the visual cortex called MT+ qualifies as an NCC for the experience of visual motion, but disagree about precisely how activity in MT+ is related to consciousness. Melanie might hold that the experience of visual motion just is MT+ activity, whereas Martine might be a dualist and hold that MT+ activity and visual experiences are distinct states that are only contingently related.

It is important to recognize that neither physicalists nor dualists are committed to the existence of neural correlates of consciousness, for although any particular experience will have a physical basis, it is an open question whether there are correlations between types of neural states and types of conscious states. Indeed, a number of authors have argued that rather than searching for the neural correlates of consciousness, the science of consciousness should instead focus on the functional or computational correlates of consciousness.

Further reading

Klein, C., T. Bayne, and J. Hohwy. 2020. Explanation in the Science of Consciousness: From the Neural Correlates of Consciousness (NCCs) to the Difference Makers of Consciousness (DMCs). *Philosophy and the Mind Sciences*, 1(2). https://doi.org/10.33735/phimisci.2020.II.60.

Noë, A. and E. Thompson. 2004. Are There Neural Correlates of Consciousness? *Journal of Consciousness Studies*, 11(1): 3–28.

9.3 Monitoring theories versus first-order theories

One of the major fault lines in the landscape of consciousness separates monitoring theories from first-order theories. Monitoring theories hold that a mental state is conscious in virtue of being monitored (or represented) in a certain way. It is impossible to give a positive characterization of first-order theories, for they are united only in their opposition to monitoring theories. As first-order theorists see it, we can explain what it is for a mental state (M) to be conscious without appealing to the fact that M is monitored (or represented) in a certain way. This section focuses on the debate between monitoring theories and first-order theories; Section 9.4 focuses on the debate between different kinds of first-order theories.

Although all monitoring theories share a commitment to the idea that a mental state is conscious in virtue of being monitored, they don't all develop that basic idea in the same way. Two main contrasts can be drawn here. The first concerns the relationship between the monitoring state and the monitored state. *Higher-order* theories hold that the monitored state must be distinct from the monitoring state (Rosenthal 1997; Gennaro 2004), whereas *same-order* (or self-representational) accounts hold that the monitoring state and the monitored state must be identical (Kriegel 2009; Kriegel & Williford 2006; Thomasson 2000). A second contrast concerns the nature of the monitoring relation. Some versions of the monitoring approach hold that mental states are conscious when they are the objects of certain kinds of thoughts (Rosenthal 1986, 2005); others hold that they are conscious when they are monitored in a quasi-perceptual manner (Armstrong 1968; Lycan 1996); and still others hold that mental states are conscious when they are monitored by a subpersonal process (Brown et al. 2019; Lau 2008). Monitoring accounts are accounts of what makes a mental state conscious, and they have nothing as such to say about phenomenal character.[8]

Rather than consider the contrasts between different versions of the monitoring approach, our focus here will be on the merits of the general approach itself. What reasons are there to think that a mental state is conscious in virtue of the fact that it is represented in a certain way?

The conceptual argument

One argument for the monitoring approach appeals to certain platitudes about consciousness. A conscious mental state, it is often claimed, just is a mental state of which one is conscious, and hence it follows that mental states are conscious in virtue of being monitored in some way. I'll call this the 'conceptual argument', for it takes the monitoring account to follow directly from conceptual truths about consciousness. Here is one version of this argument (based on Lycan 2001a; see also Kriegel 2005; Rosenthal 1997):

1   A conscious state is a mental state that one is conscious (that is, aware) of.
2   The 'of' in (1) is the 'of' of intentionality: what one is aware of is an intentional object of awareness.
3   Intentionality is representation: a state has a thing as its intentional object only if it represents that thing.
4   Awareness of a mental state involves a representation of that state (from 2 and 3)

Therefore,

C   A conscious state is a state that is represented by one of the subject's mental states (from 1 and 4).

What should we make of the conceptual argument?[9] As Ernest Sosa (2003) has pointed out, there are two ways of reading (1). The argument requires an intentional reading of (1), but it is also possible to read (1) in a deflationary way, according to which the claim that one is conscious of one's experiences is to be understood on the model of the claim that one smiles one's smiles and dances one's dances. Thus understood, (1) says nothing more than that conscious states are states that belong to a subject. This reading of (1) provides no support for the monitoring account.

A second issue concerns premise (4): 'Awareness of a mental state involves a representation of that state'. Even if being aware of a mental state requires representing it, awareness is surely a *special* kind of representational relation. Cognitive science posits all kinds of representational relations that don't involve awareness. Why do certain ways of representing a state involve being aware of it, whereas others don't? Monitoring accounts don't answer this question but simply help themselves to an unanalysed notion of awareness. The problem, however, is that 'awareness' is arguably a synonym for 'consciousness'. So, even if it's true that a mental state is conscious in virtue of the fact that one is conscious of it, that doesn't get us very far unless we already know what it is to be conscious of something. And, one might argue, knowing that it is to be conscious of something *just is* the problem of state consciousness rephrased.

The argument from subjectivity

A second argument – the argument from subjectivity – appeals to phenomenological considerations. Unlike the conceptual argument, this argument aims to establish only one version of the monitoring approach: the same-order (or self-representational) account. The idea is that we can account for the subjectivity of consciousness – its 'for-me-ness', as some theorists put it – only by supposing that conscious states represent themselves. This conception of consciousness arguably dates back to Aristotle (Carston 2002) and was developed in detail by Franz Brentano in the late 19th century. According to Brentano,

> Every [conscious] act, no matter how simple, has a double object, a primary and a secondary object. The simplest act, for example the act of hearing, has as its primary object the sound, and for its secondary object, itself, the mental phenomenon in which the sound is heard.
>
> (Brentano 1874/1973: 153–54)

How might an argument from the subjectivity of consciousness to the same-order (or self-representational) account of consciousness run?

Here is one suggestion:

1   Necessarily, a conscious state is a state that there is something that it is like for the subject of that state to be in.
2   In order for there to be something that it is like to be in a state, that state must represent itself: it must be self-representational.

Therefore,

C   a mental state is conscious in virtue of representing itself in a certain way.

The subjectivity argument begins on a firm footing, for premise (1) restates a widely accepted characterization of (phenomenal) consciousness. Premise (2), however, is less secure. Suppose that you suddenly realize that a background noise (the hum of an espresso machine, for example) has stopped. You didn't notice the noise until it stopped, but now that it has stopped you realize that the character of your experiential state has changed. Arguably, you were conscious of the hum all along – it was a component of your subjective perspective – you just hadn't been aware *of* your experience of the hum. Something similar seems to characterize many episodes of mind-wandering and reverie. Arguably, these are contexts in which you enjoy conscious states (experiences) of which you are not conscious. Conscious states can take themselves as their 'secondary objects' (as Brentano puts it), but they need not. Indeed, it seems entirely possible that creatures who lack our powers of reflection and self-consciousness (such as infants and non-human animals) are rarely, if ever, aware of their experiences.

A more general challenge for monitoring accounts is whether they can accommodate widely held views about the distribution of consciousness. On the one hand, the approach threatens to be too *conservative*, for many creatures which are ordinarily regarded as conscious (such as very young infants and non-human animals) may lack the capacity to monitor their own representations. At the same time, the approach also threatens to be too *liberal*, for many artificial systems that aren't ordinarily regarded as conscious *do* have the capacity to monitor their own representations.

Attempts to address one of these challenges threaten to exacerbate the other. For example, monitoring theorists could respond to the first challenge by suggesting that the kind of monitoring that is required for consciousness doesn't require conceptual thought and need only involve subpersonal representations of the kind that young infants and many kinds of animals possess. This response might address the 'too conservative' challenge, but only by fortifying the 'too liberal' challenge, for if concepts are not required for consciousness then it becomes harder for the monitoring theorist to explain why current artificial systems aren't conscious. Conversely, if the monitoring theorist argues that artificial systems aren't conscious on the grounds that (say) they don't represent their mental states *as* mental states, then they make it harder to accommodate the intuition that infants and animals can be conscious. We might dub this the *Goldilocks problem*, for it's a problem of developing the monitoring account so that it 'just fits' our pretheoretical intuitions regarding the distribution of consciousness. Of course, the monitoring theorists could reject those intuitions, arguing either that young infants and simple animals aren't conscious or that current AI systems are conscious. However, adopting this response would represent a cost to the plausibility of the monitoring approach.

A final problem with the subjectivity argument concerns the transition from the claim that all conscious states are self-representational to the claim that mental states are conscious in virtue of representing themselves. After all, it seems entirely conceivable that a mental state could be self-representational without being conscious. (Even relatively simple computational devices have self-referential representations.) What's needed here is an account of why certain types of self-representation generate consciousness but others don't. On the face of things, providing such an account requires going beyond the resources provided by the same-order monitoring account.

An empirical argument

A third argument for the monitoring approach is given by Hakwan Lau and David Rosenthal (2011). Cognitive neuroscience, they argue, shows that activity in sensory areas at the back of the brain gives rise to consciousness only when it is monitored by activity in cognitive areas at the front of the brain. Thus, they claim, data drawn from cognitive neuroscience converges with the conclusions of a priori arguments to justify the central tenet of the monitoring account: a mental state is conscious in virtue of being appropriately monitored.

Although Lau and Rosenthal see the empirical case for the monitoring approach as dovetailing nicely with the philosophical case for the view, on the face of things these two kinds of arguments motivate very different accounts of consciousness. The philosophical arguments employ personal-level considerations, and thus motivate a version of the monitoring view on which the monitoring state must be a kind of thought or a quasi-perceptual state. In contrast, the findings drawn from cognitive neuroscience are best understood in terms of sub-personal representations, and thus motivate a version of the monitoring view that appeals to relations between subpersonal representations. If this line of thought is right, then the empirical argument wouldn't really converge with philosophical considerations to support a single account of consciousness, but is instead best thought of as pointing towards an account of consciousness that has no philosophical support.

What of the empirical argument itself? First, it is controversial whether activity in frontal areas of the brain reflects consciousness itself. Critics point out that studies that find an association between perceptual consciousness typically require that subjects to produce reports. Thus, they argue, frontal activity might merely reflect the need to make (or prepare to make) reports, rather than consciousness itself (see Boly et al. [2017]; for a reply, see Odegaard et al. [2017]). In favour of this possibility is the fact that activity in frontal areas is significantly reduced when subjects are no longer required to report their experiences (e.g., Frässle et al. 2014). Resolving this debate requires better measures of consciousness than those which we currently possess.

Second, even if 'front-of-the-brain' activity is implicated in consciousness, it is a further question whether this activity reflects the monitoring of first-order mental states. Functionalists, for example, might argue that front-of-the-brain activity is required for consciousness only because it enables the contents of first-order states to become available to the various systems that govern thought and action, and not because it is implicated in representing those states. We explore functionalist accounts of consciousness, together with some of their first-order rivals, in the following section.

9.4 Neural theories versus functional theories

The two central first-order approaches to consciousness are neural approaches and functional approaches. Both approaches recognize the importance of neural activity in generating consciousness, but they provide very different accounts of why neural activity is important. Neural theorists focus on its distinctively neural properties, whereas functionalists hold that what matters with respect to brain activity aren't its distinctively neural features but its functional profile: what it is caused by and what it in turn causes. Each approach can be developed as an account of state consciousness and phenomenal character, or its scope can be restricted to only one of these two aspects of consciousness.

Let's begin by considering neural accounts. What reasons are there to think that consciousness is either identical to (or best explained in terms of) neural activity?[10]

The mind-brain identity theorists of the 1950s were motivated by the thought that by identifying consciousness with brain activity one could avoid both the 'spooky' metaphysics of dualism on the one hand and the implausible dispositionalism of behaviourism on the other (see, e.g., Place 1956; Feigl 1958; Smart 1959). In the current context, however, this motivation is unpersuasive, for both monitoring and functional accounts also provide alternatives to dualism and behaviourism. What's needed here is some reason to think that consciousness is grounded in (or even just correlated with) the brain's neural properties as opposed to its representational or functional ones.

Neural theorists sometimes appeal to the effects of neural interventions on consciousness as evidence for their view. Some neural interventions, such as those caused by general anaesthetics, eliminate consciousness entirely; others, however, have an impact only on specific types of experiences (e.g., Fox et al. 2020; Winawer & Parvizi 2016). For example, lesions to an area in the visual cortex called MT+ can cause akinetopsia, a deficit in the ability to see motion, whereas stimulating MT+ with transcranial magnetic stimulation (TMS) can trigger experiences of motion. Does the fact that it is possible to intervene on consciousness in these ways show that consciousness is best understood in neural terms?

No. In fact, there are multiple problems with the interventionist argument. First, the evidence for correlations between specific types of brain activity and specific conscious experiences is rather weak. Although the brain does contain areas and networks that care about certain kinds of stimuli more than others, there appear to be few one-to-one mappings from particular brain areas and networks onto particular forms of experience, and even relatively specialized areas and networks are implicated in many types of conscious state (Anderson 2014). To take just one example of this phenomenon, consider the so-called 'pain matrix', a network involving the primary and secondary somatosensory cortices, the insula, and the anterior cingulate cortex, which is typically active when people experience pain. Although the pain matrix is correlated with pain, we cannot map activity in the pain matrix onto pain, for the pain matrix is also activated by stimuli that are highly salient (i.e., attention-grabbing) but not painful (Iannetti & Mouraux 2010; Mouraux et al. 2011). Neural plasticity – the fact that brain areas that are typically used to process stimuli of one kind are, in some cases, used to process stimuli of another kind – provides a closely-related challenge to the interventionist argument (Box: Cortical dominance and cortical deference).

Box: Cortical dominance and cortical deference

What happens when the connections between the brain and the world are rewired, so that brain areas that normally receive one type of input (say, visual input) receive a novel type of input (say, auditory input)? It depends. In some cases activity in the target area leads to the kinds of experiences that are normally associated with it, but in other cases it leads to experiences associated with the new type of input. Hurley and Noë (2003) apply the label 'cortical dominance' to cases of the first type (because the nature of the experience is in line with that which is typically associated with the cortical region in question), and they apply the label 'cortical deference' to cases of the second type (because consciousness defers to the nature of the input).

Cortical dominance is illustrated by the phantom limb phenomenon. Normally, tactile input from the arm and face maps onto adjacent cortical areas. However, after amputation of part of the arm, tactile input from the face invades deafferented cortex whose normal conscious expression involves feeling one's arm being touched. When this area of cortex is activated by input from the face, it continues to retain this conscious expression. So, when the face of someone with a phantom limb is stroked, they will often experience their (missing) limb being stroked (in addition to feeling their face being stroked (Ramachandran & Hirstein 1998). Cortical deference is illustrated by neural activity in blind children, in which areas of the cortex that are ordinarily dedicated to vision are used to process speech and haptic information (Bedney et al. 2015; Hamilton & Pascual-Leone 1998).

Cortical dominance is unsurprising from the perspective of neural theories, but such theories struggle to explain cortical deference. Why should modulating the *input* to an area of cortex change its conscious expression if consciousness is to be accounted for in neural terms? By contrast, other approaches to consciousness, such as representationalism (see Section 9.5), have no difficulty accounting for cortical deference but they struggle to explain cortical dominance.

Qualitative Expression:	A-feeling	A-feeling (deference) or B-feeling (dominance)
Of Cortical Area:	1	2
Input Source:	A	B

Cortical Dominance: activation of 2 by A feels like activation of 2 by B normally would, i.e. the B-feeling. The normal qualitative expression of 2 is unchanged.

Cortical Deference: activation of 2 by A feels like activation of 1 by A, i.e. the A-feeling. The qualitative expression of 2 changes to reflect new source of input.

Based on Figure 1 from Hurley and Noë (2003)

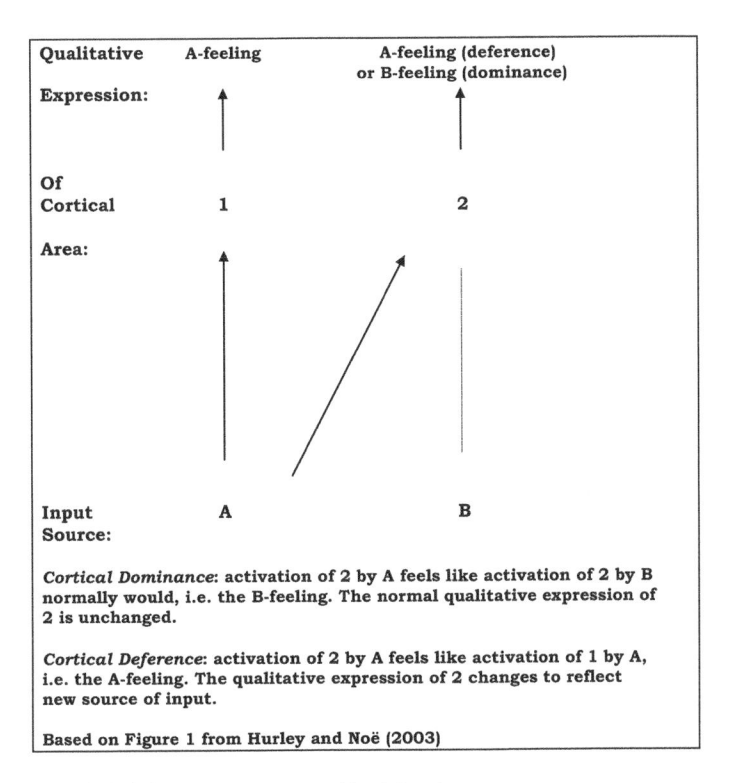

Figure 9.2 Cortical deference versus cortical dominance

Source: Reproduced from Susan Hurley and Alva Noë (2003), 'Neural Plasticity and Consciousness', *Biology and Philosophy*, 18: 131–68, with the kind permission of Alva Noë. Figure by Miriam Dym, Susan Hurley and Alva Noë.

Further reading

Hurley, S., and A. Noë. 2003. Neural Plasticity and Consciousness. *Biology and Philosophy*, 18(1): 131–68.

The second problem with the interventionist argument is that other accounts of consciousness can also explain why certain interventions on brain activity have particular effects on consciousness. Monitoring theorists can account for such effects by arguing that neural interventions alter the capacity to monitor first-order mental states or by modulating the first-order mental states themselves, and functionalists can argue that neural interventions affect consciousness by modulating the functional profile of the relevant mental states. In sum: not only is it unclear whether there are systematic relations between neural activity and consciousness, to the extent that systematicity obtains neural accounts may not provide the best explanation of it.

Let's turn now to criticisms of the neural approach. Perhaps the most influential criticism is the objection from chauvinism: because neural theories entail that consciousness is limited to entities with neural properties, they seem to be unreasonably conservative. Even if human consciousness is best explained in neural terms, is it really plausible to suppose that all possible forms of consciousness require neural activity? Couldn't a suitably constructed AI system be conscious, or at least pass all of our best tests for consciousness?

In response to this objection some theorists bite the bullet, arguing that it is simply begging the question against neural theories of consciousness to assume that non-neural systems can be conscious. In a sense they are right: the objection *does* beg the question. But that doesn't render it irrelevant or unfair. The point is that there could be systems which are unconscious (by the lights of the neural theory) but which would pass all of our current tests for consciousness. (Indeed, such systems might also pass any future test for consciousness!) It doesn't, of course, follow that such systems would be conscious, but surely there would be something peculiar in recognizing that a system has passed our best tests for consciousness but refusing to regard it as conscious.

Not only does the objection from chauvinism undermine the neural approach to consciousness, it also points towards another view: functionalism. Functionalists argue that consciousness is best understood in terms of the functional profile of brain states and processes, where a state's functional profile is typically understood in terms of its causal role: what causes it and what it in turn causes. As we noted in Chapter 3, there are many forms of functionalism.

One important contrast is between a priori functionalism (also known as analytic functionalism) and a posteriori functionalism (also known as psychofunctionalism). A priori functionalists hold that the functional roles associated with consciousness can be identified via conceptual analysis, whereas a posteriori functionalists hold that the functional roles associated with consciousness can be identified only by empirical research in (for example) psychology and neuroscience. Although a priori functionalism has been very influential as an account of certain kinds of mental states (e.g., belief, desire, and intention), it has had significantly less influence as an account of consciousness. The problem, in a nutshell, is that the central concept of consciousness, PHENOMENAL CONSCIOUSNESS, doesn't seem to be a functional concept. Phenomenal consciousness itself may turn out to be a functional property, but the concept of phenomenal consciousness does not present it as such.

For the reasons just given, most functionalist accounts of consciousness are versions of a posteriori functionalism. For example, Michael Tye's (1995) PANIC account holds that representations are conscious when they are poised for the flexible control of thought and action. Jesse Prinz's (2012) attended intermediate representations (AIR) theory is also a version of a posteriori functionalism, for it treats attention – understood in terms of access to working memory – as a key factor in explaining why certain mental states are conscious. But perhaps the most influential version of a posteriori functionalism is Bernard Baars's (1988) Global Workspace Theory (GWT). According to the GWT, representations are conscious when they enter a 'global workspace', which makes their contents available to a wide array of 'consuming systems', such as working memory, metacognition, and attention.[11]

GWT is a version of what I will call 'quasi-functionalism', for it aims to explain only why conscious mental states are conscious, and says nothing about phenomenal character. Other functionalist accounts are comprehensive, and invoke functional roles to explain not only why some mental states are conscious but also why different kinds of conscious states have different phenomenal characters. Quasi-functionalism is the more influential of the two views, but comprehensive functionalism does have its advocates (e.g. Shoemaker 1975).

So much for the differences between functional accounts. What should we make of the approach in general?

One of the leading motivations for functionalism is the fact that conscious states seem to have a functional profile that distinguishes them from unconscious states. The contents of consciousness are, in general at least, available for the direct control of thought and action. They are reportable, they guide our voluntary behaviour, and they inform our deliberations. By contrast, although the contents of unconscious states can have indirect effects on thought and action, they aren't available for the direct control of thought and action in the ways in which the contents of conscious states are. Let's call this claim the *availability thesis*. According to the *availability argument*, the best explanation for the truth of the availability thesis is that consciousness is to be explained in terms of functional properties.

Let's consider three objections to the availability argument. The first concerns the status of the availability thesis. In effect – the objection runs – we presuppose the availability thesis in deciding whether or not a mental state is conscious, for states whose contents are not generally available for the control of thought and action simply aren't regarded as conscious. In other words, it's possible that we don't see counterexamples to the availability thesis not because they don't exist but simply because our methods for detecting consciousness are blind to their possibility. Were we to adopt other criteria for the ascription of consciousness then the availability thesis might not appear to be plausible.

A second issue concerns the scope of the availability thesis. What kinds of agents does it apply to? Neurotypical adult human beings? All human beings? All mammals? All biological organisms? All agents whatsoever, irrespective of their nature? The most ambitious versions of functionalism take the view to apply to conscious agents in general. But the evidence that we have for the availability thesis (to the extent that we have any at all) concerns only human beings, a very small sample of possible conscious agents. Any attempt to apply functionalism more broadly will need to justify the assumption that the functional role associated with consciousness in humans is indicative of its functional role in systems of other kinds.

A final problem with the availability argument concerns the inference from the availability thesis to the truth of functionalism. In effect, the availability argument holds that because conscious states have a distinctive functional profile consciousness itself is to be explained or understood in terms of functional properties. But, one might argue, if consciousness is to be understood in functional terms, then one can't *explain* why conscious states have a distinctive functional profile, for that would be circular. In effect, one would be claiming that conscious states have a distinctive functional profile because they have a distinctive functional profile – true but vacuous! Instead, the objection goes, only *non-functional* theories can *explain* why conscious states have a distinctive functional profile.

Functionalism's critics don't merely take issue with the arguments for functionalism; they also provide objections to the view. One of the most influential of these is Ned Block's (1978) China-Brain argument. Block asks us to imagines a scenario in which the residents of China simulate for an hour the functional roles of the neurons in a normal human brain by communicating with each other via walkie-talkies. This activity creates a massively distributed agent: 'China-Brain'. The only difference between you and China-Brain is the medium in which the relevant functional states are realized: roughly speaking, your functional states are realized by the interactions between neurons, whereas China-Brain's functional states are realized by the interactions between Chinese citizens. For the functionalist, however, all that matters when it comes to consciousness are a system's functional properties. Thus (Block argues), the functionalist should conclude that China-Brain has the conscious states that you do. But, Block claims, it is clearly absurd to suppose that China-Brain would have conscious states of any kind, let alone the kinds of conscious states that you enjoy. In effect, Block argues that functionalists are committed to an overly liberal view of the distribution of consciousness.

There are two lines of response open to the functionalist. The first denies that the functional roles relevant to consciousness can be captured by simply duplicating the causal relations between neurons. According to 'long-arm' functionalists, the input and output states that determine consciousness involve states of the environment rather than states that are internal to the cognitive system. In this version of functionalism, China-Brain would need to interact with its environment in roughly the ways that we do in order to share our conscious states.

Other functionalists – 'short-arm' functionalists – accept that China-Brain could have the kinds of functional states on which consciousness supervenes, but they deny that it is 'clearly absurd' to ascribe consciousness to China-Brain. After all (they point out), China-Brain will share our behavioural capacities: it will produce introspective reports; it will engage in voluntary behaviour; and it will monitor its own mental states. If asked, it would be able to tell you what it's like to taste durian, how pains differ from itches, and whether it prefers Aretha Franklin to Queen. China-Brain may not in fact be conscious, but it does seem likely that we would be tempted to view it as conscious. And if that's right, then the China-Brain argument leaves functionalism unscathed.

9.5 Intentionalism

Let's bring this chapter to a close by considering an account of consciousness that focuses exclusively on the explanation of phenomenal (or experiential) character. The account in question is often known as 'representationalism', but I prefer the less common label 'intentionalism'. We encountered a restricted form of intentionalism in Chapter 4, when we considered the claim that the phenomenal character of perception is fixed by its intentional content. On this view, the phenomenal differences between tasting coffee, hearing the opening notes of Miles Davis's *Kind of Blue*, and looking at a stand of redwoods can be understood in terms of the intentional properties of these experiences. Here, our focus is on intentionalism understood as a claim about *all* forms of phenomenal character. Thus understood, the claim is that the phenomenal feel of even bodily sensations and emotions can be accounted for in terms of intentionality.

It seems evident that at least *some* phenomenal differences can be understood in terms of intentional content. For example, the phenomenal difference between seeing an object as square and seeing it as round reflects the content-involving differences between these two experiences. It would be elegant if all phenomenal differences can be understood in terms of intentional content. Another attractive feature of intentionalism is its reductive promise. Although there is vigorous debate about precisely how intentionality might be grounded in physical states and processes (see Chapter 6), it is widely held that a reductive account of intentionality will be forthcoming. The hope, in other words, is that by first accounting for phenomenal character in terms of intentionality, and then accounting for intentionality in terms of scientifically unproblematic properties (such as causal role or correlation), we might be able to solve the hard problem and close the explanatory gap.[12]

Of course, it is one thing for a position to be attractive and quite another for it to be true. One particularly acute challenge to intentionalism is that posed by moods. As Angela Mendelovici (2014) puts it, moods 'throw a wrench in the intentionalist project', for they don't seem to be about anything. Emotions typically (perhaps always) have objects – one might be angry about a perceived insult or excited about an upcoming anniversary – but moods appear to lack any kind of directness towards particular aspects of the world. One can simply wake up in a state of cheerfulness. If asked what one is happy about one might be lost for words. As far as one can tell 'from the inside', one's jovial mood might seem to be completely undirected. The same point applies to (say) melancholy and depression. The experiences associated with moods simply don't seem to be in the business of saying how things are.

Intentionalists argue that appearances are misleading, and that moods do in fact have representational content. However, intentionalists do not have a shared view of the kind of content that moods possess. Some intentionalists argue that moods represent physiological states in much the way in which sensations of thirst, hunger, and nausea do. For example, Tye claims that moods represent departures from the functional equilibrium that characterizes our normal bodily state (Tye 1995: 129). We might call this account of moods the *inward-facing* view, for it treats moods as representations of internal bodily states. Others argue that moods represent features of one's environment, and that they have more in common with perceptual experiences than they do with bodily sensations. However, unlike ordinary perceptual experiences (which ascribe properties to particular objects), moods have a global focus – their objects are 'near all-inclusive and undifferentiated', as Annette Baier (1990) has put it. Robert Solomon captures this perspective elegantly:

> Euphoria, melancholy and depression are not about anything in particular (though some particular incident might well set them off); they are about the whole of our world, or indiscriminately about anything that comes our way, casting happy glows or somber shadows on every object and incident of our experience
>
> (Solomon 1976: 173)

We might call this the *outward-facing* view of moods, for it supposes that moods are in the business of representing the state of the world rather than the state of the internal milieu.

There are various questions that could be put to each of these views. We could ask proponents of the inward-facing view how it captures the phenomenal differences between moods – why, that is, does one kind of departure from functional equilibrium feel like *this* whereas another feels like *that*. With respect to the outward-facing view, we could ask what exactly it is for a mood to cast a 'happy glow' or a 'somber shadow' on one's environment. What must the world be like in order for such an experience to be *veridical* and to represent things as they are?

But it is an objection that applies to both strategies, which seems to me to be the most problematic for the intentionalist: whatever content moods have, it doesn't seem to be the right *kind* of content to account for phenomenal character. Here's why. If intentional content is to explain phenomenal character, then that content must be accessible to its subject. This condition is met in perceptual contexts, for perceptual content *is* available to the subject. For example, an agent can match a visually presented object with another object of the same shape or hue. But whatever content moods have, it doesn't seem to inform thought and action in the ways in which personal-level content must. Thus, the content of mood experiences would appear to be subpersonal rather than personal. But in that case, it's not clear how appeals to it might account for the phenomenal character of moods, for phenomenal character is clearly a personal-level phenomenon.

9.6 Conclusion

Let's review the ground that we've covered in this chapter. We began with the central methodological challenge facing the science of consciousness: should it restrict itself to first-person (or 'subjective') measures, or should it make use of third-person (or 'objective') measures? First-person measures are problematic: not only are there doubts about their reliability and scientific standing, but there are many contexts in which they simply can't be used. At the same time, they seem to be required in order to validate potential third-person methods for identifying consciousness. Addressing this methodological challenge thus remains an ongoing task.

We then considered four of the most influential accounts of consciousness: monitoring accounts, neural accounts, functional accounts, and intentional accounts. There are no decisive arguments for or against any one of these views, and each has its advocates. In a sense, the fundamental challenge that they all face is that of extrapolating from facts about consciousness as it occurs in 'us' – adult human beings who are able to report on our experiences – to other creatures, such as human infants, non-human animals, and artificial systems. We know that consciousness emerges from the operations of the embodied brain, but we don't know whether it is the distinctively neural properties of the brain's activity that accounts for consciousness, or whether it's the brain's functional and representational properties that are most relevant. And here, perhaps, we return to the challenges discussed in the previous chapter, for addressing these questions may require closing the explanatory gap and solving the hard problem.

Further reading

For more on theories of consciousness, see William Seager's *Theories of Consciousness: An Introduction and Assessment* (2nd ed., Routledge, 2016) and Rocco Gennaro's *Consciousness* (Routledge, 2016). Anil Seth's *Being You* (Dutton, 2021) and Susan Blackmore and Emily

Troscianko's *Consciousness: An Introduction* (3rd ed., Routledge, 2018) are both engaging introductions to the science of consciousness, and each volume covers a much wider range of theories than this chapter does.

On the methodological issues confronting the science of consciousness, see Maja Spener's 'Consciousness, Introspection, and Subjective Measures', in U. Kriegel (ed.), *The Oxford Handbook of the Philosophy of Consciousness* (OUP, 2020) and Elizabeth Irvine's *Consciousness as a Scientific Concept* (Springer, 2012). Also excellent is Irvine's 'Old Problems with New Measures in the Science of Consciousness', *British Journal for the Philosophy of Science*, 63(3): 627–48 (2012).

The best anthology of papers on theories of consciousness remains *The Nature of Consciousness* (MIT, 1997), edited by Ned Block, Owen Flanagan, and Güven Güzeldere. On higher-order theories of consciousness see Rocco Generro (ed.), *Higher-Order Theories of Consciousness: An Anthology* (John Benjamins, 2004); Josh Weisberg 'Higher-Order Theories of Consciousness', in U. Kriegel (ed.), *The Oxford Handbook of the Philosophy of Consciousness* (OUP, 2020); and R. Brown, H. Lau, and J. E. LeDoux, 'Understanding the Higher-Order Approach to Consciousness', *Trends in Cognitive Sciences*, 23(9): 754–68 (2019). On self-representational approaches to consciousness, see Uriah Kriegel and Ken Williford (eds.), *Self-Representational Theories of Consciousness* (MIT, 2006) and Tom McClelland's entry on the topic in Uriah Kriegel (ed.), *The Oxford Handbook of the Philosophy of Consciousness* (OUP, 2020).

For overviews of intentionalism, see Adam Pautz's 'Representationalism about Consciousness', in Uriah Kriegel (ed.), *The Oxford Handbook of the Philosophy of Consciousness* (OUP, 2020) and Michael Tye's 'Representationalist Theories of Consciousness', in B. McLaughlin, A. Beckermann and S. Walter (eds.), *The Oxford Handbook of Philosophy of Mind* (OUP, 2009). For more on moods and intentionalism see Murat Aydede and Matthew Fulkerson, 'Affect: Representationalists' Headache', *Philosophical Studies*, 170(2): 175–98 (2014), and the debate between Amy Kind and Angela Mendelovici in Uriah Kriegel (ed.), *Current Controversies in the Philosophy of Mind* (Routledge, 2014); Mendelovici argues in favour of intentionalism about moods, whereas Kind argues against it. For more on emotion and moods more generally, see Julien Deonna and Fabrice Teroni's *The Emotions: A Philosophical Introduction* (Routledge, 2012).

Study questions

1. What is the difference between first-person methods and third-person methods in the study of consciousness? What are their respective strengths and weaknesses? Do you think that it is fair to describe first-person methods as 'subjective' and third-person methods as 'objective'?
2. What is the difference between an account of state consciousness and an account of conscious character? Which theories of consciousness aim to answer both questions, and which theories aim to answer just one of these questions?
3. Is there a single sense in which a mental state can be said to be conscious, or does the term 'consciousness' mean one thing when applied to (say) perceptual experiences and bodily sensations and another when applied to (say) thoughts?

4   What is the difference between higher-order and same-order versions of the monitoring approach to consciousness? Why do both higher-order and same-order theories of consciousness qualify as versions of the monitoring approach to consciousness?
5   Explain and evaluate the conceptual argument for monitoring theories of consciousness.
6   Why does neural plasticity pose a challenge to neural theories of consciousness? How might the advocate of a neural theory of consciousness respond to the challenge of neural plasticity?
7   Explain and evaluate Ned Block's China-Brain objection to functionalism.
8   Why do moods pose a challenge to intentionalist accounts of phenomenal character? Do intentionalists have an adequate response to that challenge?

Notes

1 For a variety of perspectives on introspection and first-person methods, see Irvine (2012b), Feest (2014), Goldman (1997), Goldman (2003), Jack and Roepstorff (2003), Jack and Roepstorff (2004), Overgaard (2006), Piccinini (2009), and Spener (2019).
2 See Chapter 12 for more on introspection.
3 For more on introspective disputes, see Bayne and Spener (2010), Hohwy (2011), Kriegel (2007), Siewert (2007), and Schwitzgebel (2008).
4 For discussion of various third-person methods, see Irvine (2012b), Sandberg et al. (2010), and Seth et al. (2008).
5 My own view is that generic consciousness and state consciousness are intimately related, and an account of the latter should deliver an account of the former. As I see it, a creature is conscious just in case it has a subjective perspective, and it has a subjective perspective just in case it has phenomenally conscious mental states.
6 Consider, for example, the taxonomies developed by Ned Block, David Rosenthal, and Christopher Hill. Block (1995) claims that four phenomena trade under the label 'consciousness': phenomenal consciousness, access consciousness, monitoring consciousness, and self-consciousness. Rosenthal (2002) argues that neither phenomenal consciousness nor access consciousness is a genuine form of consciousness, but he does distinguish two kinds of mental state consciousness: transitive consciousness and intransitive consciousness. Hill (2009) identifies six kinds of consciousness: agent consciousness, propositional consciousness, introspective consciousness, relational consciousness, phenomenal consciousness, and experiential consciousness.
7 There are, however, exceptions. For dissent, see Rosenthal (2002). For an important discussion of phenomenal consciousness, see Byrne (2004).
8 Monitoring accounts are also officially silent when it comes to the explanation of generic consciousness, although it is natural for the monitoring theorist to hold that a creature is conscious just in case it monitors some of its mental states in the appropriate manner.
9 Lycan actually presents the argument as an argument for the higher-order account of consciousness, and formulates its conclusion as follows:

(5)   A conscious state is a state that is itself represented by *another* of the subject's mental states. (my emphasis)

However, as far as I can tell, Lycan's argument provides no reason to think that the representing state must be distinct from the represented state, and I have thus revised its conclusion so as to make it acceptable to both higher-order and same-order theorists.
10 Recent advocates of neural accounts of consciousness include Block (2009), Hill (1991), Lamme (2006), McLaughlin (2007), Perry (2001), and Polger (2004). Older versions of the approach include Armstrong (1968) and Lewis (1966, 1980).
11 An influential variant of this theory is known as the global neuronal workspace theory (GNWT), for it includes claims about the neural implementation of the global workspace; namely, that it is located

in the parietal and frontal areas (Dehaene & Naccache 2001; Mashour et al. 2020). However, at its core NGWT remains a version of functionalism, for it holds that frontoparietal areas are relevant to consciousness only because they implement a global workspace architecture.

12 Because of this, the contrast between intentionalist and functionalist accounts of consciousness needs to be handled with some care. Although each view can be endorsed independently of the other, one can also combine them by appealing to functionalism as an account of why an experience has the content (and thus, according to the intentionalist, the phenomenal character) that it does.

10 Mental causation

> **Chapter overview**
>
> - Considers what lies behind our ordinary commitment to the reality of mental causation
> - Explores the exclusion argument against mental causation and considers a number of responses to it
> - Examines the tension between mental causation and externalist accounts of mental content
> - Considers an apparent challenge to mental causation posed by the work of the neuroscientist Benjamin Libet.

In his paper 'Making Mind Matter More', Jerry Fodor wrote:

> If it isn't literally true that my wanting is causally responsible for my reaching, and my itching is causally responsible for my scratching, and my believing is causally responsible for my saying. . . . If none of that is literally true, then practically everything I believe about anything is false and it's the end of the world.
>
> (Fodor 1990: 156)

Fodor's prose might be a little purple, but he is surely right to suggest that mental causation is central to our self-conception. If our mental states have no causal powers, then our practice of holding each other accountable for our actions would be threatened, the legal requirement of mens rea (a guilty mind) may be impossible to satisfy, and we would have no reason to take a person's utterances or facial expressions as a guide to what they thought or felt. Indeed, if there were no mental causation then the very existence of mentality would be in doubt, for if mental states have no causal powers then it's unclear how they could make their existence known to us.

There are, however, a number of arguments that appear to show that wants, itches, and beliefs don't – indeed, can't – cause reachings, scratchings, or sayings. One of the most significant of these challenges is the causal exclusion argument, developed in most detail by Jaegwon Kim (1934-2019). Section 10.2 first introduces you to the exclusion argument and then considers how dualists and identity theorists respond to it; Section 10.3 explores how nonreductive physicalists might respond to it. In Section 10.4, we consider a challenge to mental causation posed by content externalism – the view that mental content isn't fixed by what's 'in the head' but can depend on an agent's history and/or environment (see Chapter 7). The chapter concludes by examining a challenge to mental causation raised by Benjamin Libet's neuroscientific research into the initiation of voluntary action.

But before we consider the challenges facing mental causation, we need first to explore the roots of our commitment to it. Why exactly do we assume that wants cause reachings, itches cause scratchings, and beliefs cause sayings, and is there anything to be said in defence of this assumption?

10.1 Motivating mental causation

If you are in a situation that allows it, raise either your left hand or your right hand. Done? Now reflect for a moment on the nature of your experience. Did you experience your mental states as causally implicated in your actions? Were you aware of yourself as deliberating about which hand to raise? Did it seem to you as though your deliberation – or perhaps the intention that you formed as the result of your deliberation – caused your hand to move? If so, you would be in good company, for many claim to be introspectively aware of the causal powers of thought. As Descartes put it in a letter to Princess Elisabeth of Bohemia, even those who never philosophize 'do not doubt in the least that the soul moves the body' (Descartes 1643/2007: 69).

Although introspectively based arguments for mental causation have a wide and enduring appeal, they are also very controversial. Some reject them because they doubt that introspection is trustworthy. These theorists agree that introspection seems to tell us that mental states cause our actions, but they deny that we have good reason to treat introspection as a reliable guide to the causal structure of the mind. Others theorist doubt whether introspection even *seems* to tell us that our thoughts cause our actions. These theorists grant that we experience our movements as realizing our intentions and decisions, but they deny that we ordinarily experience our movements as *caused* by our intentions and decisions (O'Connor 1995; Horgan et al. 2003; Wakefield & Dreyfus 1991). Indeed, these authors suggest that if there is any causal content to ordinary agentive experience, it involves the *self*: I experience myself (rather than my mental states) as the source of my actions. The phenomenology of first-person agency deserves more attention than we can give it here, but suffice it to say that it is an open question whether we really do experience our mental states as the causes of our behaviour.[1]

A second (and less controversial) motivation for mental causation concerns the explanatory role of the mind. Suppose that you have arranged to meet Frederique at the Eiffel Tower at noon. We can explain why you make your way to the Eiffel Tower by appealing to your beliefs about the time and location of the appointment and your desire to meet Frederique. Explaining behaviour in terms of mental states doesn't just render it intelligible, it seems also to identify its causes. If asked why you went to the Eiffel Tower you might say, 'Because that's

180 Mental causation

where I had arranged to meet Frederique'. The 'because' in this sentence appears to identify both the *reasons* for your behaviour and its *causes*. Without mental causation, the notion that we are agents who have genuine control over our actions would be called into question.

Having considered two of the main motivations for our commitment to mental causation, let's turn now to question of what that commitment involves. What exactly would it take to vindicate mental causation? There are two components to this question: a 'mental' bit and a 'causal' bit. Let's begin with the mental bit.

Ideally, an account of mental causation should vindicate the thought that mental states are causally efficacious in virtue of their mental features. That claim isn't the platitude that it might seem to be, for an event can be causally efficacious in virtue of some of its properties but not others. Suppose that Helen sings the closing notes of Gustav Mahler's *Um Mitternacht* (At Midnight), and in so doing she causes a window to shatter. Intuitively, what caused the window to shatter wasn't the meaning of what Helen sang but the volume of her singing. The window would still have shattered had Helen sung (say) Strauss's *Four Last Songs* equally loudly, but not if she had sung *Um Mitternacht* quietly.

The demand that an account of mental causation should show that mental states are causally efficacious in virtue of their mental features is really just the demand that an account of mental causation should secure the causal efficacy of mental properties (better: instantiations of mental properties). Intuitively, my intention to lift my arm is causally efficacious in virtue of the fact that it is an intention of a specific kind (namely, to lift my arm). Following Horgan (1989), we might say that an account of mental causation should really be an account of 'mental quausation', for we want to vindicate the idea that mental states are causally efficacious *qua* (i.e., in virtue of their being) mental states.

What about the 'causal' bit of 'mental causation'? The notion of causation is about as troublesome as any notion can be, and the amount that has been written on it would fill a small library. Luckily, we can make some headway with respect to the problem of mental causation without a deep dive into the causation literature. However, there is one distinction that will prove absolutely vital in what follows, and that is the distinction between two very general accounts of causation: *productive accounts* and *difference-making accounts* (Hall 2004). The former take causation to involve the transmission of a quantity of some kind: force, power, or energy (Dowe 2000). As it is sometimes put, productive views treat causation as 'oomphy'. Difference-making accounts of causation makes no commitment to the transfer of force or energy from one event to another, but focus instead on how states of one kind depend on states of another kind (Lewis 1973; Menzies & Beebee 2019). At the heart of the difference-making approach is the idea that causal facts are essentially facts about the counterfactual structure of the world – that is, how changes to one aspect of the world would affect other aspects of the world. As we will see, the distinction between causation-as-production and causation-as-difference-making has an important bearing on certain objections to mental causation.

10.2 The causal exclusion objection

Of the many challenges to mental causation, Jaegwon Kim's causal exclusion challenge has dominated the field. The problem can be put as follows. Consider a simple action, such as raising your right hand. Intuitively, your decision to raise your right hand caused the movement of your hand. Let's call the movement of your hand 'E', for we assume that it was an

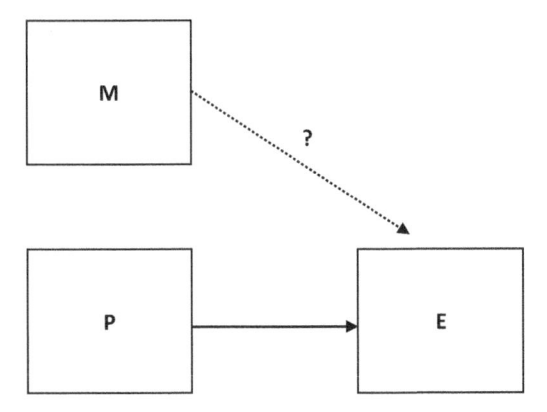

Figure 10.1 Apparent causal competition between the mental and the physical. Given that P is causally sufficient for E, what work is there for M to do?

effect of your decision. And let's call the decision to raise your right hand 'M', in honour of the fact that it is a mental state. Now, suppose that the physical realm is causally complete (or closed, as it is sometimes put), so that for any physical state there is a prior physical state that is fully sufficient for it. Given completeness, there will be a prior physical state that is causally sufficient for E. Let's call that prior state 'P'. The exclusion problem is this: given that P is causally sufficient for E, what work is there for M to do? M's causal status with respect to E seems to be undermined by the presence of P (see Figure 10.1). In effect, the exclusion problem treats mental states and physical states as causal competitors. Given that the causal credentials of physical states would seem to be impeccable, the argument appears to show that there is no causal work for mental states to do.

We can formalize the exclusion objection as follows:

1 P is causally sufficient for E. (COMPLETENESS)
2 If P is causally sufficient for E, then nothing that is distinct from P causes E unless E is overdetermined. (EXCLUSION)
3 M is distinct from (i.e., not identical to) P. (DISTINCTNESS)
4 This is not a case of overdetermination. (NON-OVERDETERMINATION)

Therefore,

5 M doesn't cause E.

The exclusion problem has generated a small mountain of literature, and there is no consensus on how it might be solved, if indeed it can be solved at all. That said, few theorists take it to show that mental causation doesn't occur; indeed, not even Kim saw it in this light. As he put it, the problem is one of showing '*how* mental causation is possible, not *whether* it is possible' (Kim 1998: 61). The challenge is to identify where the argument goes wrong, and why it goes wrong where it does.

Dualists sometimes reject COMPLETENESS, holding that there are gaps in the causal structure of the physical world that are plugged by mental phenomena. If we were to follow the causal path back from certain kinds of behaviour, they suggest, we would inevitably find a physical event that is caused by a mental event (such as an act of volition), but has no causally sufficient physical antecedents. This was Descartes's account of mental causation, and although it still has its advocates, it is widely assumed to be inconsistent with what we know from science. Although some events (such as radioactive decay) might be uncaused, it is generally held that if an event has a fully sufficient cause, then it has a fully sufficient *physical* cause. Certainly, most physicalists hold that one needn't go beyond physical theory (and in particular, neuroscience) to find the causal roots of behaviour. If one were to trace the causal path back from the activity in the motor cortex that triggers a movement, then one would never encounter anything other than a physical state.[2]

The EXCLUSION principle also seems unobjectionable, for if a previous state of my brain is causally sufficient for the movement of my hand, then it might seem as though my decision causes my hand to move only if the movement of my hand has *two* causes: a physical cause (P) and a mental cause (M). The idea that the movement of my hand has two full causes is certainly coherent, for events *can* be causally overdetermined. Consider the unlucky mafioso victim, who finds himself the target of two hitmen who just so happen to shoot him at precisely the same time. Each shot is fully sufficient to bring about the victim's demise, and it is mere coincidence that they are simultaneous. Perhaps mental states and physical states work in this way: independent causes that are each fully sufficient to bring about their effects. In other words, perhaps we should reject NON-OVERDETERMINATION.

But although it is possible for an event to have two full causes, it seems implausible to suppose that the movements of one's body are systematically overdetermined in the way in which the death of the mafioso victim is. After all, if P causes E, then it looks as though M is superfluous to requirements. But that seems wrong. Intuitively, an account of mental causation should ensure not just that mental states are causally efficacious, but that they are (at least sometimes) *needed* for their effects. At the very least, if mental causation does involve overdetermination, then the kind of overdetermination that it involves is surely not usefully modelled on the case of the unlucky mafioso victim.

But if we accept COMPLETENESS, EXCLUSION, and NON-OVERDETERMINATION, then it seems as though mental causation can be saved only by rejecting DISTINCTNESS. This is precisely the lesson that Kim draws from the exclusion argument: mental states and neural states aren't causal competitors because mental states *are* physical states. As we noted in Chapter 3, this form of reductive physicalism is known as the type identity theory, so named because it identifies mental types (i.e., properties) with physical types. In the same way that lightning is electrochemical discharge, so too - the type identity theorist claims - the decision to raise one's hand is identical to a physical state (presumably a neural state). The forest fire was caused by electrical discharge and lightning, but this isn't a case of overdetermination because lightning just is electrical discharge.

Rejecting NON-DISTINCTNESS comes at a price, for there are influential - and, to my mind, compelling - objections to the type identity account. As we noted in earlier chapters, mental properties seem to be multiply realizable: two individuals can be in the same type of mental state without being in the same type of brain state. This objection isn't decisive (see, e.g., Lewis 1980; Kim 1998), but it is certainly powerful. In my view - and indeed that of many others - reductive physicalism of the kind exemplified by the type identity theory is an option of last resort.

Of course, if the type identity account provided the only way to save mental causation, then perhaps we ought to embrace it no matter how serious the objections to it might be. (After all, one might think that rejecting mental causation is also an option of last resort!) However, we will see that mental causation can be saved without embracing reductive physicalism. Moreover, it's not clear that reductive physicalism would deliver everything that we might want from an account of mental causation. Let's dwell on this point for a minute.

Return to our example of mental causation: your decision to raise your right hand causes your hand to move. Assuming the truth of reductive physicalism, your decision is identical to a certain brain state, and will thus be causally efficacious if that brain state is causally efficacious. But although this account might save mental causation, it sheds no light on why the cause of your movement is best described in psychological terms. In a sense, reductionism 'saves' mental causation only by rebranding it as a kind of neural causation. If mental states were physical states, then psychological terms wouldn't be needed for the causal explanation of behaviour. But genuine commitment to mental causation, one might argue, requires that the causal explanations provided by psychological predicates can't be replaced by those provided by some other explanatory framework (such as neuroscience; see Box: Token identities [again]).

Box: Token identities (again)

Kim adopts the type identity theory as a solution to the exclusion problem, but there is also another form of reductionism that is sometimes taken to solve the exclusion problem: the *token* identity theory. Developed by Donald Davidson, the token identity account holds that although mental properties cannot be identified with neural properties, each particular mental event is identical to a particular neural event. The token identity view promises to secure mental causation, for if mental events are neural events, then there is no principled reason to think that mental events can't be causes. Can this promise be met?

There are two reasons to think not. The first problem is that the token identity theorist has nothing to say about the causal powers of mental properties. On the token identity view, my pain causes me to say 'Ouch!', but it doesn't play this causal role in virtue of the fact that it is a pain. Davidson was unperturbed by this criticism, for he regarded events (understood as unstructured particulars) as the relata of causation, and was a nominalist about properties. But it is widely – and, in my view, correctly – held that an account of mental causation ought to capture the idea that mental phenomena have causal powers in virtue of their mental properties.

The second problem for the token identity view concerns causal explanation. Consider a finding from research into depression, which suggests that one of the main causal factors for depression is humiliation rather than loss (Kendler et al. 2003). Generalizations of this kind are ubiquitous in psychiatry and psychology, but it is not clear how to account for them within the framework of Davidson's account, for it assumes that the only causal generalizations that apply to mental events are those that describe them in terms of physical predicates.

Further reading

Davidson, D. 1970. Thinking Causes. Reprinted in J. Heil and A. Mele (eds.), *Mental Causation*. Oxford University Press, 1993.
Davidson, D. 1995. Laws and Cause. *Dialectica*, 49(2-4): 263-80.
Honderich, T. 1982. The Argument for Anomalous Monism. *Analysis*, 42: 59-64.

We have seen that the exclusion argument doesn't trouble dualists who are prepared to reject CLOSURE, nor does it trouble those physicalists who are prepared to reject NON-DISTINCTNESS, as identity theorists are. But it does trouble non-reductive physicalists, for the non-reductive physicalist denies that mental properties are identical to neural properties. In Section 10.3, we consider some of the ways in which non-reductive physicalists have responded to the argument. But before we turn to those responses, we need to consider one very important point about the argument: it generalizes.

We have focused on the idea that there is causal competition between neural states and mental states, but there is nothing in the structure of the exclusion argument which restricts its scope to mentality. In fact, it seems as though variants of the argument could be applied to *any* high-level property. For example, one could deploy a version of the argument to make the case that biological properties must be epiphenomenal because all the causal work is really done by the chemical properties on which biological properties supervene. Indeed, given that neural states supervene on more fundamental physical states, one could even develop an exclusion argument to cast doubt on the causal efficacy of *neural* states. In short, if the exclusion argument were sound, it would threaten to drain causation from the world entirely (Block 2003b).[3]

Perhaps, you might be thinking, the real moral of the exclusion argument is that all high-level properties *are* epiphenomenal, and that causation is to be found only at the level of fundamental physics. But that conclusion is surely untenable, for causal claims are ubiquitous in the special sciences. (Indeed, there is reason to think that causation obtains *only* in the special sciences, and that causal relations have no home in fundamental physics at all.)[4] Better, then, to regard the generalizability of the exclusion argument as evidence that it goes wrong somewhere. The question is, *where*?

10.3 Causal exclusion and non-reductive physicalism

Suppose that a rock is thrown at a window causing it to break. Why did the window break? One answer to this question appeals to the window's fragility; another appeals to its molecular structure. As Frank Jackson and Philip Pettit (1990) point out, the appeal to the window's molecular structure seems to trump the appeal to its fragility if we are looking to identify the cause of the event. But, they claim, although the window's fragility doesn't cause it to break, it is *causally relevant* to its breaking, for the window's fragility ensures that it will have a molecular structure that causes it to break when struck with appropriate force. As Jackson and Pettit put it, fragility is not itself causally efficacious, but it 'programs' for properties that are.

Jackson and Pettit go on to argue that the relationship between the glass's fragility and its molecular structure provides a good model of the relationship between mental properties and their neural underpinnings. Although mental properties don't themselves have physical effects, they program for neural states which do. The decision to move your hand doesn't cause your hand to move, but it is causally relevant to its motion, for an agent who has decided to move her hand will be in a neural state that causes her hand to move.

The appeal to program explanation has some attractive features. For one thing, it captures the causal relevance of psychological explanations, and in this regard it improves on the account of psychological explanation provided by the identity theory. But it also falls far short of what we might want from an account of mental causation, for it grants that mental states *aren't* causally efficacious. In fact, the appeal to program explanation provides a response to the exclusion argument only insofar as it demonstrates that appeals to mentality are causally relevant. That's obviously better than nothing, but it's hardly the full-throated defence of mental causation for which we might have hoped.

A more robust response to the exclusion argument begins with a story told by Stephen Yablo (1992). Suppose that we wave a scarlet flag at a bull, thus provoking the bull to charge. We might, Yablo says, entertain two hypotheses about what caused the bull to charge:

1 What caused the bull to charge was the flag's being scarlet.
2 What caused the bull to charge was the flag's being red.

If the bull charges only in response to scarlet flags (and ignores other shades of red), then it would be reasonable to prefer (1) over (2). If, on the other hand, the bull would have charged no matter what shade of red the flag had been, then we should prefer (2) instead. The reason for this, Yablo suggests, is that causes must be proportionate to their effects. To cite the flag's being scarlet as the cause of the bull's charging would be to provide an overly specific factor if the bull would have charged irrespective of the flag's shade of red. But even when we have reason to prefer (2) rather than (1), it is still the case that the flag's being scarlet was *causally sufficient* for the bull to charge. Why? Well, the flag's being scarlet ensures that it is red, and we are assuming that the flag's being red is what caused the bull to charge.

Yablo's case of the charging bull provides a counterexample to EXCLUSION (see Figure 10.2). Because causation is governed by the proportionality constraint, a property can be causally sufficient for an effect without qualifying as its cause.[5] Yablo treats the proportionality constraint as intuitively compelling, and he is surely right to do so. After all, if the bull would have charged no matter what shade of red the flag had been, then we would surely have said that cause of its charging was the flag's redness rather than the fact that it was scarlet. At same time, we would be on firmer ground in rejecting EXCLUSION if we could provide some kind of theoretical backing for the proportionality constraint.

That backing can be provided by considering the nature of causation. At the end of Section 10.1, we distinguished two conceptions of causation: causation-as-production and causation-as-difference-making. The former approach sees causation as involving the transmission of some kind of force or power, whereas the latter conceives of causation in terms of relations of counterfactual dependence. Now, although the proportionality constraint might

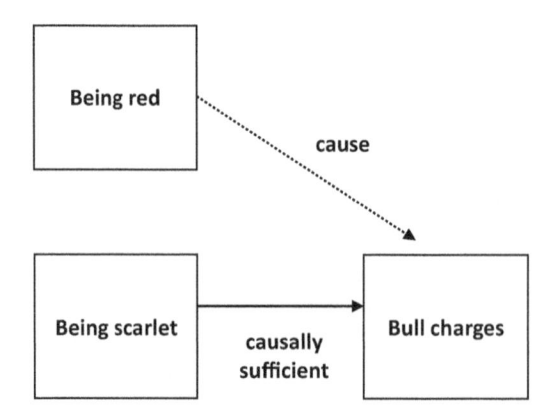

Figure 10.2 A schematic representation of Yablo's counterexample to EXCLUSION

appear to be unmotivated from the perspective of production views of causation, it falls naturally out of a difference-making conception of causation.

Consider once again Yablo's bull. The flag's being scarlet suffices for the fact that the bull charged, but it's not a difference-maker in this case, for had the flag been any other shade of red the bull would still have charged. An intuitive way to think of this is in terms of the kinds of interventions that would have altered the relevant outcome. Intervening on the redness of the flag (by, say, changing it to blue) would have prevented the bull from charging, but if indeed it is the redness of the flag that caused the bull to charge, then intervening on the flag's shade of red (by, say, changing it from scarlet to crimson) would have had no effect.

Let's apply this picture to the problem of mental causation. The problem, you will recall, is that mental states seem to be locked in causal competition with the brain states that underpin them. Thus, we seem forced to either: reject the reality of mental causation; accept that our behaviour is systematically overdetermined (having both mental states and brain states as its causes); or identify mental states with brain states. Difference-making accounts of causation provide us with a fourth option: although the brain states that underpin our mental states are causally sufficient for our behaviour, they may not qualify as its causes because the mental states that supervene on them may be better qualified to function as the difference-makers for behaviour actions than are their underlying brain states.[6]

Consider again my decision to move my right hand (M), which causes my hand to move (E). Now, suppose that you want to prevent my right hand from going up. Intuitively, the most effective way to do that would be intervene on M; that's the relevant difference-maker here. Intervening on the neural state (P) that underpins M might be less effective way of affecting whether E occurs. Why? Because P is only one of the many ways in which M might be realized, just as a flag's being scarlet is only one of the many ways in which it can be red. In short, the difference-making approach to causation provides the non-reductionist with grounds for rejecting EXCLUSION, and if EXCLUSION goes then so too does the causal exclusion argument.

It is important to recognize that this result is limited in two respects. First, although we have seen that mental properties *can* defeat neural properties insofar as they are causal competitors, we have found no reason to assume that the proportionality constraint will always (or even in general) favour mental states over the neural states with which they are in competition. Even if mental properties *can* successfully compete with neural properties with respect to causal status, it is a further question how often, and in what contexts, they might do so. Second, and more fundamentally, we haven't established that mental states have causal powers. As Karen Bennett (2007) has pointed out, the exclusion argument assumes that mental states are capable of causal work and aims to show only that they don't actually cause anything (on the grounds that there is such work for them to do).[7] There are, however, arguments which raise doubts about the very capacity of mental states to function as causes. We turn to one such argument now.

10.4 Externalism and mental causation

When Helen broke the window pane by singing the closing notes of Mahler's *Um Mitternacht*, the effect was due not to the meaning of what she sang but to the volume of her singing. But although the meaning of Helen's words didn't cause the window to break, it did have an effect on her audience, causing them to enter a mood of sombre reflection. It's not just the meaning of our words that can have an impact on the world, so too can the meaning of our thoughts. Helen sang Mahler's *Um Mitternacht* because she wanted to. Had she wanted to sing something else – Richard Strauss's *Four Last Songs*, for example – then that's what she would have done.

We take the causal efficacy of mental content for granted, but it is surely one of the most mysterious features of the mind. How can meanings be causes? This challenge faces all accounts of content, but externalists face a particularly pressing version of it. As we saw in Chapter 7, externalists hold that a person's mental states constitutively depend on how they are embedded in their environment. Different versions of externalism focus on different aspects of an agent's environment – some focus on evolutionary properties, others on the underlying nature of their physical environment, and still others on facts about an agent's social and linguistic environment – but all externalists deny that meaning is fixed by what's 'in the head'. Externalism poses a challenge to mental causation, for an object's causal powers seems to depend solely on its intrinsic properties. If a 25-cent coin can activate a vending machine, then so too can its counterfeits– objects that have the size, shape, and mass of a 25-cent coin but not its historical or relational properties. A commitment to the idea that mental states are causally efficacious in virtue of their content seems to be at odds with a commitment to content externalism.

We can put this problem in terms of what I will call the *argument from externalism*.

1. Mental states are not intrinsic, for they depend constitutively on facts about the agent's history and/or environment. (EXTERNALISM)
2. An agent's behaviour is caused only by their intrinsic states. (LOCALISM)
3. Therefore, mental states are not causally efficacious.

In the same way that the causal exclusion argument can be seen as an objection to non-reductive physicalism rather than an objection to mental causation, so too the argument from externalism can be turned on its head to provide an objection to externalism rather than an objection to mental causation. Indeed, some theorists embrace internalism precisely because they take externalism to undermine the possibility of mental causation (e.g., Crane 1991). Those who take this approach might allow that there is a kind of content that is 'wide', but they deny that this content is causally efficacious. Ordinary ascriptions of intentional states might appeal to wide content, but only narrow content (they claim) is implicated in causal accounts of an agent's behaviour.

Although this two-factor view of content represents a possible fall-back position for those troubled by the argument from externalism, we might also want to know whether externalism itself can be reconciled with a commitment to mental causation.

One attempt to do just that is due to Fred Dretske (1988, 1993). Dretske distinguishes two kinds of causes: *triggering* causes and *structuring* causes. Triggering causes are directly involved in the production of their effects. Moving a computer mouse is a triggering cause of the movement of the cursor on a laptop's screen. Structuring causes explain why a triggering cause has the effects that it does. For example, the mouse can control the cursor only if it is appropriately embedded in the relevant system. With this distinction in place, Dretske suggests that although mental states aren't triggering causes of behaviour, they can function as structuring causes of behaviour. Although an agent's neural states are directly involved in the production of behaviour (and thus function as triggering causes), their mental states explain why the agent's neural states have the causal powers that they do (thus functioning as structuring causes). In effect, Dretske accepts EXTERNALISM, and he accepts LOCALISM insofar as it applies to triggering causes, but he argues that our commitment to mental causation can be salvaged by recognizing a kind of causation, structuring causation, which doesn't depend only on intrinsic properties.

One question raised by Dretske's proposal is whether mental properties really do function as structuring causes of behaviour. Although it's certainly true that environmental factors have an impact on how an agent is wired, one might think that the impact must always be mediated by its effects on an agent's intrinsic properties. Those properties will, it seems, screen off the contribution of the organism's environment. If this line of thought is right, then the appeal to structural causation may not provide an account of how wide content can be causally efficacious.

Moreover, even if it can be shown that mental states are structuring causes, that may not deliver what we want from a defence of mental causation. On Dretske's account, your decision to get a drink of water is relevant to your behaviour only insofar as it explains your *capacity* to get a drink of water. But that's not how we typically view the causal role of decisions. Instead, we regard decisions as 'here-and-now' (or 'proximal') causes of bodily movement. Dretske's account delivers something in the vicinity of mental causation, but it falls short of what we pre-theoretically want.

Let's return to the argument from externalism, and see if it might not be possible to reconcile externalism with the view that mental states are triggering causes. Note, first, that the challenge raised by the anti-externalism argument is not specific to mental causation but arises in any context that involves relationally individuated properties. A biologist, for example, might explain facts about the behaviour of an animal by adverting to the species to which it belongs. But being the member of a particular species isn't an intrinsic property of an animal; it's a relational property. (Two animals that are molecular duplicates could belong to different species on account of their different histories.) Similarly, an economist might explain why inflation is rising by appealing to relational properties, such as a country's balance of payments or its levels of foreign investment. In the same way that the exclusion argument raises issues that go far beyond the scope of mental causation, so too does the argument from externalism. Recognizing this fact does not itself show where the argument goes wrong, but it suggests that it must go wrong somewhere. With that in mind, let's return to the argument.

Given that the externalist can't reject EXTERNALISM, it looks as though their only option is to reject LOCALISM. Must causes be local, involving only intrinsic states? Consider sunburn. Being sunburnt is not an intrinsic state, for it is constitutive of being sunburnt that you have been exposed to the sun (or at least, some form of ultraviolet radiation). But being sunburnt is also evidently a state with causal powers. Sunburn causes people to moan, to sleep badly, and to seek medical attention (when sufficiently severe).

This apparent counterexample to LOCALISM can be challenged, for a critic could argue that sunburn doesn't really have the suite of effects that it seems to. Consider two individuals, Bonnie and Clyde. Bonnie is suffering from a severe case of sunburn. Clyde's skin is also damaged, but in his case the damage was caused by being exposed to a chemical. Further, let's assume that both Bonnie and Clyde seek medical attention in order to relieve their suffering. How should we describe the cause of their behaviour? Intuitively, we might be inclined to say that Bonnie seeks medical help because she is sunburnt. After all, that is the state in which she finds herself; had she not been sunburnt then she wouldn't be seeking medical help. But - the critic might point out - we can't explain Clyde's behaviour in the same way, for he isn't sunburnt. But (the critic might continue) our intuitions here must be wrong, for Bonnie's and Clyde's actions have the same cause - after all, we are assuming that their skin is damaged in the same way. We might be tempted to say that Bonnie does what she does because she is sunburnt, but strictly speaking the cause of her actions involves only the fact that her skin is damaged (rather than the fact that it has been damaged by exposure to the sun). Similarly (the critic continues), although we talk as though externally individuated mental states are causally responsible for behaviour, strictly speaking it is only their internal analogues (such as having damaged skin) that are causally efficacious.

There are two ways to respond to this objection, one of which is more conciliatory than the other. The more conciliatory of the two responses takes a leaf out of the program explanation playbook, arguing that although mental states *aren't* causally efficacious (or at least, aren't causally efficacious in virtue of their content), reference to such states provides invaluable information about those properties that are causally efficacious (just as reference to fragility does).

The less conciliatory response rejects the assumption that the case of Bonnie and Clyde provides a good model for thinking about mental causation. In the case of Bonnie and Clyde, we are able to identify an internal state that they have in common (namely, skin damage), which might be argued to be the cause of their respective actions. But now consider Oscar and his twin on Twin Earth. The localist intuition is that we should screen off the contribution made by their respective environments and focus on the internal state that they have in common. It is this state (so the thought goes), which causes each of them to reach for a glass. Now, although that thought might seem to be a forced move from the perspective of the productive conception of causation, it is not obviously entailed by the difference-making view. Perhaps the broad (i.e., relational) state of wanting water has a better claim to being the relevant difference-maker for Oscar's behaviour than the narrow state that he shares with his twin does. I'll leave you to consider the prospects of this proposal.

10.5 Libet's challenge

Thus far, we have focused on principled objections to mental causation – that is, arguments which purport to show that mental causation is impossible. Assuming that these arguments fail, it is a further question whether mental states *are* causally efficacious. After all, it is one thing for mental causation to be possible and quite another for it to actually occur in the ways that we ordinarily think it does. In this final section, we consider some neuroscientific data that is sometimes taken to show that decisions (volitions, acts of will) aren't causally efficacious – or at least, that they don't have the kind of causal efficacy that we ordinarily ascribe to them.

The data in question derive from a series of studies conducted by the neuroscientist Benjamin Libet (1916-2007) and colleagues, in which participants were instructed to move their right hand 'whenever they felt the urge to do so' within a certain interval of time (say, 20 seconds; Libet 1985; Libet et al. 1983). At the same time, participants were instructed to monitor a timer, and (once they had acted) to report when they had 'decided', 'intended', or 'first felt the urge' to act. Libet call these reports 'W judgments' (presumably because W stands for 'will').

While participants were monitoring their intentions, Libet used electroencephalography (EEG) to record their brain activity. Earlier researchers had discovered a characteristic pattern of neural activity, known as the readiness potential (RP), that occurs prior to intentional action (Schurger et al. 2021). Libet was interested in the temporal relationship between the RP and W judgments. Does the RP anticipate the W judgment, does it follow the W judgment, or are the two events simultaneous? Libet discovered that on average the RP (what he called a 'type II RP') occurs about 350 milliseconds (ms) before the point at which participants reported that they had first been aware of their decision (urge, intention) to act (Figure 10.3). Libet's experiments have been criticized on methodological grounds (see the commentaries

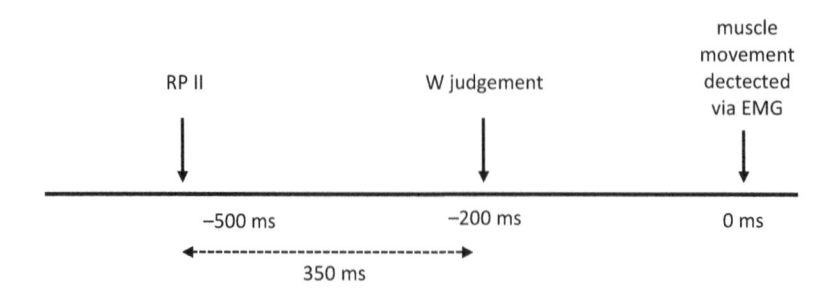

Figure 10.3 A schematic representation of Libet's data

Source: Based on Libet (1999).

on Libet 1985), but his basic finding – that simple, inconsequential, motor actions ('Libet actions') involve an RP whose onset precedes W judgments by roughly 350 ms – has been replicated by many studies and is widely accepted.

Although Libet's primary interest was in the question of free will, he took his data to have important implications for mental causation. Libet argued that because the RP occurs before the agent's decision to move their hand, that decision is epiphenomenal – or at least, it doesn't cause the motor response that the agent takes it to have caused. (Libet presumably allowed that the decision causes the W reports that participants produce.) The claim, in other words, is that Libet's data reveal our ordinary experiences of mental causation to be illusory: we think that we're in conscious control of our actions, but we're not (see, e.g., Wegner 2002). Eddy Nahmias (2014) has dubbed this view 'willusionism'.

We can reconstruct the Libet-based argument for willusionism ('the Libet argument') as follows:

1   Libet actions are caused by the RP.
2   If Libet actions are caused by the RP, then they aren't caused by the agent's decision.
3   So, Libet actions aren't caused by the agent's decision. (From 1, 2)
4   Libet actions are representative of actions in general: if they aren't causally efficacious, then actions in general aren't caused by decisions.
C   So, decisions in general aren't causally efficacious. (From 3, 4)[8]

Let's begin by considering (4): are Libet actions representative of actions in general? No. In fact, they are rather unusual. Most actions are informed by reasons of some sort or another. Even the simple act of choosing a piece of fruit from a fruit bowl is informed by rational considerations of some kind. For example, one might consider which piece of fruit is in the best condition, or which is the tastiest, or which involves the least amount of effort to reach. Libet actions, by contrast, are explicitly designed so as to be independent of any such considerations, for participants have no reason to raise their hand at one moment rather than another.

It is no great surprise, then, to discover that the neural antecedents of Libet actions differ from those of reason-based actions. The neuroscientist Uri Maoz and colleagues (2019) conducted in a study in which participants were allowed to choose which of two organizations would receive a $1,000 donation from the researchers. Not only was the RP absent on these trials, but the neural profile of these trials was very different from that of trials on which participants made only arbitrary, Libet-style decisions. In short, we have good reason to reject (4).

Nonetheless, it is still worth considering the implications of Libet's data. For one thing, it is possible that neuroscientists will discover a form of brain activity that bears the same kind of relationship to reason-based actions that the RP bears to arbitrary actions. Furthermore, the role of decisions in arbitrary actions is itself a matter of interest. Even if Libet's findings don't motivate scepticism about the role of decisions in general, they might still be at odds with our ordinary conception of mental causation (Box: What's it like to raise your hand?).

Box: What's it like to raise your hand?

Most discussions of Libet's experiments assume that participants experience themselves as deciding to act here and now, and that they experience such decisions as causing their hand to move. However, these assumptions have not gone unchallenged, and a number of theorists have argued that such descriptions misrepresent what it's like to raise one's hand in the context of a Libet-style experiment.

Some theorists, such as Owen Flanagan (1996), argue that participants exercise conscious agency only when they decide to comply with the experimental instructions; that is, when they agree to raise their hand at some point in the relevant 20-second interval. Having made that initial decision – so this line of thought goes – participants then 'outsource' the job of deciding precisely when to raise their hand to purely automatic, unconscious processes, and it is these processes that cause the agent's hand to move when it does. On this view, it's no mark against mental causation that Libet actions aren't consciously initiated, for agents don't even experience themselves as making such decisions. Another view, defended by Terry Horgan (2011) among others, is that participants do indeed experience themselves as deciding to raise their hand at a particular point in time, but they don't experience that decision as causing their hand to go up. Instead, participants experience *themselves* (rather than their decisions) as the source of their actions. On this view, talk of agent causation does a better job of capturing what it's like to raise one's hand than talk of mental state causation does.

The claims of Flanagan and Horgan return us to the issues raised at the start of this chapter concerning the introspective evidence for 'mental causation', and the question of what exactly it is that our ordinary, pre-theoretical conception of conscious agency commits us to.

Further reading

Holton, R. 2006. The Act of Choice. *Philosophers' Imprint*, 6(3): 1-15.
Horgan, T., Tienson, J. & Graham, G. 2003. The Phenomenology of First-Person Agency. In S. Walter and H.-D. Heckmann (Eds.) *Physicalism and Mental Causation: The Metaphysics of Mind and Action*. Exeter: Imprint Academic, pp. 323-40.

Let's turn now to (2): 'If Libet actions are caused by the RP, then they aren't caused by the agent's decision'. Is this claim plausible?

On the face of things, it looks like a non-starter, for it seems to assume that causes cannot themselves be caused. That assumption is false. The striking of the match caused the fuse to light, and the lighting of the fuse caused the bomb to detonate. Why couldn't something similar occur here? Perhaps the RP caused the agent's decision (or neural basis thereof), which in turn caused the agent's arm to go up.

But despite this response, it seems to me that there is something to be said for (2), for decisions aren't naturally thought of as mere cogs in a causal chain. Decisions can certainly be influenced by various factors, but treating a decision as necessitated by those factors seems to deprive it of its very function. As Richard Holton (2006) has observed, the job of a decision is to settle uncertainty, and it's hard to see what scope there could be for a decision if the factors leading up to it remove uncertainty in the way that the RP might be thought to. The question, of course, is whether the factors leading up to the agent's decision *do* remove uncertainty, or whether they merely incline an agent to make one kind of decision rather than another.[9]

With that in mind, let's turn to the first premise of the Libet argument: are Libet actions caused by the RP? Does an RP give rise to action in something akin to the way in which the lighting of a bomb's fuse gives rise to its detonation? As Mele (2009) has pointed out, we simply don't know. Because the RP on any one trial is obscured by neural noise, it can be identified only by integrating the data collected on a large number of trials. Doing that involves a process known as 'back-averaging', in which trials are aligned to the onset of the action. Thus, instances in which an RP occurs but isn't followed by an action will go undetected. For all we know, there may be many instances in which an RP occurs but isn't followed by any kind of action.[10]

10.6 Conclusion

This chapter has focused on two challenges to mental causation: the causal exclusion challenge and the challenge from semantic externalism. Both challenges focus on the very possibility of mental causation: the latter purports to show that mental properties aren't able to do any causal work (given certain influential conceptions of mental content); the former purports to show that there is no work for mental properties to do (given certain influential conceptions of the relationship between mental properties and physical properties).

Responses to these challenges can be grouped into two broad camps: the 'head-on' camp and the 'fall-back' camp. Members of the head-on camp argue that the exclusion and/or externalism arguments fail. Theorists who adopt this strategy often argue that the objections to mental causation rest on misguided assumptions about the nature of causation. Members of the fall-back camp accept that mental causation is indeed impossible, but they argue that something close enough to mental causation can be salvaged from the wreckage. Different 'fall-back' theorists develop different accounts of this something, but most theorists emphasize the explanatory credentials of the mental, holding that although mental properties are not themselves causally efficacious they can (and often do) legitimately figure in causal explanations.

Each strategy generates further questions. Evaluating the head-on approach takes us into the philosophy of causation and the question of whether causation should be understood in terms of the transmission of some kind of quality (as productive approaches have it) or whether it should be understood in terms of relations of dependence (as difference-making approaches have it). Evaluating the fall-back strategy raises questions in the philosophy of mind, epistemology, and ethics about what exactly we want from an account of mental causation. Does our pre-theoretical commitment to mental causation demand that mental properties are themselves causally efficacious, or does it require only that they are causally relevant, giving us information about causal relations without themselves functioning as causes? What implications would epiphenomenalism have for our knowledge of mental states, for debates about the existence of mental properties, or for our conception of voluntary agency – and could we live with those implications?

Finally, we considered one of the many challenges to mental causation arising out of neuroscience: Libet's challenge. Although Libet's challenge has been enormously influential in neuroscience and the popular media, we saw that its influence is unwarranted. Nonetheless, our examination of Libet's challenge proved instructive, not least because it reminded us that even if objections to the very possibility of mental causation fail, it is a further question whether our thoughts and feelings do indeed have the causal consequences that we ordinarily take them to have.

Further reading

For excellent overviews of mental causation, see Karen Bennett's 'Mental Causation', *Philosophy Compass*, 2(2): 316-37 (2007); Sophie Gibb's 'Mental Causation', *Analysis*, 74(2): 327-38 (2014); and Holly Anderson's 'Mental Causation', in N. Levy and J. Clausen (ed.), *Springer Handbook of Neuroethics* (Springer, 2015).

Mental Causation (OUP, 1993), edited by John Heil and Alfred Mele, collects together many of the classic papers on the topic. A more recent collection is *Being Reduced: New Essays on Reduction, Explanation, and Causation* (OUP, 2008), edited by Jakob Hohwy and Jesper Kallestrup, which contains many excellent discussions of the exclusion objection. Among the many places in which Jaegwon Kim discussed the exclusion argument is his paper 'The Non-Reductivist's Troubles with Mental Causation', which appears in the collection edited by John Heil and Alfred Mele mentioned above. Another good entry point into the exclusion argument is provided by Jesper Kallestrup, 'The Causal Exclusion Argument', *Philosophical Studies*, 131(2): 459-85 (2006). For a recent defence of the program explanation response see Philip Pettit's 'The Program Model, Difference-Makers, and the Exclusion Problem'. In H. Beebee, C. Hitchcock, and H. Price (eds.), *Making a Difference: Essays on the Philosophy of Causation* (OUP, 2017).

For more on mental causation and content externalism, see Pierre Jacob's 'Externalism and Mental Causation', *Proceedings of the Aristotelian Society* 92, 203-19 (1992) and Stephen Yablo's 'Wide Causation', in J. Tomberlin (ed.), *Philosophical Perspectives*, 11: 251-81 (1997).

For further discussion of Libet's argument, see Adina Roskies's paper 'Why Libet's Studies Don't Pose a Threat to Free Will', in W. Sinnott-Armstrong & L. Nadel (Eds.), *Conscious Will and Responsibility: A Tribute to Benjamin Libet* (OUP, 2010) and my 'Libet and the Case for Free Will Scepticism', in *Free Will and Modern Science* (OUP, 2011), edited by Richard Swinburne. Eddy Nahmias's paper 'Is Free Will an Illusion? Confronting Challenges from the Modern Mind Sciences', in Walter Sinnott-Armstrong (ed.), *Moral Psychology, Vol. 4: Freedom and Responsibility* (MIT Press, 2014) provides an excellent overview of 'willusionism' more generally.

Study questions

1 Section 10.1 outlines a number of reasons for believing in the reality of mental causation. Which of these arguments for mental causation do you find plausible, if any?
2 What is Jaegwon Kim's causal exclusion argument? What does the argument show, according to Kim?
3 Discussing the causal exclusion argument, Karen Bennett (2007: 325) remarks: 'There are two hurdles to becoming gainfully employed. First, one must have the requisite skills;

second, there must be employment opportunities available. It's one thing to be fit for work, and quite another to actually find a job!' Explain what relevance this comment has to the exclusion argument.

4 How does Davidson's token identity theory respond to the causal exclusion objection? What is one objection to the token identity theory?
5 Explain the role of the proportionality principle in Yablo's response to the exclusion challenge. How might the proportionality principle be defended?
6 Explain the apparent tension between mental causation and content externalism? What are the two strategies that this chapter considers for how this tension might be resolved? Do you think that either strategy is successful?
7 Explain and evaluate the Libet argument for 'willusionism'.
8 The conclusion to this chapter distinguishes two strategies for responding to the challenges facing mental causation: the head-on strategy and the fall-back strategy. Which of these two strategies do you find more plausible, and why?

Notes

1 For more on this, see Horgan (2007), Bayne (2008), and Nida-Rümelin (2007).
2 Some theorists take COMPLETENESS to be definitional of physicalism, or to at least be entailed by the definition of physicalism. However, as best I can tell, it doesn't follow from the supervenience-based conception of physicalism with which we are operating here.
3 See Kim (1998, 2005) for his reply to the claim that the exclusion objection generalizes.
4 For this point, see Field (2005), Pearl (2000), and Hitchcock (2007).
5 Yablo takes this point to be directly relevant to the exclusion argument, for on his view the nonreductive physicalist is committed to thinking of mental properties as related to their neural realizers in exactly the same way that being red is related to being scarlet. Just as an object is red by being scarlet, magenta, crimson, and so on, so too (the thought runs) an agent is in a particular mental state by being in any one of indefinitely many neural states (N1, N2, N3, etc.). And just as being scarlet necessitates being red (but not vice versa), so too being in N1 necessitates deciding to raise one's hand (but not vice versa). It is, however, controversial whether the nonreductive physicalist should treat neural properties as determinates of mental properties in the way in which scarlet is a determinate of red (see, e.g., Menzies 2008; Walter 2007). However, Yablo's central point remains secure even if neural properties aren't determinates of mental properties, for he shows that the proportionality constraint ('causes must be proportionate to their effects') is at odds with EXCLUSION.
6 For other responses to the exclusion argument that draw on the difference-making conception of causation (broadly construed), see Bennett (2003), Bennett (2008), Campbell (2007, 2008), Menzies (2003), List and Menzies (2009), Raatikainen (2010), Sinnott-Armstrong (2021), and Woodward (2008).
7 See note 2.
8 Strictly speaking, (5) doesn't entail that decisions are epiphenomenal, for it allows that they might play a role (say) in the production of an agent's verbal reports. However, it is epiphenomenal in spirit, and runs strongly counter to our ordinary views about mental causation.
9 At this point, we are on the verge of the vexed question of free will. Could a decision or act of will be free if it were caused, or does free will require the absence of causation? Although issues of mental causation are bound up with questions of free will in many ways, it is a curious fact that discussions of mental causation rarely engage with questions of free will. See Bernstein and Wilson (2016) for an interesting exception to that generalization.
10 There is also good reason to believe that certain aspects of the RP data might be statistical illusions, and that features of the relationship between (say) the RP and the W judgment might characterize the averaged data even though they do not characterize any of the individual trials that contribute to that data. For discussion, see Schurger et al. (2012).

11 Other minds

Chapter overview

- Examines three accounts of how we ascribe mental states to other people (mindreading)
- Considers an argument for the claim that applying psychological concepts to other people is incoherent
- Introduces the sceptical worry that knowledge of other minds is beyond our reach, and considers two responses to it
- Explores some of the challenges involved in detecting consciousness in non-human animals and AI systems.

Much of waking life is concerned with the mental states of other people. We feel empathy for those who have suffered misfortune, we are angry at those who have insulted us, and we are often puzzled by those who fail to see the world as we do. The capacity to understand the mental states of others – to 'mindread' or 'mentalize', as it is known – lies at the heart of social life. You cannot co-operate with someone without being able to 'read' their mind, nor can you deceive them. No wonder, then, that mindreading has attracted so much philosophical attention.

Mindreading raises three kinds of problems. The first is explanatory: how do we actually do it? What cognitive processes do we employ to identify the mental states of other people? I will call this the psychological problem of other minds, for it is a question about how our minds operate. Although the psychological problem is first and foremost a scientific problem, it does raise a number of distinctively philosophical issues, and philosophers have had a lot to say about it. We will examine some of the main accounts of mindreading in Section 11.1.

The second problem of other minds is conceptual. The practice of mindreading assumes that psychological concepts can be intelligibly applied to other people. However, an intriguing argument calls that assumption into question, for it seems to show that there is something deeply problematic in the very thought that someone else might (say) be in pain. We consider this argument (and possible responses to it) in Section 11.2.

DOI: 10.4324/9781003225348-12

A third problem raised by other minds is epistemic: under what conditions can we *know* what other beings are thinking or feeling? This is in many ways the central philosophical problem of other minds. As we will see, it takes a number of rather different forms. One focus of discussion concerns our capacity to know the minds of our fellow human beings. Our ordinary mindreading capacities are certainly not infallible, but we do assume that other people's mental states are among the kinds of things that we can know. Sceptics, however, argue that such claims are unjustified. We consider the sceptical challenge of other minds in Section 11.3.

Another aspect of the epistemic problem of other minds concerns our knowledge of other *kinds* of minds. What, if anything, can we know about the mental states of creatures that are very different from us? Section 11.4 focuses on non-human animals, while Section 11.5 addresses the challenge of artificial consciousness. These sections tackle what might be described as the *scientific* problem of other minds, for questions about our knowledge of other kinds of minds are open scientific questions in the way that questions about our knowledge of ordinary human minds are not.

11.1 The psychology of mindreading

Before we consider accounts of the psychology of mindreading, we need to consider what mindreading actually involves, for it is a multifaceted phenomenon. Three aspects of mindreading can be distinguished. First, mindreading requires a grasp of psychological concepts. Clearly, I cannot ascribe pain to you unless I have the concept PAIN. Second, mindreading requires the capacity to accurately apply psychological concepts. A competent mindreader will be able to apply the concept PAIN accurately, distinguishing those individuals who are in pain from those who aren't. Third, mindreading involves the capacity to explain and predict behaviour on the basis of mental state attributions. There is limited utility in being able to tell when someone is in pain if you can't also draw out the implications of this fact for explaining and predicting their behaviour. Some theories attempt to account for all three aspects of mindreading, whereas others are more selective in their focus.

Among the various approaches to mindreading that have been developed, three have been particularly influential.[1] The first treats mindreading as a perceptual capacity. The view here isn't that there is a specific perceptual modality for mindreading, but that the standard sensory modalities – most obviously vision, but perhaps other sensory modalities too – provide us with perceptual awareness of other people's mental states.[2]

The perceptual account is easily motivated, for we certainly *talk* as though we have perceptual access to mental phenomena. We speak of *seeing the joy* on someone's face and of *hearing impatience* in their voice. As Wittgenstein noted, our awareness of other people's states of mind often shares the directness and immediacy that characterizes perception:

> We do not see facial contortions and make inferences from them (like a doctor forming a diagnosis) to joy, grief, boredom. We describe a face immediately as sad, radiant, bored, even when we are unable to give any other description of the features. Grief, one would like to say, is personified on the face.
>
> (Wittgenstein 1953/2009: §225)

198 Other minds

Wittgenstein's comments focus on emotional states, but it is tempting to think that mental phenomena of other kinds can also be perceived. For example, it is plausible to suppose that one can simply see that someone is trying to shut a door or pick up a cup.

Despite its attractiveness, the perceptual approach to mindreading faces significant challenges. For one thing, it is incomplete: it provides no account of what is involved in grasping psychological concepts, nor does it provide any insight into our capacity to use our knowledge of mental states to explain and predict behaviour. At best, the perceptual approach explains our capacity to *detect* the mental states of others. But can it do even that?

Some theorists say 'no' on the grounds that mental properties are not observable in the way in which (say) a banana's colour or an apple's shape are. Joy, grief, and boredom might be intimately related to observable properties (such as facial expressions), but they cannot themselves be seen. Strictly speaking, what's observable is only the behavioural manifestation of an emotion and not the emotion itself.

But even if mental phenomena are not themselves observable, it can be argued that knowledge of mental phenomena could nonetheless be perceptual. The thought here is that it might be possible to perceive that an object has a certain property even when the property in question is not observable. As Dretske (1973) once noted, although weight itself is not visible, it is possible to see that someone has lost weight. In a similar vein, one might argue that it is possible to see that someone is in pain even if pains themselves cannot be seen.

A further worry concerns the *scope* of the perceptual account. The claim that certain emotional states, bodily sensations, and intentions are perceivable has some plausibility, for these states are associated with characteristic patterns of bodily responses. Although few of us can articulate what is distinctive of the facial expression associated with (say) worry, there clearly *is* such a facial expression, and we are able to recognize it when we see it (see Figure 11.1).

Figure 11.1 Migrant Mother, Dorothea Lange (1936)

But many (perhaps most) mental states are not associated with distinctive patterns of bodily responses. There is no particular way that (say) an intention to learn a foreign language manifests itself in facial expression or bodily movements. In the same way that the holistic and open-ended nature of psychological concepts undermines the plausibility of analytical behaviourism (according to which psychological concepts can be analysed in terms of behavioural dispositions), so too it undermines the idea that mental states are, in general, perceivable. Perception may well play an important role in mindreading, but there is much more to mindreading than perceiving.

Another account of mindreading is the theory-theory, an approach that is so named because its advocates take mindreading to involve the deployment of a kind of folk (or naïve) theory of the mind, often known as 'folk psychology'. The theory-theory has been developed in a number of ways (see Box: The theory-theory: little scientists, mental modules), but at its heart is the claim that we read the minds of others by drawing on a rich body of information about the causal profiles of mental states (i.e., the ways in which mental states interact with each other and with an agent's environment and behaviour). This body of information enables us identify a target's mental states on the basis of their behaviour and environment, and to make predictions about what they will do (or are likely to have done) on the basis of their mental states. For example, if you know that Kylie believes that there is beer in the fridge, and if you know that she wants a beer, then you can use your grasp of the principles of folk psychology ('Other things being equal, if someone desires that X, and if they believe that by doing Y they will secure X, then they will do Y') to predict that Kylie will go to the fridge. Alternatively, if you know that Kylie is going to the fridge, and that she thinks the fridge contains beer, then you might infer that she wants a beer.

Box: The theory-theory: little scientists, mental modules

The theory-theory has been developed in a number of quite different ways. Some theory-theorists hold that children acquire a theory of the mind by using the same general learning processes that are involved in understanding other aspects of the natural and social world (e.g., Gopnik 1993; Gopnik & Wellman 1992). This view is sometimes described as the 'child-as-scientist' account. Other theory-theorists hold that the acquisition of a theory of mind involves the operations of a dedicated mental module, akin to the modules that are implicated in language production and comprehension (e.g., Scholl & Leslie 1999; Baron-Cohen 1995). On this view, our grasp of folk psychology is either innate or is acquired by a specialized learning mechanism. A third version of the theory-theory holds that children acquire a theory of mind from their caregivers and siblings in the course of learning the meanings of psychological terms (e.g., Perner et al. 1994; Peterson & Siegal 2000). The differences between these versions of the theory-theory complicates the task of providing a general assessment of it.

Further reading

Lavelle, J. S. 2018. *The Social Mind*. Routledge.Stich,
S., and S. Nichols. 2003. *Mindreading*. Oxford University Press.

One attractive feature of the theory-theory is that it provides a unified treatment of the three aspects of mindreading that we have distinguished. We have already seen how it accounts for our capacity to both detect mental states and to use information about mental states to explain and predict behaviour. But the theory-theory also provides an account of what is involved in grasping psychological concepts. Roughly speaking, the theory-theory takes psychological concepts to be defined in terms of their functional roles and holds that what it is to grasp a psychological concept is to grasp the relevant functional role.

Critics sometimes object to the theory-theory on the grounds that ordinary people are able to articulate few (if any) of the alleged principles of folk psychology. (Indeed, even philosophers of mind struggle to formulate such principles!) This criticism seems to me to be misguided, for theory-theorists take our grasp of the principles of folk psychology to be 'implicit' or 'tacit' rather than consciously accessible. The model here is the knowledge one has of the grammar of one's native language. Just as the information that explains our capacity to distinguish grammatical sentences ('The girl chased the dog') from ungrammatical ones ('Chased girl dog the') is largely unavailable to conscious awareness, so too – theory-theorists hold – is the body of information that underlies our mindreading capacities.

A third approach to mindreading holds that we work out what mental states another person is in by adopting their perspective, and (roughly speaking) attributing to them the kinds of mental states that we would be in if we were in their situation. This is known as the simulationist account, for it assumes that mindreading involves using one's own mind to simulate the mental states of another person.[3] The idea of simulation-based knowledge is a familiar one. Suppose that you want to know how an Airbus A380 aeroplane will behave in a hurricane. Instead of applying a physical theory to this problem, one might simply build a model of an A380 and see how it behaves when exposed to hurricane-like conditions. So too, simulationists argue, one can track the mental states of another person – the mindreading 'target' – by using one's own mind as a model of theirs. Crucially, simulation-based mindreading doesn't require a theory of how minds work.[4]

Here's an example of how simulation-based mindreading might work. Suppose that we are playing chess and I am trying to predict your next moves. Rather than draw on a theory of people's chess-playing behaviour, I might simply pretend to have your aims and beliefs, and then feed those states into my own decision-making processes. ('Suppose that I were Black. What would I do? Let's see. I could take White's bishop, but then . . .'). If the upshot of this simulation is a decision to move my queen, then I will ascribe that decision to you. More generally, simulationists hold that mindreading involves adopting the target's position, letting one's own psychology run 'offline' on the mental states that are generated by the pretend states, and then ascribing the resulting mental states to the target.

Of course, not all minds are alike. We differ from each other both in our specific mental states (you might have beliefs and desires that I don't) and in our psychological capacities (you might be better at chess than I am). But if our minds differ, how then am I able to use my mind to model yours?

In response, simulationists argue that our mindreading efforts are successful only to the extent that we are able to compensate for such differences. Suppose that you are playing chess with Magnus Carlsen, the current world champion. Although you can pretend to have his aims, you probably won't be able to predict his next move. But the fact that simulation wouldn't be able to support effective mindreading in this context is actually a mark in favour of the simulationist account, for this is precisely the kind of situation in which most of us would fail to be effective mindreaders.

Another objection is that merely pretending to have someone else's perspective can't do the kind of work that the simulationist account requires. After all, imagining being in a *physical* state rarely has the effects associated with actually being in the relevant state. For example, drinking hemlock causes death, but merely imagining that one has drunk hemlock has no adverse effects on one's health whatsoever. Thus, critics ask, why should we assume that 'pretend' mental states will trigger the same kinds of psychological processes that are generated by their genuine counterparts?

This is a good question, and providing a comprehensive response to it goes beyond the scope of this chapter. That said, it is clear that there is significant overlap between the causal roles of genuine mental states and that of their imagined counterparts. Horror films generate feelings of fear and heart palpitations despite the fact that one doesn't really believe that one is in danger. One explanation for the commonalities in causal roles between genuine mental states and their imagined counterparts involves the fact that they have content in common. For example, believing that one is facing a grizzly bear is likely to elicit the thought that one is in danger, while pretending that one is facing a grizzly is likely to elicit the (pretend) thought that one is in danger.

We have outlined the three main accounts of mindreading, but we have barely scratched the surface of the debate between these views. In particular, we have not considered the extensive body of research in developmental psychology, psychopathology, and neuroscience which bears on this issue (see, e.g., Apperly 2010; Baron-Cohen et al. 2013; Koster-Hale & Saxe 2013; Lavelle 2018). Unfortunately, we must leave that fascinating work to one side, and turn instead to an argument that challenges the very intelligibility of third-person mindreading.

11.2 The conceptual problem of other minds

Mindreading is woven into the fabric of everyday life, and there would seem to be nothing more natural than applying psychological concepts to other people. There is, however, an influential argument for the claim that it is incoherent to ascribe psychological concepts to other people. This problem is known as the conceptual problem of other minds.[5]

The conceptual problem begins with the idea that grasping a psychological concept requires introspective attention to mental states of the relevant kind. On this view, grasping the concept PAIN (for example) involves attending to one's own pains, and noting that they share a distinctive phenomenal quality (painfulness). This account of what is involved in grasping psychological concepts is attractive and widely endorsed. (Indeed, we saw in Chapter 8 that it lies at the heart of the phenomenal concept response to the knowledge argument.) But – the argument continues – if it's right, then it would be impossible to conceive of someone else's pains. As Wittgenstein put it, 'If one has to imagine someone else's pain on the model of one's own, this is none too easy a thing to do: for I have to imagine pain which I *do not feel* on the model of the pain which I *do* feel' (1953/2009: §302). The problem, in a nutshell, is not that I can't *know* whether you're in pain, but that I can't even formulate the hypothesis that you might be in pain, for my concept PAIN can be applied only to my own experiences. I can conceive of a pain that is *located* in your body, but I would – so the argument goes – have to think of this pain as mine rather than yours.

We can put the argument as follows:

1. Grasping the concept PAIN is a matter of grasping how pains feel.
2. Given (1), for me to conceive of pain in your body is for me to conceive of a state, located in your body, that feels a certain way.
3. But if a state feels a certain way, then it must feel a certain way *to me*.
4. But a state that feels a certain way to me must be my pain.

Thus,

C it is not possible to intelligibly apply the concept PAIN to someone else.

Since we clearly can intelligibly apply the concept PAIN to other people, there must be something wrong with the argument, but where exactly does it go wrong?

Wittgenstein rejects the first premise. On his account, pains are not 'inner states', and the concept PAIN is not acquired by attending to the phenomenology of one's own pains. Although Wittgenstein doesn't explicitly deny the existence of inner states (feelings of pain), the point of his famous 'beetle in the box' thought experiment is to undermine the idea that grasping psychological concepts involves attending to inner states (see Box: The beetle in the box).

Box: The beetle in the box

One of the most delightful thought experiments in the whole of philosophy is Wittgenstein's famous 'beetle in the box' scenario (1953/2009: §293). Suppose, Wittgenstein says, that everyone has a box into which only they can peer, and that each box contains an object that the owner of the box refers to as a 'beetle'. Because no one has access to the contents of anyone else's box, it is impossible to tell whether any two boxes contain objects of the same kind. Wittgenstein's point is that if terms like 'pain' referred to sensations that were accessible to only one person (in the way that each beetle is accessible to only one person), then there would be a real question about whether different people mean the same thing by 'pain'. But, Wittgenstein continues, since we clearly *do* mean the same thing by 'pain' (and other psychological terms), it follows that 'pain' (and psychological terms more generally) cannot be the name of a private object (a 'beetle in a box'). Wittgenstein concludes that psychological terms acquire meaning on the basis of their links to publicly accessible behaviour rather than on the basis of their relations to inner states of consciousness.

Further reading

Budd, M. 1989. *Wittgenstein's Philosophy of Psychology*. Routledge.
Wittgenstein, L. 1953/2009. *Philosophical Investigations*. 4th ed. P.M.S. Hacker and Joachim Schulte (eds. and trans.). Oxford: Wiley-Blackwell.

Although theory-theorists distance themselves from what they regard as the overly behaviouristic flavour of Wittgenstein's account, they share his rejection of (1). Understanding the concept PAIN, they hold, isn't a matter of grasping how pains *feel* but of understanding the role that the concept of pain plays within folk-psychological theory – roughly, that is, understanding what causes pain and what pains in turn cause.

Many theorists, however, will have qualms about rejecting (1). Although it's certainly plausible to suppose that *some* psychological concepts can be grasped in the absence of introspective engagement with their objects, that doesn't seem to be true of the concept PAIN. Arguably, grasping PAIN requires knowing what it's like to be in pain. Someone who has never experienced pain might be able to acquire a *kind* of concept of pain, but – the thought is – they won't have a full grasp of the ordinary concept of pain. Thus, it is a matter of some interest whether the conclusion of the conceptual argument can be resisted without rejecting (1).

The answer, I think, is that it can. Premise (3) is surely implausible: a state can feel a certain way without feeling that way *to me*. Even if the concept PAIN can be acquired only via introspective attention to one's own pains, it doesn't follow that one cannot intelligibly apply it to other people. The key here is the distinction between one's own subjectivity and subjectivity as such. It may indeed be incoherent to suppose that a pain can feel a certain way without feeling a certain way *to someone*, but it doesn't follow that the person feeling the pain must be identical to the person deploying the concept PAIN. The idea that we grasp psychological concepts by attending to our own mental states might indeed be false, but the fact that it is intelligible to apply psychological concepts to other people doesn't show that it is false.

11.3 The sceptical problem of other minds

We ordinarily assume that the individuals with whom we interact on a daily basis have minds, and that we know quite a bit about their mental lives. The sceptic, however, argues that these assumptions are unjustified, and that we know little (if anything) about the minds of others. Mindreading, according to the sceptic, is not a source of knowledge. Indeed, the radical sceptic argues that we don't even have the capacity to form warranted beliefs about other minds.

There are two ways of engaging with the sceptical problem of other minds. The first aims to prove the sceptic wrong, and to demonstrate to the sceptic's satisfaction that our ordinary mindreading methods deliver knowledge. In my view, this position is misguided, for it seems to me that we are justified in assuming that the sceptic is wrong (Box: Solipsism). To my mind, a better way of engaging with the sceptical problem is to treat it as issuing a challenge regarding the nature of our knowledge of other minds. The aim, then, is not to prove *that* we have knowledge of the minds of our follow human beings, but to identify the *basis* of this knowledge. With that thought in mind, let's consider what the three accounts of mindreading that we canvassed in Section 11.2 (the perceptual theory, the theory-theory, and the simulation-theory) have to say with respect to the sceptical challenge.[6]

> **Box: Solipsism**
>
> Most philosophers assume that there are other minds, and that we can (and do) know quite a bit about them. Solipsists reject these assumptions, for the solipsist thinks of herself/himself as the only conscious subject that there is. The solipsistic perspective is eloquently captured by Sylvia Plath in the opening verse of her poem *Soliloquy of the Solipsist*:
>
> > I?
> > I walk alone;
> > The midnight street
> > Spins itself from under my feet;
> > When my eyes shut
> > These dreaming houses all snuff out;
> > Through a whim of mine
> > Over gables the moon's celestial onion
> > Hangs high.
>
> Solipsism is a vanishingly rare view – indeed, there is a sense in which no two solipsists hold the same view, for each denies the other's existence. However, the threat of solipsism frames the sceptical challenge of other minds, for it is often held that an adequate response to the sceptical challenge must show that solipsism is unreasonable.
>
> Plath, S. 1981. Soliloquy of the Solipsist. *Collected Poems*. Harper Perennial.

Let us begin with the perceptual account of mindreading. If mindreading is perceptual, then its epistemic credentials would seem to be secure, for perception is surely a source of knowledge. Just as my belief that there is (say) a barn in front of me is justified by the fact that it looks like there is a barn in front of me, so too – one might argue – my belief that you are angry is justified by the fact that you look angry. Of course, perceptually based beliefs *can* turn out to be false (perhaps what looks to be a barn is just a barn façade; perhaps you are merely pretending to be angry), but to acknowledge that perception can mislead is not to say that it ordinarily misleads or that it is typically unwarranted. At the very least, if our access to other minds is perceptual, then it is no worse off than our access to many other features of the external world.

It is, however, very much an open question whether our primary mode of access to other minds *is* perceptual. As we noted earlier, although we may have perceptual access to certain kinds of mental states (such as emotions), it is unlikely that mindreading is in general perceptual. Thus, any response to the sceptical challenge that appealed only to perception would be severely impoverished indeed.

What about the simulationist account of mindreading? Would mindreading generate knowledge if it were primarily a matter of simulating another person's perspective? The simulationist account of mindreading goes hand in glove with what is known as the *analogical* account, a view that is most closely associated with the writings of J. S. Mill (1865/1979) and Bertrand Russell (1948).[7] The idea is this: because groaning and wincing are associated with pain in my case, I can infer that you are in pain from the fact that you are groaning and wincing. More generally, the analogical response holds that mindreading generates knowledge because it is reasonable to suppose that the correlations between mental states and behaviour which apply in one's own case will apply also to other people.

Let's consider three objections to the analogical account. The first derives from the fact that it is relatively rare for behaviours to be uniquely associated with particular mental states. Suppose that you see me run from my house. I might be running because: I believe that my house is on fire and I want to escape from it; I am going to the aid of a neighbour; or because I am exercising. But if a single type of behaviour can be associated with indefinitely many mental states, how could inferences from behaviour to mentality ever be justified (let alone underpin claims to knowledge)?

The response to this objection involves recognizing that the interpretation of behaviour needn't rest on a single, narrowly defined item of behaviour. Instead, we interpret behaviour on the basis of the target's overall behavioural profile. If that profile is consistent with a number of mindreading interpretations (as it often is), then it may be the case that no single interpretation of the target's behaviour will yield knowledge.

A second objection is that the analogical account cannot deliver knowledge because it involves one-shot induction – in other words, it's an inference from a single case. But – the worry runs – one-shot inductions don't underwrite knowledge. Suppose that you suffer from migraines after eating blueberries. Would that give you good reason to think that I too suffer from migraines after eating blueberries? Surely not. You might, of course, happen to be right if you were to draw that inference, but you surely wouldn't *know* that I have a migraine merely because you've seen me eat blueberries. But – the sceptic continues – the blueberry argument (as we can call it) is no worse than ordinary ascriptions of mentality as the analogical account conceives of them. Put another way, the problem is to explain why one-shot induction is legitimate in the pain/wincing case but illegitimate in the migraine/blueberries case.

There is a serious challenge here, but it needs to be carefully formulated. The problem (as I see it) isn't with one-shot induction as such, for one-shot induction *can* yield knowledge. Suppose that you have examined only one female wombat and have observed her give birth to live young. On the basis of this one case, it would be reasonable to conclude that female wombats in general give birth to live young. Whether or not a one-shot induction is warranted depends on how the property in question is distributed in the relevant population. One-shot induction can generate knowledge when dealing with properties that are highly correlated (being female / giving birth to live young) in a particular population (say, wombats), but it can lead one astray when dealing with properties that are not highly correlated (e.g., eating blueberries / having migraines) in the relevant population.

At this point, there are various strategies open to the sceptic. One strategy would be to argue that we have positive reason to doubt that mental properties and behavioural properties are highly correlated. The problem with this strategy is that it requires knowledge of other minds, which is precisely what the sceptic claims we lack. A less ambitious sceptical strategy would be to argue that we have no good reason to think that mental properties are highly correlated with behavioural properties, and that without such a reason it would be sheer hubris to employ one-shot induction in this domain.

This strategy is more promising, but it too faces objections. For one thing, it is reasonable to think that there are robust connections between mental states and certain patterns of behaviour. One needn't think that these connections are discernible a priori or that they capture the essence of mental phenomena. All that is required, rather, is that the relations between mental states on the one hand and behavioural responses on the other are relatively stable across individuals. This reply can be motivated by noting that mental properties are evolved properties, and selection pressures are likely to ensure that there is at least broad uniformity in how they are distributed within a species (Sober 2000).

Of course, as we move away from the typical members of our own species and consider the members of other species (and atypical members of our own species), we have less reason to think that one-shot induction will yield knowledge. But this is not a mark against the analogical account, for that account is concerned with *ordinary* mindreading, and, for the most part, ordinary mindreading is restricted to neurotypical, adult members of our own species. After all, we often *don't* know what to say about the mental states of non-human animals, infants, or our fellow human beings who have suffered severe brain damage (see Box: Detecting consciousness in the 'vegetative state').

Box: Detecting consciousness in the 'vegetative state'

Patients with severe brain damage often enter a state of unresponsive wakefulness, known as the 'vegetative state' or the 'unresponsive wakefulness syndrome'. These patients show signs of wakefulness – they exhibit a sleep/wake cycle and spontaneously open their eyes – but they do not produce any behavioural indicators of awareness (hence the term 'vegetative'). However, recent brain-imaging and EEG studies indicate that as many as 20% of these patients may retain some form of awareness (Edlow et al. 2020; Kondziella et al. 2016). The first study of this kind involved a 23-year-old woman who was in a vegetative state as the result of a car accident (Owen et al. 2006). On some trials she was instructed to imagine playing tennis, and on other trials she was instructed to imagine walking around her house. Astonishingly, neuroimaging revealed brain activity in just those brain areas that are known to be involved in motor imagery and spatial navigation. Even more impressive was the temporal profile of this neural activity: it began immediately after the imagery instruction was given and ceased immediately after she was told to stop imagining herself playing tennis or walking around her house.

The advocate of the analogical account might argue that this patient was conscious on the grounds that she displayed the kinds of brain activity that is correlated with consciousness in neurotypical individuals. The advocate of the inference to the best explanation (IBE) account (see below) might argue for the same conclusion on the grounds that ascribing consciousness to this patient provides the best explanation of her brain activity. Whatever the fate of these arguments, it is clear that the problem of other minds has profound moral and clinical significance.

Further reading

Fernández-Espejo, D., and A. M. Owen. 2013. Detecting Awareness after Severe Brain Injury. *Nature Reviews Neuroscience*, 14: 801–9.
Owen, A. M. et al. 2006. Detecting Awareness in the Vegetative State. *Science*, 313: 1402.
Shea, N., and T. Bayne. 2010. The Vegetative State and the Science of Consciousness. *British Journal for the Philosophy of Science*, 61: 459–84.

What might the sceptical challenge look like from the perspective of the theory-theory? Recall that the theory-theory takes mindreading to involve the application of a theory of mind (folk psychology), which explains behaviour in terms of interactions between an agent's environment and a range of psychological states (perception, beliefs, desires, intentions, etc.). From this perspective, the sceptical challenge can be met by showing that the explanations of behaviour provided by folk psychology are good explanations (or at least, are better than their competitors). This response to the sceptical challenge is known as the *inference to the best explanation* account (Melnyk 1994; Pargetter 1984).

Inference to the best explanation (IBE) is a form of explanation in which one argues for the truth of a hypothesis on the grounds that it provides the best explanation for a certain phenomenon (Lipton 2004). For example, one might defend the hypothesis that it rained last night ('H') on the grounds that this hypothesis provides the best explanation of the fact that the streets are wet. Other explanations are possible (perhaps a water main burst), but if they are weaker (all things considered) than H, then it's reasonable to adopt H (and one might count as knowing H). Similarly, the advocate of the IBE approach argues that we are justified in ascribing folk-psychological states to other people on the grounds that doing so provides the best explanation of their behaviour. Other explanations may be possible, but they will be inferior to those provided by folk psychology.

There are two ways of pushing back against the IBE account. First, one might accept that the ascription of mental states is in the business of explaining behaviour but argue that it is not particularly successful in this regard. As we saw in Chapter 3, eliminativists such as Paul Churchland argue that many of the explanations provided by folk psychology are poor and will be displaced by those that appeal to neuroscience and scientific psychology. Here is not the place for a detailed evaluation of the eliminativist challenge, but it is important to recognize that in some sense there are as many varieties of eliminativism as there are components of folk psychology. Even if certain facets of folk psychology are vulnerable to elimination, others seem to be relatively immune to the eliminativist threat. My own view is that the explanatory credentials of many of the central folk-psychological categories (most notably belief, desire, and intention) are secure.

A second challenge to the IBE account concerns mental phenomena that don't appear to be in the business of explaining behaviour, such as states that are characterized in terms of their phenomenal character. Consider 'inverted spectra' scenarios of the kind that we discussed in Chapter 4, in which properties that produce one kind of experience in me (say, that associated with the colour of ripe strawberries) produce another kind of experience in you (say, that associated with the colour of broccoli). The possibility of spectrum inversion seems to be irrelevant as far as predicting and explaining your behaviour is concerned. When it comes to figuring out what you're going to do, what matters is not the phenomenal character of your experiences but whether your representation of a class of objects is stable across changes in context. To put the point in Wittgensteinian terms, it doesn't matter whether the beetles in our respective boxes have the same intrinsic nature; instead, all that matters is that they have the same causal profile. As long as we agree on a sufficiently wide range of judgments ('this one is red; that one is green'), it doesn't matter whether the things that look red to me look the way that green things look to you or vice versa.[8]

What should we say then about our knowledge of the phenomenal states of others? Arguably, we have two options. On the one hand, we could embrace the analogical account. Even if the analogical account cannot justify our claim to *know* the phenomenal states of other people, it might be able to provide our beliefs about this domain with a rational foundation. Alternatively, we could reject the 'raw feels' account of phenomenal states, and argue that phenomenal properties are really just intentional/functional states of a certain kind (and as such can, perhaps, be accommodated within the IBE framework). Whether phenomenal states can be reduced to intentional/functional states is, of course, another question.

11.4 Other kinds of minds I: non-human animals

A very different version of the epistemic problem of other minds concerns minds that are unlike ours. When it comes to our fellow human beings, we generally assume that our ordinary mindreading practice can (and often does) generate knowledge. (At least, this is true of adult neurotypical humans: ordinary mindreading struggles to identify the mental states of infants and individuals suffering from severe brain damage.) By contrast, it is very much an open question whether knowledge of the minds of non-human animals and AI systems *is* available to us. At the very least, it is not something that we take for granted. Genuine doubt about whether your friends and family members are conscious is a sign of psychiatric illness, but uncertainty about consciousness in birds, bees, or Data, the android depicted in *Star Trek: The Next Generation* is – one might argue – the appropriate attitude to adopt. Let's postpone for now the problem of artificial consciousness, and consider some of the many challenges posed by consciousness in non-human animals.

One challenge concerns the distribution of consciousness. Is consciousness restricted to (say) mammals, or does it also include reptiles, birds, or fish? What about invertebrates such as bees, lobsters, and spiders? Indeed, might the circle of sentience even encompass plants? (See Box: Plant mentality.) Many of the issues raised by these questions can be brought into focus by considering one particularly intriguing animal: the octopus.[9]

> **Box: Plant mentality**
>
> Botanists often describe plants as perceiving, learning, and even communicating with each other. Most theorists view such talk as metaphorical, arguing that plants no more try to grow towards the sun or tell each other about the presence of pests than laptops try to print documents or smartphones tell their owners about upcoming appointments. Others, however, hold that we should take talk of plant mentality quite literally, arguing that plants perceive, learn, and communicate in much the same sense in which you and I do. In defence of this view, they point out that plants respond adaptively to their environment, they integrate information from different sources, and they track the spatial and temporal gradient trajectories of resource availability. Indeed, some theorists argue that we should even take seriously the idea that plants are conscious - that they have a subjective point of view (Calvo 2017; Gagliano 2017).
>
> Given our ignorance of the physical basis of consciousness, it would surely be premature to dismiss the possibility of consciousness in plants. (Certainly those who take panpsychism seriously have every reason to give the hypothesis of plant consciousness a sympathetic hearing!) At the same time, the case for admitting plants to the consciousness club is far from overwhelming. Rather than think of plants as having an experiential perspective in the way that animals do, it may be more plausible to compare them to the kinds of subpersonal information-processing systems involved in interpreting speech, returning a tennis serve, and picking up a cup of coffee. These systems do indeed have representational states, but there is little reason to treat them as conscious agents in their own right.
>
> **Further reading**
>
> Calvo, P. 2017. What Is It Like to Be a Plant? *Journal of Consciousness Studies*, 24(9-10): 205-27.
> Gagliano, M. 2017. The Mind of Plants: Thinking the Unthinkable. *Communicative and Integrative Biology*, 10(2): e1288333.
> Maher, C. 2017. *Plant Minds: A Philosophical Defense*. Routledge.

Octopuses have relatively large brains - the common octopus has roughly 500 million neurons - and they display many features of general intelligence. For example, they have been found using their ability to generate jets of water from their arms to clean out sites to use as a home, repel scavenging fish and pesky experimenters, and short out the lighting in their aquarium that appears to be bothering them (Mather 2019; Godfrey-Smith 2016). Behavioural complexity of this kind in a mammal would generally be regarded as good evidence of consciousness, and it is tempting to regard it as evidence of consciousness in the octopus.

At the same time, there are important differences between us and the octopus, some of which might undermine the plausibility of ascribing consciousness to the octopus. One consideration is evolutionary: the octopus belongs to a very different branch of the tree of life from that on which we (and other mammals) are located. Thus, either our last common ancestor – which was likely some kind of a small, flattened worm that lived roughly 600 million years ago (Godfrey-Smith 2013) – was also conscious, or consciousness has evolved more than once. Although one (or even both) of these hypotheses might be true, the point is that there are evolutionary considerations against ascribing consciousness to an octopus that don't apply to mammals who display comparable levels of cognitive and behavioural complexity.

Another difference between us and the octopus concerns the structure of cognitive control. Like all cephalopods, the octopus has a decentralized nervous system, and only two-fifths of its neurons are located in its brain; the remainder are in its arms. This distributed control structure appears to provide each of the octopus's arms with significant degrees of autonomy. There is evidence that each arm can process information about its environment without needing to send signals to the brain, and much of what the octopus does seems to be under the control of one or more of its arms acting of its/their own accord. (Hochner et al. 2006).

What implications does this distributed structure of octopus cognition have for the question of consciousness? On the one hand, one could argue that consciousness is necessarily unified, and that an organism is conscious only if it has a single, integrated, point of view on its environment. Those tempted by this response will see the distributed nature of control and perceptual processing in the octopus as evidence that it is a zombie – smart, perhaps, but not conscious. Another view (and one with which I'm more sympathetic) is that the distributed nature of octopus cognition doesn't undermine the case for ascribing consciousness to the octopus, but merely suggests that what it's like to be an octopus is surely very different from what it's like to be a human being (Carls-Diamante 2017). The problem we confront here is that of determining whether a particular feature of human consciousness (in this case, its unity) is essential to consciousness as such, or whether it merely characterizes the form of consciousness that we (together, perhaps, with the members of some other species) enjoy.

Let's turn now from consciousness as such to the *contents* of consciousness. Assuming that we can tell whether a particular kind of animal is conscious, it's a further question whether we can also tell what kinds of conscious states that creature is capable of. A particularly important aspect of this question concerns *self*-consciousness: do other species have the capacity for self-consciousness, or is self-consciousness a uniquely human phenomenon?

Investigations of self-consciousness in humans often focus on mastery of the first-person pronoun ('I'), but obviously that approach cannot be employed when dealing with non-linguistic creatures. Instead, many experimenters employ the mirror test. Developed by Gordon Gallup in the 1970s (Gallup 1970; Gallup et al. 2002), the mirror test involves placing a mark on an animal's head that it can see only with the use of a mirror. An animal is taken to have passed the mirror test when it uses the mirror to engage in self-regarding behaviour (such as attempting to rub the mark off). Chimpanzees pass the mirror test, as do most great apes (other than gorillas); monkeys, by contrast, do not. There is suggestive evidence of mirrored-self recognition in elephants, dolphins, magpies, and even fish.[10]

Is the mirror test a good test for self-consciousness? Failing to pass the mirror test certainly doesn't show that an animal isn't self-conscious, for there are many reasons why an animal could be conscious of itself but refrain from using mirrors to engage in self-directed behaviours. (For example, it might not be interested in removing a mark from its face, or it might find mirrors aversive.) Instead, the question is whether passing the mirror test is good evidence of self-consciousness. More specifically, we need to ask what *kind* of self-consciousness might be involved in mirrored-self recognition.

The puzzle here is that most animals are clearly aware of themselves in some sense, for they treat their own body parts very differently from the ways in which they treat the body parts of other animals. In this sense, then, even animals that fail the mirror test can be said to have some kind of self-awareness. What does the use of mirrors to inspect one's body add to this? Why should using a mirror to remove a mark from a body part that can be seen only with a mirror indicate a more sophisticated form of self-consciousness than attempting to remove a mark from a body part that can be seen without the aid of a mirror?

One plausible answer is that passing the mirror test requires appreciating how one's body appears from other points of view, and that it is one object among other objects. This is a more sophisticated form of self-consciousness than the kind of self-consciousness that is involved in the fact that an animal will treat its own limbs differently from the way in which it treats the limbs of its conspecifics.

Yet another form of self-consciousness involves what psychologists refer to as *mental time travel* (MTT; Corballis & Suddendorf 2007). This term refers to the ability that you and I have to remember the past and anticipate the future 'from the inside'. For example, I can recall visiting Darjeeling as a child, and I can also anticipate returning to Darjeeling in the future.

MTT is a distinctively human trait, but is it also a *uniquely* human trait? Do other species also have the capacity to remember the past and anticipate the future from the inside? The psychologists Nicola Clayton and Anthony Dickinson (1998) attempted to answer this question by giving scrub jays worms and peanuts to cache in different locations. Scrub jays prefer fresh worms to peanuts, but they prefer peanuts to worms that have been cached for some time (and may have become inedible). Clayton and Dickinson found that the scrub jays retrieved freshly cached worms before they retrieved peanuts, but they retrieved peanuts in preference to worms that weren't fresh.

It is tempting to take these results to show that scrub jays engage in MTT. The thought here is that they attempt to retrieve freshly cached worms first because the anticipated pleasure of eating fresh worms is greatest; and they are able to retrieve the freshly cached worms because they are guided by their experiential memories of when and where they stored the worms. Another possibility, however, is that although the behaviour of scrub jays is guided by their preferences and propositional knowledge, none of that information involves MTT. According to this account, the preference that scrub jays have for fresh worms over peanuts does not involve anticipating what it would be like eat a fresh worm as opposed to a peanut, but is simply a matter of stored information to the effect that fresh worms are tastier than peanuts. Similarly, the propositional account holds that although the behaviour of the scrub jays is guided by information about when and where they cached certain foods, scrub jays don't remember their acts of caching from the inside in the way that you and I might.[11]

It is not clear how we might decide between these two interpretations of the scrub jays' behaviour. The propositional interpretation might be defended on the grounds that it is apparently more parsimonious, requiring only mechanisms of preference formation and propositional memory which we already know non-animals have. At the same time, the MTT interpretation might be defended on the grounds that *we* would employ MTT to execute tasks like this, and that the methods which we would use are unlikely to be unique to us. The overarching challenge here, of course, is to identify experimental methods that might enable us to distinguish the experiential aspects of 'mental time travel' from its informational aspects in non-verbal creatures.[12]

11.5 Other kinds of minds II: artificial consciousness

As challenging as the problems of consciousness in non-human animals are, it is questions about consciousness in AI systems that threaten to pose the most serious version of the problem of other minds. From Ridley Scott's *Blade Runner* to Alex Garland's *Ex Machina* and Kazuo Ishiguro's *Klara and the Sun*, questions about artificial consciousness have long fascinated fans of science fiction, but with the increasing sophistication of AI they are now being taken seriously within science itself. Indeed, questions about the possibility of consciousness in AI systems – and, indeed, in artificially created biological systems (Box: Consciousness in cerebral organoids?) – are attracting the attention of ethicists, policymakers, and legal theorists.

Box: Consciousness in cerebral organoids?

Derived from stem cells, cerebral organoids are laboratory-made 3D structures that display certain features of the developing human brain, such as spiking activity and complex oscillatory waves (Sakaguchi et al. 2019; Trujillo et al. 2018). Although current cerebral organoids lack many of the neurophysiological features of human brains, the neurofunctional profile of future organoids is likely to increasingly approximate that of the developing human brain.

Because organoids have neither sensory nor motor systems, standard tests for the presence of consciousness cannot be applied to them. One possible solution to this problem involves the redeployment of measures of neural complexity that have been used to identify consciousness in brain-damaged patients. The leading example of such measures is the *perturbational complexity index* (PCI), in which the cortex is first stimulated by transcranial magnetic stimulation (TMS) and then electroencephalography (EEG) is used to measure the complexity of the resulting neural response (Casali et al. 2013). PCI has proven effective in detecting consciousness in a variety of contexts in which the capacity for verbal report and voluntary behaviour is compromised, such as dreaming, ketamine-induced anaesthesia, and severe brain injury (Sarasso et al. 2015; Casarotto et al. 2016), and in principle it might be used to identify consciousness in organoids.

Further reading

Bayne, T., A. Seth, and M. Massimini. 2020. Are There Islands of Awareness? *Trends in Neurosciences*, 43(1): 6-16.

The challenge of artificial consciousness is often approached via the Turing test. Turing, of course, proposed his test as a test for thought, but we can consider its plausibility as a test for consciousness. (Indeed, if thought requires consciousness – as some theorists hold – then the Turing test is a test for thought only if it is also a test for consciousness.) As we noted in Chapter 5, the Turing test involves three individuals: an interrogator, an ordinary human, and an AI system ('the target'). Let's call our target 'Ava', in honour of the protagonist at the centre of *Ex Machina*. Ava and the human are assigned to separate rooms, and Ava can be said to have passed the Turing test if, after an extended session of questioning, the interrogator is unable to tell which room contains the human and which contains her.

Failing the Turing test surely tells us nothing about whether or not Ava is conscious. In the same way that a non-human animal might be conscious but be unable to pass the Turing test, so too we should allow that an artificially conscious agent's mode of consciousness is so unlike ours that its identity would be easily unmasked by the interrogator. But what if Ava *passes* the Turing test? Would that justify the conclusion that she was conscious?

The issue is an open one. What we can say, however, is neither of the two arguments that we considered in connection with the sceptical problem of other minds – the argument from analogy and the inference to the best explanation – is all that promising. The problem with the argument from analogy is there is little reason to assume that the correlations between cognitive/behavioural capacities and consciousness that apply to human beings (and, to some degree perhaps, other species) will apply also to AI systems such as Ava. Of course, if we knew that Ava's cognitive architecture mirrored our own at every level of description then we would be on firmer ground in thinking that she was conscious, but it is surely unlikely that Ava's cognitive architecture will mirror our own at every level of description. Ava is likely to resemble us at some levels of description and to be very different from us at other levels of description. The argument from analogy doesn't tell us which levels of description matter with respect to the question of consciousness. Appeals to inference to the best explanation are equally problematic, for the explanatory role of consciousness in us – let alone in artificial agents – remains obscure. Would an AI system need to be conscious in order to pass the Turing test, or could it display the conversational agility of an ordinary human without possessing even a whiff of subjectivity? At this point, we simply don't know.

In fact, questions about the distribution of consciousness in artificial systems might be beyond our capacity to answer. Here is an argument for precisely that conclusion:

1   A validated test for artificial consciousness must either compare the target AI system to us, or it must appeal to a reductive theory of consciousness.
2   Tests of consciousness that compare the target AI system to us are unfairly parochial.
3   Developing a reductive theory of consciousness requires closing the explanatory gap.
4   We can't close the explanatory gap.

So,

C   We can't develop a validated test for artificial consciousness.

Let's call the conclusion of this argument the 'pessimistic inference'. How might it be challenged? As I see it, premise (1) is secure. Premise (2) is also compelling, for it seems likely that most forms of artificial consciousness will differ greatly from the mode of consciousness that we enjoy; indeed, it seems likely that they will differ greatly from any biologically based mode of consciousness. The controversial premises are (3) and (4), although they will be challenged in different ways by different theorists. These issues are best explored by returning to the contrast between Type-A physicalists and Type-B physicalists (see Chapter 8).

The Type-A physicalist may well grant (3), but they are likely to challenge (4). As they see it, identifying the distribution of consciousness in artificial systems is possible, for there are certain kinds of physical/functional states that necessitate consciousness, and progress in philosophy and/or science will unmask those necessitation relations, thus closing the explanatory gap. And once the explanatory gap is closed, we will be able to tell whether a target AI system is conscious by identifying its physical/functional profile. Of course, whether the Type-A theorist is right to assume that we have the capacity to close the explanatory gap is a contested matter.

The Type-B physicalist is likely to grant (4) but will challenge (3), arguing that it is possible to provide an account of consciousness without fully closing the explanatory gap. The problem, however, is that theories of consciousness are developed by studying consciousness as it occurs in human beings (and, to a lesser extent, other mammals). Thus, any reason to think that a particular theory can be applied to systems that are very different to us must, it seems, diminish in direct proportion to the cognitive gulf between us and the target system. In a nutshell, artificial consciousness confronts us with the following challenge. The more an artificial system differs from us, the less appropriate it is to subject it to tests of human consciousness, but the less a test for consciousness is tailored to us, the more difficult it is to validate. The pessimistic inference is not unassailable, but it should certainly give pause to anyone who is tempted to treat the problem of artificial consciousness with insouciance.

11.6 Conclusion

We began this chapter by considering the three main accounts of the mechanics of mindreading: the perceptual theory, the simulationist theory, and the theory-theory. We saw that although perception might make a contribution to mindreading, much of our everyday understanding of the minds of those around us is likely to be done either by simulation-based processes or by the deployment of a rich body of information about how minds work.

We then turned to more distinctively philosophical terrain, beginning with the question of what our psychological concepts must be like in order for them to be applicable to other people. We considered Wittgenstein's argument for thinking that our capacity to intelligibly apply psychological concepts to other people shows that such concepts are not grasped on the basis of attending to 'private' sensations. I suggested that that argument fails: psychological concepts can be coherently applied to other beings even if they are acquired by attending to the character of one's own experiences.

In the second half of this chapter, we turned our attention to the epistemic challenges raised by other minds. We began with the problem of other human minds, and the sceptic's claim that we cannot – or at any rate, do not – know what other people are thinking and feeling. We then considered two ways in which claims to knowledge of other minds might be justified – the analogical response and the inference to the best explanation response – noting some of the main challenges facing each account. Finally, we explored the question of consciousness in non-human animals and artificial systems. It is here that the weaknesses of the analogical approach and the IBE approach are most evident. The analogical approach provides us with little guidance, for it doesn't tell us what kinds of properties are most relevant to the ascription of consciousness. The IBE approach is perhaps more promising, but it requires an account of what consciousness does (and does not) explain, and at present we have no such account (or at least, not one that elicits general agreement). Perhaps progress in science or philosophy will enable us to get a better grip on how consciousness is distributed in the animal kingdom and artificial systems. Another possibility, however, is that there are principled limits on our capacity to identify consciousness in beings that are radically unlike us.

Further reading

Excellent introductions to the psychology of mindreading debate can be found in Suilin Lavelle's *The Social Mind: A Philosophical Introduction* (Routledge, 2018) and Ian Apperly's *Mindreaders: The Cognitive Basis of 'Theory of Mind'* (Psychology Press, 2010). A number of the foundational papers in the debate about the psychology of mindreading can be found in a pair of volumes edited by Martin Davies and Tony Stone: *Folk Psychology: The Theory of Mind Debate* (Wiley-Blackwell, 1995) and *Mental Simulation: Evaluation and Applications* (Wiley-Blackwell, 1995). Important monographs on the topic include Alvin Goldman's *Simulating Minds: The Philosophy, Psychology and Neuroscience of Mindreading* (OUP, 2006); Stephen Stich and Shaun Nichols's *Mindreading* (OUP, 2003); and Gregory Currie and Ian Ravenscroft's *Recreative Minds: Imagination in Philosophy and Psychology* (OUP, 2002). Peter Godfrey-Smith's 'Folk Psychology as a Model', *Philosophers' Imprint*, 5(6): 1-16 (2005) provides an thought-provoking treatment of the debate between the simulation-theory and the theory-theory, while Shannon Spaulding's 'Mindreading beyond Belief: A More Comprehensive Conception of How We Understand Others', *Philosophy Compass*, 13(11): e12526 (2018) examines aspects of mindreading that have not traditionally received the attention they deserve.

Discussion of the conceptual and sceptical problems of other minds can be found in Anita Avramides's *Other Minds* (Routledge, 2001) and Alec Hyslop's *Other Minds* (Kluwer, 1995). For more on the analogical account, see Alec Hyslop and Frank Jackson, 'The Analogical Inference to Other Minds', *American Philosophical Quarterly*, 9: 168-76 (1972). A recent collection of papers that address both conceptual and empirical issues relating to our knowledge of other minds can be found in *Knowing Other Minds* (OUP, 2019), edited by Anita Avramides and Matthew Parrott.

The literature on the philosophy of animal minds is vast. A good place to begin is with Kristin Andrews's *The Animal Mind: An Introduction to the Philosophy of Animal Cognition* (2nd ed., Routledge, 2020). Two excellent collections of essays on animal thought are *Rational Animals?* (OUP, 2006), edited by Susan Hurley and Matthew Nudds, and *The Philosophy of Animal Minds* (CUP, 2009), edited by Robert Lutz. For an interesting discussion of the mirror test see Alexandra Boyle's 'Mirror Self-Recognition and Self-Identification', *Philosophy and Phenomenological Research*, 97/2: 284-303 (2018). For discussions that focus specifically on animal consciousness, see Andrew Barron and Colin Klein, 'What Insects Can

Tell Us about the Origins of Consciousness', *PNAS*, 113(18): 4900-4908 (2016); Jonathan Birch, 'The Search for Invertebrate Consciousness', *Noûs*, forthcoming; Michael Tye, *Tense Bees and Shell-Shocked Crabs: Are Animals Conscious?* (OUP, 2017); and Simona Ginsberg and Eva Jablonka, *The Evolution of the Sensitive Soul: Learning and the Origins of Consciousness* (MIT Press, 2019). Also highly recommended is David Foster Wallace's 'Consider the Lobster', in *Consider the Lobster and Other Essays* (Little, Brown, 2005).

Ned Block's 'The Harder Problem of Consciousness', *Journal of Philosophy*, 99(8): pp. 391-425 (2002) explores some of the challenges raised by artificial consciousness. For a thought-provoking treatment of the possibility of love with an AI system, see Spike Jonze's film *Her* and the related discussion in Troy Jollimore's '"This Endless Space between the Words": The Limits of Love in Spike Jonze's *Her*', *Midwest Studies in Philosophy*, 39(1): 120-43 (2015).

Study questions

1. This chapter distinguishes three elements of mindreading. What are they, and how are they related to each other?
2. What are the three accounts of the mechanics of mindreading presented in this chapter? What do you regard as the main strengths and weaknesses of each account?
3. What is the conceptual problem of other minds? Why is it more fundamental than the sceptical (epistemic) problem of other minds? Which of the two solutions to it that are presented in Section 11.2 do you prefer, and why?
4. This chapter distinguishes two conceptions of the sceptical problem of other minds. What is the difference between these two conceptions, and which do you think is more compelling?
5. What is the analogical response to the sceptical problem of other minds? What are its strengths and weaknesses?
6. What is the inference to the best explanation response to the sceptical problem of other minds? What are its strengths and weaknesses?
7. In what sense are the challenges posed by other kinds of minds similar to those that are posed by other human minds, and in what sense are they distinctive? In answering this question, you might like to reflect on the problems posed by ascribing mental states to non-linguistic human beings, such as babies or severely brain-damaged patients.
8. What is the pessimistic inference as outlined in Section 11.5? Do you find the argument for it plausible? If not, how would you challenge it?

Notes

1. Another approach to mindreading, which we won't discuss here, is given by Dennett's intentional stance. See Chapter 6 for discussion.
2. For discussion of perceptual accounts of mindreading, see Carruthers (2015), Cassam (2007), Dretske (1973), Green (2010), Lavelle (2012), McDowell (1998), McNeill (2012), and J. Smith (2015).
3. See Currie and Ravenscroft (2002), Gallese (2005), Goldman (1989, 2006), Gordon (1986), Harris (1992), and Heal (1986).
4. The use of simulation does require that one make certain theoretical assumptions (e.g., in determining what counts as subjecting a model to hurricane-like conditions), but these assumptions don't

drive simulation-based mindreading in the way that they drive theory-based mindreading. See Goldman (1989) for further discussion.
5 For discussion, see Avramides (2001), Gomes (2011), McGinn (1984), and Nagel (1986).
6 Curiously, discussions of the sceptical problem of other minds rarely engage with the psychology of mindreading, and it is sometimes tempting to read certain authors as concerned with the question of whether we could in principle have knowledge of other minds as opposed to engaging with the question of whether our ordinary mindreading practices do in fact deliver knowledge.
7 Although J. S. Mill is associated with the analogical account, Thomas (2001) argues convincingly that Mill's view was actually closer to the inference to the best explanation account that we consider next.
8 Indeed, there is some reason to think that qualia inversion might actually occur. See Nida-Rümelin (1996b) for discussion.
9 For more on octopus consciousness, see Godfrey-Smith (2013, 2016), Mather (2008, 2019), and Seth (2016).
10 For elephants, see Plotnik et al. (2006); for dolphins, see Mitchell (1995) and (Reiss & Marino 2001); for magpies, see Prior et al. (2008); and for fish, see Kohda et al. (2019).
11 For more on the debate between these two interpretations, see Suddendorf and Busby (2003), Suddendorf and Corballis (2007), Clayton et al. (2003a, 2003b).
12 See Boyle (2020-a) for an interesting solution to this challenge.

12 Self-knowledge

Chapter overview

- Considers ways in which the access one has to one's own mental states differs from the access that one has to the mental states of other people
- Examines four of the leading accounts of self-knowledge and identifies their respective strengths and weaknesses.

Even with the benefits of modern science, visits to the dentist often involve considerable amounts of discomfort. In an attempt to minimize that discomfort, your dentist might ask you to (say) raise your hand when the pain becomes too intense. Your dentist doesn't have direct access to your pain, but they will assume that you do, and that you can 'just tell' whether or not your tooth really hurts or is just mildly uncomfortable.

It's not only dentists who assume that a person knows whether or not they are in pain: we *all* tend to make that assumption. Indeed, we make similar assumptions with respect to make kinds of mental states. Suppose that you proclaim that you believe Earth to be flat. Your audience might question your sincerity or wonder if you're joking, but they are unlikely to think that you are mistaken about what it is that you believe.

Philosophers use the term 'self-knowledge' to refer to the kind of knowledge that we have of our own mental states. This chapter wrestles with the problem of self-knowledge, focusing on four very different accounts of the phenomenon. We begin, however, by considering what is distinctive of self-knowledge, for we need an account of the features of self-knowledge in order to be able to evaluate accounts of how self-knowledge is possible. In what ways does the knowledge that one has of one's own mind (first-person mindreading) differ from the knowledge that one has of the minds of others (third-person mindreading)?

12.1 The scope and status of self-knowledge

Self-knowledge appears to involve processes and procedures that cannot be used to gain information about another person's mental states. I might be able to know what you're thinking or feeling, but my knowledge of your thoughts and feelings will always be mediated in some way. Typically, I rely on what you do or say in order to know what you think or feel. By contrast, I don't need to examine my own behaviour in order to know what I think or feel. We can capture this thought by saying that the sources of self-knowledge appear to be *peculiar* to it.

Of course, one *can* discover things about one's own mind by reflecting on one's behaviour. One might realize that one is jealous of a friend by noting one's treatment of them, and conversations with a therapist might enable one to become aware of one's fear of commitment. These insights qualify as forms of 'self-knowledge' insofar as they involve knowledge of oneself, but they differ in fundamental ways from the kind of self-knowledge that philosophers of mind are interested in when they refer to 'the problem of self-knowledge'.

A second distinctive feature of self-knowledge is that it is (or at least seems to be) epistemically privileged. I might know that you are in pain, but my beliefs about your pain are vulnerable to forms of sceptical doubt to which my beliefs about my own pain are immune. I can wonder whether your tooth hurts quite as much as you seem to say it does, but it doesn't seem to make much sense for me to wonder whether *my* tooth hurts quite as much as it seems to. Similarly, although it may often be reasonable to doubt whether I have reliable access to your beliefs, desire, and intentions, but it is much harder to tell a story on which it is reasonable to doubt the reliability of one's access to one's own beliefs, desires, and intentions. We can capture this thought by saying that self-knowledge seems to be epistemically privileged when contrasted with our knowledge of other minds.

There are various conceptions of what the privileged nature of self-knowledge amounts to. For example, some philosophers have held that self-knowledge is privileged because it is infallible (i.e., incapable of being wrong). Certain instances of self-knowledge might indeed be infallible. Consider the thought 'I am now thinking'. Arguably this thought is infallible, for the very having of it appears to guarantee its truth.[1] However, it is doubtful whether infallibility extends much beyond self-verifying statements of this kind, and there is good reason to allow that self-knowledge can go wrong in various ways (see Chapter 9).

What is the scope of self-knowledge? What kinds of things can one know about one's own mind in this distinctively first-person manner? Philosophers have traditionally taken a very broad view of the scope of self-knowledge. David Hume once remarked that 'the actions and sensations of the mind are wholly transparent – they must necessarily appear in every particular what they are' (1739–40/2000). There are, however, good reasons to doubt that the mind is fully transparent to itself.

One source of resistance to the transparency thesis (as we can call Hume's claim) concerns the kinds of psychological processes involved in (say) executing a tennis serve, remembering a familiar tune, or understanding these words. These processes are not immediately accessible from the first-person perspective; instead, one needs to employ the tools of neuroscience and psychology in order to identify them. However, the advocate of the transparency thesis can sidestep this objection by arguing that it was only ever meant to apply to personal-level mental phenomena, and that the processes involved in executing a tennis serve, remembering a familiar tune, and understanding these words are subpersonal.

But there are problems with the transparency thesis even if its scope is restricted to personal-level phenomena. Consider character traits, such as introversion. It is possible to be introverted without knowing (or even being in a position to know) that one is introverted. Arguably, identifying one's own character traits requires adopting a third-person perspective on oneself and examining one's behaviour in the way in which one might examine the behaviour of another person. We also seem to lack distinctively first-person access to many of our psychological dispositions. What would you do if you discovered an intruder in your house? Would winning the lottery make you happy? How would you respond if given the opportunity to make a large amount of money by breaking the law? Psychologists have discovered that we are often poor at predicting our own behaviour, and that other people may have a better understanding of our own behavioural dispositions than we ourselves do.

But although some mental phenomena may not be characterized by transparency, others certainly are. We can group such phenomena into three classes. First, there are sensations and perceptual experiences. We seem to enjoy a distinctive kind of access to our own aches, pains, tingles, and perceptual experiences. You might wonder whether these experiences accurately represent the state of your body or your perceptual environment, but it would be relatively unusual to wonder whether you're right about what the experiences *themselves* are like. Second, there are conscious thoughts of various kinds: memories, imaginings, judgments, decisions, and so on. We typically assume that in having a thought we are aware of both its attitude (e.g., that it's a *decision*) and its content (e.g., that it's a decision *to feed the cat*). Third, there are standing propositional attitude states, such as intentions, beliefs, and desires. For example, we assume that if someone believes that Neil Armstrong was the first person to walk on the moon, then they have a kind of direct access to this fact. Uncertainty about what one believes (desires, intends) isn't typically a matter of ignorance but instead reflects the fact that one isn't sure about what to believe (desire, intend).

Our commitment to the idea that these phenomena are directly accessible from the first-person perspective is reflected in our attitude to ordinary first-person uses of mental terms, what are often called 'avowals'. When someone says, 'I'm in pain', 'I'm deciding what to have for dinner', or 'I hope to visit Marrakesh', we tend to assume that they are indeed in pain, that they are deliberating about what to have for dinner, and that they do hope to visit Marrakesh. We do, of course, realize that people can be insincere or mistaken about what their words mean, but bracketing such concerns we typically regard avowals as authoritative. Only rarely do we think it appropriate to challenge them. Most theorists assume that the authority of avowals derives from their epistemically privileged nature (Box: Avowals and expressivism). What I say about my own mental states is authoritative because the access that I have to my own mind is generally more secure than the access that you have to it. In short, the authority of avowals is typically taken to derive from the fact that knowledge of one's own mind is epistemically privileged. As we will see, the problem of self-knowledge is, in large part, the problem of explaining what accounts for its privileged nature.

> **Box: Avowals and expressivism**
>
> Most accounts of self-knowledge assume an epistemic treatment of avowals: avowals are authoritative because the speaker *knows* what their own mental states are. Expressivists reject this assumption, and hold that statements of the form 'I'm feeling sad' have the kind of authority with respect to sadness that crying does. That authority isn't epistemic; rather, it's the authority that derives from the fact that crying is a 'natural expression' of pain. In infants and non-human animals, pain is expressed by non-verbal behaviours such as crying, whimpering, and protective responses. Expressivists argue that in mature humans these non-verbal expressions of pain are supplemented by avowals, such as 'Ouch!' or 'My ankle hurts'.
>
> Expressivists are surely right to point out that avowals are often – perhaps even ordinarily – used to express mental states rather than to report them. ('I love you' is not typically a report of one's attitude to someone; it's an *expression* of that attitude.) But it doesn't follow that we don't know our own mental states, or that there is no genuine problem of first-person mindreading. What one says is one thing; what one knows is another. I needn't say anything (even to myself) in order to know how I'm feeling or what I'm thinking.
>
> **Further reading**
>
> Bar-On, D. 2004. *Speaking My Mind: Expression and Self-Knowledge*. Clarendon Press.
> Finkelstein, D. 2003. *Expression and the Inner*. Harvard University Press.

12.2 The inner-sense account

Let's begin with the inner-sense account of self-knowledge. This account is so named because it takes self-knowledge to involve a kind of internally directed sensory mechanism (or suite of mechanisms). Just as we have sensory mechanisms for detecting the states of our body and environment, so too – advocates of the inner-sense account hold – we have mechanisms for detecting our own states of mind. According to inner-sense theorists, the privileged nature of self-knowledge derives from the fact that the mechanisms of inner sense are more reliable than the mechanisms that we use to identify the mental states of other people.

The roots of the inner-sense account extend back to John Locke and Immanuel Kant, and versions of it remain popular.[2] One reason for its abiding appeal is that it promises to demystify self-knowledge. After all, there are many mechanisms for monitoring the states of one's own body (such as one's level of hydration): why shouldn't self-knowledge not also involve a suite of monitoring mechanisms?

But despite its prima facie plausibility, there are a number of robust objections to the inner-sense account. One objection is that perceptual systems generate experiences with distinctive phenomenal characters, whereas there seems to be no distinctive phenomenal character associated with self-knowledge (Shoemaker 1994). I might be aware of my mental states, but I don't experience them in the way in which I experience my bodily states or the states of the objects in my environment. Call this the *no distinctive phenomenology* objection.

Some advocates of the inner-sense view argue that there *is* a distinctive phenomenology associated with self-knowledge – what we might call the phenomenology of 'inner attention'. William Lycan puts this point as follows:

> If I have never particularly noticed what Pittsburgh tapwater tastes like to me, I can attend carefully the next time I drink some, and find out. If my doctor asks me to describe my wrist pain, I can resist distraction, focus my attention on the pain, and give the doctor more detail than I had previously been aware of.
>
> (Lycan 2003: 21)

I agree with Lycan that there is such a thing as the phenomenology of inner attention, but I am not persuaded that sensory phenomenal character characterizes all instances of self-knowledge in the way in which it characterizes all instances of perceptual and bodily experience.

A more compelling response to the objection, it seems to me, is to deny that mechanisms of 'inner-sense' would need to resemble the mechanisms of 'outer-sense' in all respects. Perhaps the mechanisms of inner-sense are more akin to the kinds of subpersonal monitoring mechanisms that control homeostatic processes (and which lack any phenomenal character) than they are to the mechanisms that are involved in perceptual or bodily experience. All that the 'inner-sense' view is committed to is that self-knowledge involves a mechanism (or suite of mechanisms) that generates accurate representations of one's mental states by monitoring them.

A very different challenge to the inner-sense account concerns its capacity to account for the privileged nature of self-knowledge. There are two kinds of worries here. The first concerns what Sydney Shoemaker (1988) has called 'self-blindness'. If self-knowledge involves a monitoring mechanism, then it ought to be possible for that mechanism to malfunction, and for one to be systematically unaware of a mental state that one is in. For example, if the mechanisms responsible for monitoring one's intentions were damaged, then one would no longer have distinctively first-person knowledge of what one was doing. In such a situation, one would be forced to identify one's intentions by examining one's behavioural patterns.

Is self-blindness of this form really possible? Perhaps not. Shoemaker argues that the very nature of many kinds of mental states entails that a rational agent who is equipped with the relevant concepts must be able to self-ascribe them. Shoemaker's argument for this view turns on an appeal to functionalism, but one needn't embrace functionalism to think that there is something incoherent in the idea of systematic self-blindness. Self-blindness might be possible with respect to certain kinds of mental phenomena (such as character traits), but it is far less obvious that one could be self-blind with respect to one's experiences, thoughts, and standing states.

A second worry relating to the privileged nature of self-knowledge concerns the possibility of false positives. If there are mechanisms of inner-sense, why wouldn't it be possible for them to misfire in the way in which the mechanisms involved in sensory perception can, thus generating representations of mental states that one is not actually in. But – the objection continues – it's doubtful whether self-knowledge really *can* go wrong in this way (or at least, not systematically). Could one seem to be having an auditory experience as of a loud siren without actually having such an experience? Could one seem to be deliberating about which of two jobs to take without actually doing so? Could one seem to experience an excruciating toothache without actually being in pain? If you think that the answers to these questions must be no, then perhaps you ought to have doubts about the inner-sense account (Box: Acquaintance).

> ### Box: Acquaintance
>
> Acquaintance theorists argue that we can do justice to the particularly intimate relation that we bear to our own experiences only by recognizing the existence of a unique kind of relation known as 'acquaintance'. The roots of this approach go back to Bertrand Russell's *The Problems of Philosophy* (1912), and although it was neglected for many decades, it is currently undergoing a renaissance. At its heart is the idea that if one is acquainted with a mental state, then there is no possibility of a gap between the way in which that state appears and the way in which it is. States with which one is acquainted must be exactly as they appear. Most acquaintance theorists restrict its scope to bodily sensations and perceptual experiences, although Russell himself extended the approach to include knowledge of our own thoughts.
>
> Appeals to acquaintance face two main challenges. The first concerns the inherent obscurity of the acquaintance relation itself. What exactly is it to be acquainted with a mental state? Some theorists treat the notion as a primitive, but that is profoundly unsatisfying. Others give an account of it in mereological (i.e., part-whole) terms, suggesting that to be acquainted with an experience is for that experience to be a part (or component) of one's awareness of it. However, this proposal doesn't explain the epistemic features of self-knowledge that acquaintance theorists want to account for, for the mere fact that a mental state is embedded in one's awareness of it does not itself explain one's direct and certain knowledge of it. A second challenge to the acquaintance account concerns the possibility of introspective error. If there is no possibility of a gap between the way in which an experience appears and the way in which it is, then it becomes difficult to explain how we could ever be wrong about the character of our own experiences (as we sometimes are).
>
> ### Further reading
>
> Balog, K. 2012. Acquaintance and the Mind-Body Problem. In Simone Gozzano and Christopher S. Hill (eds.), *New Perspectives on Type Identity: The Mental and the Physical*. Cambridge University Press.
> Duncan, M. 2021. Acquaintance. *Philosophy Compass*, 16(3): e12727.
> Gertler, B. 2012. Renewed Acquaintance. In D. Smithies and D. Stoljar (eds.), *Introspection and Consciousness*. Oxford University Press, pp. 89–123.

But it is a third challenge to the inner-sense account that is perhaps the most interesting – and the most serious. The challenge concerns the mechanics of monitoring. How could a self-scanning device identify one's mental states as the kinds of states they are? Suppose that you intend to visit Marrakesh. According to the inner-sense account, your awareness of this intention involves the operation of a mechanism that is not only able to distinguish intentions from mental states of other kinds (e.g., beliefs and desires), but can also distinguish the intention *to visit Marrakesh* from (say) the intention *to become an astronaut* or the intention *to learn Mandarin*. How could a subpersonal mechanism do either of these things?

One might argue that if the intention to visit Marrakesh is (or is realized by) a distinctive kind of brain state, then a self-scanner would be able to detect this intention by detecting the relevant kind of brain state. But this won't quite do, for even if the intention to visit Marrakesh is (or is realized by) a distinctive kind of brain state, the self-scanner would need to be aware of the relevant state as a mental state (and not just as a brain state). It is unclear, however, that a self-scanner would have the resources to do that.

In fact, there are really two problems here. The first problem concerns the content of the target state, for the self-scanner needs to be able to distinguish an intention to *visit Marrakesh* from an intention to *become an astronaut* or *learn Mandarin*. On the face of things, this looks like a tall challenge, especially for externalists, who hold that the content of a mental state is determined by its relations to the agent's environment (see Chapter 7, esp. 7.4). In response, some argue that the self-scanner wouldn't need to 'decode' the contents of its targets, but could simply copy them in the way in which one might copy sentences that are written in a language that one doesn't understand (see, e.g., Nichols & Stich 2003). As long as this copying process preserved the features in virtue of which the target states had their contents, then the monitoring state would have access to those contents (albeit, perhaps, in an embedded form).

The second problem concerns the attitude (or mode) of the target state. It is one thing for the monitoring mechanism to have access to the content of the target state, but it must also have access to the attitude that the agent takes to this content. How does the scanner know that the target state is an *intention* to visit Marrakesh as opposed to (say) a *desire* to visit Marrakesh? To identify intentions as such, the self-scanner may need access to the properties that distinguish intentions from mental states of other kinds. The leading proposal here is functional: intentions differ from other attitudes in virtue of the kinds of states that tend to cause them and the kinds of states that they in turn tend to cause. But if that's right, then a self-scanner may need to have access to information about the functional roles of its targets. I will leave you to consider how much of a challenge that might pose to the inner-sense account.

12.3 The inferentialist account

One of the most influential passages in the literature on self-knowledge is due to Gareth Evans (1946-80):

> In making a self-ascription of belief, one's eyes are, so to speak, or occasionally literally, directed outward – upon the world. If someone asks me 'Do you think there is going to be a third world war?', I must attend, in answering him, to precisely the same outward phenomena as I would attend to if I were answering the question 'Will there be a third world war?'
>
> (1982: 225)

The thought that Evans is gesturing at here is that it is possible to acquire knowledge of what one believes by attending to the world as one believes it to be.

Among the many accounts of self-knowledge that Evans's comments have inspired is Alex Byrne's inferentialist account.[3] Byrne's account is so called because he takes self-knowledge to involve the deployment of a suite of inference rules. These rules are a bit like the rules of logic, such as conjunction elimination, which allows one to infer '*p*' from '*p* and *q*'. In the case of self-knowledge for belief, Byrne argues, we use an inference rule that he calls the 'doxastic schema', which allows one to go from '*p*' to 'I believe that *p*'. Thus, if one believes that there's a fox in the chicken coop, then the doxastic schema allows one to infer that one believes that there's a fox in the chicken coop. In other words, the doxastic schema takes one from a belief to self-knowledge (or at least, self-belief) of that belief.

How might inferentialism explain the peculiar and privileged nature of self-knowledge? Accounting for peculiarity is relatively straightforward, for the doxastic schema can be applied only to one's own beliefs. (I can't apply the doxastic scheme to your belief that there's a fox in the chicken coop, for example.) Accounting for the privileged nature of self-knowledge, however, is less straightforward. Indeed, on the face of things the doxastic schema would seem to entail that self-knowledge is anything but privileged. After all, the inference from '*p*' to 'I believe that *p*' 'isn't deductively valid, nor does it conform to any standard pattern of good inference', as André Gallois (1996: 47) once observed. But the doxastic schema does have one epistemic virtue: it is self-verifying. If one believes that one believes *p* as a result of following the doxastic schema, then the belief that one believes *p must* be true.

One challenge to inferentialism concerns when to apply the doxastic schema. After all, the contents of most (perhaps all) beliefs can also occur in the context of other propositional attitudes. In addition to *believing* that the fox is in the chicken coop, one can also *hope* that the fox is in the chicken coop, *intend* for the fox to be in the chicken coop, or merely *wonder* whether the fox is in the chicken coop. Applying the doxastic schema to (say) the state of *hoping that the fox is in the chicken coop* would generate a *failure* of self-knowledge, for one would have mistaken a hope for a belief. In order to apply the doxastic schema appropriately, it looks as though one must have *already* determined whether one's attitude to *p* is that of belief. But if that's the case, then inferentialism fails to provide the full story as to how we know what we believe.

A second challenge to inferentialism concerns its *scope*: can the approach be extended beyond belief to account for other kinds of self-knowledge? Some ways of extending the inferentialist approach look to be relatively unproblematic. For example, it is plausible to suppose that perception can be treated on the model of belief. The idea here is that we come to know our perceptual experiences by applying a schema that involves as inference from '*q*' to 'I perceive that *q*', where *q* stands for a perceptual content rather than a belief content. Perhaps the account can also be successfully applied to desire. Here is Byrne's sketch of how such an account might go:

> Do I want to stay home and crochet or go out to the John Tesh concert? In answering the question, my attention is 'directed outward', in Evans' phrase, to the two options and their merits. Going to the concert is desirable: hence, I want to go.
>
> (Byrne 2011: 213)

The idea here is that we find out what we desire by focusing our attention on various possible states of the world, and asking what it is that we find desirable (see also Fernández 2007).

But there are cases of self-knowledge that are harder for inferentialism to accommodate. Consider knowledge of one's own intentions. Byrne (2011) suggests that we identify our intentions by directing our attention to what we will do. But that seems to get things the wrong way around: intuitively, knowledge of what one will do seems to be grounded in knowledge of one's intentions. Even more challenging, perhaps, is knowledge of the thoughts that populate the stream of consciousness. What outward-directed questions should one focus on in order to identify one's memories, imaginings, deliberations, or decisions? Suppose that you find yourself wondering how your grandmother is. Do you know that you are currently thinking about your grandmother by considering your grandmother? Surely not; indeed, as Dorit Bar-On has noted, it's not even clear what that would amount to (Bar-On 2015: 140). In short, even if inferentialism can account for certain aspects of self-knowledge, it appears unlikely to provide a satisfactory account of self-knowledge in general.

12.4 The deliberative account

Another view of self-knowledge that builds on Evans's remark – 'I get myself into a position to answer the question whether I believe that *p* by putting into operation whatever procedures I have for answering the question whether *p*' – is the *deliberative account*, a view that has been developed by Richard Moran (2001, 2003).[4]

At the heart of the deliberative account is the idea that self-knowledge is a practical enterprise rather than a theoretical one. One knows what one believes because belief involves an exercise of reason-based deliberation. Moran takes the main point of Evans's remarks to be that the question of what one believes cannot be dissociated from the question of what one thinks one has reason to believe. 'A person is credited with first person authority', he concludes, 'when we take the question of what he does believe to be settled by his decision as to what he is to believe' (2001: 134).

How might the deliberative account explain the peculiar and privileged nature of self-knowledge? The explanation of peculiarity is straightforward, for your deliberative capacities do not extend beyond your own mind. (You can make up your own mind, but you can't make up the mind of someone else.) But the deliberative expanation for why self-knowledge is privileged is rather more complicated. Here, Moran makes much of the contrast between ordinary self-knowledge and the kind of self-knowledge that can be obtained from third-person sources, such as the testimony of a therapist. The fundamental difference here, he argues, isn't that in relying on third-person sources one's knowledge of one's own mind is less secure than it ordinarily is, but that third-person cases involve a kind of alienation that is absent from ordinary self-knowledge. This alienation can be accounted for, Moran holds, only by recognizing that the authority of ordinary self-knowledge derives from our capacity to see ourselves as the authors of our mental lives.

What is the potential *scope* of the deliberative account? What forms of self-knowledge might it accommodate? Moran excludes sensations and perceptual experiences from the ambit of the view on the grounds that these states are not subject to deliberation. Memories, imaginings, ponderings, and so on might also to be excluded from the account for the same reasons. Indeed, Byrne (2011) and Shoemaker (2003) have argued that the view cannot even be plausibly applied to all instances of belief. They point out that becoming aware of a belief isn't always a matter of 'making up one's mind', for in some cases one's mind is already settled, while in other cases the reasons for or against the relevant proposition are decisive and there is no need for deliberation.

In response, Moran (2003) argues that insofar as one's attitude to *p* is one of belief, one must actively reaffirm one's commitment to *p*, even if one has previously endorsed *p* or finds the case in favour of *p* overwhelming. Beliefs are not like tattoos, states that one might simply be stuck with irrespective of one's current attitude to them; instead they must be actively maintained. I may have previously endorsed the claim that there will be a third world war, but if I am now presented with new evidence that bears on the issue then I ought, as a rational agent, consider the question again.

This response might be effective in rebutting the objection raised by Byrne and Shoemaker, but it does highlight a further challenge to the deliberative account: there is a difference between what I *ought* to do as a rational agent and what I *will* do. Ordinary human reasoning does not always conform to the norms of rationality, and a mental state can be the kind of state that is responsive to reasons without actually *being* responsive to reasons. Consider phobias. Although fear ought to be (and usually is) responsive to reasons, one can also be irrationally afraid. But the fact that a mental state fails to be responsive to reasons doesn't prevent one from becoming aware of it in the normal, first-personal manner. One can be aware of one's (irrational) fear of spiders in much the same way in which one is aware of one's (rational) fear of snakes. Indeed, we may even need to recognize the possibility of a gap between what one takes oneself to have reason to believe and what one actually believes.

The idea that self-knowledge can derive from our role in authoring a mental state is an intriguing one, and it may play *a* role in a comprehensive account of self-knowledge (Box: Anscombe on agent's knowledge). However, the scope of that role is likely to be limited at best. There are many mental phenomena that aren't subject to deliberation, and even when a particular kind of mental state does fall within the scope of deliberation, the question of whether one *is* in the relevant state cannot always settled by asking whether one *ought* to be in it.

Box: Anscombe on agent's knowledge

In her important book *Intention*, G.E.M. Anscombe presented an intriguing contrast between two types of knowledge: speculative (or contemplative) knowledge and agent's knowledge. Speculative knowledge is knowledge that is derived from the objects that are known. Here, she says, 'the facts, reality, are prior and dictate what is to be said, if it is knowledge'. Agent's knowledge has a different structure. Rather than being derived from its objects, agent's knowledge is 'the cause of what it understands' (Anscombe 1963: 57).

An example might help to illustrate what Anscombe has in mind. Consider an architect who has designed a house, which is then built in accordance with her plans. Does the architect need to see or in some way receive information about the house in order to know its layout? Arguably not. The architect knows the house's layout because she designed it: she is its source. She doesn't need to inspect it in the way that she would if the house were designed by another architect. Similarly, Anscombe claims, as agents we know what we are doing 'without observation or inference' because we are the source of our actions.

Further reading

Newstead, A. 2006. Knowledge by Intention? In S. Hetherington (ed.), *Aspects of Knowing*. Elsevier, 183-202.

O'Brien, L. 2003. On Knowing One's Own Actions. In J. Roessler and N. Eilan (eds.), *Agency and Self-Awareness*. Clarendon Press, pp. 358-82.

Schwenkler, J. 2012. Non-observational Knowledge of Action. *Philosophy Compass*, 7(10): 731-40.

12.5 Neo-Rylean approaches

The accounts of self-knowledge that we have examined thus far are each committed to the idea that first-person mindreading is both peculiar and privileged. We turn now to an approach that rejects both assumptions, holding that although first-person mindreading does indeed differ from third-person mindreading in various ways, in many respects it is not different in kind. In effect, this approach holds that first-person mindreading is really just a special case of third-person mindreading – it's third-person mindreading directed towards oneself.

The founding figure in this tradition is Gilbert Ryle (1900-76). Ryle argued that there is nothing distinctive about the kind of access that one has to one's own states of mind:

> The sort of things I can find out about myself are the same as the sorts of things I can find out about other people, and the methods of finding them out are much the same. A residual difference in the supplies of the requisite data makes some difference in degree between what I can know about myself and what I can know about you, but these differences are not all in favour of self-knowledge. In certain quite important respects it is easier for me to find out what I want to know about you then it is for me to find out the same sorts of things about myself. In certain other important respects it is harder. But in principle, as distinct from practice, John Doe's ways of finding out about John Doe are the same as John Doe's ways of finding out about Richard Roe.
>
> (Ryle 1949: 155-56)

Ryle's claims are startling, for it seems evident both that the kinds of things that I can find out about myself go beyond the kind of things that I can find out about other people, and that the methods I employ for finding things out about my own mental life differ from those that I employ to find out about the mental lives of others. I don't need to examine my facial expressions in order to know that my head is throbbing, nor do I need to consult my patterns of behaviour to know that I intend to make a cup of coffee. Ryle's account of self-knowledge might seem plausible to those who are sympathetic to behaviourism (as he was), but that merely demonstrates the implausibility of behaviourism.

But although 'full-strength' Ryleanism has few contemporary advocates, a number of authors – most notably Alison Gopnik (1993) and Peter Carruthers (2011) – have developed 'neo-Rylean' accounts of self-knowledge.[5] Unlike Ryle, both Gopnik and Carruthers allow that we have privileged access to either some (Gopnik) or all (Carruthers) forms of *sensory* experience, but they join Ryle in denying that we have privileged access to our own thoughts and propositional attitudes. Here is how Carruthers puts it:

> When attributing attitudes to ourselves, we can make use of the evidence provided by our own inner speech, our visual and motor imagery, our own affective feelings, and so on. In contrast, while we have access to other people's overt speech, we never have access to their inner speech or other forms of imagery. Nor do we have access to any of their affective reactions, except insofar as these are manifested in their behaviour. There is therefore generally *more* sensory data available when we attribute propositional attitudes to ourselves than when we attribute them to others. But it still requires interpretation for attitudes to be ascribed.
>
> (Carruthers 2011: 2–3; emphasis in original)

On this view, we fail to recognize that access to our own thoughts is interpretative because, as adults, we have had so much experience in interpreting ourselves that we typically find self-interpretation effortless. But, Gopnik and Carruthers argue, that impression is illusory, for the access that we have to our own thoughts is no more direct than the access that we have to the thoughts of others.

Both Gopnik and Carruthers develop their accounts on the basis of findings in cognitive science. Gopnik herself is a developmental psychologist, and she draws on studies that she and others have conduced which indicate that young children make the same kinds of mistakes about their own beliefs, desires, and intentions that they make about the beliefs, desires, and intentions of other people. In one study, three-year-olds were shown a candy box which turned out to be full of pencils (Perner et al. 1987). When asked what another person would think is in the box if it were shown to them, the children said that the other person would think that there are pencils in the box. But three-year-olds also have problems ascribing false beliefs to their earlier selves. When they were asked, 'When you first saw the box, before we opened it, what did you think was inside it?', two-thirds of the children said they had originally thought that there were pencils in the box (Gopnik & Astington 1988). Here, the children seem to be making an incorrect inference about their own (immediately past) beliefs. Only when they are about four years of age are children able to reliably report the beliefs that they held in the immediate past (but no longer hold).

For his part, Carruthers draws on research in social psychology which suggest that we have a strong propensity to confabulate – that is, to ascribe thoughts and propositional attitudes to ourselves that we don't in fact have.[6] Although other accounts of self-knowledge allow that confabulation is possible – after all, everyone agrees that it is possible to apply third-person mind-reading processes to oneself – Carruthers argues that the extent and nature of our tendency to confabulate is best explained by supposing that we lack direct access to our own thoughts, and that we rely instead on cues derived from the sensory data to which we do have direct access.

Although the evidence marshalled by Gopnik and Carruthers raises questions about the degree to which we have direct and transparent access to the contents of our own minds, it is far from decisive. Even if children don't acquire a full grasp of the concept of belief (for example) until the age of four, it's possible that once they acquire it children can apply it to themselves in distinctive ways. This line of thought allows that grasping psychological concepts such as BELIEF is indeed a theoretical achievement, but it resists the claim that there is nothing peculiar or privileged about the self-application of these concepts. Carruthers's interpretation of the 'confabulationist' literature can also be challenged, for it can be argued that the relevant experiments show not that we are prone to form false beliefs about our own propositional attitudes (as he holds), but that we are prone to *change* our propositional attitudes on the basis of relatively trivial reasons (Box: Making sense of oneself).

Box: Making sense of oneself

In studies of counter-attitudinal behaviour, participants are instructed to write an essay which supports a position that they themselves reject. For example, individuals who oppose an increase in university fees might be induced to write an essay in support of increasing university fees. Participants write these 'counter-attitudinal' essays in one of two conditions: a 'no-choice' condition and a 'free-choice' condition. Those assigned to the no-choice condition are given cues (such as being reminded that the essay topic has been set by the experimenter) that undermine their sense of agency, whereas those assigned to the free-choice condition are given cues (such as being asked to sign a consent form) which prime them to feel responsible for what they have written. Studies typically find that participants in the free-choice condition – and only these participants – change their attitude once they have written their counter-attitudinal essay. For example, those who had previously opposed an increase in university fees might say that they no longer oppose such an increase, or even that they support it.

Carruthers holds that these findings are best explained by supposing that participants are mistaken about their own attitudes, arguing as follows. First, writing a counter-attitudinal essay generates adverse feelings, which in turn leads individuals to engage in some form of 'dissonance reduction' to manage those feelings. Individuals in the no-choice condition can manage these feelings by reminding themselves that what they wrote wasn't really up to them, but those in the free-choice conditions don't have that option. Instead, they engage in dissonance reduction by reporting attitudes that are in line with the views expressed in their essay. Since a person's sincere reports provide evidence of what they believe, participants in the free-choice condition have evidence that they have changed their attitudes, and thus come to believe that they have changed their mind. But that self-interpretation is false, for (Carruthers claims) their attitude to the topic in question *hasn't* changed.

Another possibility, of course, is that the process of writing a counter-attitudinal essay under free-choice conditions does in fact cause individuals to change their mind.

> This change wouldn't be prompted by the presentation of new evidence, but would instead result from the same kinds of mechanisms of dissonance reduction to which Carruthers appeals. Deciding between this proposal and Carruthers's proposal requires addressing complex questions about what exactly attitudes are, and the degree to which an agent's attitudes can dissociate from the attitudes that they self-ascribe.

In addition to challenging the arguments given by Gopnik and Carruthers, critics also claim that the neo-Rylean view is vulnerable to various objections. One kind of objection focuses on disorders of mindreading. Here, it has been argued that certain individuals with schizophrenia (Robbins 2009) and autism (Nichols & Stich 2003) have difficulty identifying other people's thoughts, but they don't suffer from comparable difficulties in identifying their own thoughts. If true, such claims would put pressure on the neo-Rylean account, for it predicts that difficulties in third-person mindreading ought to be accompanied by difficulties in first-person mindreading. However, it is controversial whether such claims are true, for there is some evidence that individuals with schizophrenia and autism often *do* have difficulties in identifying their own thoughts (see Carruthers 2011).

In my view, the most serious objection to the neo-Rylean account derives from worries about what we might call the 'poverty of the stimulus'. Suppose that you are sitting quietly in your chair, and someone asks you what you're thinking about. You respond: 'I was thinking about going to the bank'. How did you arrive at this answer? The neo-Rylean can't appeal to either situational or behavioural cues here, for there are none. Arguably, the only data to which they might appeal is inner speech. Perhaps (the thought is), one knows that one is thinking about going to the bank because one is aware of an episode of inner-speech in which this thought is expressed.

But this proposal presents the neo-Rylean with the following dilemma. Either access to the meaning of inner speech is interpretative, or it isn't. If it is interpretative, then it ought to be subject to the kind of ambiguity and equivocation to which the interpretation of ordinary speech is subject. (If I say 'I'm going to a bank', you might be unsure whether I mean to go to a river or to a financial institution). But one's awareness of one's own thoughts is never subject to ambiguity of this form. After all, you never need to ask yourself what kind of bank you have in mind when you think to yourself, 'I should go to the bank today'. Thus, it looks though the neo-Rylean must hold that our access to the meaning of inner speech is direct (i.e., non-interpretative). However, this position seems to be equally problematic. For one thing, it is controversial whether the meaning of speech can be perceived (O'Callaghan 2011), and if the meaning of ordinary speech is not perceivable then it's not clear why the meaning of inner speech should be. Worse, allowing that the meaning of inner speech can be directly apprehended would undercut much of the motivation for the neo-Rylean view, for if we have non-interpretive access to the meaning of inner speech, then it's hard to see why we couldn't also have non-interpretative access to the meaning of our thoughts.

12.6 Conclusion

Let's review the territory that we've covered in this chapter by considering some of the major points of disagreement surrounding self-knowledge.

First, there is disagreement concerning the scope of self-knowledge. Some theorists hold that we have a distinctive kind of access to a great many kinds of mental phenomena (bodily sensations, perceptual experiences, conscious thoughts, standing propositional attitudes); others hold that the range of distinctively first-person access to the mind is highly restricted, and perhaps includes little more than bodily sensations and perceptual experiences.

Second, there is disagreement about the kind of authority that accompanies self-knowledge. Some theorists regard self-knowledge as characterized by a kind of epistemic security that doesn't extend to our beliefs about other people's mental states, whereas others argue that the contrast between knowledge of one's own mind and knowledge of the minds of others is (at most) one of degree rather than one of kind.

But perhaps the most fundamental disagreement concerns the sources of self-knowledge. As we have seen, some theorists take self-knowledge to involve the operation of certain kinds of self-scanning devices; others argue that it is based on the use of inference rules (such as the doxastic schema); still others hold that it is grounded in exercises of rational agency; and a final group of theorists maintain that it involves nothing more than the self-directed application of the methods that we use to read the minds of others. I have presented these accounts as competitors, but we should also take seriously the possibility that self-knowledge is grounded in a variety of mechanisms and procedures. Indeed, given the diversity of mental phenomena themselves, pluralism with respect to self-knowledge is surely to be expected. But it is one thing to think that a comprehensive account of self-knowledge might have various elements, and quite another to know what exactly those elements are or how they might be knitted together.

Further reading

Excellent introductions to the problem(s) of self-knowledge include Brie Gertler's *Self-Knowledge* (Routledge, 2011) and Annalisa Coliva's *The Varieties of Self-Knowledge* (Palgrave, 2016). There are also a number of very good collections of papers on self-knowledge, including Annalisa Coliva's (ed.), *The Self and Self-Knowledge* (OUP, 2012); Anthony Hatzimoysis's (ed.), *Self-Knowledge* (OUP, 2011); and Brie Gertler's *Privileged Access: Philosophical Accounts of Self-Knowledge* (Ashgate, 2003). Older collections include Crispin Wright, Barry Smith, and Cynthia Macdonald (eds.), *Knowing Our Own Minds* (OUP, 1998) and Quassim Cassam, *Self-Knowledge* (OUP, 1994).

For more on inner-sense approaches to self-knowledge, see Shaun Nichols and Stephen Stich's 'How to Read Your Own Mind: A Cognitive Theory of Self-Consciousness', in Quentin Smith and Aleksandar Jokic (eds.), *Consciousness: New Philosophical Perspectives* (OUP, 2003). For a recent collection of essays on the notion of acquaintance see *Acquaintance: New Essays* (OUP, 2019), edited by Jonathan Knowles and Thomas Raleigh.

For more on the inferentialist approach see Jordi Fernández's *Transparent Minds: A Study of Self-Knowledge* (OUP, 2013) and Alex Byrne's *Transparency and Self-Knowledge* (OUP, 2018). The classic defence of the deliberative approach is Richard Moran's *Authority and Estrangement: An Essay on Self-Knowledge* (Princeton University Press, 2001). For a critical discussion of Neo-Rylean views of self-knowledge, see S. Nichols and S. Stich, 'Reading One's Own Mind: Self-Awareness and Developmental Psychology', *Canadian Journal of Philosophy*,

30: 297–339 (2004) and Dorit Bar-On and Jordan Ochs, 'The Role of Inner Speech in Self-Knowledge: Against Neo-Rylean Views', *Teorema*, 37(1): 5–22 (2018).

Study questions

1 What does it mean to say that self-knowledge is 'peculiar' and 'privileged'? Which account of self-knowledge best explains these features of self-knowledge?
2 What is the difference between expressing a mental state and reporting it? Explain how this distinction might be relevant to the question of why self-knowledge is privileged.
3 What is the 'no distinctive phenomenology' objection to the inner-sense account of self-knowledge? Is this objection compelling?
4 What is Shoemaker's self-blindness objection to the inner-sense account of self-knowledge? How might the advocate of the inner-sense account respond to it?
5 What two accounts of self-knowledge draw inspiration from Gareth Evans' remark that 'I get myself into a position to answer the question whether I believe that *p* by putting into operation whatever procedures I have for answering the question whether *p*'? How, exactly, do these two accounts of self-knowledge differ from each other?
6 What is the idea at the heart of deliberative accounts of self-knowledge? What kinds of mental states is the deliberative approach well placed to explain, and what kinds of mental states does it struggle to explain?
7 How do the neo-Rylean accounts developed by Gopnik and Carruthers differ from Ryle's own account of self-knowledge?
8 What attitude do neo-Ryleans take to the claim that self-knowledge is peculiar and privileged? Do you think that this attitude is warranted?

Notes

1 There is, however, a question about whether 'I' succeeds in referring to anything. If there is no self, then 'I am now thinking' wouldn't be infallible for it wouldn't even be true. We consider 'no-self' theories in Chapter 13.
2 See, e.g., Armstrong (1968), Goldman (2006), Lycan (1996), and Nichols and Stich (2003).
3 See, e.g., Byrne (2011, 2018), Dretske (1995, 1999), Fernández (2013), and Gallois (1996).
4 See also McGeer (1996) and especially Boyle (2009, 2011) for accounts that have much in common with Moran's deliberative approach to self-knowledge.
5 Note, however, that neither Gopnik nor Carruthers refers to their view as neo-Rylean. Gopnik calls her account the 'theory-theory', whereas Carruthers calls his account the 'interpretative-sensory access' (ISA) theory.
6 Note that 'confabulation' in this sense of the term should be distinguished from another sense of 'confabulation' which refers to a syndrome associated with disturbances of autobiographical memory.

13 The self

Chapter overview

- Identifies various roles played by the concept of the self
- Considers various pathologies of self-awareness
- Examines three leading conceptions of the self: dualism, animalism, and neo-Lockean views
- Discusses the claim that the self is an illusion.

One of the most celebrated passages in the work of the Chinese philosopher Zhuang Zhou, also known as Zhuangzi (4th century BCE), is known as 'the dream of the butterfly':

> Once Zhuang Zhou dreamt he was a butterfly, a butterfly flittering and fluttering around, happy with himself and doing as he pleased. He didn't know he was Zhuang Zhou. Suddenly he woke up and there he was, solid and unmistakable Zhuang Zhou. But he didn't know if he was Zhuang Zhou who had dreamt he was a butterfly, or a butterfly dreaming he was Zhuang Zhou. Between Zhuang Zhou and a butterfly there must be some distinction! This is called the Transformation of Things.
>
> (Watson 1968: 49)

One of the questions with which Zhuangzi wrestles in this passage concerns the nature of the self: what, exactly, is he? Is he a human being, something 'solid and unmistakable'; or is he some kind of immaterial substance, something that could just as easily be associated with a butterfly as with a human being? And if he is an immaterial substance, then what exactly is the difference between him and a butterfly?[1]

This chapter introduces you to the philosophical debate surrounding the self. Some philosophers argue that you are an immaterial substance, an entity whose existence is not tied to any particular organism. Others argue that you are an animal of a certain kind, a member of a particular species. Still others argue that you are a psychological network, an integrated collection of mental states and capacities. And perhaps most radically, some theorists argue

DOI: 10.4324/9781003225348-14

that the self is an illusion, and that you are at best a fictional device, if indeed you are any kind of thing at all.

13.1 Putting the self to work

We begin not with accounts of the self but with the *concept* of the self, for unless we have some grip on what the concept of the self involves, we will be ill-equipped to judge the merits of competing accounts of what self.

Some theorists doubt whether the term 'self' is associated with a coherent concept. Here, for example, is Eric Olson:

> People often speak as if there were a serious philosophical problem about selves. Is there a self? Is the self knowable? How does the self relate to the body? These and other questions are thought to make up something called the problem of the self. I doubt seriously that there is any such problem. Not because the self is unproblematic, or because there are unproblematically no such thing as selves. My trouble is that a problem must be a problem *about* something: even if there are no selves, there must be at least some problematic idea or concept of a self, if there is to be a problem of the self. As far as I can see there is no such idea.
>
> (Olson 2007: 262)

Olson's worries are not unreasonable, for the 'self' is indeed used in many ways. Some theorists use the term to refer to a certain kind of experience, the kind of experience that involves (as we might put it) 'self-awareness'. Some theorists use 'self' to refer to social roles and relations, as when one might distinguish the self that one presents to one's closest friends and confidantes from the self that one presents to one's colleagues and the wider world. And some theorists use 'self' to refer to those aspects of one's character with which one identifies most closely. These uses of 'self' are perfectly legitimate, but they are at best only indirectly related to the notion of the self with which we are concerned.

An account of the self (in our sense of the term) is an answer to the question, 'What, most fundamentally, are you?' In asking this question, we aren't looking for a list of any old properties that you might happen to have. If asked, 'What are you?', you might reply, 'I am a student'. This answer might be true, but being a student is a property that you happen to have (we can suppose), rather than one which is required for your very existence. There was once a time when you weren't a student, and it's likely that at some point you will no longer be a student. So, although you are a student, you aren't most fundamentally a student. In looking for an account of the self, we are looking for an account of your essential nature.

To guide our search, it will be useful to distinguish some of the roles (or jobs) that we associate with the self. The best account of the self will be the one that best fits that job description that we draw up.

First, the self functions as the referent of first-person thought. It is the thing that you refer to when you think to yourself, 'I'm hungry' or 'I wonder where I am'. Consider Lucy Lawless, star of the 1990s television series *Xena: Warrior Princess*. Lucy Lawless can use the name

'Lucy Lawless' to refer to herself, but she can also refer to herself by using the first-person pronoun 'I'. Of course, there are important differences between 'I' and a proper name. Anyone can use 'Lucy Lawless' to refer to Lucy Lawless, but the only person who can use 'I' to refer to Lucy Lawless is Lucy Lawless herself. In this sense, then, 'I' is a kind of private name. Whether the peculiar nature of I-thoughts might tell us anything about the nature of the self is a question to which we will return.

Another job that we expect the self to play is that of 'anchoring' thoughts and experiences. In Charles Dickens's novel *Hard Times*, a character called Mrs. Gradgrind remarks, 'I think there's a pain somewhere in the room but I couldn't positively say that I have got it'. Mrs. Gradgrind's statement strikes us as odd, not just because we assume a person always knows whether or not a particular pain is their own, but also because she seems to take seriously the possibility of 'free-standing pains' – pains that are not anchored to (or had by) any particular subject of experience. That idea is as strange as the idea that a cat could disappear but leave its grin behind. Just as a grin is always the grin of some particular grinner, so too any thought or experience must, it seems, be the thought or experience of some particular self.

Third, selves guide a distinctive kind of moral and prudential concern, what we might call *self-directed concern*. Suppose that you stumble upon the report of a murder and suspect that you might have been the murderer. (Perhaps you have amnesia for a certain period of your past.) You are unlikely to be indifferent to questions about the identity of the perpetrator. Or suppose that you are told that someone in your town will be tortured tomorrow, but the identity of the victim will be revealed only at the last minute. Here too questions about identity are surely something about which you care. Is it *you* who will be tortured or someone else? No matter how altruistic we may be, the attitudes that we take to ourselves – to what *we* do and experience – differ in fundamental ways from those that we take to other people.

Fourth, the self is (or at least appears to be) manifest in experience. It is not just a theoretical entity that we posit in order to solve various problems in metaphysics or the philosophy of language, but is something of which we seem to have 'direct sensible acquaintance', as William James once put it (1890/1983: 286). Arguably, any viable account of the self must accommodate the ways in which the self is presented in experience.

That said, it must be recognized that we are sailing into contested waters here, for many deny that the self is ever given to us as an object of experience. In a passage that may have been inspired by Buddhism (Gopnik 2009), David Hume famously denied being able to find any trace of the self in his own experience:

> When I enter most intimately into what I call *myself*, I always stumble on some particular perception or other, of heat or cold, light or shade, love or hatred, pain or pleasure. I never can catch *myself* at any time without a perception, and never can observe any thing but the perception.... If any one upon serious and unprejudic'd reflexion, thinks he has a different notion of *himself*, I must confess I can reason no longer with him. All I can allow him is, that he may be in the right as well as I, and that we are essentially different in this particular. He may, perhaps, perceive something simple and continu'd, which he calls *himself*; tho' I am certain there is no such principle in me.
>
> (*Treatise* 252)

Hume's point is not that there is no self, but that we don't even have *experiences* of selfhood. We are, he says, aware only of mental particulars ('perceptions', in his terminology), but not of anything that *has* these particulars. And just as many theorists agree with James, so too many side with Hume, claiming to find no trace of the self in their own experience. Here is not the place to attempt to resolve this dispute (see Box: Losing oneself).[2] The important point to note is that those who take the self to be presented in experience have reason to regard this fact as placing an important constraint on an account of the self. On this view, selves must be the kinds of things of which we can be experientially aware.

Box: Losing oneself

There are many contexts in which the ordinary sense of the self is disrupted. For example, patients suffering from anarchic hand syndrome experience a loss of control over a hand, often describing it as having 'a mind of its own' (Marchetti & Della Sala 1998); and patients suffering from delusions of thought insertion experience a loss of control over their own thoughts, claiming that are under the direct control of other agents (Sass & Parnas 2003). But the psychopathology in which the experience of selfhood is most acutely compromised is depersonalization. Individuals who suffer from this condition often report feeling unreal in some way. One patient remarked, 'often I have to … enter a shop to talk, to ask for something, in order to get a new proof that I really am myself' (quoted in Billon 2014). In extreme cases, depersonalization takes the form of Cotard's delusion, in which patients assert that they are dead or that they no longer exist. One of the striking features of Cotard's delusion is that patients can be reluctant to use 'I', preferring to refer to themselves via the demonstrative 'it' or their proper name.

It is tempting to draw two lessons from these conditions. The first is that those who deny that there is an experience of selfhood are wrong, for we need to recognize such an experience in order to understand what is lost in these cases. The second lesson is that those who take the experience of selfhood to be a necessary feature of consciousness (as many do) are also wrong, for these conditions indicate that consciousness can survive the loss of the sense of 'I'. A similar argument can be made with reference to meditation and the psychedelic state, for many subjects in these conscious states reports a sense of egoless consciousness (Metzinger 2020; Millière 2017).

Further reading

Billon, A. 2014. Why Are We Certain That We Exist? *Philosophy and Phenomenological Research*, 91(3): 723-59.

Duncan, M. 2019. The Self Shows Up in Experience. *Review of Philosophy and Psychology*, 10(2): 299-318.

Young, A. W., and K. M. Leafhead. 1996. Betwixt Life and Death: Case Studies of the Cotard Delusion. In P. Halligan and J. Marshall (eds.), *Method in Madness: Case Studies in Cognitive Neuropsychiatry*. Psychology Press.

238   The self

Let's take stock. Selves, as we conceive of them, are the objects of first-person thought; they anchor mental phenomena, they guide self-directed concern, and they are (widely thought to be) manifest in experience. In effect, we have provided a job description for the self. It might, of course, turn out that no single thing plays all four of these roles. (That might be because some of the jobs that we associate with the self aren't done by anything at all; or it might be because although every job is done by something or other, no one thing does them all.) If it does turn out that nothing fits the job description provided here, then our ordinary conception of the self would be in need of fundamental revision. That is precisely the position held by illusionist accounts of the self. We consider illusionism in the final section of this chapter. First, however, we must examine some of the leading realist views of the self, according to which something fits the job description outlined here – or at least, fits it well enough to qualify as 'the self'.

13.2   Dualism

Substance dualists (hereinafter 'dualists') hold that the self is a kind of non-physical thing that functions as the substrate for one's mental life. In Western philosophy, this non-physical entity is often referred to as the soul, while in Hinduism it is often known as *atman*. If dualism is right, then you are not identical to the human being who wears your socks, sits in your armchair, and sleeps in your bed. Instead, you are merely embodied in that human being. Some versions of dualism hold that the self must always be embodied but can migrate from one body to another, while others allow that it can exist fully disembodied.

There is some reason to think that dualism is the default view of the self, and that we are 'natural-born dualists', as the psychologist Paul Bloom (2004) has put it.[3] One reason for dualism's appeal may lie in the possibilities it appears to offer for life after death. Indeed, if you are an immaterial substance, then not only might you survive the demise of the animal with which you are associated, it's also possible that you existed before it did.

Our main interest, however, is not with dualism's appeal but with its truth. Let's begin with what I will call the *existence question*: is there any reason to think that our mental lives involve the operations of an immaterial substance – a 'soul'?

One argument for the soul's existence appeals to certain distinctive features of first-person thought. As we noted earlier, 'I' is peculiar in that you alone can use it refer to yourself. Now, one might be tempted to infer that because 'I' is private, then the object to which it refers must also be private, something that you alone have access to. And of course, souls would indeed be private in just this sense, for they are not observable in the way that physical objects (such as human beings) are.

This argument might be attractive, but its appeal should be resisted. The fact that I-thoughts are private (in the sense that we have identified) doesn't entail that what they refer to must also be private. For all the argument shows, you could be a perfectly ordinary physical object, albeit one that has the capacity to refer to itself in ways that are not available to anyone else.

A more promising argument for dualism appeals to our capacity to imagine ourselves occupying very different forms of embodiment (consider Zhuanghi's dream of a butterfly) or indeed no embodied perspective at all. An important example of this approach is the *Flying Man argument*, proposed by the medieval Iranian philosopher Avicenna (Ibn Sina) (Avicenna 1959; Adamson & Benevich 2018). Imagine, Avicenna says, a person who is directly created by

God in mid-air and who receives no sensory input of any form. This 'flying man' has no perceptual experience of the world or of his own body. He doesn't even experience the position of his limbs in space; indeed, for all he knows he has no body, for having just been created he will have no memories of embodiment. But despite any experience of embodiment, Avicenna claims, the flying man will be aware of himself. This fact, Avicenna argues, shows that the self is an immaterial substance that is distinct from the body.

One point at which Avicenna's argument might be challenged concerns the assumption that the flying man could be self-aware. Perhaps self-awareness requires either some form of bodily awareness or a history of interaction with other agents, so that even an omnipotent God couldn't create a self-conscious individual 'out of thin air' (so to speak). Avicenna takes it for granted that the flying man could be self-conscious, but perhaps he has no right to that assumption.

Granting (if only for the sake of argument) that the flying man could be aware of himself, it is not entirely clear how this fact might show the self to be essentially immaterial. Avicenna seems to assume that in being aware of himself the flying man would be aware of his essence, and that part of what it is to be aware of one's essence is to be aware of the kind of thing that one is. Thus, if the continued existence of one's body were required for one's continued existence, then the flying man would not be conceivable (which, Avicenna assumes, he clearly is).[4]

Avicenna isn't alone in making optimistic assumptions about our capacity to tell, on the basis of self-awareness alone, which of one's properties belong to one's essence. Here is René Descartes's conceivability argument for dualism:

> I know that everything which I clearly and distinctly understand is capable of being created by God so as to correspond exactly with my understanding of it. Hence the fact that I can clearly and distinctly understand one thing apart from another is enough to make me certain that the two things are distinct, since they are capable of being separated, at least by God. Thus, simply by knowing that I exist and seeing at the same time that absolutely nothing else belongs to my nature or essence except that I am a thinking thing, I can correctly infer that my essence consists solely in the fact that I am a thinking thing. It is true that I may have a body that is very closely joined to me. But nevertheless, on the one hand I have a clear and distinct idea of myself, in so far as I am simply a thinking, non-extended thing; and on the other hand I have a distinct idea of body, in so far as this is simply an extended, non-thinking thing. And accordingly, it is certain that I am really distinct from my body, and can exist without it.
>
> (Descartes 1641/1996: 54)

Although there are important differences between Descartes's conceivability argument and Avicenna's flying man argument, both arguments appear to assume that self-awareness enables one to fully grasp one's essential attributes. Given that assumption, if the self were essentially embodied, then that fact would be apparent on the basis of what one can (and cannot) imagine from the first-person perspective.

It is, however, doubtful whether self-awareness does reveal one's essential attributes as such. In fact, many would argue that very little can be gleaned about one's fundamental nature from what one is (or isn't) able to imagine from the first-person perspective. Can you imagine being Napoleon at Waterloo? One might think so. Certainly it doesn't seem any harder to imagine being Napoleon than it is to imagine being a disembodied subject of pure thought. But could you *really* have been Napoleon? Surely not (Williams 1966/1973). What one can apparently imagine from the first-person perspective may be a poor guide to the structure of reality, for the first-person concept contains so little information about the kind of thing that one is. As Kant remarked, '"I" is the poorest of all representations' (1781/1998: B408).[5] Self-awareness may perhaps be trusted to reveal *that* one is (but see Section 13.5), but it reveals very little about *what* one is.[6]

There are other arguments for the existence of an immaterial soul, but we must leave them to one side and turn to a second challenge facing the dualist: even if the existence of the soul can be established, what grounds are there for identifying the soul with the self? Why not think of the soul as one thing and the self as another? Call this the *identification question*.

One answer to this question appeals to the role that the self plays in anchoring mental phenomena. 'You are a particular immaterial substance', the dualist might say, 'because the thoughts and experiences of which you are directly aware are the thoughts and experiences of that substance'. This reply has some merit, for we do indeed think of the self as the thing that anchors mental phenomena. But we also saw that anchoring is only one of the roles that we expect the self to play. Could an immaterial substance play the other roles associated with the self?

Consider first the role of I-thoughts. On the face of things, many I-thoughts are at odds with dualism. Suppose that you think to yourself, 'I am 24 years old' or 'I am 6 feet tall'. Strictly speaking, if dualism were true, then these statements (and many others like them) would be false, for no immaterial substance is 24 years old or 6 feet tall. There is indeed a challenge for the dualists here, but it is far from insurmountable. To deal with it, the dualist will distinguish between two ways of understanding I-thoughts (and their verbal expression). Strictly speaking, they might say, claims such as 'I am 24 years old' are indeed false, but there is a less strict interpretation on which they can qualify as true, for we can take such claims to refer to the human being in which one is currently embodied rather than one's self.

So far, perhaps, so good; but the dualist may have more trouble with other aspects of the self. Consider the role of the self in guiding self-regarding concern. Drawing on a suggestion that Locke once made, suppose that we were to discover that souls swap experiences each night, so that the experiences that you seem to remember having had yesterday were in fact had by the soul that has my current experiences and vice versa. Would this discovery give me any reason to distance myself from the experiences that I remember having (but you don't) and think of them as your experiences rather than mine? I don't think so. To take an even more exotic scenario, suppose that I was to discover that the immaterial self that underpins my current experiences will tomorrow swap places with the immaterial self that currently underpins the experiences of a butterfly. If dualism were right, then I should be prepared to extend my self-related concern to the butterfly: I should think of the butterfly's future experiences as *my* experiences. But that doesn't seem right.

Let's take stock. We have seen that dualism faces two formidable challenges. The first challenge concerns the very existence of an immaterial substance (the soul) that might underpin mentality. As we have seen, some of the leading arguments for the soul's existence are unconvincing. But even if the soul's existence can be established, dualists still face questions about whether we should identify the self with the soul. Dualism's critics generally focus on the first of these two challenges, but to my mind the second challenge is equally daunting.

13.3 Animalism

When you look at yourself in the bathroom mirror, what you see is an animal of a certain kind, a member of the species *Homo sapiens*. According to animalists, the object that you see is quite literally your self, for you are an animal. You came into existence when a particular human being came into existence, and you will go out of existence when (and only when) that same human being goes out of existence. Animalism is also known as 'the biological account', for it holds that an account of the self – or at least, the kinds of selves that we are – can be given in biological terms (van Inwagen 1990; Olson 1997; Snowdon 2014).[7]

There is much that is attractive about animalism. For one thing, it appears able to accommodate all four aspects of the self that we explored in Section 13.1. It can account for first-person thought, for there is nothing particularly mysterious in the fact that certain types of animals have the capacity to refer to themselves. It can explain the self's anchoring role: what makes my mental states the states of a single self is the fact that they are the states of a single organism. It seems to align with our ordinary expressions of self-directed concern, for I care about the fate of one particular human being (the one who wears my socks, sits in my chair, sleeps in my bed) in ways that I don't care about the fate of other human beings. And, finally, it appears to do justice to the experience of selfhood. Although there are disorders of consciousness in which a person can feel alienated from their body (and the parts thereof), one ordinarily experiences a kind of identification with one's body. Indeed, even Descartes noted that one doesn't experience one's body in the way in which a sailor might experience their ship, but instead experiences oneself as 'intermingled' with one's body (1641/1996: 56).

In addition to appearing to deliver what we want from an account of the self, animalism also avoids a number of tricky questions faced by those who reject it. If you aren't identical to the human being who wears your socks, sits in your chair, and sleeps in your bed, how precisely *are* you related to it? If this animal can have thoughts (and why shouldn't it?) how are its thoughts related to yours? Could there be two thinkers – one of whom is you, and one of whom is an animal – wearing your socks, sitting in your chair, and sleeping in your bed? That hardly seems plausible.[8]

Despite the case in favour of animalism, there are a number of scenarios that are widely regarded as fatal to its prospects. At its core, each of these scenarios aim to show that the identity conditions of human beings pull apart from the identity conditions of selves. One scenario of this kind involves conjoined twins. Consider Abigail and Brittany Hensel, conjoined twins from Minnesota (Wallis 2013).[9] The Hensel twins have separate heads, spinal cords, hearts and stomachs, but they share a single liver, large intestine, and bladder. Despite their physical entanglement, Abigail's I-thoughts refer to one self and Brittany's I-thoughts refer to another self – at least, that would appear to be the most natural thing to say. Each twin appears to have her own thoughts, perceptions, and sensations (although there are intriguing suggestions that they can 'share' experiences too). The two twins certainly care about each other, but their self-regarding attitudes seem to have distinct objects. Family members appear to treat them as distinct subjects of moral concern, and what Brittany is answerable for is not the same as what Abigail is answerable for. All of these facts are difficult to square with animalism if the Hensel twins constitute a single organism.

Of course, one might argue that the Hensel twins don't constitute a single organism, but are rather distinct human beings who share certain body parts (e.g., Olson 2014; Liao 2006). This might be the right thing to say about the Hensel twins – indeed, it might even be the right thing to say about conjoined twins in general (but see Boyle 2020-b) – but it seems to me to avoid the central issue here. The mere fact that there is some uncertainty about how many human beings figure in cases of conjoined twinning is itself at odds with animalism, for intuitively there is no such uncertainty when it comes to counting selves. The question of whether conjoined twinning is best understood in terms of overlapping organisms (who share body parts) or in terms of a single organism (with duplicate body parts) might be of interest in its own right, but it is surely irrelevant to the question of whether Abigail and Brittany Hensel are distinct selves.[10]

Box: One organism, two selves?

Another source of pressure on the biological account derives from the split-brain syndrome. This syndrome is so named because it involves an operation in which most of the fibres connecting the two hemispheres of the brain are cut. (This is done in order to prevent epileptic seizures migrating from one hemisphere to the other.) Although the split-brain procedure has limited effects on the patient's everyday life, laboratory studies suggest that the patient may have two streams of consciousness – one associated with each hemisphere.

In these studies, information is presented to the patient so that it is restricted to a single hemisphere of the brain. (This can be done by exploiting the brain's contralateral structure, in which stimuli projected to the left half of the visual field are processed in the right hemisphere of the brain and vice versa.) So, the word 'key-ring' might be presented to the patient so that 'key' falls only within the patient's left visual field (and is sent to the right hemisphere) and 'ring' falls only within the patient's right visual field (and is send to the left hemisphere). When asked to report what she sees a patient may say that she sees only the word 'ring' (because speech production is generally localized in the left hemisphere), but with her left hand she may select a picture of a key and ignore pictures of a ring and a key-ring (because movements of the left hand are primarily under the control of the right hemisphere). The patient's behaviour suggests that she is conscious of both 'key' and 'ring', but her failure to integrate these representations suggests that these experiences are not co-conscious (i.e., are not elements of a single stream of consciousness.) This puts pressure on animalism if one holds – as many theorists do – that the simultaneous experiences of a single self must be co-conscious.

> **Further reading**
>
> Nagel, T. 1971. Brain Bisection and the Unity of Consciousness. *Synthese*, 22: 396–413.
> Schechter, E. 2018. *Self-Consciousness and 'Split' Brains*. Oxford University Press.

The conjoined twins objection puts pressure on animalism, for it suggests that multiple selves can be associated with a single organism. But what about the converse possibility? Could a single self be associated with more than one organism?

Consider the possibility of a brain (or rather, cerebrum) transplant (Shoemaker 1984; Shoemaker 2011). Suppose that the cerebrum of one individual (Donor) is transplanted into the cranium of another individual (Recipient), whose own cerebrum has been removed and destroyed. (Despite the loss of their cranium, Recipient remains alive due to the continued functioning of their brainstem.) We might even suppose that the transplanted cerebrum continues to support consciousness during the procedure, so that there is a continuous stream of thoughts and experiences associated with it ('What's happening?' 'Is the operation over yet?' 'Where am I?'). The thoughts and experiences which occur at the start of this procedure are centred on Donor's body, but as the procedure continues they give way to thoughts and experiences that are centred on Recipient's body.

How should we describe this scenario? If animalism is correct, then the experiences that belong to this stream of consciousness must be assigned to distinct selves: the earlier experiences belong to Donor, whereas the later experiences belong to Recipient. (After all, only the cerebrum is transplanted – and an organism can survive the loss of its cerebrum.) But this description is surely implausible. Suppose that once the procedure has finished, there is a memory of an experience that occurred at the start of the procedure, such as hearing a bell. Animalists must describe this as a case in which one self (Recipient) remembers an experience had by another self (Donor). Surely, one might think, it is more plausible to say that in this scenario a single self remembers one of *its* earlier experiences, an experience that it had when it was associated with a different human being.[11]

Where does this leave animalism? It certainly has one significant advantage over dualism, for there is no doubt that organisms exist (whereas the existence of the soul is far from evident). But it is less clear that animalists have established that we are identical to particular animals. There is, no doubt, an intimate connection between you and the human being who wears your socks, sits in your chair, and sleeps in your bed. But if the arguments given here are sound, then you are not identical to that animal, for its identity conditions are not your identity conditions.

13.4 The psychological approach

According to many, the lesson to be learnt from the problems with dualism and animalism is that an account of the self must be fundamentally psychological in nature. Psychological approaches are often referred to as 'Lockean' (or 'neo-Lockean') views, for they have their roots in John Locke's discussion of personal identity. Locke argued that the referent of the term 'self' – or, to use the term that he more frequently employed, 'person' – is distinct from that of 'man' (i.e., human being). The latter is a biological notion, whereas the former is to be understood in psychological terms. As Locke put it in his *An Essay Concerning Human Understanding*, a person is a 'thinking intelligent Being, that has reason and reflection, and can consider it self as itself, the same thinking thing in different times and places' (1690/1975: 2.27.9). According to neo-Lockeans, it is our psychological properties which gives us our identity conditions.

Although all version of the psychological approach take their inspiration from Locke, they develop his approach in very different ways. These differences can be highlighted by considering *the binding problem*: what is it that binds together all of the mental states of a single self *as* the states of a single self? Why aren't your mental states the states of different selves, or indeed no selves at all?[12] The binding problem has two aspects. The first concerns mental phenomena that are simultaneous with each other. For example, you might be watching waves break against a sea wall, hearing the cry of gulls, and enjoying the taste of fish and chips. What unifies these experiences and makes them all yours? This is the synchronic binding problem. The second aspect of the problem is concerned with mental unity as it obtains across time. What unifies an experience that you had at the age of five with an experience that you are having right now, such that they are both your experiences? This is the diachronic binding problem

Dualists and animalists have straightforward answers to these questions, for they can each appeal to the activity of a single substance. (The dualist will identify this substance with an immaterial soul; the animalist will identify it with an organism.) But the Lockean cannot provide an answer of this kind, for Lockeans are reductionists about the self: as they see it, selves are constituted by mental phenomena and the relations that hold between them.[13] Thus, the Lockean must appeal to relations between mental phenomena to explain what binds them together as the states of a single self. Crucially, different versions of the psychological approach appeal to different kinds of relations here.

One version of the view focuses on causal relations. According to this account, mental states are bound together as the states of a single self because they are causally integrated with each other in ways in which the states of different selves are not. An influential advocate of this version of the Lockean approach is Sydney Shoemaker. It is, Shoemaker says,

> a commonplace that an important part of the functional role of a mental state is to give rise, in combination with other mental states, to yet other mental states. This happens when people reason and deliberate. But it also happens in ways that involve no exercise of agency. The 'cognitive dynamics' and 'cognitive kinematics' of mental states is such that over time they change in certain ways depending on what other mental states accompany them. An expectation of something as being in the remote future evolves into an expectation of something immediately forthcoming, given normal awareness of the passage of time. And one need not engage in any deliberate reasoning or deliberation for one's understanding of a situation to mature over time, or for separate items of knowledge or belief to merge into a unified conception. . . . So given our person who starts at a particular time with a certain set of mental states, we expect there to be a

series of mental states which develops from that set of mental states and exhibits a certain kind of continuity.

(Shoemaker 1997: 295)

Shoemaker argues that many of the causal relations that obtain between the mental states of a single self are essential to their identity as the kinds of states that they are. In other words, he sees the psychological account of the self as intimately related to a certain kind of functionalism.[14]

Barry Dainton (2004, 2008) has developed a very different version of the psychological approach, one which appeals to relations of phenomenal unity and continuity (co-consciousness) to solve the binding problems. Roughly speaking, the idea is that experiences belong to a single self in virtue of occuring within a unified stream of consciousness. This approach has some plausibility with respect to simultaneous experiences, but it struggles when confronted with the diachronic binding problem. Consider again an experience that you had as a five-year-old child and an experience that you are having right now. These two experiences are not parts of a single, uninterrupted stream of consciousness, for there is surely some point between them at which you completely lost consciousness. Dainton responds to this challenge by appealing to the notion of an experience-producing system: we survive interruptions in the flow of experience because we are, most fundamentally, experience-producing systems. This is still at heart a phenomenal approach to the self, he claims, because what it is to be an experience-producing system is defined in terms of co-consciousness.[15]

A third version of the psychological approach appeals to narrative relations. According to this view, the various mental states that compose a self – or at least, the kinds of selves that we are – are the states of a single self because they are woven together as parts of a single story. Marya Schechtman, one of the leading architects of this view, puts it as follows:

We constitute ourselves as persons by forming a narrative self-conception according to which we experience and organize our lives. This self-conception and its operations are largely implicit and automatic. As we are socialized into human culture, we are taught to operate with a background conception of ourselves as continuing individuals, leading the lives of persons. What this means more specifically is that we experience the present in the context of a larger life-narrative. In order to have a narrative self-conception in the relevant sense, the experienced past and anticipated future must condition the character and significance of present experiences and actions. When I have a self-constituting narrative, what happens to me is not interpreted as an isolated incident, but as part of an ongoing story.

(Schechtman 2007: 162)

Schechtman's primary claim isn't that we tend to regard our lives as having some kind of story-like structure. Instead, her claim is that taking a narrative attitude to a mental episode is at the heart of what *makes* that episode yours. Selves, on this view, are self-constituting (Schechtman 1996).

The contrast between these three versions of the Lockean approach is striking. Consider again the question of what makes it the case that an experience which you had as a five-year-old is *your* experience. On Shoemaker's view, this experience is yours because it is causally integrated with your current experiences in the right kinds of ways; on Dainton's view, it's yours because it's produced by the same experience-producing systems that are producing your current experiences; and on Schechtman's view, this experience is yours because you identify with it in a distinctive kind of way, incorporating it into the story of your life.

Let's leave to one side the differences between these versions of the Lockean approach and focus instead on what they have in common. All three accounts identify the self with a psychological system of some kind, a network of mental states and capacities. Can a view of this kind, irrespective of how it's developed, deliver a viable account of the self?

It appears to be well placed to account for certain features of the self. Consider, for example, the role of I-thoughts. As we observed earlier, it is natural to suppose that the I-thoughts of Abigail Hensel refer to one self, whereas those of Brittany Hensel refer to a distinct self. The Lockean approach can accommodate this fact, for the two kinds of I-thoughts are embedded in different psychological networks. The Lockean can also account for the role that selves play in 'anchoring' mental phenomena. Because the Lockean approach is reductive, it cannot explain why mental states are anchored to selves (and why different mental states are anchored to different selves) in the way that the Cartesian or animalist can (i.e., by appealing to a substance), but the Lockean can appeal to the fact that different mental states are embedded in distinct psychological networks to explain why we assign them to distinct selves.

There are, however, aspects of the self that are potentially more challenging for the Lockean to accommodate. One such aspect concerns the role of the self in guiding self-directed concern, for it is an open question whether our self-regarding attitudes always track the kinds of relations that Lockeans take to be essential to the identity of the self. Consider a scenario first described by Bernard Williams (1970), in which you are told that your body will be tortured at some future time, but that in the interval between now and the torture, your brain will be wiped of all its current psychological states. If the Lockean view is right, then you have no grounds to worry about whether it's really you who will be tortured, for the Lockean self wouldn't survive the wiping procedure. However, it is far from clear that that would be the right attitude to take to this scenario. Perhaps, as Williams points out, it would be appropriate to think of the future pain as one's own pain, even if the wiping procedure removes the kinds of psychological connections that are, on the Lockean view, required for the continued existence of the self across time.

There are also questions about whether the Lockean can account for the nature of self-awareness. Arguably we don't experience ourselves as entities that are in some sense constructed out of mental states and their relations. Rather, we experience ourselves as entities that *have* mental states. In this sense, then, the reductionism that is inherent in the psychological approach seems to be at odds with the experience of selfhood.

For many, however, the central objection to the Lockean approach concerns the determinacy of the self. The kinds of relations that Lockeans appeal to can hold to greater or lesser degrees, and there seems to be no principled way to say how tight these relations must be in order to constitute a single self. If that is right, then there will be scenarios in which there may be no fact of the matter as to whether two experiences are had by the same self or not. This indeterminacy would be ontological rather than epistemic, and couldn't be resolved by the acquisition of further information about mental phenomena and the relations between them.

The thought that the existence of the self might be vague and fuzzy is a disquieting one, for it is tempting to assume that given any possible scenario, either one continues to exist or one doesn't. It might (of course) be difficult to tell which of these two possibilities would occur, but that's a purely epistemic matter: the existence of the self (one might think), can admit of no vagueness or ambiguity. As the Scottish philosopher Thomas Reid (1710-96) put it,

> The identity of a person is a perfect identity: where it is real it admits of no degrees; and it is impossible that a person should be in part the same, and in part different ... The evidence of identity in other persons other than ourselves does indeed admit of all degrees, from what we account certainty, to the least degree of probability. But still it is true, that the same person is perfectly the same, and cannot be so in part, or in some degree only.
> (Reid 1785/1975: 111)

Reid's claim is undeniably attractive, but perhaps its allure should be resisted. Consider degenerative conditions, such as Alzheimer's disease. Those who witness the effects of Alzheimer's disease on a loved one often describe it as 'eating away' at the self. In such conditions, perhaps it is appropriate to think of the self as fading out over a period of time rather than being extinguished in an instant (see Box: Who wants to live forever?). A parallel point can be made with respect to the emergence of the self. Your psychological states, capacities, and dispositions didn't originate all at once but instead took shape gradually and incrementally. As strange as it may sound, perhaps there was no precise moment at which you came into existence.

Box: Who wants to live forever?

Different accounts of the self have very different implications for what it would take to secure some form of personal immortality.

If you are most fundamentally an animal, then you survive only as long as the particular human being that you are survives. When it goes out of existence, so too do you. Thus, if animalism is correct, then the only way to become immortal would be to avoid – or perhaps reverse – the event of death.

In contrast, if dualism is correct, then immortality requires only the continued existence of the soul. What that requires is, however, an open question. In the *Phaedo*, Plato argued that the soul is naturally immortal on the grounds that it is simple and has no parts, and only that which has parts can decay. But Plato's argument is not wholly convincing, for not only is the simplicity of the soul questionable, but it is also doubtful whether only that which has parts can go out of existence. And even if the soul is naturally immortal, it 'guarantees no immortality of the sort we care for', as Williams James (1890/1983: 273) once pointed out.

It is sometimes suggested that the Lockean view offers the strongest prospects of immortality. If you are nothing but a psychological system, the argument goes, then your immortality could be secured by simply uploading your mind into a storage system and downloading it into a suitable brain as and when required. But would this really secure any kind of *personal* immortality? Here is one puzzle to consider.

Suppose that something goes wrong with the downloading process, and instead of being downloaded into just a single brain, your memories, beliefs, desires, and so on are downloaded into the brains of multiple individuals, all of whom go on to lead independent lives. On the face of things, each of your descendent 'selves' would have an equally good claim to being you. Does it then follow that each of them *would* be you? Indeed, could you achieve a kind of immortality (or something close to it) not by living a single life of unlimited duration, but by living, in parallel, infinitely many lives of finite duration? Or are each of these selves distinct from you (and, presumably, each other), despite the fact that each of them has as much psychological continuity with your current self as your current self has with the self that you were yesterday?

Further reading

Blackford, R., and D. Broderick (eds.). 2014. *Intelligence Unbound: The Future of Uploaded and Machine Minds*. Wiley-Blackwell.

Chalmers, D. 2010. The Singularity: A Philosophical Analysis. *Journal of Consciousness Studies*, 17(9-10): 7-65.

Schneider, S. 2009. Mindscan: Transcending and Enhancing the Human Brain. In S. Schneider (ed.), *Science Fiction and Philosophy*. Blackwell, 241-55.

13.5 The self as an illusion

Let's bring this chapter to a close by considering one of the most radical responses to the problem of the self: illusionism. As the label indicates, illusionists hold that our ordinary conception of the self is fundamentally flawed, and that the self is in some important sense an illusion. Illusionism has been defended since the time of the Buddha (5th-4th centuries BCE) and is currently the subject of much attention. We will consider two rather different forms of illusionism.

The most straightforward version of illusionism is the 'no-self' view. No-self theorists are eliminativists about the self. They accept that thoughts, actions, and experiences exist, but, they claim, there are no thinkers, agents, or subjects of experience. Some no-self theorists accept that we have *experiences* of selfhood, but they deny that such experiences succeed in latching on to anything.

There are various arguments for the no-self view, but arguably the most influential begins with the dualist conception of the self that we encountered at the start of this chapter. The idea here is that dualism provides the right account of what the self would have to be, for only an immaterial substance could have the kind of unity and permanence that a genuine self requires. But – the argument continues – there are no immaterial substances of the kind that the dualist posits, and hence there is no self.

Dualists, of course, will take issue with this argument, but so too will animalists and neo-Lockeans. Animalists will ask why organisms don't qualify as selves, while neo-Lockeans will ask why the self can't be identified with a psychological network. In order to respond to these challenges, no-self theorists need to show that there are demands on what it is to be a self that neither animalists nor neo-Lockeans can meet. For example, they might argue that the self would need to be indivisible, or that its identity would need to be perfectly determinate. Animalists and neo-Lockeans, of course, will deny that selves must meet these demands. Settling this debate requires engaging with difficult questions about what the concept of the self involves, and that is beyond our remit here. What is clear, however, is that if the no-self view is indeed the bold and provocative claim that it is often taken it to be, then it can't simply be equated with the rejection of dualism, for one can reject dualism without denying the existence of the self (as both animalists and neo-Lockeans do).

A rather different form of illusionism is known as 'fictionalism'. Instead of simply denying that selves exist (as the no-self theorist does), the fictionalist holds that ordinary thought is profoundly mistaken about the *kind* of thing the self is. One of the most influential versions of fictionalism is that developed by Daniel Dennett (1992), who argues that selves are 'imaginary points' around which we structure our interpretation of behaviour. On this view, the self is not a concrete thing in the way in which an organism, soul, or even a psychological network would be. Instead, Dennett says, it is an abstractum, an explanatory posit. Dennett likens selves to centres of gravity, dubbing them 'centres of narrative gravity'.

In certain respects, Dennett's fictionalism is akin to the neo-Lockean views of the self that we discussed in Section 13.4. However, instead of identifying the self with a psychological network, Denntt identifies the self with the character around which that network is structured. Thus, Dennett's view can accommodate the phenomenology of selfhood, and the fact that we experience ourselves as something 'over and above' mere networks of psychological states. Like the neo-Lockean, Dennett holds that although there is usually one self per human being, there could be cases – involving, for example, split-brain individuals or those who suffer from dissociative identity disorder (Dennett & Humphrey 1989) – in which we need to invoke multiple centres of narrative gravity in order to explain the behaviour of a single human being. 'All that has to be the case', he writes, 'is that the story doesn't cohere around one self, one imaginary point, but coheres (coheres much better, in any case) around two different imaginary points' (Dennett 1992: 246).

Fictionalism might also look a lot like the no-self view, but there is an important contrast between these two positions. The no-self theorist holds that realism about the self could have been true, for souls – had they turned out to exist – would qualify as selves. By contrast, fictionalism excludes the very possibility of realism about the self. Even if your mental life involves the activity of an immaterial substance, that substance could no more qualify as your self than an atom lodged in the middle of the Eiffel Tower could qualify as its centre of gravity. Thus, although both the fictionalists and the no-self theorists take our ordinary conception of the self to be fundamentally mistaken, they differ in their conception of the nature of this mistake.[16]

Illusionism strikes many people as outrageous, a view that perhaps borders on the incoherent. But what, if anything, is wrong with it?

One objection appeals to the nature of I-thoughts. Doesn't Descartes' cogito argument ('I think, therefore I am') guarantee the referential success of 'I'? Even if the cogito doesn't shed any light on what one is, surely (one might think) it does guarantee *that* one is. In response, no-self theorists argue that Descartes has no right to take the cogito ('I am thinking') for granted. All we really know from the first-person perspective, they claim, is that thought, perception, and action are occurring. It doesn't follow from this that there is a self which is the subject (or agent) of thought.[17]

Even if these replies suffice to address the cogito-based objection – and it's far from obvious that they do – there are many other challenges facing illusionism. Could anything but a realist self anchor mental phenomena? Can an illusionist conception of the self be reconciled with a realist conception of mental phenomena, or does illusionism about the self entail illusionism about thoughts, actions, and experiences? And what of the practical consequences of illusionism? Do our ethical attitudes, legal frameworks, and political institutions presuppose realism about the self, or could they survive the adoption of illusionism? (See Box: Doing without the self.) I will leave you to reflect on these questions.

Box: Doing without the self

Over and above questions about the truth of illusionism, there are questions about its attractiveness. Would the rejection of the realist self be a good thing, or is illusionism a thesis that we should embrace only with great reluctance?

Buddhists believe that there is much to be gained from accepting illusionism. Doing without the self, they argue, would reduce suffering, reveal the fundamental irrationality associated with the fear of death, and make us less prone to egoism. Of course, Buddhists recognize that it is not easy to rid 'oneself' of the illusion of selfhood (Nichols et al. 2018), but they maintain that the benefits of doing so more than compensate for the effort required.

Some of illusionism's consequences may indeed be salutary, but others are more troubling. We ('our selves') make promises to each other, we direct praise and blame towards each other, and we care for each other. It is unclear how much of our ordinary ethical framework – not to mention the social and legal practices with which it is bound up – could survive the loss of the self. Can illusions stand in moral relation to each other? Can they praise and blame each other? Can they care about anything, or indeed be the objects of care?

Further reading

Chadha, M., and S. Nichols. 2019. Self-Conscious Emotions without a Self. *Philosophers' Imprint*, 19(38): 1-16.

Siderits, M., E. Thompson, and D. Zahavi (eds.). 2011. *Self, No-Self? Perspectives from Analytical, Phenomenological, and Indian Traditions*. Oxford University Press.

13.6 Conclusion

We began this chapter by considering the concept of the self, for without a grip on the kind of work selves are meant to do, we aren't able to evaluate competing accounts of the self. The job of the self, I suggested, is to function as the object of first-person thought, to anchor mental particulars, to serve as the focus of a distinctive kind of concern (self-directed concern), and to function as the object of self-awareness.

We then turned to the question of what exactly it is that, in our case at least, plays the role of the self. Dualists take it to be played by an irreducible mental substance, a 'soul'. Animalists argue that the self role is played by organisms. Lockeans hold that it is played by a psychological network of a certain kind. And illusionists, as we have just seen, hold either that the role of the self is not played by anything at all (the no-self view), or that it is played only by an explanatory fiction – an abstractum of a certain kind.

Dualism may be intuitively attractive, but it faces formidable challenges. Not only is the existence of the soul questionable (the existence challenge), but there are also questions about whether the soul (should it exist) would deserve to be thought of as the self (the identification challenge). Animalists face no problems with respect to the question of existence, but they too face challenges with respect to the question of identification. It seems possible that two minds can be associated with a single organism, and that a single stream of consciousness could migrate from one organism to another. Arguably, these scenarios show that the notion of the self is most fundamentally psychological rather than biological in nature. Neo-Lockean accounts attempt to exploit this thought, suggesting that the self is nothing over and above mental states and the relations that bind them together. The neo-Lockean approach promises to deliver much of what we want from an account of the self, but in denying that selves have precise and determinate identity conditions it runs counter to the intuitions of many. Illusionism avoids many of the challenges facing realist views of the self, but in rejecting the existence of a concrete self, illusionists face questions about what exactly it is that anchors mental phenomena or guides self-directed concern.

We began this chapter noting that the problem of the self is an ancient one, dating back at least as far as Zhuangzi's dream of the butterfly. There is, I think, something sobering in the thought that the problem of the self remains unresolved despite centuries of reflection. But perhaps it is also reassuring to recognize that the problem of the self is not restricted to one particular culture or social group but has instead been a perennial concern of those who are philosophically inclined. Whatever else we might be, we are certainly the kinds of beings that find questions about our own nature deeply puzzling.

Further reading

Amy Kind's *Personal Identity* (Polity Press, 2015), Barry Dainton's *Self* (Penguin, 2014), and Harold Noonan's *Personal Identity* (3rd ed., Routledge, 2019) all provide thought-provoking treatments of the issues that we've examined in this chapter. For a broader approach to the self than the approach taken here, see *The Oxford Handbook of the Self* (OUP, 2011), edited by Shaun Gallagher and *The Self* (OUP, 2021), edited by Patricia Kitcher.

An excellent collection of essays on various pathologies of self-consciousness can be found in *Disturbed Consciousness: New Essays on Psychopathology and Theories of Consciousness* (MIT Press, 2015), edited by Rocco J. Gennaro. For more on the phenomenology of selfhood, see Galen Strawson's *Selves: An Essay in Revisionary Metaphysics* (OUP, 2009) and

Evan Thompson's *Waking, Dreaming, Being* (Columbia University Press, 2014). *The Subject's Matter: Self-Consciousness and the Body* (MIT Press, 2017), edited by Frederique de Vignemont and Adrian Alsmith, contains an excellent set of essays on precisely that topic.

For further reading on substance dualism see *The Blackwell Companion to Substance Dualism* (Blackwell, 2018), edited by J. Loose, A. Menuge, and J. P. Moreland. For defence of a rather different version of dualism to the one on which I focused here see Martine Nida-Rümelin's 'The Non-descriptive Individual Nature of Conscious Individuals', in G. Gasser and M. Stefan (eds.), *Personal Identity. Complex or Simple?* (CUP, pp. 157-76, 2012).

For more on animalism see Hud Hudson's 'I Am Not an Animal!', in Peter van Inwagen and Dean Zimmerman (eds.), *Persons: Human and Divine* (OUP, pp. 216-34, 2007) and *New Essays on Persons, Animals, and Identity* (OUP, 2016), edited by Stephan Blatti and Paul F. Snowdon.

Much of the influence of neo-Lockean accounts of the self is due to Derek Parfit's monumental *Reasons and Persons* (Clarendon Press, 1984). For more on Sydney Shoemaker version of the neo-Lockean view, see his contribution to *The Oxford Handbook of the Self* (OUP, 2011), edited by Shaun Gallagher. For more on the phenomenal approach to the self, see Matt Duncan's 'A New Argument for the Phenomenal Approach to Personal Persistence', *Philosophical Studies*, 177: 2031-49 (2020). Marya Schechtman's 'Stories, Lives, and Basic Survival', *Royal Institute of Philosophy Supplements, Vol. 60: Narrative and Understanding Persons* (CUP, 2007) provides an excellent introduction to her account of the self.

For more on illusionism see Miri Albahari's *Analytical Buddhism. The Two-Tiered Illusion of Self* (Palgrave, 2006); Monima Chadha's 'Reconstructing Memories, Deconstructing the Self', *Mind & Language*, 34(1): 121-38 (2019); Mark Sideritis's *Personal Identity and Buddhist Philosophy* (2nd ed, Routledge, 2015); and Jenann Ismael and John Pollock's 'So You Think You Exist?', in T. M. Crisp, M. Davidson, and D. Vander Laan (eds.), *Knowledge and Reality* (Springer, 2006). David Velleman's 'The Self as Narrator', in *Self to Self: Selected Essays* (CUP, 2006) is a thought-provoking response to Dennett's fictionalist treatment of the self.

Study questions

1 Section 13.1 identifies four roles that (it is claimed) are associated with the concept of the self. Do you agree that we think of selves as playing all four roles? Are there other roles that we want an account of the self to accommodate?

2 What can we learn about the sense of self from meditation, the psychedelic state, and disorders of consciousness such as depersonalization?

3 What is the dualist account of the self? Why is dualism sometimes known as the 'further fact' view of the self?

4 Compare and contrast Descartes's conceivability argument for the existence of an immaterial self with Avicenna's 'flying man' argument. Which of the two arguments is the stronger?

5 How might animalists respond to the conjoined twins and brain transplant objections? Do you find these responses persuasive?

6 Section 13.4 distinguishes three very different versions of the psychological (neo-Lockean) approach to the self. How do these three views differ from each other? Do you find any version of the psychological approach plausible?

7   Is illusionism with respect to the self a view that should be taken seriously, or is it in some way self-refuting?
8   What difference, if any, might embracing illusionism make to our moral, legal, and political practices and institutions?

Notes

1   The dream of the butterfly is typically understood in terms of the sceptical problem of how we can discern what is real from what is merely a dream. However, I follow Cheng (2014) in reading Zhuangzi as using it to raise questions about the nature of the self.
2   One possibility is that the self is present in the experience of some people but absent in the experience of others. Hume himself raises this as a possibility ('All I can allow him is, that he may be in the right as well as I, and that we are essentially different in this particular'), but he doesn't seem to take it particularly seriously. A second – and arguably more promising – possibility is that James and Hume mean different things by 'an experience of the self'. Hume seems to think that an experience of the self must be unaccompanied by an experience of anything else ('I never can catch *myself* at any time without a perception'), and that it must also be the experience of an entity that is unaltered by any change in psychological state (something 'simple and continued'). James, however, may be committed to neither of these assumptions.
3   There is, however, debate over the extent to which dualism represents a psychological universal. For discussion, see Hodge (2008), Slingerland and Chudek (2011), and Wierzbicka (2006).
4   Another interpretation of the flying man argument focuses on the idea that the flying man wouldn't be capable of enjoying self-awareness (as, Avicenna assumes, he clearly is) if the self were identical to the body. On this reading of the argument, the implicit assumption is that if the self were identical to the body, then self-awareness would need to involve some form of sense perception, but by hypothesis, the floating man enjoys no capacity for sense-person. For discussion, see Adamson (2018).
5   Kant also remarks: 'In attaching "I" to our thoughts, we designate the subject only transcendentally . . . without noting in it any quality whatsoever – in fact, without knowing anything of it either directly or by inference [A355]'.
6   I am indebted here to Nichols's (2008) insightful paper. See also Velleman (1996) for further reflections on imagination and the first-person perspective.
7   This way of putting things is admittedly tendentious, for animalists don't typically present their view as an account of the self, and some animalists (such as Olson) deny that the notion of the self is coherent. However, insofar as animalism is an account of our identity and the referent of 'I', it is certainly a rival to both dualism and the neo-Lockean views that we discuss in the next section.
8   This argument is known as the 'too many thinkers' argument (Carter 1988; McDowell 1997; Snowdon 1990). For some responses to it, see the essays by Baker, Parfit, and Shoemaker in Blatti and Snowdon (eds.), *Animalism: New Essays on Persons, Animals and Identity* (Oxford University Press, 2016).
9   See Bayne (2010) and Campbell and McMahon (2010).
10 Another way of grasping this point is to consider the case of Cerberus, an imaginary being described by Peter van Inwagen (1990: 91) who is a single organism but has two brains, each of which is a distinct centre of thought and perception. The animalist is committed to the view that I-thoughts that occur in each of Cerberus's brains refer to the same thing (i.e., Cerberus), but that would seem to be the wrong result if the thoughts located in one brain were not integrated with those located in the other brain.
11 For further discussions of the cerebrum transplant objection, see Olson (1997), Snowdon (2014), and Parfit (2016).
12 Note that this phrase is also used to refer to a problem in neuroscience relating to how various perceptual features (colour, shape, size, location, etc.) are bound together to form a single perceptual object, representing (say) a red ball in the middle of one's visual field.
13 Note, however, that there are different senses in which an account of the self might be said to be reductive, and not all versions of the psychological approach are reductive in the same sense. For discussion see Shoemaker (1997) and Parfit (1999).
14 See Shoemaker (1997: 292-3) for a defence of this view.

15 Some experience-based accounts deny that a self can survive interruptions of consciousness. For such a view, see Strawson (1999).
16 The following might help to clarify the difference between eliminativist and fictionalist treatments of 'I'. Astronomers once believed that perturbations in the orbit of Mercury were caused by a planet that they hadn't detected and which they dubbed 'Vulcan'. Vulcan turned out to be a non-referring term, for the perturbations in Mercury's orbit were due to relativistic effects and not an undetected planet. The eliminativist thinks of 'I' on the model of 'Vulcan': both terms are in the business of referring to a concrete entity, but neither manages to do so. Fictionalists treat 'I' in a very different way, for they deny that 'I' is in the business of referring to a concrete entity. From the fictionalist's point of view, claiming that 'I' is non-referring on the grounds that it fails to identify a concrete entity would be as misleading as claiming that 'the Eiffel Tower's centre of gravity' is non-referring on the grounds that it doesn't pick out a concrete entity: the relevant terms simply aren't *intended* to play that role.
17 For their part, the fictionalist can allow that the cogito does indeed guarantee that 'I' refers to something, but she will argue that the cogito is perfectly consistent with thinking that what 'I' refers to it an abstractum - a centre of narrative gravity - rather than a concrete particular.

Conclusion
The mind-body problem

The philosophy of mind is often taken to be centred on something called 'the mind-body problem'. Let's reflect on some of the central themes of this book in light of that phrase.

The first point to emphasize is that there is no single mind-body problem, for different aspects of the mind give rise to different mind-body problems. In varying ways, we have explored three of these problems: the 'intentionality-body' problem, the 'consciousness-body' problem, and the 'self-body' problem. We have also seen that there is debate as to how these problems are related to each other. Those who regard intentionality and consciousness as relatively distinct phenomena are likely to think that the intentionality-body problem and the consciousness-body problem need to be tackled on their own terms, while those who regard them as intimately related will suspect that these two problems may have a single solution. Exactly how the intentionality-body and consciousness-body problems are related to the self-body problem is also an open question. On some views of the self, the question of how the self relates to the body cannot be fully prised apart from the question of how consciousness and intentionality relate to the body, while other views of the self entail that an account of how the self relates to the body may have relatively little to do with how intentionality and consciousness relate to the body.

We also saw that the notion of 'the body' is as problematic as 'the mind', if not more so. Arguably, the fundamental question for the philosophy of mind is concerned with how mental states and processes are related to physical states and processes, whether or not those states and processes relate specifically to the human body. This in turn generates three questions.

First, how should the notion of the 'physical' be understood? For the most part, discussions of the mind-body problem assume a notion of the physical that is either couched in terms of physics or in terms of a special science (such as neuroscience) that is taken to be unproblematically related to physics. We have seen, however, that there is some debate as to what exactly counts as physical. Some theorists, known as 'Russellian monists', identify conscious states with the intrinsic properties of the fundamental entities described by physics. Russellian monists describe their position as a form of physicalism, but it is clearly a very different kind of physicalism from the physicalism of (say) the identity theorist who identifies conscious states with macro-level physical states such as brain states.

The second question concerns which parts of the physical world are most directly implicated in mentality. The very phrase 'the mind-body problem' suggests that our focus should

DOI: 10.4324/9781003225348-15

be on the relationship between mental states and states of the *body*, but that assumption is controversial. Some theorists argue that our focus should be narrower, and that it's really only states of the brain that matter when it comes to mentality. Others argue that our focus should be broader, and that an agent's environment and history can be as intimately related to their mental states as the states of their body or brain are.

The third question concerns how mental phenomena and physical phenomena are related. Are mental phenomenal something over and above physical phenomena, or are they nothing more than what we get if we put certain kinds of physical phenomena together in the right kinds of ways, as physicalists claim? If the latter is the case, which exactly is the relationship between mental phenomena and the kinds of physical phenomena studies by neuroscience? Are mental states nothing over and above neural states because they are identical to neural states (as type identity theorists hold), or are they nothing over and above neural states because they are realized by neural states (as functionalists hold)?

As we have seen, debates about these questions are informed by a number of considerations. One kind of consideration is semantic. Here, for example, theorists argue that an account of how psychological terms acquire their meaning places important constraints on the nature of mental phenomena. A second kind of consideration is metaphysical. Here, for example, theorists appeal to claims about what is (or, as the case may be, isn't) conceivable to argue for or against a particular conceptions of the relationship between physical phenomena and mental phenomena. A third kind of consideration is epistemic. Here, for example, theorists argue that facts about our knowledge of minds (both our own and those of others) should constrain accounts of mental phenomena. A final issue concerns mental causation. Here, some theorists argue that the nature of mental causation requires a reductive form of physicalism, while others argue that it requires a commitment to internalism.

Taking a step back from the details of these debates, one might find oneself pulled in two quite different directions. On the one hand, one might be drawn to the view that mental phenomena are related to the fundamental physical features of the world in roughly the same kind of ways that other high-level phenomena are. On this view, the mind/body nexus does not involve primitive relations of dependence between the mental and the physical but can be explained in the same kinds of ways that (say) chemical, biological, and geological phenomena can be. On the other hand, mental phenomena appear to have properties that sets them apart from other high-level phenomena in profound ways. The subjective and qualitative dimensions of consciousness have no obvious analogues in chemistry, biology, or geology, while intentionality exhibits a kind of normativity that is not evident elsewhere in nature.

Setting to one side many qualifications, we can group responses to this dilemma into three camps. Those in the first camp take the apparently problematic aspects of the mind at face value, but they hold that a story can be told as to how purely physical processes might give rise to them. Those in the second camp argue that the apparently problematic aspects of the mind shouldn't be taken at value, but should (and indeed can) be explained away as illusions. And those in the third camp argue for a kind of primitivism about mental phenomena, rejecting the eliminativism of the second camp and the reductionism of the first camp.

None of these positions is at all attractive. The problem with reductionism is that it is far from clear that an account can be given, even if only in outline form, as to how purely physical processes give rise to the most problematic aspects of the mind. Illusionism has its attractions, but explaining why the mind merely seems to have various problematic features may not be any easier than accounting for those features themselves. Primitivism takes the problematic aspects of mental phenomena seriously, but there is a sense in which it merely restates the mind-body problem rather than offering a solution to it.

In the introduction, I promised to provide you with a map of the central problems in the philosophy of mind; I didn't, however, promise to solve those problems. Figuring out how the mind fits into the natural order is a challenge that you must take up for yourself. It's not an easy challenge, but you will find that any serious attempt to engage with it has its own rewards.

GLOSSARY

Acquaintance: A mode of awareness with an object which is unmediated and involves no possibility of a gap between how that object appears to one and how it actually is. Acquaintance is sometimes invoked to account for distinctive features of knowledge of one's own mental states, particularly phenomenal states.

Analytic: A sentence or proposition whose truth is guaranteed by the meanings of its constituent terms. 'A vixen is a female fox' is plausibly regarded as an analytic truth.

Analytical behaviourism: The view that the meaning of psychological terms can be fully analysed in terms of claims about behavioural dispositions. Also known as 'logical behaviourism' and 'philosophical behaviourism'. Contrasted with psychological behaviourism (also known as scientific or methodological behaviourism), which holds that the study of the mind should be based only on behaviour and/or that the entities posited by psychology should be defined in terms of behaviour.

Animalism: The view that you and I are most fundamentally animals and that our identity conditions are purely biological.

Anomalous monism: A view associated with the work of Donald Davidson. The anomalous monist holds that although there are no strict laws relating mental predicates to physical predicates (that's the anomalous bit), mental events just are physical events (that's the monistic bit). See also **token identity theory**.

A posteriori: Literally, after experience. An a posteriori claim is a claim that is based on experience or empirical methods. A posteriori claims are contrasted with a priori claims.

A posteriori functionalism: A version of functionalism according to which scientific research is required in order to identify the functional roles that are definitive of mental states. Usually known as 'psychofunctionalism'. Contrasted with **a priori functionalism** (usually known as 'analytic functionalism').

A posteriori physicalism: A conception of the nature of physicalism, according to which physicalism does not entail that the mental truths can be derived a priori from the complete set of physical truths.

A priori: Literally, prior to experience. An a priori claim is one that can be established without recourse to experience or empirical methods. A priori claims are contrasted with a posteriori claims.

A priori functionalism: A form of functionalism according to which information about the functional roles that determine the nature of mental phenomena is available via conceptual analysis, and is often taken to be implicit in the meaning of the relevant psychological terms. Usually known as 'analytic functionalism'. Contrasted with **a posteriori functionalism** (usually known as 'psychofunctionalism').

A priori physicalism: A conception of the nature of physicalism, according to which the physicalist is committed to the claim that the mental truths can be derived a priori from the complete set of physical truths.

Awareness: Sometimes used as a synonym for consciousness in general, at other times used for a specific form of consciousness that is contrasted with phenomenal consciousness. Can take various objects, including objects, properties, events, and facts.

Behaviourism: See **analytical behaviourism**.

Brentano's thesis: The claim that intentionality is the 'mark of the mental'; that is, all and only intentional states are mental. Named in honour of Franz Brentano (1838–1917).

Dualism: In the philosophy of mind, dualism is the view that mental phenomena involve non-physical substances and/or properties. It is useful to distinguish two forms of dualism: substance dualism and property dualism. Substance dualists hold that the self (subject of experience) is a non-physical entity. Property dualists hold that (certain types of) mental events and/or properties are non-physical.

Easy problems of consciousness: A term coined by David Chalmers to describe the problem of explaining the cognitive and behavioural aspects of consciousness.

Eliminativism: In its purist form, eliminativism about the Xs is the view that the term 'X' is non-referring. For example, eliminativism about belief is the claim that there are no beliefs. Some versions of eliminativism allow that the term in question refers and deny only that it picks out a genuine scientific kind.

Emergentism: The view that mental properties are metaphysically necessitated by physical properties in some way but cannot be reduced to or identified with them. Some versions of emergentism include the claim that the necessitation of the mental by the physical cannot be explained but must be accepted as a primitive fact.

Epiphenomenalism: The view that mental phenomena are not causally efficacious.

Explanatory gap: A phrase coined by Joseph Levine to describe the gap between physical/functional properties of a system and its phenomenal (experiential) properties, which (many hold) cannot be bridged by familiar modes of explanation.

Folk psychology: The psychological framework that is used in everyday life to explain, predict, and understand human behaviour. Also known as 'naïve psychology' and 'commonsense psychology'.

Hard problem of consciousness; Coined by David Chalmers, the phrase refers to the problem of giving a reductive explanation of **phenomenal consciousness**. Closely related to the **explanatory gap** and contrasted with the **easy problems of consciousness**.

Identity theory: See **type identity theory**.

Illusionism: Broadly speaking, illusionism about Xs is the idea that our conception of Xs is mistaken in fundamental respects. Some versions of illusionism collapse into a kind of **eliminativism**: we think that Xs (e.g., beliefs, selves, consciousness) are real, but they are in fact just illusions.

Inseparatism: The view that intentionality and phenomenal consciousness are closely related, and that the analysis of at least one of these properties requires appealing to the other. Contrasted with **separatism**.

Intentionalism: The view that the phenomenal character of a conscious state supervenes on its intentional properties. Also (and more commonly) known as 'representationalism'.

Introspection: The faculty (or exercise thereof) that we use to become aware of our own mental states in a distinctly first-person manner.

Materialism: See **Physicalism**.

Mindreading: The practice of ascribing mental states to other individuals (and oneself). Also known as 'mentalizing'.

Nomological: Involving a law of nature (from *nomos*, which is Greek for 'law').

Nomological dangler: A term coined by Herbert Feigl (and popularized by J.J.C. Smart) that refers to experiences as conceived of by dualists (and certain kinds of emergentists). The idea is that on these views, experiences cannot be accommodated within a scientific conception of reality but 'dangle' from primitive laws that relate mental states to physical states.

Non-reductive physicalism: A conception of the mind which holds that mental phenomena are nothing over and above physical phenomena (that's the physicalism bit) but denies that mental properties can be identified with the properties of any other science, such as neuroscience (that's the non-reductive bit).

Normativity: A phenomenon is normative when it requires or supports evaluative judgments of some kind. In the philosophy of mind, normativity is associated most closely with intentional content.

Panpsychism: The view that all concrete objects (or at least, those that are most fundamental) have some form of consciousness.

Phenomenal character: The experiential aspect of a mental state that makes it the kind of mental state that it is. Often referred to as 'qualitative character'.

Phenomenal concept: A concept that refers to a type of experience in terms of what it's like to have it.

Phenomenal consciousness: The form of consciousness that is typically defined by appeal to the phrase 'what it's like', and is most closely associated with the **hard problem of consciousness** and the **explanatory gap**.

Physicalism: The view that the mental facts are 'nothing over and above' the physical facts. Chapter 2 provides a more detailed account.

Representationalism: See **Intentionalism**.

Russellian monism: The view that the intrinsic/categorical properties of matter are experiential, and that science can tell us only about matter's dispositional properties. Named in honour of Bertrand Russell (1872-1970).

Separatism: The view that intentionality and phenomenal consciousness are fundamentally distinct phenomena. Contrasted with **inseparatism**.

Subjectivity: Sometimes used to refer to the fact that conscious states are always the states of a particular subject of experience; sometimes used to refer to the sense of selfhood that is taken to accompany most (some say all) conscious states.

Supervenience: A modal relation between two types of properties (or, according to some uses, between two types of predicates). It takes various forms, depending on the strength of the relationship and the conception of supervenience base.

Synthetic: A sentence or proposition is synthetic when its truth is not a function of the meaning of its constituent terms. Contrasted with **Analytic**.

Token identity theory: A form of non-reductive physicalism, which holds that particular mental states/events are identical to particular neural states/events, but that mental properties aren't identical to neural properties. See also **Anomalous Monism**.

Transparency (of perceptual experience): The claim that in attending to one's own perceptual experiences, one is only ever aware of those aspects of the world that are represented by those experiences, and is not aware of features of the experiences themselves. Also referred to as the 'diaphanousness of perceptual consciousness'.

Transparency thesis: Used in relation to perceptual experience, the transparency thesis is usually understood as the claim that perceptual experience is transparent. Used in relation to self-knowledge, the transparency thesis is the claim that the contents of the mind are always accessible from the first-person perspective.

Type-A physicalism: A version of physicalism according to which the mental truths are entailed by the complete set of physical truths. Contrasted with **Type-B physicalism**. See also **a priori physicalism**.

Type-B physicalism: A version of physicalism which denies that the mental truths are entailed by the complete set of physical truths. Contrasted with **Type-A physicalism** See also **a posteriori physicalism**.

Type identity theory: The view that mental properties are identical to neural properties. Also known as 'central state materialism' in the older literature.

Qualia (singular: quale): A problematic term that has various uses and is best avoided. In its broadest sense, it refers to any phenomenal (or experiential) aspect of the mind.

In a narrower sense, it refers to those phenomenal aspects of the mind that cannot be accounted for in functional or intentional terms.

Zombie: A creature with the physical, functional, and behavioural profile of a normal human being but (by definition) is not conscious. Your zombie twin shares your physical, functional, and behavioural properties but none of your conscious properties.

BIBLIOGRAPHY

Aaronson, S. 2014. My Conversation with 'Eugene Goostman', the Chatbot that's All Over the News for Allegedly Passing the Turing Test, Shtetl-Optimized. *Shtetl-Optimized: The Blog of Scott Aaronson*, 9 June, https://www.scottaaronson.com/blog/?p=1858 [accessed 18 August 2021].
Adams, F. & Aizawa, K. 2001. The Bounds of Cognition. *Philosophical Psychology*, 14(1): 43–64.
Adams, F. & Aizawa, K. 2008. *The Bounds of Cognition*. Malden: Blackwell.
Adamson, P. 2018. *Philosophy in the Arabic World*. Oxford: Oxford University Press.
Adamson, P. & Benevich, F. 2018. The Thought Experimental Method: Avicenna's Flying Man Argument. *Journal of the American Philosophical Association*, 4(2): 147–64.
Aizawa, K. 1997. Explaining Systematicity. *Mind and Language*, 12: 115–36.
Aizawa, K. 2014. Tough Times to Be Talking Systematicity. In P. Calvo and J. Symons (Eds.) *The Architecture of Cognition: Rethinking Fodor and Pylyshyn's Systematicity Challenge*. Cambridge, MA: MIT Press, pp. 77–101.
Akins, K. 1993a. A Bat without Qualities? In M. Davies and G.W. Humphreys (Eds.) *Consciousness: Psychological and Philosophical Essays*. Oxford: Blackwell, pp. 345–58.
Akins, K. 1993b. What Is It Like to Be Boring and Myopic? In B. Dahlbom (Ed.) *Dennett and His Critics*. Oxford: Blackwell.
Alexander, S. 1920. *Space, Time, and Deity*. London: Macmillan & Co.
Alter, T. 2001. Know-How, Ability, and the Ability Hypothesis. *Theoria*, 67: 229–39.
Alter, T. 2007. Does Representationalism Undermine the Knowledge Argument? In T. Alter and S. Walter (Eds.) *Phenomenal Concepts and Phenomenal Knowledge: New Essays on Consciousness and Physicalism*. New York: Oxford University Press, pp. 65–76.
Anderson, M. 2014. *After Phrenology: Neural Reuse and the Interactive Brain*. Cambridge, MA: MIT Press.
Anscombe, G.E.M. 1963. *Intention* (2nd ed.). Oxford: Blackwell.
Apperly, I. 2010. *Mindreaders: The Cognitive Basis of 'Theory of Mind'*. London: Psychology Press.
Armstrong, D. 1968. *A Materialist Theory of the Mind*. London: Routledge and Kegan Paul.
Audi, R. 2013. *Moral Perception*. Princeton, NJ: Princeton University Press.
Austin, J. L. 1962. *Sense and Sensibilia*. Oxford: Oxford University Press.
Auvray, M. & Spence, C. 2008. The Multisensory Perception of Flavour. *Consciousness and Cognition*, 17: 1016–31.
Avicenna. 1959. On the Soul. In Fazlur Rahman (Ed.) *Avicenna's De Anima: Being the Psychological Part of Kitāb al-Shifā*. Oxford: Oxford University Press.
Avramides, A. 2001. *Other Minds*. London: Routledge.
Ayer, A. J. 1956. *Problems of Knowledge*. London: Penguin.
Baars, B. 1988. *A Cognitive Theory of Consciousness*. Cambridge, MA: CUP.
Bach, K. 1987. *Thought and Reference*. Oxford: Oxford University Press.
Bach, K. 1997. Review Essay: Engineering the Mind. *Philosophy and Phenomenological Research*, 57(2): 459–68.
Ball, D. 2009. There Are No Phenomenal Concepts. *Mind*, 118: 935–62.
Baier, A. 1990. What Emotions Are About. *Philosophical Perspectives*, 4: 1–29.
Balog, K. 2012. In Defense of the Phenomenal Concept Strategy. *Philosophy and Phenomenological Re-

search, 84(1): 1-23.

Barbur, J., Ruddock, K. & Waterfield, V. 1980. Human Visual Responses in the Absence of the Geniculo-Calcarine Projection. *Brain*, 103(4): 905-28.

Bar-On, D. 2015. Transparency, Expression, and Self-Knowledge. *Philosophical Explorations*, 18(2): 134-52.

Baron-Cohen, S. 1995. *Mindblindness: An Essay on Autism and Theory of Mind*. Cambridge, MA: MIT Press.

Baron-Cohen, S., Lombardo, M. & Tager-Flusberg, H. 2013. *Understanding Other Minds: Perspectives from Developmental Social Neuroscience* (3rd ed.). Oxford: Oxford University Press.

Barwich, A. S. 2020. *Smellosophy: What the Nose Tells the Mind*. Cambridge, MA: Harvard University Press.

Batty, C. 2010. Scents and Sensibilia. *American Philosophical Quarterly*, 47: 103-18.

Batty, C. 2011. Smelling Lessons. *Philosophical Studies*, 153: 161-74.

Bayne, T. 2008. The Phenomenology of Agency. *Philosophy Compass*, 3(1): 182-202.

Bayne, T. 2010. *The Unity of Consciousness*. Oxford: Oxford University Press.

Bayne, T. 2013. Agency as a Marker of Consciousness. In T. Vierkant, J. Kiverstein and A. Clark (Eds.) *Decomposing the Will*. Oxford: Oxford University Press, pp. 160-80.

Bayne, T. & Spener, M. 2010. Introspective Humility. In E. Sosa and E. Villanueva (Eds.) *Philosophical Issues*, 20: 1-22.

Bechtel, W. & Mundale, J. 1999. Multiple Realizability Revisited: Linking Cognitive and Neural States. *Philosophy of Science*, 66(2): 175-207.

Bedney, M., Richardson, H. & Saxe, R. 2015. 'Visual' Cortex Responds to Spoken Language in Blind Children. *The Journal of Neuroscience*, 35(33): 11674-81.

Beebee, H. 2003. Seeing Causing. *Proceedings of the Aristotelian Society*, 103: 257-80.

Bennett, K. 2003. Why the Exclusion Problem Seems Intractable, and How, Just Maybe, to Tract It. *Noûs*, 37: 471-97.

Bennett, K. 2007. Mental Causation. *Philosophy Compass*, 2(2): 316-37.

Bennett, K. 2008. Exclusion Again. In J. Hohwy and J. Kallestrup (Eds.) *Being Reduced*. Oxford: Oxford University Press, pp. 280-305.

Bermúdez, J. L. 2003. *Thinking without Words*. Oxford: Oxford University Press.

Bernstein, S. & Wilson, J. 2016. Free Will and Mental Quausation. *Journal of the American Philosophical Association*, 2(2): 310-31.

Billon, A. 2014. Why Are We Certain That We Exist? *Philosophy and Phenomenological Research*, 91(3): 723-59.

Block, N. 1978. Troubles with Functionalism. In W. Savage (Ed.) *Perception and Cognition* (Vol. 9). Minneapolis: University of Minnesota Press, pp. 261-325. Reprinted in Block, N. (Ed.) *Readings in Philosophy of Psychology* (Vols. 1 and 2). Cambridge, MA: Harvard University Press, pp. 268-305.

Block, N. 1981. Psychologism and Behaviourism. *Philosophical Review*, 90(1): 5-43.

Block, N. 1986. Advertisement for a Semantics for Psychology. *Midwest Studies in Philosophy*, X: 615-78.

Block, N. 1995. On a Confusion about the Function of Consciousness. *Behavioral and Brain Sciences*, 18(2): 227-87.

Block, N. 1996. Mental Paint and Mental Latex. In E. Villanueva (Ed.) *Philosophical Issues*, 7, Perception: 19-49.

Block, N. 2003a. Mental Paint. In M. Hahn and B. Ramberg (Eds.) *Reflections and Replies: Essays on the Philosophy of Tyler Burge*. Cambridge, MA: MIT Press.

Block, N. 2003b. Do Causal Powers Drain Away? *Philosophy and Phenomenological Research*, 67: 133-50.

Block, N. 2007. Consciousness, Accessibility, and the Mesh between Psychology and Neuroscience. *Behavioral and Brain Sciences*, 30: 481-548.

Block, N. 2009. Comparing the Major Theories of Consciousness. In M. S. Gazzaniga (Ed.) *The Cognitive Neurosciences*. Cambridge, MA: MIT Press, pp. 1111-22.

Block, N. 2014. Rich Conscious Perception Outside Focal Attention. *Trends in Cognitive Sciences*, 18(9): 445-47.

Block, N. & Stalnaker, R. 1999. Conceptual Analysis, Dualism, and the Explanatory Gap. *Philosophical Review*, 108: 1-46.

Bloom, P. 2004. *Descartes' Baby*. New York: Basic Books.

Boghossian, P. 1989. Content and Self-Knowledge. *Philosophical Topics*, 17: 5-26.

Boghossian, P. 1997. What the Externalist Can Know A Priori. *Proceedings of the Aristotelian Society*, 97: 161-175.

Boly, M., Massimini, M., Tsuchiya, N., Postle, B. R., Koch, C. & Tononi, G. 2017. Are the Neural Correlates of Consciousness in the Front or in the Back of the Cerebral Cortex? Clinical and Neuroimaging Evidence. *Journal of Neuroscience*, 37(40): 9603-13. https://doi.org/10.1523/JNEUROSCI.3218-16.2017.
Boyle, A. 2020-a. The Impure Phenomenology of Episodic Memory. *Mind and Language*, 35: 641-60.
Boyle, A. 2020-b. Conjoined Twinning and Biological Individuation. *Philosophical Studies*, 177(8): 2395-415.
Boyle, M. 2009. Two Kinds of Self-Knowledge. *Philosophy and Phenomenological Research*, 78(1): 133-64.
Boyle, M. 2011. Transparent Self-Knowledge. *Proceedings of the Aristotelian Society*, 85(1): 223-41.
Brentano, F. 1874/1973. *Psychology from an Empirical Standpoint*. London: Routledge and Kegan Paul.
Brewer, B. 2011. *Perception and Its Objects*. Oxford: Oxford University Press.
Broad, C. D. 1925. *The Mind and Its Place in Nature*. London: Routledge and Kegan Paul.
Brogaard, B. 2014. *Does Perception Have Content?* Oxford: Oxford University Press.
Brogaard, B. 2015. Perceptual Reports. In M. Matthen (Ed.) *Oxford Handbook to the Philosophy of Perception*. Oxford: Oxford University Press.
Brown, J. 1995. The Incompatibility of Anti-Individualism and Privileged Access. *Analysis*, 55(3): 149-156.
Brown, J. 2004. *Anti-Individualism and Knowledge*. Cambridge, MA: MIT Press.
Brown, J. 2008. Semantic Externalism and Self-Knowledge. In A. Beckermann, B. McLaughlin and S. Walter (Eds.) *Oxford Handbook of the Philosophy of Mind*. Oxford: Oxford University Press.
Brown, R., Lau, H. & LeDoux, J. 2019. Understanding the Higher-Order Approach to Consciousness. *Trends in Cognitive Sciences*, 23(9): 754-68.
Brueckner, A. 2007. Externalism and Privileged Access Are Consistent. In B.P. McLaughlin and J.D. Cohen (Eds.) *Contemporary Debates in Philosophy of Mind*. Oxford: Blackwell, pp. 37-52.
Buckner, C. 2019. Deep Learning: A Philosophical Introduction. *Philosophy Compass*, 14(10): e12625.
Burge, T. 1979. Individualism and the Mental. *Midwest Studies in Philosophy*, 4(1): 73-122.
Burge, T. 1986. Individualism and Psychology. *Philosophical Review*, 95: 3-45.
Burge, T. 1988. Individualism and Self-Knowledge. *Journal of Philosophy*, 85: 649-93.
Burge, T. 1996. Our Entitlement to Self-Knowledge. *Proceedings of the Aristotelian Society*, 96: 91-116.
Butterfill, S. 2009. Seeing Causings and Hearing Gestures. *The Philosophical Quarterly*, 59(236): 405-28.
Byrne, A. 1999. Cosmic Hermeneutics. In J. Tomberlin (Ed.) *Philosophical Perspectives*, 13: 347-83.
Byrne, A. 2001. Intentionalism Defended. *Philosophical Review*, 110(2): 199-240.
Byrne, A. 2004. What Phenomenal Consciousness Is Like. In R. Gennaro (Ed.) *Higher-Order Theories of Consciousness: An Anthology*. Amsterdam: John Benjamins, pp. 203-25.
Byrne, A. 2009. Experience and Content. *Philosophical Quarterly*, 59: 429-51.
Byrne, A. 2011. Transparency, Belief, Intention. *Proceedings of the Aristotelian Society* (Supplementary Volume), 85(1): 201-21.
Byrne, A. 2018. *Transparency and Self-Knowledge*. Oxford: Oxford University Press.
Byrne, A. & Hilbert, D. 2003. Color Realism. *Behavioral and Brain Sciences*, 26: 791-94.
Byrne, A. & Tye, M. 2006. Qualities Ain't in the Head. *Noûs*, 40(2): 241-55.
Calvo, P. 2017. What Is It Like to Be a Plant? *Journal of Consciousness Studies*, 24(9-10): 205-27.
Camp, E. 2009. A Language of Baboon Thought? In A. Lurz (Ed.) *The Philosophy of Animal Minds*. Cambridge: Cambridge University Press, pp. 108-27.
Campbell, J. 2002. *Reference and Consciousness*. Oxford: Oxford University Press.
Campbell, J. 2007. An Interventionist Approach to Causation in Psychology. In A. Gopnik and L. Schulz (Eds.) *Causal Learning: Psychology, Philosophy, and Computation*. Oxford: Oxford University Press, pp. 58-66.
Campbell, J. 2008. Interventionism, Control Variables and Causation in the Qualitative World. *Philosophical Issues*, 18: 426-45.
Campbell, T. & McMahon, J. 2010. Animalism and the Varieties of Conjoined Twinning. *Theoretical Medicine and Bioethics*, 31: 285-301.
Carls-Diamante, S. 2017. The Octopus and the Unity of Consciousness. *Biology and Philosophy*, 32: 1269-87.
Carruthers, P. 1996. *Language, Thought and Consciousness*. Cambridge: Cambridge University Press.
Carruthers, P. 2002. The Cognitive Functions of Language. *Behavioural and Brain Sciences*, 25: 657-726.
Carruthers, P. 2004. On Being Simple-Minded. *American Philosophical Quarterly*, 41: 205-20.
Carruthers, P. 2008. Meta-Cognition in Animals: A Skeptical Look. *Mind & Language*, 23(1): 58-89.
Carruthers, P. 2011. *The Opacity of Mind*. Oxford: Oxford University Press.
Carruthers, P. 2015. Perceiving Mental States. *Consciousness and Cognition*, 36: 498-507.
Carston, V. 2002. Aristotle on Consciousness. *Mind*, 111(444): 751-815.

Carter, W.R. 1988. Our Bodies, Our Selves. *Australasian Journal of Philosophy*, 66(3): 308-19.
Cartwright, N. 1999. *The Dappled World*. Cambridge: Cambridge University Press.
Casali, A. G. et al. 2013. A Theoretically Based Index of Consciousness. *Science Translational Medicine*, 5: 198ra105.
Casarotto, S. et al. 2016. Stratification of Unresponsive Patients by an Independently Validated Index of Brain Complexity. *Annals of Neurology*, 80: 718-29.
Casati, R. & Dokic, J. 2005. Sounds. In Edward N. Zalta (Ed.) *The Stanford Encyclopedia of Philosophy* (Spring 2009 ed.). https://plato.stanford.edu/archives/spr2009/entries/sounds/.
Cassam, Q. 2007. *The Possibility of Knowledge*. Oxford: Clarendon Press.
Cath, Y. 2009. The Ability Hypothesis and the New Knowledge-How. *Noûs*, 43(1): 137-56.
Cavedon-Taylor, D. 2018. Odors, Objects, and Olfaction. *American Philosophical Quarterly*, 55(1): 81-94.
Chalmers, D. J. 1993. Connectionism and Compositionality: Why Fodor and Pylyshyn Were Wrong. *Philosophical Psychology*, 6(3): 305-19.
Chalmers, D. J. 1995. Facing up to the Problem of Consciousness. *Journal of Consciousness Studies*, 2(3): 200-19.
Chalmers, D. J. 1996. *The Conscious Mind*. New York: Oxford University Press.
Chalmers, D. J. 1997. Moving Forward on the Problem of Consciousness. *Journal of Consciousness Studies*, 4(1): 3-46.
Chalmers, D. J. 2000. What Is a Neural Correlate of Consciousness? In T. Metzinger (Ed.) *Neural Correlates of Consciousness: Empirical and Conceptual Questions*. Cambridge, MA: MIT Press pp. 17-39.
Chalmers, D. J. 2002. The Components of Content. In D. J. Chalmers (Ed.) *Philosophy of Mind: Classical and Contemporary Readings*. Oxford: Oxford University Press.
Chalmers, D. J. 2004a. Phenomenal Concepts and the Knowledge Argument. In P. Ludlow, Y. Nagasawa and D. Stoljar (Eds.) *There's Something about Mary: Essays on Frank Jackson's Knowledge Argument Against Physicalism*. Cambridge, MA: MIT Press, pp. 269-98.
Chalmers, D. J. 2004b. The Representational Character of Experience. In B. Leiter (Ed.) *The Future for Philosophy*. Oxford: Oxford University Press, pp. 153-81.
Chalmers, D. J. 2012. *Constructing the World*. Oxford: Oxford University Press.
Chalmers, D. J. 2016. Panpsychism and Panprotopsychism. In G. Bruntrup and L. Jaskolla (Eds.) *Panpsychism: Contemporary Perspectives*. Oxford: Oxford University Press, pp. 19-47.
Chalmers, D. J. & Jackson, F. 2001. Conceptual Analysis and Reductive Explanation. *Philosophical Review*, 110(3): 315-61.
Cheng, K.-Y. 2014. Self and the Dream of the Butterfly in the *Zhuangzi*. *Philosophy East and West*, 64/3: 563-97.
Cheney, D. L. & Seyfarth, R. M. 2007. *Baboon Metaphysics: The Evolution of a Social Mind*. Chicago: University of Chicago Press.
Chisholm, R. M. 1957. *Perceiving*. Ithaca: Cornell.
Chomsky, N. 1995. Language and Nature. *Mind*, 104: 1-61.
Church, J. 2010. Seeing Reasons. *Philosophy and Phenomenological Research*, 80(3): 638-70.
Churchland, P. M. 1981. Eliminative Materialism and the Propositional Attitudes. *Journal of Philosophy*, 78: 67-90.
Churchland, P. S. 1996. The Hornswoggle Problem. *Journal of Consciousness Studies*, 3(5-6): 402-8.
Clark, A. 1991. Systematicity, Structured Representations and Cognitive Architecture: A Reply to Fodor and Pylyshyn. In T. Horgan and J. Tienson (Eds.) *Connectionism and the Philosophy of Mind*. Dordrecht: Kluwer, pp. 198-218.
Clark, A. 1998. Magic Words: How Language Augments Human Computation. In P. Carruthers and J. Boucher (Eds.) *Language and Thought*. Cambridge: Cambridge University Press, pp. 162-83.
Clark, A. 2005. Intrinsic Content, Active Memory and the Extended Mind. *Analysis*, 65(1): 1-11.
Clark, A. 2006. Material Symbols. *Philosophical Psychology*, 19: 291-307.
Clark, A. 2009. Spreading the Joy? Why the Machinery of Consciousness is (Probably) Still in the Head. *Mind*, 118(472): 963-93.
Clark, A. & Chalmers, D. 1998. The Extended Mind. *Analysis*, 58: 10-23.
Clayton, N. S., Bussey, T. J. & Dickinson, A. 2003a. Can Animals Recall the Past and Plan for the Future? *Nature Reviews Neuroscience*, 4: 685-91.
Clayton, N. S., Bussey, T. J., Emery, N. J. & Dickinson, A. 2003b. Prometheus to Proust: The Case for Behavioural Criteria for 'Mental Time Travel'. *Trends in Cognitive Sciences*, 7(10): 436-37.

Clayton, N. S. & Dickinson, A. 1998. Episodic-Like Memory During Cache Recovery by Scrub Jays. *Nature*, 395: 272-78.
Cohen, J. 2001. Color, Content, & Fred: On a Proposed Reductio of the Inverted Spectrum Hypothesis. *Philosophical Studies*, 103: 121-44.
Cohen, J. D. 2017. Cognitive Control: Core Constructs and Current Considerations. In T. Egner (Ed.) *Wiley Handbook of Cognitive Control*. New York, NY: Wiley, pp. 3-28.
Coleman, S. 2016. Panpsychism and Neutral Monism: How to Make Up One's Mind. In G. Bruntrup and L. Jaskolla (Eds.) *Panpsychism: Contemporary Perspectives*. Oxford: Oxford University Press, pp. 249-82.
Copeland, B. J. 1993. *Artificial Intelligence: A Philosophical Introduction*. Oxford: Blackwell.
Copeland, B. J. (Ed.). 1999. A Lecture and Two Radio Broadcasts by Alan Turing. In K. Furukawa, D. Michie and S. Muggleton (Eds.) *Machine Intelligence, 15*. Oxford: Oxford University Press.
Copeland, B. J. 2000. The Turing Test. *Minds and Machines*, 10: 519-39.
Copenhaver, R. & Shields, C. (Eds.). 2019. *The History of the Philosophy of Mind*. Abingdon: Routledge.
Corballis, M. & Suddendorf, T. 2007. The Evolution of Foresight: What Is Mental Time Travel, and Is It Unique to Humans? *Behavioral and Brain Sciences*, 30(3): 299-313.
Cowey, A. 2010. The Blindsight Saga. *Experimental Brain Research*, 200: 3-23.
Crane, T. 1991. All the Difference in the World. *Philosophical Quarterly*, 41: 1-25.
Crane, T. 2003. The Intentional Structure of Consciousness. In Quentin Smith and Aleksandar Jokic (Eds.) *Consciousness: New Philosophical Perspectives*. Oxford: Oxford University Press, pp. 33-56.
Crane, T. 2005. Papineau on Phenomenal Concepts. *Philosophy and Phenomenological Research*, 71(1): 155-62.
Crane, T. 2010. Cosmic Hermeneutics versus Emergence: The Challenge of the Explanatory Gap. In Graham Macdonald and Cynthia Macdonald (Eds.) *Emergence in Mind*. Oxford: Oxford University Press, pp. 22-34.
Crowther, T. & Mac Cumhaill, C. 2018. *Perceptual Ephemera*. Oxford: Oxford University Press.
Cullison, A. 2010. Moral Perception. *European Journal of Philosophy*, 18(2): 159-75.
Cummins, R. 1989. *Meaning and Mental Representation*. Cambridge, MA: MIT Press.
Cummins, R. 1996. Systematicity. *Journal of Philosophy*, 93(22): 561-614.
Currie, G. & Ravenscroft, I. 2002. *Recreative Minds*. Oxford: Oxford University Press.
Cutter, B. & Tye, M. 2011. Tracking Representationalism and the Painfulness of Pain. *Philosophical Issues: The Epistemology of Perception*, 21: 90-109.
Dainton, B. 2004. The Self and the Phenomenal. *Ratio*, 365.
Dainton, B. 2008. *The Phenomenal Self*. Oxford: Oxford University Press.
Dasgupta, S. 2014. The Possibility of Physicalism. *The Journal of Philosophy*, 111(9): 557-92.
Davidson, D. 1973. Radical Interpretation. *Dialectica*, 27: 313-28.
Davidson, D. 1974. Belief and the Basis of Meaning. *Synthese*, 27: 309-23, 14.
Davidson, D. 1987. Knowing One's Own Mind. *Proceedings and Addresses of the American Philosophical Association*, 60(3): 441-58.
Davies, M. 1991. Concepts, Connectionism and the Language of Thought. In W. Ramsey, S. P. Stich & D. Rumelhart (Eds.) *Philosophy and Connectionist Theory*. Hillsdale, NJ: Lawrence Erlbaum Associates, pp. 485-503.
Davies, M. 1992. Aunty's Own Argument for the Language of Thought. In J. Ezquerro and J. M. Larrazabal (Eds.) *Cognition, Semantics and Philosophy: Proceedings of the First International Colloquium on Cognitive Science*. Dordrecht: Kluwer Academic Publishers, pp. 235-71.
Davies, M. 1997. Externalism and Experience. In N. Block, O. Flanagan and G. Güzeldere (Eds.) *The Nature of Consciousness: Philosophical Debates*. Cambridge, MA: MIT Press, pp. 309-28.
Davies, M. 1998. Language, Thought, and the Language of Thought (Aunty's Own Argument Revisited). In P. Carruthers and J. Boucher (Eds.) *Language and Thought*. Cambridge: Cambridge University Press, pp. 226-47.
Davies, M. 2012. Consciousness and Explanation. In L. Weiskrantz and M. Davies (Eds.) *Frontiers of Consciousness*. Oxford: Oxford University Press.
Davies, M., Aimola Davies, A. M. & Coltheart, M. 2005. Anosognosia and the Two-Factor Theory of Delusions. *Mind & Language*, 20(2): 209-36.
Dehaene, S. & Naccache, L. 2001. Towards a Cognitive Neuroscience of Consciousness: Basic Evidence and a Workspace Framework. *Cognition*, 79: 1-37.
Dennett, D. C. 1969. *Content and Consciousness*. London: Routledge and Kegan Paul.

Dennett, D. C. 1978a. Why you Can't Make a Computer That Feels Pain. *Synthese*, 38: 415-56.

Dennett, D. C. 1978b. A Cure for the Common Code. In *Brainstorms: Philosophical Essays on Mind and Psychology*. Montgomery, VT: Bradford Books. pp. 90-108.

Dennett, D. C. 1982. Beyond Belief. In A. Woodfield (Ed.) *Thought and Object: Essays on Intentionality*. Oxford: Oxford University Press, pp. 1-96.

Dennett, D. C. 1987. True Believers. In *The Intentional Stance*. Cambridge, MA: MIT Press.

Dennett, D. C. 1988. Quining Qualia. In A. Marcel and E. Bisiach (Eds.) *Consciousness in Contemporary Science*. Oxford: Oxford University Presspp, pp. 42-77.

Dennett, D. C. 1991a. Mother Nature versus the Walking Encyclopedia: A Western Drama. In W. Ramsey, S. Stich and D. E. Rumelhart (Eds.) *Philosophy and Connectionist Theory*. Hillsdale, NJ: Lawrence Erlbaum, pp. 21-30.

Dennett, D. C. 1991b. *Consciousness Explained*. Boston: Brown and Little.

Dennett, D. C. 1991c. Real Patterns. *Journal of Philosophy*, 88(3): 27-51.

Dennett, D. C. 1992. The Self as a Centre of Narrative Gravity. In F.S. Kessel, P. M. Cole and D. L. Johnson (Eds.) *Self and Consciousness: Multiple Perspectives*. Hillsdale, NJ: Lawrence Erlbaum.

Dennett, D. C. 1996. *Kinds of Minds: Toward an Understanding of Consciousness*. New York: Basic Books.

Dennett, D. C. 2006. What Robomary Knows. In T. Alter and S. Walter (Eds.) *Phenomenal Concepts and Phenomenal Knowledge: New Essays on Consciousness and Physicalism*. Oxford: Oxford University Press, pp. 15-31.

Dennett, D. C. 2016. Illusionism as the Obvious Default Theory of Consciousness. *Journal of Consciousness Studies*, 23(11-12): 65-72.

Dennett, D. C. & Humphrey, N. 1989. Speaking for Ourselves: An Assessment of Multiple Personality Disorder. *Raritan*, 9(1): 68-98.

Descartes, R. 1641/1996. *Meditations on First Philosophy*. Trans. and ed. J. Cottingham. Cambridge: Cambridge University Press.

Descartes, R. 1643/2007. Letter to Elisabeth. In *The Correspondence between Princess Elisabeth of Bohemia and René Descartes*, edited and translated by Lisa Shapiro. Chicago, IL: The University of Chicago Press.

de Vignemont, F. 2009. Hysteria: The Reverse of Anosognosia. In T. Bayne and J. Fernandez (Eds.) *Delusions and Self-Deception: Affective Influences on Belief-Formation*. London: Psychology Press, pp. 241-60.

Dorsch, F. & Macpherson, F. (Eds.). 2018. *Phenomenal Presence*. Oxford: Oxford University Press.

Dou, E. & Geng, O. 2019. *Humans Mourn Loss after Google Is Unmasked as China's Go Master*. The Wall Street Journal, April.

Dowe, P. 2000. *Physical Causation*. Cambridge: Cambridge University Press.

Dretske, F. 1973. Perception and Other Minds. *Noûs*, 7: 34-44.

Dretske, F. 1981. *Knowledge and the Flow of Information*. Cambridge, MA: MIT Press.

Dretske, F. 1988. *Explaining Behavior: Reasons in a World of Causes*. Cambridge, MA: MIT Press.

Dretske, F. 1993. Mental Events as Structuring Causes of Behavior. In J. Heil and A. Mele (Eds.) *Mental Causation*. Oxford: Clarendon Press.

Dretske, F. 1995. *Naturalizing the Mind*. Cambridge, MA: MIT Press.

Dretske, F. 1996. Phenomenal Externalism or If Meanings Ain't in the Head, Where Are Qualia? *Philosophical Issues*, 7(Perception): 143-58.

Dretske, F. 1999. The Mind's Awareness of Itself. *Philosophical Studies*, 95: 103-24.

Dretske, F. 2006. Perception without Awareness. In T. S. Gendler and J. Hawthorne (Eds.) *Perceptual Experience*. Oxford: Oxford University Press, pp. 147-80.

Dretske, F. 2010. What We See: The Texture of Conscious Experience. In B. Nanay (Ed.) *Perceiving the World: New Essays on Perception*. Oxford: Oxford University Press, pp. 54-67.

Edlow, B. L., Claassen, J., Schiff, N. & Greer, D. M. 2020. Recovery from Disorders of Consciousness: Mechanisms, Prognosis, and Emerging Therapies. *Nature Reviews Neurology*, 17: 135-56.

Evans, G. 1982. *The Varieties of Reference*. Oxford: Clarendon Press.

Ewing, A. C.1962. *The Fundamental Questions of Philosophy*. New York: Collier Books.

Farkas, K. 2003. What is Externalism? *Philosophical Studies*, 112(3): 187-208.

Farkas, K. 2008a. Phenomenal Intentionality without Compromise. *The Monist*, 91(2): 273-93.

Farkas, K. 2008b. *The Subject's Point of View*. Oxford: Oxford University Press.

Farrell, B. A. 1950. Experience. *Mind*, 59: 170-98.

Feest, U. 2014. Phenomenal Experiences, First-Person Methods, and the Artificiality of Experimental Data. *Philosophy of Science*, 81: 927-39.
Feigl, H. 1958. The 'Mental' and the 'Physical'. *Minnesota Studies in the Philosophy of Science*, 2: 370-497.
Fernández, J. 2007. Desire and Self-Knowledge. *Australasian Journal of Philosophy*, 85(4): 517-36.
Fernández, J. 2013. *Transparent Minds: A Study of Self-Knowledge*. Oxford: Oxford University Press.
Field, H. 2005. Causation in a Physical World. In M. J. Loux and D. W. Zimmerman (Eds.) *The Oxford Handbook of Metaphysics*. Oxford: Oxford University Press.
Fish, W. 2009. *Perception, Hallucination and Illusion*. Oxford: Oxford University Press.
Flanagan, O. 1996. Neuroscience, Agency, and the Meaning of Life. In *Self-Expressions*. Oxford: Oxford University Press, pp. 53-64.
Fodor, J. 1974. Special Sciences, or the Disunity of Sciences as a Working Hypothesis. *Synthese*, 28: 97-115.
Fodor, J. 1984. Semantics, Wisconsin Style. *Synthese*, 59: 231-50.
Fodor, J. 1985. Fodor's Guide to Mental Representation: The Intelligent Auntie's Vade-Mecum. *Mind*, 94: 76-100.
Fodor, J. 1987. *Psychosemantics: The Problem of Meaning in the Philosophy of Mind*. Cambridge, MA: MIT/Bradford.
Fodor, J. 1990. Making Mind Matter More. In his *A Theory of Content and Other Essays*. Cambridge, MA: MIT Press.
Fodor, J. 1998. *Critical Condition*. Cambridge, MA: MIT Press.
Fodor, J. 2009. Where Is My Mind? *London Review of Books*, 31(3): 13-15.
Fodor, J. & McLaughlin, B. P. 1990. Connectionism and the Problem of Systematicity: Why Smolensky's Solution Doesn't Work. *Cognition*, 35(2): 183-205.
Fodor, J. & Pylyshyn, Z. 1988. Connectionism and Cognitive Architecture: A Critical Analysis. *Cognition*, 28(1-2): 3-71.
Forde, E.M.E. & Wallesch, C. W. 2003. A Psychological Review of Anton's Syndrome. In C. Code, C. W. Wallesch, E. ggg and A. R. Lecours (Eds.) *Classic Cases in Neuropsychology* (Vol. 2). New York: Psychology Press, pp. 199-222.
Fox, K.C.R. et al. 2020. Intrinsic Network Architecture Predicts the Effects Elicited by Intracranial Electrical Stimulation of the Human Brain. *Nature Human Behavior*, 4: 1039-52.
Frankish, K. 2010. Dual-Process and Dual-System Theories of Reasoning. *Philosophy Compass*, 5(10): 914-26.
Frankish, K. 2016a. Illusionism as a Theory of Consciousness. *Journal of Consciousness Studies*, 23(11-12): 11-39.
Frankish, K. 2016b. Not Disillusioned: Reply to Commentators. *Journal of Consciousness Studies*, 23(11-12): 256-89.
Frässle, S., Sommer, J., Jansen, A., Naber, M. & Einhäuser, W. 2014. Binocular Rivalry: Frontal Activity Relates to Introspection and Action But Not to Perception. *The Journal of Neuroscience*, 34(5): 1738-47.
French, R. 1990. Subcognition and the Limits of the Turing Test. *Mind*, 99: 53-65.
French, R. 2000. The Turing Test: The First 50 Years. *Trends in Cognitive Sciences*, 4(3): 115-22.
Frith, C., Perry, R. & Lumer, E. 1999. The Neural Correlates of Conscious Experience: An Experimental Framework. *Trends in the Cognitive Sciences*, 3: 105-114.
Gagliano, M. 2017. The Mind of Plants: Thinking the Unthinkable. *Communicative and Integrative Biology*, 10(2): e1288333.
Gallese, V. 2005. Embodied Simulation: From Neurons to Phenomenal Experience. *Phenomenology and the Cognitive Sciences*, 4(1): 23-48.
Gallois, A. 1996. *The World without, the Mind Within: An Essay on First-Person Authority*. Cambridge: Cambridge University Press.
Gallup, G. G., Jr. 1970. Chimpanzees: Self-Recognition. *Science*, 167: 86-87.
Gallup, G. G., Jr., Anderson, J. R. & Shillito, D. J. 2002. The Mirror Test. In M. Bekoff, C. Allen and G. M. Burghardt (Eds.) *The Cognitive Animal*. Cambridge, MA: MIT Press.
Gendler, T. S. 2008a. Alief and Belief. *Journal of Philosophy*, 105(10): 634-63.
Gendler, T. S. 2008b. Alief in Action (and Reaction). *Mind & Language*, 23: 552-85.
Gennaro, R. 2004. *Higher-Order Theories of Consciousness: An Anthology*. Amsterdam: John Benjamins.
Gertler, B. 2002. Explanatory Reduction, Conceptual Analysis, and Conceivability Arguments about the Mind. *Noûs*, 36: 22-49.
Gertler, B. (Ed.). 2003. *Privileged Access: Philosophical Accounts of Self-Knowledge*. Aldershot: Ashgate.
Gertler, B. 2011. *Self-Knowledge*. Abingdon: Routledge.

Glüer, K. 2009. In Defence of a Doxastic Account of Experience. *Mind and Language*, 24(3): 297-327.
Glüer, K. 2014. Looks, Reasons, and Experiences. In B. Brogaard (Ed.) *Does Perception Have Content?* Oxford: Oxford University Press, pp. 76-102.
Godfrey-Smith, P. 2004. On Folk Psychology and Mental Representation. In *Representation in Mind*. Amsterdam: Elsevier, pp. 147-62.
Godfrey-Smith, P. 2005. Folk Psychology as a Model. *Philosophers' Imprint*, 5(6).
Godfrey-Smith, P. 2013. Cephalopods and the Evolution of the Mind. *Pacific Conservation Biology*, 19: 4-9.
Godfrey-Smith, P. 2016. *Other Minds: The Octopus, the Sea, and the Deep Origins of Consciousness*. New York: Farrar, Strauss, and Giroux.
Godfrey-Smith, P. 2020. In the Beginning There Was Information? *Studies in History and Philosophy of Science Part C: Studies in History and Philosophy of Biological and Biomedical Sciences*, 80: 101239.
Goff, P. 2012. Does Mary Know I Experience Plus Rather Than Guus? A New Hard Problem. *Philosophical Studies*, 160(2): 223-35.
Goff, P. 2017a. *Consciousness and Fundamental Reality*. Oxford: Oxford University Press.
Goff, P. 2017b. Panpsychism. In S. Schneider and M. Velmans (Eds.) *The Blackwell Companion to Consciousness* (2nd ed.). Oxford: Blackwell.
Goff, P. & Coleman, S. 2020. Russellian Monism. In U. Kriegel (Ed.) *Oxford Handbook of the Philosophy of Consciousness*. Oxford: Oxford University Press.
Goldberg, S. 2006. Brown on Self-Knowledge and Discriminability. *Pacific Philosophical Quarterly*, 87(3): 301-14.
Goldberg, S. (Ed.). 2015. *Externalism, Self-Knowledge, and Skepticism: New Essays*. Cambridge: Cambridge University Press.
Goldenberg, G., Müllbacher, W. & Nowak, A. 1995. Imagery without Perception: A Case Study of Anosognosia for Cortical Blindness. *Neuropsychologia*, 33: 1373-82.
Goldman, A. 1989. Interpretation Psychologised. *Mind and Language*, 4: 161-85. Reprinted in M. Davies and T. Stone (Eds.). 1995. *Folk Psychology*. Oxford: Blackwell, pp. 74-99.
Goldman, A. 1997. Science, Publicity, and Consciousness. *Philosophy of Science*, 64(4): 525-45.
Goldman, A. 2003. Epistemology and the Evidential Status of Introspective Reports. In A. Jack and A. Roepstorff (Eds.) *Trusting the Subject* (Vol. 2). Thorverton: Imprint Academic, pp. 1-16.
Goldman, A. 2006. *Simulating Minds: The Philosophy, Psychology, and Neuroscience of Mindreading*. Oxford: Oxford University Press.
Gomes, A. 2011. Is There a Problem of Other Minds? *Proceedings of the Aristotelian Society*, 111: 353-73.
Gopnik, A. 1993. How We Know Our Own Minds: The Illusion of First-Person Knowledge. *Brain and Behavioral Sciences*, 16: 1-14.
Gopnik, A. 2009. Could David Hume Have Known about Buddhism? *Hume Studies*, 35(1-2): 5-28.
Gopnik, A. & Astington, J. W. 1988. Children's Understanding of Representational Change and Its Relation to the Understanding of False Belief and the Appearance-Reality Distinction. *Child Development*, 59: 26-37.
Gopnik, A. & Wellman, H. 1992. Why the Child's Theory of Mind Really Is a Theory. *Mind and Language*, 7: 145-71.
Gordon, R. 1986. Folk Psychology as Simulation. *Mind and Language*, 1(2): 158-71.
Goupil, L. & Kouider, S. 2016. Behavioral and Neural Indices of Metacognitive Sensitivity in Preverbal Infants. *Current Biology*, 26(22): 3038-45.
Goupil, L., Romand-Monnier, M. & Kouider, S. 2016. Infants Ask for Help When They Know They Don't Know. *PNAS*, 113(13): 3492-96.
Green, M. 2010. Perceiving Emotions. *Proceedings of Aristotelian Society, Supplementary Volume*, 84: 45-61.
Hall, N. 2004. Two Concepts of Causation. In J. Collins, N. Hall and L. Paul (Eds.) *Causation and Counterfactuals*. Cambridge, MA: MIT Press.
Hamilton, R. H. & Pascual-Leone, A. 1998. Cortical Plasticity Associated with Braille Learning. *Trends in Cognitive Sciences*, 2: 168-72.
Harman, G. 1990. The Intrinsic Quality of Experience. In J. Tomberlin (Ed.) *Philosophical Perspectives, 4: Action Theory and Philosophy of Mind*. Atascadero, CA: Ridgeview, pp. 31-52.
Harman, G. 1996. Qualia and Colour Concepts. *Philosophical Issues*, 7(Perception): 75-79.
Harris, P. 1992. From Simulation to Folk Psychology: The Case for Development. *Mind and Language*, 7(1-2): 120-44.

Haugeland, J. 1985. *Artificial Intelligence: The Very Idea*. Cambridge, MA: MIT Press.
Haugeland, J. 1998. Mind Embodied and Embedded. In *Having Thought*. Cambridge, MA: Harvard University Press, pp. 207-37.
Haynes, J-D., Sakai, K., Rees, G., Gilbert, S., Frith, C. & Passingham, R. E. 2007. Reading Hidden Intentions in the Human Brain. *Current Biology*, 17: 323-28.
Heal, J. 1986. Replication and Functionalism. In J. Butterfield (Ed.) *Language, Mind and Logic*. Cambridge: Cambridge University Press, pp. 135-50.
Heil, J. 1998. *Philosophy of Mind: A Contemporary Introduction*. London: Routledge.
Heil, J. & Mele, A. (Eds.). 1993. *Mental Causation*. Oxford: Clarendon Press.
Hempel, C. 1969. Reduction: Ontological and Linguistic Facets. In S. Morgenbesser, P. Suppes and M. White (Eds.) *Philosophy, Science and Method: Essays in Honour of Ernest Nagel*. New York: St. Martin's Press, pp. 179-99.
Hempel, C. 1980. Comment on Goodman's Ways of Worldmaking. *Synthese*, 45: 193-99.
Hill, C. S. 1991. *Sensations: A Defense of Type Materialism*. Cambridge: Cambridge University Press.
Hill, C. S. 2009. *Consciousness*. Cambridge: Cambridge University Press.
Hill, C. S. & McLaughlin, B. P. 1999. There Are Fewer Things in Reality Than Are Dreamt of in Chalmers' Philosophy. *Philosophy and Phenomenological Research*, 59(2): 445.
Hitchcock, C. 2007. What Russell Got Right. In H. Price and R. Corry (Eds.) *Causation, Physics, and the Constitution of Reality: Russell's Republic Revisited*. Oxford: Oxford University Press.
Hochner, B., Shomrat, T. & Fiorito, G. 2006. The Octopus: A Model for a Comparative Analysis of the Evolution of Learning and Memory Mechanisms. *Biological Bulletin*, 210: 308-17.
Hodge, K. M. 2008. Descartes' Mistake: How Afterlife Beliefs Challenge the Assumption That Humans Are Intuitive Cartesian Substance Dualists. *Journal of Cognition and Culture*, 8: 387-415.
Hohwy, J. 2002. Privileged Self-Knowledge and Externalism: A Contextualist Approach. *Pacific Philosophical Quarterly*, 83: 235-52.
Hohwy, J. 2011. Phenomenal Variability and Introspective Reliability. *Mind & Language*, 26(3): 261-86.
Holton, R. 2006. The Act of Choice, *Philosophers' Imprint*, 6(3): 1-15.
Horgan, T. 1983. Supervenience and Cosmic Hermeneutics. *Southern Journal of Philosophy*, 22(Supplement): 19-38.
Horgan, T. 1984a. Functionalism, Qualia, and the Inverted Spectrum. *Philosophy and Phenomenological Research*, 44: 453-69.
Horgan, T. 1984b. Jackson on Physical Information and Qualia. *Philosophical Quarterly*, 34(135): 147-52.
Horgan, T. 1989. Mental Quausation. *Philosophical Perspectives*, 3: 47-76.
Horgan, T. 1993. From Supervenience to Superdupervenience: Meeting the Demands of the Material World. *Mind*, 102(408): 555-86.
Horgan, T. 1997. Kim on Mental Causation and Causal Exclusion. *Philosophical Perspectives*, 11: 165-84.
Horgan, T. 2001. Causal Compatibilism and the Exclusion Problem. *Theoria*, 16(40): 95-116.
Horgan, T. 2007. Mental Causation and Agent Exclusion Problem. *Erkenntnis*, 67: 183-200.
Horgan, T. 2011. The Phenomenology of Agency and the Libet Results. In W. Sinnott-Armstrong and L. Nadel (Eds.), *Conscious Will and Responsibility*. Oxford: Oxford University Press, pp. 159-72.
Horgan, T. & Tienson, J. 2002. The Intentionality of Phenomenology and the Phenomenology of Intentionality. In D.J. Chalmers (Ed.) *Philosophy of Mind: Classical and Contemporary Readings*. Oxford: Oxford University Press.
Horgan, T., Tienson, J. & Graham, G. 2003. The Phenomenology of First-Person Agency. In S. Walter and H.-D. Heckmann (Eds.) *Physicalism and Mental Causation: The Metaphysics of Mind and Action*. Exeter: Imprint Academic, pp. 323-40.
Horgan, T. & Woodward, J. 1985. Folk Psychology Is Here to Stay. *Philosophical Review*, 94: 197-226.
Hume, D. 1739-1740/2000. *A Treatise of Human Nature* (ed. D. F. Norton and M. J. Norton). Oxford: Oxford University Press.
Hurley, S. L. 1998. Vehicles, Contents, Conceptual Structure and Externalism. *Analysis*, 58(1): 1-6.
Hurley, S. L. 2010. Varieties of Externalism. In R. Menary (Ed.) *The Extended Mind*. Cambridge, MA: MIT Press, pp. 101-53.
Hurley, S. L. & Noë, A. 2003. Neural Plasticity and Consciousness. *Biology and Philosophy*, 18:131-68.
Hutchins, E. 1995. *Cognition in the Wild*. Cambridge, MA: MIT Press.
Iannetti, G. D. & Mouraux, A. 2010. From the Neuromatrix to the Pain Matrix (and Back). *Experimental Brain Research*, 205: 1-12.
Irvine, E. 2012a. *Consciousness as a Scientific Concept*. Dordrecht: Springer.

Irvine, E. 2012b. Old Problems with New Measures in the Science of Consciousness. *The British Journal for the Philosophy of Science*, 63(3): 627-48.
Irvine, E. & Sprevak, M. 2020. Eliminativism about Consciousness. In U. Kriegel (ed.) *The Oxford Handbook of the Philosophy of Consciousness*. Oxford: OUP, pp. 348-70.
Ismael, J. 1999. Science and the Phenomenal. *Philosophy of Science*, 66: 351-69.
Jack, A. I. & Roepstorff, A. 2003. Trusting the Subject I. *Journal of Consciousness Studies*, 10(Special Issue): 9-10.
Jack, A. I. & Roepstorff, A. 2004. Trusting the Subject II. *Journal of Consciousness Studies*, 11(Special Issue): 7-8.
Jackson, F. 1982. Epiphenomenal Qualia. *Philosophical Quarterly*, 32: 127-36.
Jackson, F. 2003. Mind and Illusion. *Royal Institute of Philosophy Supplements*, 53: 251-71.
Jackson, F. 2006a. On Ensuring That Physicalism Is Not a Dual Attribute Theory in Sheep's Clothing. *Philosophical Studies*, 131(1): 227-49.
Jackson, F. 2006b. The Epistemological Objection to Opaque Teleological Theories of Content. In G. Macdonald and D. Papineau (Eds.) *Teleosemantics*. Oxford: Oxford University Press, pp. 85-99.
Jackson, F. 2007. A Priori Physicalism. In B. McLaughlin and J. Cohen (Eds.) *Contemporary Debates in Philosophy of Mind*. Oxford: Blackwell.
Jackson, F. & Pettit, P. 1990. Program Explanation: A General Perspective. *Analysis*, 50: 107-17.
Jackson, F. & Pettit, P. 1993. Folk Belief and Common-Place Beliefs. *Mind and Language*, 8: 298-305.
James, W. 1890/1983. *The Principles of Psychology* (ed. F. Burkhardt). Cambridge, MA: Harvard University Press.
Jiang, Y., Costello, P., Fang, F., Huang, M. & He, S. 2006. A Gender- and Sexual Orientation-Dependent Spatial Attentional Effect of Invisible Images. *Proceedings of the National Academy of Science*, 103: 17048-52.
Johnson, K. 2004. On the Systematicity of Language and Thought. *Journal of Philosophy*, 101: 111-39.
Johnston, M. 2014. The Problem with the Content View. In B. Brogaard (Ed.) *Does Perception Have Content?* Oxford: Oxford University Press.
Kahneman, D. & Frederick, S. 2002. Representativeness Revisited: Attribute Substitution in Intuitive Judgment. In T. Gilovich, D. Griffin and D. Kahneman (Eds.) *Heuristics and Biases: The Psychology of Intuitive Judgment*. Cambridge: Cambridge University Press, pp. 49-81.
Kallestrup, J. 2006. The Causal Exclusion Argument. *Philosophical Studies*, 131(2): 459-85.
Kant, I. 1781/1998. *Critique of Pure Reason* (trans. and ed. P. Guyer and A. Wood). Cambridge: Cambridge University Press.
Kendler, K.S., Hettema, J. M., Butera, F., Gardner, C. O. & Prescott, C. A. 2003. Life Event Dimensions of Loss, Humiliation, Entrapment, and Danger in the Prediction of Onsets of Major Depression and Generalized Anxiety. *Archives of General Psychiatry*, 60: 789-96.
Kim, J. 1972. Phenomenal Properties, Psychophysical Laws and the Identity Theory. *The Monist*, 56: 178-92.
Kim, J. 1984. Concepts of Supervenience. Reprinted in J. Kim. 1993. *Supervenience and Mind: Selected Philosophical Essays*. Cambridge: Cambridge University Press, pp. 53-78.
Kim, J. 1985. Psychophysical Laws. In B.P. Mclaughlin and E. Lepore (Eds.) *Actions and Events*. Oxford: Blackwell.
Kim, J. 1993a. The Non-Reductivist's Troubles with Mental Causation. In J. Heil and A. Mele (Eds.) *Mental Causation*. Oxford: Clarendon Press, pp. 189-210.
Kim, J. 1993b. The Myth of Non-Reductive Physicalism. In *Supervenience and Mind: Selected Philosophical Essays*. New York: Cambridge University Press, pp. 265-84.
Kim, J. 1998. *Mind in a Physical World*. Cambridge, MA: MIT Press.
Kim, J., 2005. *Physicalism, or Something Near Enough*. Princeton, NJ: Princeton University Press.
Kim, J. 2011. *Philosophy of Mind* (3rd ed.) London: Routledge.
Kind, A. 2003. What's So Transparent about Transparency? *Philosophical Studies*, 115: 225-44.
Kirk, R. 1974. Zombies v. Materialists. *Proceedings of the Aristotelian Society*, 48(Supplementary): 135-52.
Kirk, R. 2005. *Consciousness and Zombies*. Oxford: Clarendon Press.
Klein, C. 2015. *What the Body Commands: The Imperative Theory of Pain*. Cambridge, MA: MIT Press.
Kohda, M. et al. 2019. If a Fish Can Pass the Mark Test, What Are the Implications for Consciousness and Self-Awareness Testing in Animals? *PLoS Biology*. https://doi.org/10.1371/journal.pbio.3000021.
Kondziella, D., Friberg, C. K., Frokjaer, V. G., Fabricius, M. & Møller, K. 2016. Preserved Consciousness in

Vegetative and Minimal Conscious States: Systematic Review and Meta-Analysis. *Journal of Neurology, Neurosurgery and Psychiatry*, 87: 485-92.
Koster-Hale, J. & Saxe, R. 2013. Theory of Mind: A Neural Prediction Problem. *Neuron*, 79(4): 836-48.
Kriegel, U. 2005. Naturalizing Subjective Character. *Philosophy and Phenomenological Research*, 71(1): 23-57.
Kriegel, U. 2007. The Phenomenologically Manifest. *Phenomenology and the Cognitive Sciences*, 6: 115-36.
Kriegel, U. 2009. *Subjective Consciousness: A Self-Representational Theory*. Oxford: Oxford University Press.
Kriegel, U. 2011. *The Sources of Intentionality*. Oxford: Oxford University Press.
Kriegel, U. (Ed) 2013. *Phenomenal Intentionality*. New York: Oxford University Press.
Kriegel, U. 2015. *The Varieties of Consciousness*. Oxford University Press.
Kriegel, U. 2019. The Intentional Structure of Moods. *Philosophers' Imprint*, 19(49): 1-19.
Kriegel, U. & Williford, K. 2006. *Self-Representational Approaches to Consciousness*. Cambridge, MA: MIT Press.
Kripke, S. 1980. *Naming and Necessity*. Cambridge, MA: Harvard University Press.
Kripke, S. 1982. *Wittgenstein on Rules and Private Language*. Oxford: Basil Blackwell.
Lake, B. M., Ullman, T. D., Tenenbaum, J. B. & Gershman, S. J. 2017. Building Machines That Learn and Think Like People. *Behavioral and Brain Sciences*, 40: e253.
Lamme, V.A.F. 2006. Towards a True Neural Stance on Consciousness. *Trends in Cognitive Sciences*, 10(11): 494-501.
Langland-Hassan, P. & Vicente, A. 2018. *Inner Speech*. Oxford: Oxford University Press.
Lau, H. 2008. A Higher-Order Bayesian Decision Theory of Consciousness. *Progress in Brain Research*, 168: 35-48.
Lau, H. & Rosenthal, D. 2011. Empirical Support for Higher-Order Theories of Conscious Awareness. *Trends in Cognitive Sciences*, 15(8): 365-73.
Laudan, L. 1981. A Confutation of Convergent Realism. *Philosophy of Science*, 48(1): 19-49.
Laureys, S. 2005. The Neural Correlate of (Un)awareness: Lessons from the Vegetative State. *Trends in Cognitive Sciences*, 9(12): 556-9.
Lavelle, J. S. 2012. Theory-Theory and the Direct Perception of Mental States. *Review of Philosophy and Psychology*, 3: 213-30.
Lavelle, J. S. 2018. *The Social Mind: A Philosophical Introduction*. London: Routledge.
LeCun, Y., Bengio, Y. & Hinton, G. 2015. Deep Learning. *Nature*, 521(7553): 436-44.
Leibniz, G. W. 1714/1989. *Monadology*. In *Leibniz: Philosophical Essays*. Ed. and Trans. R. Ariew and D. Garber. Indianapolis: Hackett.
Levin, J. 1991. Analytic Functionalism and the Reduction of Phenomenal States. *Philosophical Studies*, 61: 211-68.
Levine, J. 1983. Materialism and Qualia: The Explanatory Gap. *Pacific Philosophical Quarterly*, 64: 354-61. Reprinted in O'Connor and Robb (Eds.). 2003. *Philosophy of Mind: Contemporary Readings*. Abingdon: Routledge.
Levine, J. 1995. Qualia: Intrinsic, Relational or What? In T. Metzinger (Ed.) *Conscious Experience*. Paderborn: Schoeningh.
Levine, J. 2007. Phenomenal Concepts and the Materialist Constraint. In T. Alter and S. Walter (Eds.) *Phenomenal Concepts and Phenomenal Knowledge*. Oxford: Oxford University Press.
Levine, J. 2009. The Explanatory Gap. In B. McLaughlin et al. (Eds.) *The Oxford Handbook of Philosophy of Mind*. Oxford: Oxford University Press.
Levine, J. 2020. A Posteriori Physicalism: Type-B Materialism and the Explanatory Gap. In U. Kriegel (Ed.) *The Oxford Handbook of the Philosophy of Consciousness*. Oxford: Oxford University Press.
Lewis, D. 1966. An Argument for the Identity Theory. *Journal of Philosophy*, 63: 17-25.
Lewis, D. 1972. Psychophysical and Theoretical Identifications. *Australasian Journal of Philosophy*, 50: 249-58. Reprinted in Block, N. (Ed.) *Readings in the Philosophy of Psychology* (Vol. 1). Cambridge, MA: MIT Press, pp. 207-15.
Lewis, D. 1973. Causation. *Journal of Philosophy*, 70: 556-67. Reprinted in his 1986. *Philosophical Papers* (Vol. 2). New York: Oxford University Press.
Lewis, D. 1974. Radical Interpretation. *Synthese*, 23: 331-44.
Lewis, D. 1980. Mad Pain and Martian Pain. In Ned Block (Ed.), *Readings in the Philosophy of Psychology*. Cambridge, MA: Harvard University Press, pp. 216-22.

Lewis, D. 1983. New Work for a Theory of Universals. *Australasian Journal of Philosophy*, 61: 343-77.
Lewis, D. 1994. Reduction of Mind. In S. Guttenplan (Ed.) *A Companion to the Philosophy of Mind*. Oxford: Blackwell, pp. 412-31. Reprinted in his 1999. *Papers in Metaphysics and Epistemology*. Cambridge: Cambridge University Press, pp. 291-324.
Lewis, D. 1997. What Experience Teaches. In N. Block, O. Flanagan and G. Güzeldere (Eds.) *The Nature of Consciousness: Philosophical Debates*. Cambridge, MA: MIT Press, pp. 159-72.
Liao, S. M. 2006. The Organism View Defended. *Monist*, 89: 334-50.
Libet, B. 1985. Unconscious Cerebral Initiative and the Role of Conscious Will in Voluntary Action. *Behavioral and Brain Sciences*, 8: 529-66.
Libet, B. 1999. Do We Have Free Will? *Journal of Consciousness Studies*, 6(8-9): 47-57.
Libet, B., Gleason, C. A., Wright, E. W. & Pearl, D. 1983. Time of Unconscious Intention to Act in Relation to Onset of Cerebral Activity (Readiness-Potential). *Brain*, 106: 623-42.
Lipton, P. 2004. *Inference to the Best Explanation* (2nd ed.). Abingdon: Routledge.
List, C. & Menzies, P. 2009. Non-Reductive Physicalism and the Limits of the Exclusion Principle. *Journal of Philosophy*, 106(9): 475-502.
Loar, B. 1988. Social Content and Psychological Content. In R. Grimm and P. Merrill (Eds.) *Contents of Thoughts*. Tucson: University of Arizona Press, pp. 99-110.
Loar, B. 1997. Phenomenal States (Second Version). In N. Block, O. Flanagan and G. Güzeldere (Eds.) *The Nature of Consciousness: Philosophical Debates*. Cambridge, MA: MIT Press.
Loar, B. 2003. Phenomenal Intentionality as the Basis of Mental Content. In M. Hahn and B. Ramberg (Eds.) *Reflections and Replies: Essays on the Philosophy of Tyler Burge*. Cambridge, MA: MIT Press, pp. 229-58.
Locke, J. 1690/1975. *An Essay Concerning Human Understanding* (Ed. P. H. Nidditch). Oxford: Clarendon Press.
Loewer, B. 2017. A Guide to Naturalizing Semantics. In B. Hale, C. Wright and A. Miller (Eds.) *A Companion to the Philosophy of Language* (2nd ed.). Chichester: Wiley-Blackwell, pp. 173-96.
Lopes, D. 2000. What Is It Like to See with Your Ears? *Philosophy and Phenomenological Research*, 60: 455-59.
Lupyan, G. 2012. What Do Words Do? Toward a Theory of Language-Augmented Thought. In B. H. Ross (Ed.) *Psychology of Learning and Motivation* (Vol. 57). New York: Academic Press, pp. 155-297.
Lycan, W. G. 1987. *Consciousness*. Cambridge, MA: MIT Press.
Lycan, W. G. 1990. What Is the 'Subjectivity' of the Mental? *Philosophical Perspectives*, 4: 109-30.
Lycan, W. G. 1995. A Limited Defense of Phenomenal Information. In T. Metzinger (Ed.) *Conscious Experience*. Paderborn, Germany: Frederick Schoeningh, pp. 243-58.
Lycan, W. G. 1996. *Consciousness and Experience*. Cambridge, MA: MIT Press.
Lycan, W. G. 2001a. A Simple Argument for a Higher-Order Representation Theory of Consciousness. *Analysis*, 61(1): 3-4.
Lycan, W. G. 2001b. The Case for Phenomenal Externalism. *Philosophical Perspectives*, (Metaphysics), 15: 17-35.
Lycan, W. G. 2003. Dretske's Ways of Introspecting. In B. Gertler (Ed.) *Privileged Access: Philosophical Accounts of Self-Knowledge*. Aldershot: Ashgate.
Macdonald, C. 2004. Mary Meets Molyneux: The Explanatory Gap and the Individuation of Phenomenal Concepts. *Noûs*, 38(3): 503-24.
Macdonald, C. & Macdonald, G. (Eds.). 1995. *Connectionism: Debates on Psychological Explanation*. Oxford: Basil Blackwell.
Macpherson, F. 2006. Ambiguous Figures and the Contents of Experience. *Noûs*, 40(1): 82-117.
Maoz, U. et al. 2019. Neural Precursors of Decisions That Matter: An ERP Study of Deliberate and Arbitrary Choice. *eLife*, 8.
Marchetti, C. & Della Sala, S. 1998. Disentangling the Alien and Anarchic Hand. *Cognitive Neuropsychiatry*, 3(3): 191-207.
Marcus, G. 1998. Rethinking Eliminative Connectionism. *Cognitive Psychology*, 37: 243-82.
Martin, M. G. F. 2002. The Transparency of Experience. *Mind and Language*, 17(4): 376-425.
Martin, M. G. F. 2004. The Limits of Self-Awareness. *Philosophical Studies*, 120: 37-89.
Martin, M. G. F. 2010. What's in a Look? In B. Nanay (Ed.) *Perceiving the World*. Oxford: Oxford University Press.
Martínez, M. 2013. Teleosemantics and Productivity. *Philosophical Psychology*, 26(1): 47-68.
Mashour, G. A., Roelfsema, P., Changeux, J.-P. & Dehaene, S. 2020. Conscious Processing and the Global

Neuronal Workspace Hypothesis. *Neuron*, 105: 776-98.
Matthen, M. 2010. On the Diversity of Auditory Objects. *Review of Philosophy and Psychology*, 1: 63-89.
Mather, J. A. 2008. Cephalopod Consciousness: Behavioural Evidence. *Consciousness and Cognition*, 17: 37-48.
Mather, J. A. 2019. What's in an Octopus's Mind? *Animal Sentience*, 26(1).
Matthews, R. J. 1994. Three Concept Monte: Explanation, Implementation and Systematicity. *Synthese*, 101: 347-63.
McClamrock, R. 1995. *Existential Cognition: Computational Mind in the World*. Chicago: University of Chicago Press.
McClelland, J. L. et al. 2010. Letting Structure Emerge: Connectionist and Dynamical Systems Approaches to Cognition. *Trends in Cognitive Sciences*, 14(8): 348-56.
McDowell, J. 1997. *Reductionism and the First Person*. In J. Dancy (Ed.) *Reading Parfit*. Oxford: Blackwell, pp. 230-50.
McDowell, J. 1998. On 'The Reality of the Past'. In his *Meaning, Knowledge and Reality*. Cambridge, MA: Harvard University Press, pp. 295-313.
McGeer, V. 1996. Is 'Self-Knowledge' an Empirical Problem? Renegotiating the Space of Philosophical Explanation. *Journal of Philosophy*, 92: 485-515.
McGinn, C. 1983. *The Subjective View*. Oxford: Oxford University Press.
McGinn, C. 1984. What Is the Problem of Other Minds? *Proceedings of the Aristotelian Society*, 58: 119-37.
McGinn, C. 1988. Consciousness and Content. *Proceedings of the British Academy*, 74: 219-39.
McGinn, C. 1989. Can we Solve the Mind-Body Problem? *Mind*, 98: 349-66.
McKinsey, M. 1991. Anti-Individualism and Privileged Access. *Analysis*, 51: 9-16.
McLaughlin, B. 1992. The Rise and Fall of British Emergentism. In A. Beckermann, H. Flohr and J. Kim (Eds.) *Emergence or Reduction?: Prospects for Nonreductive Physicalism*. New York: De Gruyter, 19-59.
McLaughlin, B. 2007. On the Limits of a Priori Physicalism. In B. McLaughlin and J. Cohen (Eds.) *Contemporary Debates in Philosophy of Mind*. Oxford: Blackwell, pp. 200-24.
McMullen, C. 1985. 'Knowing What It's Like' and the Essential Indexical. *Philosophical Studies*, 48: 211-33.
McNeill, W. 2012. On Seeing That Someone Is Angry. *European Journal of Philosophy*, 20(4): 575-97.
Mele, A. 2009. *Effective Intentions: The Power of Conscious Will*. New York: Oxford University Press.
Melnyk, A. 1994. Inference to the Best Explanation and Other Minds. *Australasian Journal of Philosophy*, 72: 482-91.
Melnyk, A. 2003. *A Physicalist Manifesto: Thoroughly Modern Materialism*. Cambridge: Cambridge University Press.
Melnyk, A. 2008. Can Physicalism Be Non-Reductive? *Philosophy Compass*, 3(6): 1281-96.
Menary, R. 2010. The Holy Grail of Cognitivism: A Response to Adams and Aizawa. *Phenomenology and the Cognitive Sciences*, 9(4): 459-63.
Mendelovici, A. 2014. Pure Intentionalism about Moods and Emotions. In U. Kriegel (Ed.) *Current Controversies in Philosophy of Mind*. Abingdon: Routledge, pp. 135-57.
Mendelovici, A. 2018. *The Phenomenal Basis of Intentionality*. Oxford: Oxford University Press.
Mendola, J. 2008. *Anti-Externalism*. Oxford: Oxford University Press.
Menzies, P. 2003. The Causal Efficacy of Mental States. In S. Walter and H. D. Heckmann (Eds.) *Physicalism and Mental Causation: The Metaphysics of Mind and Action*. Exeter: Imprint Academic, pp. 195-223.
Menzies, P. 2008. The Exclusion Problem, the Determination Relation, and Contrastive Causation. In J. Hohwy and J. Kallestrup (Eds.) *Being Reduced: New Essays on Reduction, Explanation and Causation*. Oxford: OUP, pp. 196-218.
Menzies, P. & Beebee, H. 2019. Counterfactual Theories of Consciousness. In E. Zalta (Ed.) *Stanford Encyclopedia of Philosophy*. https://plato.stanford.edu/entries/causation-counterfactual/ [accessed 18 August 2021].
Metzinger, T. 2020. Minimal Phenomenal Experience: Meditation, Tonic Alertness, and the Phenomenology of "Pure" Consciousness. *Philosophy and the Mind Sciences*, 1: 7.
Mill, J. S. 1865b/1979. *An Examination of Sir William Hamilton's Philosophy* (Vol. 9, Ed. J. M. Robson). Collected Works of John Stuart Mill. Toronto: University of Toronto Press.
Millière, R. 2017. Looking for the Self: Phenomenology, Neurophysiology and Philosophical Significance of Drug-induced Ego Dissolution. *Frontiers in Human Neuroscience*, 11: 245.
Millikan, R. G. 1984. *Language, Thought and Other Biological Categories*. Cambridge, MA: MIT Press.
Millikan, R. G. 1989. Biosemantics. *Journal of Philosophy*, 86: 281-97.
Millikan, R. G. 2000. *On Clear and Confused Concepts*. Cambridge: Cambridge University Press.
Millikan, R. G. 2010. On Knowing the Meaning: With a Coda on Swampman. *Mind*, 119(473): 43-81.

Mitchell, R. W. 1995. Evidence of Dolphin Self-Recognition and the Difficulties of Interpretation. *Consciousness and Cognition*, 4: 229-34.
Moore, G. E. 1903. The Refutation of Idealism. *Journal of Philosophy, Psychology and Scientific Methods*, 1(3): 76-77.
Moran, R. 2001. *Authority and Estrangement: An Essay on Self-Knowledge*. Princeton, NJ: Princeton University Press.
Moran, R. 2003. Responses to O'Brien and Shoemaker. *European Journal of Philosophy*, 11(3): 402-19.
Mørch, H.H. 2017. Is Matter Conscious? *Nautilus*, 47. Reprinted in Chalmers, D. (Ed.) 2021. *Philosophy of Mind: Classical and Contemporary Readings* (2nd ed.). Oxford: Oxford University Press.
Mouraux, A. et al. 2011. A Multisensory Investigation of the Functional Significance of the 'Pain Matrix'. *Neuroimage*, 54: 2237-49.
Nagel, T. 1974. What Is It Like to Be a Bat? *The Philosophical Review*, 83(4): 435-50.
Nagel, T. 1979. Panpsychism. In *Mortal Questions*. Cambridge: Cambridge University Press.
Nagel, T. 1986. *The View from Nowhere*. Oxford: Oxford University Press.
Nahmias, E. 2014. Is Free Will an Illusion? Confronting Challenges from the Modern Mind Sciences. In W. Sinnott-Armstrong (Ed.) *Moral Psychology, Vol. 4: Freedom and Responsibility*. Cambridge, MA: MIT Press.
Nanay, B. 2011. Do We See Apples as Edible? *Pacific Philosophical Quarterly*, 92: 305-22.
Nanay, B. 2015. Perceptual Representation/Perceptual Content. In M. Matthen (Ed.) *Oxford Handbook for the Philosophy of Perception*. Oxford: Oxford University Press, pp. 153-67.
Neander, K. 1995. Malfunctioning and Misrepresenting. *Philosophical Studies*, 79: 109-41.
Neander, K. 1996. Swampman Meets Swampcow. *Mind and Language*, 11(1): 118-29.
Neander, K. 1998. The Division of Phenomenal Labor: A Problem for Representational Theories of Consciousness. *Philosophical Perspectives, 12: Language, Mind and Ontology*, 32: 411-34.
Neander, K. 2006. Content for Cognitive Science. In G. Macdonald and D. Papineau (Eds.) *Teleosemantics: New Philosophical Essays*. Oxford: Oxford University Press, pp. 167-94.
Neander, K. 2017. *A Mark of the Mental: In Defense of Informational Teleosemantics*. Cambridge, MA: MIT Press.
Nemirow, L. 1990. Physicalism and the Cognitive Role of Acquaintance. In Lycan, 490-99.
Nemirow, L. 2007. So This Is What It's Like: A Defense of the Ability Hypothesis. In T. Alter and S. Walter (Eds.), *Phenomenal Concepts and Phenomenal Knowledge: New Essays on Consciousness and Physicalism*. New York: Oxford University Press, pp. 32-51.
Ney, A. 2008. Defining Physicalism. *Philosophy Compass*, 3(5): 1033-48.
Ney, A. 2016. Grounding in the Philosophy of Mind: A Defense. In K. Aizawa and C. Gillett (Eds.) *Scientific Composition and Metaphysical Ground*. London: Palgrave-Macmillan.
Nichols, S. 2008. Imagination and the I. *Mind and Language*, 23(5): 518-35.
Nichols, S. & Stich, S. 2003. *Mindreading: An Integrated Account of Pretence, Self-Awareness, and Understanding Other Minds*. Oxford: Oxford University Press.
Nichols, S., Strohminger, N., Rai, A. & Garfield, J. 2018. Death and the Self. *Cognitive Science*, 42(1): 314-32.
Nickel, B. 2007. Against Intentionalism. *Philosophical Studies*, 136: 279-304.
Nida-Rümelin, M. 1996a. What Mary Couldn't Know. In T. Metzinger (Ed.) *Phenomenal Consciousness*. Schoeningh: Paderborn.
Nida-Rümelin, M. 1996b. Pseudonormal Vision. *Philosophical Studies*, 82: 145-57. Reprinted in Chalmers, D. (Ed.) *Philosophy of Mind: Classical and Contemporary Readings* (2nd ed.). Oxford: Oxford University Press.
Nida-Rümelin, M. 1998. On Belief about Experiences: An Epistemological Distinction Applied to the Knowledge Argument. *Philosophy and Phenomenological Research*, 58(1): 51-73.
Nida-Rümelin, M. 2007. Doings and Subject Causation. *Erkenntnis*, 67: 255-72.
Niklassen, L. F. & van Gelder, T. 1994. On Being Systematically Connectionist. *Mind and Language*, 9(3): 288-302.
Noë, A. 2004. *Action in Perception*. Cambridge, MA: MIT Press.
Noë, A. 2005. Real Presence. *Philosophical Topics*, 33(1): 235-64.
Nudds, M. 2001. Experiencing the Production of Sounds. *European Journal of Philosophy*, 9: 210-29.
Nudds, M. & O'Callaghan, C. 2009. *Sounds and Perception: New Philosophical Essays*. Oxford: Oxford University Press.
O'Callaghan, C. 2007. *Sounds: A Philosophical Theory*. Oxford: Oxford University Press.

O'Callaghan, C. 2011. Against Hearing Meanings. *Philosophical Quarterly*, 61: 783-807.
O'Connor, T. 1995. Agent Causation. In T. O'Connor (Ed.) *Agents, Causes, Events*. New York: Oxford University Press, pp. 173-200.
O'Dea, J. 2006. Representationalism, Supervenience, and the Cross-Modal Problem. *Philosophical Studies*, 130: 285-95.
Odegaard, B., Knight, R. & Lau, H. 2017. Should a Few Null Findings Falsify Prefrontal Theories of Conscious Perception? *Journal of Neuroscience*, 37(40): 9593-602.
Olson, E. 1997. *The Human Animal: Personal Identity without Psychology*. Cambridge: Cambridge University Press.
Olson, E. 2007. There Is No Problem of the Self. In B. Gertler and L. Shapiro (Eds.) *Arguing about the Mind*. Abingdon: Routledge.
Olson, E. 2014. The Metaphysical Implications of Conjoined Twinning. *Southern Journal of Philosophy*, 52(S1): 24-40.
O'Regan, J. K. & Noë, A. 2001. A Sensorimotor Account of Vision and Visual Consciousness. *Behavioural and Brain Sciences*, 24: 939-1011.
Overgaard, M. 2006. Introspection in Science. *Consciousness and Cognition*, 15: 629-33.
Overgaard, M. 2012. Blindsight: Recent and Historical Controversies on the Blindness of Blindsight. *WIREs Cognitive Science*, 3: 607-14. https://doi.org/10.1002/wcs.1194.
Overgaard, M., Fehl, K., Mouridsen, K., Bergholt, B. & Cleeremans, A. 2008. Seeing without Seeing? Degraded Conscious Vision in a Blindsight Patient. *PLoS One*, 3(8): e3028. https://doi.org/10.1371/journal.pone.0003028.
Owen, A. M., Coleman, M. R., Boly, M., Davis, M. H., Laureys, S. & Pickard, J. D. 2006. Detecting Awareness in the Vegetative State. *Science*, 313: 1402.
Papineau, D. 1984. Representation and Explanation. *Philosophy of Science*, 51(4): 550-72.
Papineau, D. 1993. *Philosophical Naturalism*. Oxford: Blackwell.
Papineau, D. 2001. The Status of Teleosemantics, or How to Stop Worrying about Swampman. *Australasian Journal of Philosophy*, 79(2): 279-89.
Papineau, D. 2002. *Thinking about Consciousness*. Oxford: Oxford University Press.
Papineau, D. 2011. Phenomenal Concepts and the Private Language Argument. *American Philosophical Quarterly*, 48(2): 175-84.
Papineau, D. 2014. Sensory Experience and Representational Properties. *Proceedings of the Aristotelian Society*, 114: 1-33.
Parfit, D. 1999. Experiences, Subjects and Conceptual Schemes. *Philosophical Topics*, 26(1&2): 217-70.
Parfit, D. 2016. We Are Not Human Beings. In S. Blatti and P. Snowdon (Eds.), *Animalism: New Essays on Persons, Animals and Identity*. Oxford: Oxford University Press, pp. 31-49.
Pargetter, R. 1984. The Scientific Inference to Other Minds. *Australasian Journal of Philosophy*, 62: 158-63.
Patterson, S. 1990. The Explanatory Role of Belief Ascriptions. *Philosophical Studies*, 59: 313-32.
Pautz, A. 2006. Sensory Awareness Is Not a Wide Physical Relation: An Empirical Argument Against Externalist Intentionalism. *Noûs*, 40(2): 205-40.
Pautz, A. 2010. Why Explain Visual Experience in Terms of Content? In B. Nanay (Ed.) *Perceiving the World*. Oxford: Oxford University Press.
Pautz, A. 2020. Representationalism about Consciousness. In U. Kriegel (Ed.) *The Oxford Handbook of the Philosophy of Consciousness*. Oxford: Oxford University Press.
Peacocke, C. 1983. *Sense and Content*. Oxford: Oxford University Press.
Pearl, J. 2000. *Causality: Models, Reasoning, and Inference*. Cambridge: Cambridge University Press.
Penn, D. C., Holyoak, K. J. & Povinelli, D. J. 2008. Darwin's Mistake: Explaining the Discontinuity between Human and Nonhuman Minds. *Behavioral and Brain Sciences*, 31(2): 109-30.
Pereboom, D. 2014. Russellian Monism and Absolutely Intrinsic Properties. In U. Kriegel (Ed.) *Current Controversies in Philosophy of Mind*. Abingdon: Routledge, pp. 40-69.
Perenin, M. & Jeannerod, M. 1978. Visual Function within the Hemianopic Field Following Early Cerebral Hemidecortication in Man. *Neuropsychologia*, 16: 1-13.
Perner, J., Leekam, S. & Wimmer, H. 1987. 3-Year-Olds' Difficulty Understanding False Belief: Cognitive Limitation, Lack of Knowledge or Pragmatic Misunderstanding. *British Journal of Developmental Psychology*, 5: 125-37.
Perner, J., Ruffman, T. & Leekam, S. 1994. Theory of Mind Is Contagious: You Catch It from Your Sibs. *Child Development*, 65: 1228-38.
Perry, J. 2001. *Knowledge, Possibility, and Consciousness*. Cambridge, MA: MIT Press.

Peterson, C. C. & Siegal, M. 2000. Insights into Theory of Mind from Deafness and Autism. *Mind and Language*, 15(1): 123-45.
Phillips, I. 2011. Perception and Iconic Memory: What Sperling Doesn't Show. *Mind and Language*, 26(4): 381-411.
Phillips, I. 2013. Afterimages and Sensation. *Philosophy and Phenomenological Research*, 87(2): 417-53.
Phillips, I. 2018. Unconscious Perception Reconsidered. *Analytic Philosophy*, 59(4): 471-514.
Phillips, I. 2021. Blindsight Is Qualitatively Degraded Conscious Vision. *Psychological Review*, 128(3): 558-84.
Piccinini, G. 2009. First-Person Data, Publicity, and Self-Measurement. *Philosophers' Imprint*, 9(9).
Pitt, D. 2004. The Phenomenology of Cognition or What Is It Like to Think That P? *Philosophy and Phenomenological Research*, 69: 1-36.
Place, U. T. 1956. Sensations and Brain Processes. *British Journal of Psychology*, 47: 44-50.
Plotnik, J., de Waal, F.B.M. & Reiss, D. 2006. Self-Recognition in an Asian Elephant. *PNAS*, 103: 17053-57.
Polger, T. 2004. *Natural Minds*. Cambridge, MA: MIT Press.
Polger, T. 2008. H2O, 'Water', and Transparent Reduction. *Erkenntnis*, 69(1): 109-30.
Price, H. H. 1932. *Perception*. London: Methuen.
Prinz, J. J. 2011. The Sensory Basis of Cognitive Phenomenology. In T. Bayne and M. Montague (Eds.) *Cognitive Phenomenology*. Oxford: Oxford University Press, pp. 174-96.
Prinz, J. J. 2012. *The Conscious Brain*. New York: Oxford University Press.
Prior, H. H., Schwarz, A. & Gunturkun, O. 2008. Mirror-Induced Behavior in the Magpie (Pica pica): Evidence of Self-Recognition. *PLoS Biology*, 6: e202.
Putnam, H. 1963. Brains and Behavior. In R. Butler (Ed.) *Analytical Philosophy* (2nd series). Oxford: Blackwell. Reprinted in his Philosophical Papers, vol. 2. (Cambridge: University of Cambridge Press, 1975).
Putnam, H. 1967. Psychological Predicates. In W. H. Capitan and D. D. Merrill (Eds.) *Art, Mind, and Religion*. Pittsburgh: University of Pittsburgh Press, pp. 37-48.
Putnam, H. 1975a. Philosophy and Our Mental Life. In H. Putnam (Ed.) *Mind, Language and Reality: Philosophical Papers* (Vol. 2). Cambridge: Cambridge University Press, pp. 291-303.
Putnam, H. 1975b. The Meaning of 'Meaning'. In *Philosophical Papers, Vol. II: Mind, Language, and Reality*. Cambridge: Cambridge University Press.
Raatikainen, P. 2010. Causation, Exclusion, and the Special Sciences. *Erkenntnis*, 73: 349-63.
Ramachandran, V. S. & Hirstein W. (1998). The Perception of Phantom Limbs: The D. O. Hebb Lecture. *Brain: A Journal of Neurology*, 121(9): 1603-30.
Reid, T. 1785/1975. Of Identity. In J. Perry (Ed.) *Personal Identity*. Berkeley, CA: University of California Press, pp. 107-12.
Reiss, D. & Marino, L. 2001. Mirror Self-Recognition in the Bottlenose Dolphin: A Case of Cognitive Convergence. *Proceedings of the National Academy of Sciences*, 98: 5937-42.
Rescorla, M. 2009. Chrysippus's Dog as a Case Study in Non-Linguistic Cognition. In R.W. Lurz (Ed.) *The Philosophy of Animal Minds*. Cambridge: Cambridge University Press, pp. 52-71.
Richards, W. 1973. Visual Processing in Scotomata. *Experimental Brain Research*, 17: 333-47.
Richardson, L. 2013. Flavour, Taste and Smell. *Mind and Language*, 28(3): 322-41.
Rips, L. J. 2011. Causation from Perception. *Perspectives on Psychological Science*, 6(1): 77-97.
Robbins, P. 2009. Guilt by Dissociation: Why Mindreading Might Not Be Prior to Metacognition after All. *Behavioral and Brain Sciences*, 32(2): 159-60.
Robinson, H. 1994. *Perception*. London: Routledge.
Robinson, W. 2011. A Frugal View of Cognitive Phenomenology. In T. Bayne and M. Montague (Eds.) *Cognitive Phenomenology*. Oxford: Oxford University Press, pp. 197-214.
Roelofs, L. 2019. *Combining Minds: How to Think about Composite Subjectivity*. Oxford: Oxford University Press.
Rorty, R. 1979. *Philosophy and the Mirror of Nature*. Princeton, NJ: Princeton University Press.
Rosenthal, D. 1986. Two Concepts of Consciousness. *Philosophical Studies*, 49: 329-59.
Rosenthal, D. 1997. A Theory of Consciousness. In N. Block, O.J. Flanagan and G. Güzeldere (Eds.) *The Nature of Consciousness*. Cambridge, MA: MIT Press.
Rosenthal, D. 2002. How Many Kinds of Consciousness? *Consciousness and Cognition*, 11(4): 653-65.
Rosenthal, D. 2005. *Consciousness and Mind*. Oxford: Clarendon Press.
Rumelhart, D., McClelland, J. L. & the PDP Research Group. 1987. *Parallel Distributed Processing, Volume 1*. Cambridge, MA: MIT Press.
Rupert, R. D. 1999. The Best Test Theory of Extension: First Principle(s). *Mind & Language*, 14: 321-55.

Rupert, R. D. 2004. Challenges to the Hypothesis of Extended Cognition. *Journal of Philosophy*, 101(8): 389-428.
Russell, B. 1912. *The Problems of Philosophy*. London: Williams and Norgate.
Russell, B. 1921. *The Analysis of Mind*. London: Allen & Unwin.
Russell, B. 1948. *Human Knowledge: Its Scope and Limits*. London: Routledge.
Ryder, D. 2004. SINBAD Neurosemantics: A Theory of Mental Representation. *Mind and Language*, 19(2): 211-40.
Ryder, D. 2019. Problems of Representation II: Naturalizing Content. In F. Garzon and J. Symons (Eds.) *The Routledge Companion to the Philosophy of Psychology* (2nd ed.). London: Routledge, pp. 251-79.
Ryle, G. 1949. *The Concept of Mind*. London: Hutchinson.
Sakaguchi, H., Ozaki, Y., Ashida, T., Matsubara, T., Ishi, N., Kihara, S., & Takahashi, J. 2019. Self-Organized Synchronous Calcium Transients in a Cultured Human Neural Network Derived from Cerebral Organoids. *Stem Cell Reports*. S2213-6711(19)30197-3z.
Sandberg, K., Timmermans, B., Overgaard, M. & Cleeremans, A. 2010. Measuring Consciousness: Is One Measure Better Than the Other? *Consciousness and Cognition*, 19(4): 1069-78.
Sarasso, S. et al. 2015. Consciousness and Complexity during Unresponsiveness Induced by Propofol, Xenon, and Ketamine. *Current Biology*, 25: 3099-105.
Sass, L. A. & Parnas, J. 2003. Schizophrenia, Consciousness and the Self. *Schizophrenia Bulletin*, 29: 427-44.
Sawyer, S. 1998. Privileged Access to the World. *Australasian Journal of Philosophy*, 76: 523-33.
Schaffer, J. 2009. On What Grounds What. In D. Chalmers, D. Manley and R. Wasserman (Eds.) *Metametaphysics*. New York: Oxford University Press, pp. 247-383.
Schaffer, J. 2017. The Ground between the Gaps. *Philosophers' Imprint*, 17(11).
Schechtman, M. 1996. *The Constitution of Selves*. Ithaca, NY: Cornell University Press.
Schechtman, M. 2007. Stories, Lives, and Basic Survival. *Royal Institute of Philosophy Supplements, Vol. 60: Narrative and Understanding Persons*, 155-78.
Schellenberg, S. 2011. Perceptual Content Defended. *Noûs*, 45(4): 714-50.
Scholl, B. & Leslie, A. 1999. Modularity, Development and 'Theory of Mind'. *Mind and Language*, 14(1): 131-53.
Schurger, A., Sitt, J. D. & Dehaene, S. 2012. An Accumulator Model for Spontaneous Neural Activity Prior to Self-Initiated Movement. *Proceedings of the National Academy of Sciences*, 109(42): E2904-13.
Schurger, A., Hu, P., Pak, J. & Roskies, A. 2021. What Is the Readiness Potential? *Trends in Cognitive Sciences*, 25(7): 558-70.
Schwitzgebel, E. 2008. The Unreliability of Naïve Introspection. *The Philosophical Review*, 117(2): 245-73.
Schwitzgebel, E. & Gordon, M.S. 2011. Human Echolocation. In E. Schwitzgebel (Ed.) *Perplexities of Consciousness*. Cambridge, MA: MIT Press.
Seager, W. 1995. Consciousness, Information and Panpsychism. *Journal of Consciousness Studies*, 2(3): 272-88.
Searle, J. 1980. Minds, Brains and Programs. *The Behavioral and Brain Sciences*, 3(3). Reprinted in Haugeland (Ed.). 1981. *Mind Design*. Bradford: MIT.
Searle, J. 1983. *Intentionality*. Cambridge: Cambridge University Press.
Searle, J. 1992. *The Rediscovery of the Mind*. Cambridge, MA: MIT Press.
Segal, G. 2000. *A Slim Book about Narrow Content*. Cambridge, MA: MIT Press.
Sellars, W. 1962. Philosophy and the Scientific Image of Man. In R. Colodny (Ed.) *Science, Perception, and Reality*. New York: Humanities Press/Ridgeview, pp. 35-78.
Seth, A. 2016. Aliens on Earth: What Octopus Minds Can Tell Us about Alien Consciousness. In J. Al-Khalili (Ed.) *Aliens*. London: Profile Books.
Seth, A., Dienes, Z., Cleeremans, A., Overgaard, M. & Pessoa, L. 2008. Measuring Consciousness: Relating Behavioural and Neurophysiological Approaches. *Trends in Cognitive Sciences*, 12(8): 314-21.
Shea, N. 2013. Naturalizing Representational Content. *Philosophy Compass*, 8(5): 496-509.
Shoemaker, S. 1975. Functionalism and Qualia. *Philosophical Studies*, 27(5): 291-315. Reprinted in *Shoemaker Identity, Cause, and Mind*. Cambridge: Cambridge University Press, pp. 184-205.
Shoemaker, S. 1982. The Inverted Spectrum. *Journal of Philosophy*, 79: 357-81.
Shoemaker, S. 1984. Personal Identity: A Materialist's Account. In S. Shoemaker and R. Swinburne (Eds.) *Personal Identity*. Oxford: Blackwell.
Shoemaker, S. 1988. On Knowing One's Own Mind. In *The First Person Perspective and Other Essays*. Cambridge: Cambridge University Press.

Shoemaker, S. 1994. Self-Knowledge and 'Inner Sense'. *Philosophy and Phenomenological Research*, 54: 249–314.
Shoemaker, S. 1997. Self and Substance. *Philosophical Perspectives*, 11: Mind, Causation and World: 283–304.
Shoemaker, S. 2003. Moran on Self-Knowledge. *European Journal of Philosophy*, 11(3): 391–401.
Shoemaker, S. 2011. On What We Are. In S. Gallagher (Ed.) *The Oxford Handbook of the Self*. Oxford: Oxford University Press.
Siegel, S. 2006. Which Properties Are Represented in Perception? In T. Gendler and J. Hawthorne (Eds.) *Perceptual Experience*. Oxford: Oxford University Press, pp. 481–503.
Siegel, S. 2007. How Can We Discover the Contents of Experience? *Southern Journal of Philosophy*, 45(Supplement): 127–42.
Siegel, S. 2010a. Do Visual Experiences Have Contents? In B. Nanay (Ed.) *Perceiving the World*. Oxford: Oxford University Press.
Siegel, S. 2010b. *The Contents of Visual Experience*. Oxford: Oxford University Press.
Siegel, S. 2014. Affordances and the Contents of Perception. In B. Brogaard (Ed.) *Does Perception Have Content?* Oxford: Oxford University Press, pp. 39–76.
Siewert, C. 1998. *The Significance of Consciousness*. Princeton, NJ: Princeton University Press.
Siewert, C. 2004. Is Experience Transparent? *Philosophical Studies*, 117: 15–41.
Siewert, C. 2007. Who's Afraid of Phenomenological Disputes? *Southern Journal of Philosophy*, 45: 1–21.
Sinnott-Armstrong, W. 2021. Contrastive Mental Causation. *Synthese*, 198: 861–83.
Slingerland, E. & Chudek, M. 2011. The Prevalence of Mind-Body Dualism in Early China. *Cognitive Science*, 35: 997–1007.
Smart, J.J.C. 1959. Sensations and Brain Processes. *Philosophical Review*, 68: 141–56.
Smith, B. C. 2015a. The Chemical Senses. In M. Matthen (Ed.) *The Oxford Handbook of Philosophy of Perception*. Oxford: Oxford University Press.
Smith, J. D. 2015b. The Phenomenology of Face to Face Mindreading. *Philosophy and Phenomenological Research*, 90(2): 274–93.
Smith, J. D. 2009. The Study of Animal Metacognition. *Trends in Cognitive Sciences*, 13: 389–96.
Smith, J. D., Shields, W. E. & Washburn, D. A. 2003. The Comparative Psychology of Uncertainty Monitoring and Metacognition. *Behavioral and Brain Sciences*, 26(3): 317–39.
Smolensky, P. 1991. Connectionism, Constituency, and the Language of Thought. In B.M. Loewer and G. Rey (Eds.) *Meaning in Mind: Fodor and His Critics*. Cambridge, MA: Blackwell, pp. 201–27.
Snowdon, P. 1990. Persons, Animals, and Ourselves. In C. Gill (Ed.) *The Person and the Human Mind: Issues in Ancient and Modern Philosophy*. Oxford: Clarendon Press, pp. 83–107.
Snowdon, P. 2014. *Persons, Animals, Ourselves*. Oxford: Oxford University Press.
Sober, E. 2000. Evolution and the Problem of Other Minds. *Journal of Philosophy*, 97: 365–87.
Solomon, R. 1976. *The Passions*. New York: Anchor Press/Doubleday.
Sosa, E. 2003. Privileged Access. In Q. Smith and A. Jokic (Eds.) *Consciousness: New Philosophical Perspectives*. Oxford: Oxford University Press, pp. 273–92.
Speaks, J. 2005. Is Mental Content Prior to Linguistic Meaning? *Noûs*, 40(3): 428–67.
Speaks, J. 2009. Transparency, Intentionalism, and the Nature of Perceptual Content. *Philosophy and Phenomenological Research*, 79(3): 539–73.
Speaks, J. 2011. Spectrum Inversion without a Difference in Representation is Impossible. *Philosophical Studies*, 156: 339–61.
Spener, M. 2019. Introspecting in the 20th Century. In A. Kind (Ed.) *Philosophy of Mind in the Twentieth and Twenty-First Century*. Abingdon: Routledge.
Sperling, G. 1960. The Information Available in Brief Visual Presentations. *Psychological Monographs*, 74(11).
Stalnaker, R. C. 1989. On What's in the Head. *Philosophical Perspectives*, 3: 287–316.
Stalnaker, R. C. 1990. Narrow Content. In C. Anthony Anderson and J. Owens (Eds.) *Propositional Attitudes: The Role of Content in Logic, Language, and Mind*. Stanford: CSLI.
Stalnaker, R. C. 1996. Varieties of Supervenience. *Philosophical Perspectives*, 10: 221–41.
Stalnaker, R. C. 2008. *Our Knowledge of the Internal World*. Oxford: Oxford University Press.
Stampe, D. 1977. Toward a Causal Theory of Linguistic Representation. In P. French, H. K. Wettstein, and T. E. Uehling (Eds.) *Midwest Studies in Philosophy*, vol. 2, Minneapolis: University of Minnesota Press, pp. 42–63.
Stazicker, J. 2011. Attention, Visual Consciousness, and Indeterminacy. *Mind and Language*, 26(2): 156–84.
Sterelny, K. 2010. Minds: Extended or Scaffolded? *Phenomenology and the Cognitive Sciences*, 9: 465–81.

Sterelny, K. 2012. *The Evolved Apprentice*. Cambridge, MA: MIT Press.
Stinson, S. 2018. Explanation and Connectionist Models. In M. Colombo and M. Sprevak (Eds.) *The Routledge Handbook of the Computational Mind*. Abingdon: Routledge.
Stoljar, D. 2000. Physicalism and the Necessary a Posteriori. *Journal of Philosophy*, 97: 33–54.
Stoljar, D. 2004. The Argument from Diaphanousness. *Canadian Journal of Philosophy*, 34(Supplementary Volume 30: The Philosophy of Language and Mind): 341–90.
Stoljar, D. 2014. Four Kinds of Russellian Monism. In U. Kriegel (Ed.) *Current Controversies in Philosophy of Mind*. Abingdon: Routledge, pp. 17–39.
Stotz, K. 2010. Human Nature and Cognitive-Developmental Niche Construction. *Phenomenology and the Cognitive Sciences*, 9: 483–501.
Strawson, G. 1994. *Mental Reality*. Cambridge, MA: MIT Press.
Strawson, G. 1999. The Self and the SESMET. *Journal of Consciousness Studies*, 6(4): 99–135.
Strawson, G. 2006. Realistic Monism: Why Physicalism Entails Panpsychism. *Journal of Consciousness Studies*, 13(10–11): 3–31.
Strawson, G. 2011. Cognitive Phenomenology: Real Life. In T. Bayne and M. Montague (Eds.) *Cognitive Phenomenology*. Oxford: Oxford University Press.
Suddendorf, T. & Busby, J. 2003. Mental Time Travel in Animals. *Trends in Cognitive Sciences*, 7: 391–96.
Suddendorf, T. & Corballis, M. 2007. The Evolution of Foresight: What Is Mental Time Travel, and Is It Unique to Humans? *Behavioral and Brain Sciences*, 30: 299–51.
Sutton, J. 2010. Exograms and Interdisciplinarity: History, the Extended Mind, and the Civilizing Process. In R. Menary (Ed.) *The Extended Mind*. Cambridge, MA: MIT Press.
Thaler, L. & Goodale, M. A. 2016. Echolocation in Humans: An Overview. *Wiley Interdisciplinary Reviews: Cognitive Science*, 7(6): 382–93.
Thomas, J. 2001. Mill's Argument for Other Minds. *British Journal for the History of Philosophy*, 9(3): 507–23.
Thomasson, A. L. 2000. After Brentano: A One-Level Theory of Consciousness. *European Journal of Philosophy*, 8(2): 190–210.
Thompson, B. 2008. Representationalism and the Conceivability of Inverted Spectra. *Synthese*, 160: 203–13.
Thompson, B. 2009. Senses for Senses. *Australasian Journal of Philosophy*, 87(1): 99–117.
Thompson, R.K.R., Oden, D. L. & Boysen, S. T. 1997. Language-naïve chimpanzees (Pan troglodytes) Judge Relations between Relations in a Conceptual Matching-to-Sample Task. *Journal of Experimental Psychology: Animal Behavior Processes*, 23: 31–43.
Travis, C. 2004. The Silence of the Senses. *Mind*, 113(449): 57–94.
Trujillo, C. A. et al. 2018. Nested Oscillatory Dynamics in Cortical Organoids Model Early Human Brain Network Development. *bioRxiv*. https://doi.org/10.1101/358622.
Turing, A. 1950. Computing Machinery and Intelligence. *Mind*: 433–60.
Tye, M. 1995. *Ten Problems of Consciousness*. Cambridge, MA: MIT Press.
Tye, M. 1999. Phenomenal Consciousness: The Explanatory Gap as a Cognitive Illusion. *Mind*, 108: 705–25.
Tye, M. 2000a. *Consciousness, Color, and Content*. Cambridge, MA: MIT Press.
Tye, M. 2000b. Knowing What It Is Like: The Ability Hypothesis and the Knowledge Argument. In G. Preyer (Ed.) *Reality and Humean Supervenience: Essays on the Philosophy of David Lewis*. Lanham, MD: Rowman & Littlefield.
Tye, M. 2002. Representationalism and the Transparency of Experience. *Noûs*, 36(1): 137–51.
Tye, M. 2003. Blurry Images, Double Vision, and Other Oddities: New Problems for Representationalism? In Q. Smith and A. Jokic (Eds.) *Consciousness: New Philosophical Perspectives*. Oxford: Oxford University Press, pp. 7–32.
Tye, M. & Wright, B. 2011. Is There a Phenomenology of Thought? In T. Bayne and M. Montague (Eds.) *Cognitive Phenomenology*. Oxford: Oxford University Press, pp. 326–44.
Tyndall, J. 1871. *Fragments of Science for Unscientific People*. London: Longmans.
Usher, M. 2001. A Statistical Referential Theory of Content: Using Information Theory to Account for Misrepresentation. *Mind & Language*, 16(3): 311–34.
Van Cleve, J. 2015. Troubles for Radical Transparency. In T. Horgan, M. Sabatés and D. Sosa (Eds.) *Qualia and Mental Causation in a Physical World*. Cambridge: Cambridge University Press, pp. 209–30.
van Gulick, R. 2004. So Many Ways of Saying No to Mary. In P. Ludlow, Y. Nagasawa and D. Stoljar (Eds.) *There's Something about Mary*. Cambridge, MA: MIT Press, pp. 365–405.
van Inwagen, P. 1990. *Material Beings*. Ithaca, NY: Cornell University Press.

Velleman, D. 1996. Self to Self. *The Philosophical Review*, 105(1): 39–76.
Wakefield, J. & Dreyfus, H. 1991. Intentionality and the Phenomenology of Action. In E. Lepore and R. van Gulick (Eds.) *John Searle and His Critics*. Oxford: Blackwell, pp. 259–70.
Wallis, L. 2013. Living a Conjoined Life. *BBC Magazine*. www.bbc.com/news/magazine-22181528.
Walter, S. 2007. Determinables, Determinates, and Causal Relevance, *Canadian Journal of Philosophy*, 37(1): 217–43.
Watson, B. 1968. *The Complete Works of Chuang Tzu*. New York: Columbia UniversityPress.
Wegner, D. 2002. *The Illusion of Conscious Will*. Cambridge, MA: MIT Press.
Weiskopf, D. 2008. Patrolling the Mind's Boundaries. *Erkenntnis*, 68(2): 265–76.
Weiskrantz, L. 1998. *Blindsight* (2nd ed.). Oxford: Oxford University Press.
Weissglass, D. E. 2020. Greatest Surprise Reduction Semantics: An Information Theoretic Solution to Misrepresentation and Disjunction. *Philosophical Studies*, 177: 2185–2205.
White, S. 1982. Partial Character and the Language of Thought. *Pacific Philosophical Quarterly*, 63: 347–65.
Wierzbicka, A. 2006. On Folk Conceptions of Mind, Agency and Morality. *Journal of Cognition and Culture*, 6: 165–79.
Wikforss, Å. 2004. Externalism and Incomplete Understanding. *Philosophy Quarterly*, 54: 287–94.
Williams, B. 1966/1973. Imagination and the Self. In *Problems of the Self*. Cambridge: Cambridge University Press.
Williams, B. 1970. The Self and the Future. *The Philosophical Review*, 79(2): 161–80.
Wilson, J. 2018. Grounding-Based Formulations of Physicalism. *Topoi*, 37(3): 1–18.
Wilson, R. 1994. Wide Computationalism. *Mind*, 103: 351–72.
Wilson, R. 2004. *Boundaries of the Mind: The Individual in the Fragile Sciences-Cognition*. Cambridge: Cambridge University Press.
Winawer, J. & Parvizi, J. 2016. Linking Electrical Stimulation of Human Primary Visual Cortex, Size of Affected Cortical Area, Neuronal Responses, and Subjective Experience. *Neuron*, 92: 1213–19.
Wittgenstein, L. 1953/2009. *Philosophical Investigations* 4th ed. P.M.S. Hacker and Joachim Schulte (trans. and eds.). Oxford: Blackwell.
Wittgenstein, L. 1967. *On Certainty* (ed. and trans. of Zettel by G.E.M Anscombe and G. H. von Wright). Oxford: Blackwell.
Woodward, J. 2008. Mental Causation and Neural Mechanisms. In J. Hohwy and J. Kallestrup (Eds.) *Being Reduced: New Essays on Reductive Explanation and Special Science Causation*. Oxford: Oxford University Press, pp. 218–62.
Yablo, S. 1992. Mental Causation. *Philosophical Review*, 101: 245–80.

Index

Note: Page numbers in *italic* indicate a figure, and page numbers followed by an 'n' indicate a note on the corresponding page.

Aaronson, Scott 91-2
ability hypothesis 138-40
accessibility constraint 99, 101, 106
acquaintance 153n14, 223
Adams, Frederick 128
afterimages 15
Aizawa, Kenneth 128
Akins, Kathleen 141-2
Alexander, Samuel 30
aliefs 79
AlphaZero 77, 93
analogical account (of other minds) 204-7, 213
analytic functionalism 46, 253n10
animalism 241-3, 252, 253n7; *see also* dualism
animals 208-12; *see also* evolution
anomalous monism 41-2, 183-4
anosognosia 10, 23n1
Anscombe, G.E.M. 227-8
anti-individualism 117-20; *see also* externalism
Anton's syndrome 10
a priori physicalism *see* physicalism
a posteriori physicalism *see* physicalism
Armstrong, David 41-2, 51-2, 55n9, 163
Aristotle 1, 67, 165
artificial consciousness/mind 47, 212-15
artificial intelligence 3, 47; *see also* Turing test
attended intermediate representations (AIR) 170
auditory experiences 57, 67, 68, 75n1, 96n1, 168
Austin, J. L. 57, 115n3
availability argument 171
Avicenna 1, 238-9, 252
avowals 221

Baars, Bernard 170
baboons 80
Baier, Annette 173
bat argument 134, 141-2
Bechtel, William 43
'beetle in the box' scenario 202
behaviourism 3, 38-41, 42, 43, 47, 51, 54, 167, 198-9, 229; analytical (philosophical, logical) behaviourism 39-41, 43, 47, 51, 53, 198-9; psychological (scientific) behaviourism 38-9, 51
belief 7, 13, 18, 19, 21, 50-1
Bennett, Karen 187
binding problem 244-6, 253n12
blindsight 71-2, 73, 76n14, 159
Block, Ned 63, 74, 75n6, 92-3, 157-8, 172, 176n6, 184, 216
Blockhead 92
Bloom, Paul 238
blurry vision 65-6
brain in a vat 117
brain-reading 9; *see also* mindreading
brain transplants 243, 253n11
Brentano, Franz 11-12, 14-15, 165
Brentano's thesis 11-12, 15, 22; *see also* intentionality
British emergentism *see* emergence and emergentism
Broad, C. D. 30
Brown, Jessica 124-5
Buddhism 248, 250
Burge, Tyler 118, 119-22, 124-5, 131n6
Byrne, Alex 122, 225-6, 227

Camp, Elisabeth 80, 84
Carruthers, Peter 23n2, 159, 229-31, 233n5
Cartwright, Nancy 49
causal exclusion objection 180-4, *186*, 194
causation 26, 180, 184, 185-6
Caine, Michael 144-5
Chalmers, David 3, 121, 125-9, 133, 135-7, 162
character traits 18, 19, 220, 222
China-Brain 172
Chinese room argument 88-90; *see also* Searle, John
Churchland, Patricia 140
Churchland, Paul 37n6, 48-50, 55n7, 55n8, 207
Clark, Andy 23n2, 87, 125-9
Clayton, Nicola 211
cognitive phenomenology 109-10, 156
colour 68, 135
combination problem (for panpsychism) 150
compositional fallacy 96
confabulation 230-1, 233n6
conjoined twins 241-3, 246
connectionism 85-6
connection principle 18
consciousness 2, 3, 16-18, 134-8, 160-2; explanatory targets 160-3; first-person methods 155-9, 175; and intentionalism 172-4; monitoring *versus* first-order theories 163; neural correlates of 162-3, 166-7, 168; neural *versus* functional theories 167-72; and physicalism 132-4; theories of 154-5; third-person methods 159-60, 175
content 98-101; broad (wide) *versus* narrow 121-2, 124, 188-90; and intentional stance 111-13; normativity of 103; and phenomenal approach 108-10; and teleosemantic approach 104-8; and tracking approach 101-4
content externalism 117, 118-20, 130, 131n1, 131n11
content view of perception 57-62
continuous flash suppression (CFS) 71-3
cortical deference 168-9
cortical dominance 168-9

Dainton, Barry 245
Darwin, Charles 153n16
Davidson, Donald 42, 107, 116n13, 183-4
Davies, Martin 83, 121

death 247-8
Dennett, Daniel 10-11, 49-50, 86, 111-13, 118, 140, 146-8, 155-6, 249-50
depersonalization 237
derived intentionality 14, 127-8
Descartes, René 1, 25, 34, 179, 241, 250, 252; *see also* dualism
determinism 31
Dickinson, Anthony 211
disjunction problem 102, 104
disjunctivism 60-1, 75
doppelgänger arguments 120-5, 130, 131n4, 131n6, 189-90
dreaming 16, 126-7, 160-1
Dretske, Fred 69, 104, 121-2, 159, 188, 198
dualism 25-6, 148-51, 181, 184, 253n3; and self 238-41; *see also* animalism; Descartes, René; self
duplication argument 108-9

eliminativism 3, 47-51, 55n5, 55n6, 207, 254n16
emergence and emergentism 28-31, 36
emotion 7, 173, 197
epiphenomenalism 26, 181, 184, 191-3, 195n8
Evans, Gareth 224-5, 233
evolution 153n16, 209; *see also* animals
explanatory gap(s) 136-7, 140-1, 143, 173-4, 213-14
expressivism 221
extended conscious mind hypothesis (ECM) 126-7
extended mind hypothesis 125-9, 131n13
externalism 3, 100, 117-18, 195; content (semantic) 118-20, 187-9; and the doppelgänger arguments 120-1; and mental causation 187-90; perceptual 121; phenomenal 121-2; vehicle 125-9

Farkas, Katalin 122-3
Farrell, Brian 147
Feigl, Herbert 41, 51-2, 55n9, 148, 167
fictionalism 249, 254n16, 254n17
Flanagan, Owen 192
flavour 57, 75n1
flying man argument 238-9, 253n4
Fodor, Jerry 44, 81-6, 96n4, 97n11, 104, 128, 178
folk psychology 18-20, 23, 48, 199-201
free will 195n9

French, Robert 92, 94
Frith, Chris 155
functionalism 3, 44-7, 51-3, 167-72, 176n11, 177n12; long-arm *versus* short-arm 45-6, 172; a priori *versus* a posteriori 46, 52-3, 55n9, 170

Gallois, André 225
Gallup, Gordon 210
Gendler, Tamar 79
generic consciousness 176n5
ghosts 34, 36; *see also* zombies
global neuronal workspace theory (GNWT) 176n11; *see also* Global Workspace Theory (GWT)
global states of consciousness 160-1
Global Workspace Theory (GWT) 170-1
Goldilocks problem 166
Goostman, Eugene 91-2
Gopnik, Alison 229-31, 233n5, 236

hallucination 12-13, 58-9
hard problem of consciousness 136-7
Harman, Gilbert 65, 75n6, 75n7
Haugeland, John 83, 97n9
Heil, John 112
Hempel, Carl 26
Hempel's dilemma 26-8
Hill, Christopher 176n6
Holton, Richard 193
Horgan, Terry 21, 31, 108-10, 180, 192
Hume, David 1, 80, 219, 236-7, 253n2
Hurley, Susan 126, 131n3, 168-9

identity theory *see* mind-brain identity theory
illusions 10, 58, 60, 127, 256; cognitive 81
illusionism: with respect to consciousness 146-8, 153n12, 153n13; with respect to the self 248-51
imitation game 91-2; *see also* Turing test
immortality 247-8
inference to the best explanation (IBE) 207-8, 213
inferentialism (as an account of self-knowledge) 224-6
inner-sense account of self-knowledge 221-4
inscrutability argument 138-42, 153n13
inseparatism 21-2, 63, 108, 173; *see also* separatism

intentional content 12-15, 21, 57-71, 98-114, 141-2, 172-4
intentionalism 62-9, 73, 75, 75n10, 76n11, 109, 122, 141-2, 154, 172-3, 177n12
intentionality 2, 11-16, 21, 98-101; and the intentional stance 111-13; and the phenomenal approach 108-10; and the teleosemantic approach 104-8; and the tracking approach 101-4; *see also* Brentano's thesis
intentional systems theory (IST) 111-14, 116n14, 216n1
internalism 3, 100, 117-18, 123-5
interpretivism 111, 116n13
introspection 155-9; *see also* consciousness
inverted spectrum 67-8, 208, 217n8

Jackson, Frank 24, 27, 32, 35, 116n9, 133, 135, 152n5, 184-5
James, William 236, 240, 253n2

Kant, Immanuel 87, 221, 240, 253n5
Kim, Jaegwon 180-2, 194, 195n3
Klein, Colin 64
knowledge argument 133, 135-40, 144-6, 152n3, 152n5, 153n9, 153n10, 153n11
Kriegel, Uriah 110
Kripke, Saul 103, 143-4

language 14, 19, 23n2, 81, 84, 86-7, 100, 119, 120, 128-9, 200
language of thought (LOT) hypothesis 77, 81-7, 96, 96n2
Laplace, Pierre Simon 31-2
Laplacean demon 137, 152, 153n11
Lau, Hakwan 166-7
levels of consciousness 161; *see also* global states of consciousness
Levine, Joseph 136
Lewis, David 46, 51-2, 55n2, 55n4, 55n9, 116n13, 138-9
Libet, Benjamin 179
Libet's challenge *190*, 190-4
Loar, Brian 108, 109
localism 187-9
Locke, John 1, 67, 221, 243-4
logical behaviourism *see* behaviourism
Loewer, Barry 100

Lovelace, Ada 92-3
Lycan, William 121, 164, 176n9, 222

machine functionalism 55n3
Maoz, Uri 191
Marianna 139
materialism 24, 37n1, 37n6
McGinn, Colin 121, 141
Mele, Alfred 193
Melnyk, Andrew 30-1, 45
memory 7, 211-12, 233n6, 240, 243, 245
Mendelovici, Angela 110, 173
mental causation 4, 123, 178-9; and the causal exclusion objection 180-4, *181*; and externalism 187-90; and internalism 123; and Libet's challenge 190-4; motivation for 179-80; and non-reductive physicalism 184-7
Mentalese *see* language of thought (LOT) hypothesis
mentality: aspects of 6-8, 20-2; and consciousness 16-18, 22; and folk psychology 18-20, 23; and intentionality 11-16; privacy of 8-11, 22
mental latex 63, 66
mental paint 63, 66, 75n6
mental properties 7-8
mental states 7-8
mental time travel (MTT) 211-12
metacognition 159
metaphysical supervenience *see* supervenience
Mill, J. S. 205, 217n7
Millikan, Ruth 104-6, 113
mind-brain identity theory 41-4, 51-3, 167-70, 182
mindreading 4, 9, 197-201, 215, 216n4
mirror-test 210-11
MOMA argument 125-9
monitoring theories of consciousness 163-7, 176n8
moods 15, 173-4
Moore, G. E. 65, 75n7
Moran, Richard 226-7
multiple realization 43-4, 167-8, 182
Mundale, Jennifer 43
mysterianism 141

Nagel, Thomas 3, 133, 134
Nahmias, Eddy 191
naïve realism 56, 59-62

narrow content *see* content, broad (wide) *versus* narrow
Neander, Karen 107, 116n8
necessity 29-30
neo-Ryleanism 228-32
neural correlates of consciousness (NCCs) 162-3
neural plasticity 44, 168
neural theories of consciousness 167-72, 176n10
Nida-Rümelin, Martine 139, 217n8, 252; *see also* ability hypothesis
no-circularity constraint 100, 101, 106, 109
Noë, Alva 125, 127, 168-9
nomological dangler 148
nomological supervenience *see* supervenience
normativity 103, 109, 256

octopus 151, 208-10, 217n9
olfaction 57, 75n1
Olson, Eric 235
optimistic induction 140-1
O'Regan, Kevin 127
organoids, cerebral 106-7, 212
other minds 196-7; and artificial consciousness 212-15; conceptual problem of 201-3, 215; and mindreading 197-201; and non-human animals 208-12; sceptical problem of 203-8, 217n6

pain 21, 39-43, 45, 47, 49-50, 64, 168, 218, 221
panpsychism 149, 153n15, 153n16, 209
panprotopsychism 149-50
Papineau, David 107, 116n9, 122
Pascal, Blaise 77
Pautz, Adam 122
perception 56-62, 75, 75n5; and admissible contents 69-71; alleged transparency of 65-6, 75n7; border between perception and thought 78-9; and intentionalism 62-9; unconscious 71-3
perceptual account of mindreading 197-8, 204, 216n2
perceptual learning 70-1
perceptual presence 59-62, 75
personal-level explanation 10-11
perspicuity constraint 100, 102, 106, 109, 116n2
perturbational complexity index (PCI) 212
pessimistic inference 217
Pettit, Philip 184-5

phenomenal approach to content 108-10, 113, 116n5
phenomenal character 17, 59, 63-9, 108-10, 121-2, 141-2, 145, 146, 156, 161-2, 167, 171, 172-4, 177n12, 208, 221-2
phenomenal concepts 144-5, 150, 151, 153n10, 153n11, 201
phenomenal concept strategy (PCS) 144-6, 145, 153n9
phenomenal consciousness 16-17, 161
phenomenal contrast argument 70-1
phenomenal externalism 121-3
phenomenal overflow 157-8
Phillips, Ian 15, 72, 158
philosophical behaviourism see behaviourism
physicalism 3, 36, 37n1, 37n3, 152n2, 255-6; and the ability hypothesis 138-40; a priori physicalism 31-3, 37n5, 55n9, 137-42, 153n13; a posteriori physicalism 31-3, 37n3, 55n9, 137-8, 142-4; and the bat argument 134; and behaviourism 38-41; and consciousness 132-4; definitions of 24, 26-31, 37n3; and dualism 148-51; and eliminativism 47-51; and functionalism 44-7; and Hempel's dilemma 26-8, 36; and illusionism 146-8; and intentionalism 141-2; and the knowledge argument 135; and mind-brain identity theory 41-4; motivations for 24-6; non-reductive 41, 44-7, 184-7; and optimism 140-1; and phenomenal concept strategy 144-6; prospects of 33-5; reductive 41-3; and role of science 51-3; and scrutability 142-4; and supervenience 28-31, 36; Type-A physicalism 32, 138, 141-2, 146, 214; Type-B physicalism 32, 133, 142, 146, 151-2, 153n13, 214; and zombies 135-8
Place, U.T. 41, 51-2, 55n9, 167
plants 209
Plato 1, 247
possibility 29-30, 34, 40, 83, 86, 92, 135, 142, 151
Prinz, Jesse 170
privacy 8-11, 25, 40, 42, 46, 218, 228
productivity of thought 83-6, 96n3, 96n4
program explanation 184-5, 189
properties 7-8, 16, 26-8, 41-2, 44, 45, 57, 61, 66-7, 180, 183-4; intrinsic versus relational 46-7, 57, 66, 100, 107, 118, 187-8
proportionality principle 195

propositional attitudes 12-14, 21, 46, 48-50, 61, 78, 96n2, 99, 112, 224-5, 229-31
psychophysical laws 25-6, 29-30, 33, 42, 51, 135, 148-9, 151
Putnam, Hilary 40, 42-3, 118, 119-22, 131n5, 131n6

qualia 17, 37n6, 63, 121-2, 147, 161, 217n8

Ramsification 55n4
readiness potential (RP) 190, 193
realizer functionalism 55n2
reasoning 81, 82
Reid, Thomas 247
representationalism see intentionalism
revisionism 48-9
robot response to the Chinese room argument 90
role functionalism 55n2
Rorty, Richard 21
Rosenthal, David 163-4, 167, 176n6, 176n7
Russell, Bertrand 27, 148-51, 223
Russellian monism 27, 36, 255
Ryle, Gilbert 39, 228-9

Schechtman, Marya 245
Schwitzgebel, Eric 152n1, 156-7
science 2, 20, 27-8, 42, 48-9, 51-3, 73, 140, 142, 149, 155-6, 166, 170, 183-4, 190-3
scrub jays 211
scrutability 142-4
Searle, John 18, 23, 88-90, 140; see also Chinese room argument
self 234-5; and animalism 241-3; and the body 255; and dualism 238-41; as illusion 248-51; psychological approach to 243-8; see also dualism
self-blindness 222, 233
self-consciousness 210-11
self-directed concern 236, 241, 246
self-knowledge 4, 123-5, 131n12, 218-21, 233; deliberative account of 226-8; inferentialist account of 224-6; inner-sense account of 221-4; neo-Rylean approaches to 228-32
Sellars, Wilfrid 20
sensationalism 63, 66
sense data 58-9
separatism 21, 23; see also inseparatism

Shoemaker, Sydney 221-2, 227, 243-6
Siegel, Susanna 70, 74
simulation-based mindreading 200, 204, 216n3, 216n4
Solomon, Robert 173
Sosa, Ernest 164
Skinner, B. F. 39, 51
Smart, J. J. C. 41, 51-2, 55n9, 167
solipsism 203
Solomon, Robert 173
Sperling, George 157-8
split-brain syndrome 242, 249
state consciousness 176n5
Stazicker, James 158
structural resemblance accounts 115n1
subjectivity 28, 47, 50, 122, 134, 150, 160, 164-6, 176n5, 203, 209, 237
subject of experience 50, 235-7, 241-2, 250; see also self
subpersonal explanations 10-11
substitution principle 144
super-spartans 40
supervenience 28-31, 34, 35, 37n2, 40, 42, 55n1, 63-4, 66, 118, 131n3, 195n2
Sutton, John 128
Swampman 107
symbols, mental 77, 81-4, 88-90, 97n9, 100-1, 106n4
systematicity of thought 83-6, 96n3, 96n4, 96n5

teleosemantics 104-8, 116n7
theory-theory 199-200, 203, 207-8
thought 77-8; boundaries of 90-4; and Chinese room argument 88-90; language of 81-7; scaffolding of 87; varieties of 78-81
Tienson, John 21, 108-10
token identity theory 41-2, 54, 183, 195

touch 67, 168
tracking approach 101-4
transparency (of perception) 65-6, 75n7
transparency thesis 219-20
Turing, Alan 91, 97n10
Turing test 77, 91-4, 213; see also artificial intelligence
Twin Earth 119-25, 131n4, 131n5, 189-90
Tye, Michael 15, 64, 122, 170, 173
Type-A physicalism see physicalism, Type-A physicalism
Type-B physicalism see physicalism, Type-B physicalism
type identity theory see mind-brain identity theory

unconscious perception 71-3
underived intentionality 14

vegetative state 206-7
vehicle externalism 125-9, 131n2
virtual reality 62
vitalism 140

wakefulness 16, 160, 206
Watson, J. B. 39, 51
Weiskopf, Daniel 128-9
Williams, Bernard 246
willusionism 191, 195
Wittgenstein, Ludwig xiv, 39, 145, 197-8, 201-3
Wodehouse, P.G. 84
Woodfield, Andrew 106

Yablo, Stephen 185-6, 195n5

Zhuangzi (Zhuang Zhou) 1, 234, 251
zombies 34, 36, 133, 135-8; see also ghosts

For Product Safety Concerns and Information please contact our
EU representative GPSR@taylorandfrancis.com Taylor & Francis
Verlag GmbH, Kaufingerstraße 24, 80331 München, Germany